Semi-State Actors in Cybersecurity

Semi-State Actors in Cybersecurity

FLORIAN J. EGLOFF

OXFORD
UNIVERSITY PRESS

OXFORD
UNIVERSITY PRESS

Oxford University Press is a department of the University of Oxford. It furthers
the University's objective of excellence in research, scholarship, and education
by publishing worldwide. Oxford is a registered trade mark of Oxford University
Press in the UK and certain other countries.

Published in the United States of America by Oxford University Press
198 Madison Avenue, New York, NY 10016, United States of America.

© Florian J. Egloff 2022

Library of Congress Cataloging-in-Publication Data
Names: Egloff, Florian J. (Florian Johannes), author.
Title: Semi-state actors in cybersecurity / Florian J. Egloff.
Description: New York, NY : Oxford University Press, [2022] |
Includes bibliographical references and index.
Identifiers: LCCN 2021037341 (print) | LCCN 2021037342 (ebook) |
ISBN 9780197579282 (paperback) | ISBN 9780197579275 (hardback) |
ISBN 9780197579312 | ISBN 9780197579299 | ISBN 9780197579305 (epub)
Subjects: LCSH: Computer crimes. | Computer security—International cooperation. |
Non-state actors (International relations) | Cyberspace operations (Military science)
Classification: LCC HV6773 .E35 2022 (print) | LCC HV6773 (ebook) |
DDC 005.8—dc23
LC record available at https://lccn.loc.gov/2021037341
LC ebook record available at https://lccn.loc.gov/2021037342

DOI: 10.1093/oso/9780197579275.001.0001

1 3 5 7 9 8 6 4 2

Paperback printed by LSC Communications, United States of America
Hardback printed by Bridgeport National Bindery, Inc., United States of America

Contents

CONTENTS

Tables and Figures

Tables

Figures

INTRODUCTION AND
RESEARCH STRATEGY

1

Introduction

In the 2020s, as the rollout of the fifth-generation mobile networks is picking up steam, a large Chinese telecommunications technology company, Huawei, has become a national security concern for many states outside China. The risks emanating from technological dependency to a very large technology company with special, perhaps opaque, ties to its home country's national security agencies feature prominently in national security conversations about cybersecurity—and not just with regards to companies domiciled in China.

A second concern is the private offensive outfits operating in the interests of their client states and companies (with some claiming to sell only to governments). For example, in summer 2020, researchers from the Citizen Lab, a University of Toronto–based research team, uncovered a massive India-based hack-for-hire operation they labelled Dark Basin, compromising government officials, multiple industries, as well as civil society from six different continents.[1]

A third concern is cybercriminals, particularly when effective law enforcement in their domiciled state is either lacking the capacity to or is unwilling to rein in cybercriminals' activities. It appears that some governments have found the existence of sophisticated cybercrime to be advantageous for capability building as well as for deniability for their own operations.

In this book, I will show that these seemingly disconnected concerns are connected: they all involve diverse types of relationships of states to actors with significant cyber capabilities. I examine these relationships in-depth and show that the actors all inhabit a common realm.

Through so doing, the book aids international relations scholars to better understand the global politics of cybersecurity and develops a historically informed perspective on how these actors are connected to the state. We will see that rather than the diffusion of power, an argument often made with regard to cyber capabilities (i.e. that smaller actors profit asymmetrically), relationships between the state and various actors shape each other.[2] Rather than diminishing the state, the actors observed are reconfigured by, and in turn reconfigure, the state in particular ways. Specifically, the semi-state

Semi-State Actors in Cybersecurity. Florian J. Egloff, Oxford University Press. © Florian J. Egloff 2022.
DOI: 10.1093/oso/9780197579275.003.0001

actors looked at in this book have historically been, and continue to be, crucial participants in the political contestations on what sovereignty and statehood mean.

The analytic perspective adopted will highlight the fluidity of the legitimacy of the state. I am interested in topics such as private hacking, state interactions with cybercriminals, and large technology companies and their various interactions with states. Are states able to deny access to markets and restrict activities of large technology companies and service providers? Are these corporations depending on 'peace' in cyberspace provided and enforced by states? Is cybercrime 'just' a crime or does it play a different function in international security?[3]

To the cybersecurity scholarship, the book contributes a historical lens with which to analyse changing relationships and tensions between different types of actors and the state. Thereby, the cybersecurity literature already has significant works detailing some of these relationships. For example, some have looked at particular types of actors (states, terrorists, hacktivists, etc.) and characterized their cyber strategies and operations.[4] Others have looked at proxy actors—though most assume a fixed state and non-state identities.[5]

I will add a historical perspective of countervailing tensions and a co-presence in a joint security ecosystem of actors with varying proximity to the state. By countervailing, I mean, for example, it is not just the state that 'uses' other actors but sometimes also the reverse. Furthermore, the different types of actors, such as the ones just detailed, exist in the same universe and jointly create an intelligible cyber(in-)security ecosystem that we all inhabit.

Thus, the focus of the book lies in examining complex relationships between different actors in cybersecurity and the state. I introduce nuance to the discussion on how actors are connected to the state and what sort of security challenges and opportunities those relationships entail. To do this, I use a historical analogy to pirates, privateers, and mercantile companies, which I will now briefly introduce.

Pirates, privateers, and mercantile companies were integral to maritime security between the 16th and 19th centuries. They traded, explored, plundered, and controlled sea lanes and territories across the world's oceans. State navies often lagged behind. Working for a navy was associated with lower pay, more hierarchical organisations, and less flexibility to accommodate other foreign power structures. In contrast, working for another more unconventional actor enabled sailors to thrive in the seams between state powers. The seas thereby offered opportunity and peril. Opportunity because crews expected to profit directly from the journeys. Peril because life on the seas was rough—the business of long-distance trade and violence at sea fraught with the risk of death.

Today, people are again seeking their fulfilment, destiny, and luck with more unconventional actors. As cyberspace is weaved into the fabric of all aspects of society, the provision and undermining of security in digital spaces have become a new arena for digital pirates, privateers, and mercantile companies. This book details their actions at the seams between state powers. Through collaboration and competition with states, these actors thrive due to the ever-increasing extension of human interaction into this newer global domain. Power, money, and the thrill to explore still drive individuals. In different forms of organisations, large technology companies, patriotic hackers, and cybercriminals have all presented difficult political challenges, defying the largely state-centric political paradigms in international politics.

I use the historical analogy as a methodological tool to illuminate the relationships of actors with significant cyber capabilities to states. This is important, as both historically on the sea and in cyberspace, states are not the main actors but are reliant on private actors to act in their interests. Drawing on the results of a five-year investigation at the University of Oxford, including significant archival research, I will show how the historical analogy can aid us to better understand the roles of semi-state actors with varying degrees of state proximity. We will see, first, empirically how the issues raised by naval security arrangements during the 16th–19th centuries, when states attempted to increase their influence over the high seas through cooperation with or toleration of other actors, can be analogized to the security dynamics observed in cyberspace. Second, I will show how such an application of the concepts, derived from a particular historical understanding of mercantile companies, privateers, and pirates, changes our understanding of cyber(in-)security. Thereby, the underlying domains—cyberspace and the sea—have some important commonalities and differences, which will be discussed in detail.[6] For now, suffice it to say that the focus will be on the relationships of these unconventional actors to states and not primarily on the domain itself.

Relatively little work on privateering and mercantile companies exists in the field of international relations. The small body of work that does highlights the merit of integrating early modern historical development into contemporary international relations; for example, Janice E. Thomson highlighted the process of eradication of private violence looking at mercantile companies, privateers, and pirates.[7] However, dealing with early modern history comes with the temptation to submit to a teleological story in favour of the nation-state. Thus, one has to be attuned that history could have taken a different course.[8] Consequently, whilst the historical analogy evaluated here reconceptualizes cyber(in-)security in particular ways, it should not be read as a judgement favouring the consolidation of state control in cyberspace.

To examine the unconventional actors, I challenge the clean divide international relations often makes between state and non-state actors. Our actors of interest defy a neat bifurcation of the world. State-sponsored hackers are behind many high-profile network intrusions, some governments collaborate with cybercriminals, and large technology companies are collaborating and competing with various states. I will show that these important actors exist in-between the two categories, which I designate as semi-state actors (see Table 2.2). They are neither non-state actors, as their special relationships with states imbricates them into the realm of international political conflict, nor are they state actors, as their partial independence and arm's length relationship keeps them from joining the state fold. In the realm of cyber(in-)security, those actors fundamentally shape the security and insecurity experienced worldwide. Calling them non-state actors would obscure their deep interlinkages with the international political system.

Thus, I will re-examine the relations between actors in ways unavailable within the current public/private and foreign/domestic divides.[9] Breaking up

Table 1.1 Comparison between actors on the sea and in cyberspace

Actor Type	Sea	Cyberspace
State actors	Navy (including mercenaries)	Cyber armies, intelligence, police forces, state contractors, offensive security providers
Semi-state actors	Mercantile companies	Technology champions, major telecommunications companies
	Privateers	Patriotic hackers, private contractors to companies, some security vendors Some cybercriminal elements
Non-state actors	Pirates	Independent hackers, cybercriminal elements (incl. organized crime)

Source: A similar table was published in Florian J. Egloff, 'Cybersecurity and the Age of Privateering: A Historical Analogy', *University of Oxford Cyber Studies Working Papers*, no. 1 (2015). Published electronically 4 March 2015, https://perma.cc/XC33-GT7W.

the state/non-state divide into a more continuous set of relationships allows for a richer understanding of cyber(in-)security and international politics more broadly. The book will show that cyber contestations, cybersecurity policies, and accounts of cyber(in-)security are better understood after investigating the relationships between governments and other, sometimes unconventional, actors—some of them motivated predominantly by economic interests.

This book details the complex interplay of cooperation and competition between the non- and semi-state actors and states in cyber(in-)security. By introducing semi-state actors and their interactions with non-state actors and states, it demonstrates a middle way between two opposed theoretical positions about the status of non-state actors in cybersecurity. On the one hand, some argue that cyberspace is 'just' a new medium of international competition and that it mostly reinforces existing power structures, privileging existing state structures (as opposed to non-state actors).[10] On the other hand, others posit that cyberspace presents a fundamental revolution in technological possibilities, enabling radical challengers to the state-system, including revisionist states and radical non-state actors (e.g. terrorists).[11] I position myself in the middle of those positions. I advance the thesis that state competition in cyberspace fundamentally involves concurrent collaboration and competition with a different set of actors, namely, semi-state actors.

Before turning to the main arguments, I should clarify the terminological understanding of cyber(in-)security used. This book builds its definition of security with an awareness of developments in the literature broadly associated with critical security studies.[12] It takes the classical security dilemma as a starting point for investigating (in-)security. The security dilemma captures the potential of protective actions by actor A to secure itself, leading to (unintended) perceived insecurity for actor B. Thus, the provision of security often reproduces insecurities in ways that can undermine the production of security.[13] For these reasons, this book uses the term *(in-)security* to denote that whether certain practices produce security or insecurity depends on the perspective taken.

This has implications on the way cyber(in-)security is defined. The book adopts a critical security studies approach to security. It is key that cyber(in-)security always refers to securing some part of cyberspace from a particular threat for a particular referent actor.[14] Clearly, such challenges vary among referent actors. For individuals, cyber(in-)security challenges may take the form of the protection of one's privacy, whereas for businesses, it may concern the stability of operations. Thus, as explained, *cyber(in-)security* points to the simultaneous security and insecurity that certain practices produce, depending on the actor's perspective.[15]

The Main Arguments Up Front

Overall, I will put forward three main claims that together reward us with a new lens of understanding the international politics of cyber(in-)security. First, by analysing contestations in cyber(in-)security against the background of the history of contestations in piracy and privateering, one can better understand how state proximity is used politically by both attackers and defenders. In the cases investigated, both the attacking and defending governments had significant influence shaping the public narrative about how the attacking 'hackers' are linked to a state. This mirrors the historical evolution of the pirate and privateer: governments and mercantile companies used different types of constructions politically, which, over time, shaped the normative space of what behaviour was tolerated on the seas. This also changes our understanding of attribution, a key element in the strategic use of cyber means, by shifting our focus on the political drivers of public attribution.[16] Based on the historical investigation of pirates and privateers, the book will show that one can better understand attribution claims made by defenders as political claims, in which they select from different types of narratives of how to construct the proximity to the state. The categories of the pirate and privateer were significantly reshaped over the time span investigated in this book. Thus, the historically informed view on how public attributions of individual cyber incidents interact with shaping actor categories over time is an element the analogy is uniquely placed to contribute.

Second, the longevity and path dependencies of historical privateering setups refine our understanding of the constancy, as well as the long-term risks and rewards, of state collaboration with cybercriminals. I will examine the alignment between Russian cybercriminal networks and Russian state interests and analogize the relationship between Russian cybercrime and the Russian state to historical privateers and pirates. Analytically privateering is a particular type of incentive structure in which one actor (the sovereign/the state/the mercantile company) tries to channel the self-interested capacities to become active in the actor's interest. The historical analysis of longevity and depth of privateering structures suggests a prolonged period of blurred lines between state and non-state actors. Thus, if one follows the argument about the alikeness of privateering and some of the overlapping activity between states and criminal networks, then a (historically existing) lock-in effect suggests that this policy has a self-stabilizing quality. Through that, one can understand the difficulty of exiting a policy based on a political cybercriminal nexus and explain the stability of politically constituted cyber insecurity. Again, using this historical analogy enables one to make this long-term observation, as one interprets the state-criminal relationships from a historical perspective.

Third, by treating large technology companies, such as Apple, Google, or Huawei, as political actors of their own kind, the mercantile company lens sharpens the focus on how cooperative and conflictive relations to states, as well as practices of self-protection, influence cyber(in-)security. Particularly, the historical investigation will show how mercantile companies used strategies of expansion and monopolization and how they used their state association strategically. Thus, in different contexts, companies asserted themselves either as 'mere merchants' or as sovereigns. Similarly, as the case studies will show, our understanding of the political behaviour of modern, large technology companies in the domain of cyber(in-)security can be better understood when drawing on such historical experience. Thus, our understanding of the role these companies play in providing cyber(in-)security will be refined. Particularly, the transformation from companies having to completely provide their own protection to starting to demand some state protection mirrors a key turning point in the late 17th century that will be explored in this book.

By examining a diverse range of state and semi-state agency and interaction, the book can shed new light on the politicization of cyber(in-)security and on particular aspects of international relations theory. In the spirit of critical security studies, the book develops and clarifies the understandings of the agency of actors who are neither state nor non-state actors. Special attention is paid to how actions are constituted with reference to a particular relationship to the state. When interrogating the empirical cases, I will show how activities are being rendered as an activity of the state or as activities of another actor.

One of the theoretical contributions the book makes is to elaborate how cyberspace alters rather than diminishes state sovereignty.[17] Actors that share the stage with states do not directly challenge states in as much as they change them: they create 'new wealth, new coalitions, and new attitudes'.[18] Joseph Nye concluded that 'cyberspace will not replace geographical space and will not abolish state sovereignty, but like the town markets in feudal times, it will coexist and greatly complicate what it means to be a sovereign state or a powerful country in the twenty-first century'.[19] My interest lies in developing this further theoretically, that is, how these metaphorical town markets *interact* with states. That is, how new actors are linked to states and what security dynamics are triggered by the perceived existence of such relationships.

Thus, the insights into how categories of the pirate, privateers, and mercantile companies and their configurations to states changed over time enable a new analysis of the current (re-)configuration of the analogical cyber actors. For example, I will look at how cyber mercantile companies are using their status of quasi-sovereigns and 'mere merchants' to order their relations to states. This allows for a deeper insight into how cyber(in-)security politics takes place among and across these actors.

The analogical analysis will illuminate both pathways for optimism and pessimism. Pessimism is warranted, as the historical phenomena changed slowly and over centuries. I will identify political path-dependent policy choices that can explain why cyber privateers and pirates will continue to exist and show instances where cyber mercantile companies fight for their own political agendas, leaving little hope that cybersecurity could be a good enjoyed by everyone. However, the book will end on an optimistic note: countervailing trends do exist. Cyber mercantile companies need not be a menace. Rather, they could also become anchors of stability as their interest in a stable environment coupled with their political power open new pathways for change. For example, their resistance to excessive government surveillance and their insistence on globally compatible jurisdictional solutions to cyberspace can curtail some states' extraterritorial ambitions.

The hope is that the perspective developed contributes to a more stable, cooperative, and secure cyberspace for its users. As the discussions around cyber(in-)security often focus on the asymmetric ways actors can profit from insecurity, I hope that by offering a holistic understanding, the foundations are laid for designing innovative and more durable approaches to cyber(in-)security challenges.

A Few Methodological Considerations

Just as these historical actors interacted amongst one another and with states, similarly today, a variety of actors are operating in concert with states to make use of the insecurity of cyberspace to further their own interests. However, the types of interactions between the actors and the effects of their undertakings are poorly understood. The book addresses this gap by providing a more nuanced understanding of the state's relationships to private actors both historically on the sea and contemporarily in cyberspace.[20] The analogical analysis enables observing the interaction between these actors over time, particularly with respect to state proximity, to better understand the type of challenges witnessed in a loosely governed cyberspace.

The analogy has never been explored in depth. Previous work referring to the analogy examined in this book has either been very short, focused on cyberwarfare or centred on privateering as a policy option.[21] This is problematic as 'the choice of a metaphor carries with it practical implications about contents, causes, expectations, norms, and strategic choices'.[22] In cyber(in-)security, academic work has discussed both how analogies are used and offered various alternative analogies.[23] Some have pointed out that the Cold War concepts used in cyber(in-)security are misleading and that privateering may offer an alternative perspective.[24] Thus, this book evaluates this alternative perspective by investigating one composite analogy further, namely the one to mercantile companies, privateers, and pirates.

To do that, I will develop a conceptual lens with which to capture state proximity and a macro-historical process focus (detailed in Chapter 2). The state-proximity lens views state proximity as a continuum, enabling a broad categorization of actors into state, semi-state, and non-state actors. Thereby, mercantile companies are a special type of semi-state actor due to their functional agency that, in some respects, they resemble a quasi-sovereign.

The focus on interactive macro-historical processes leads to three specific ways of investigating the actors in history. First, due to the interest in state proximity of the actors over time, the question of interest is on how an actor renders itself and is being rendered as proximate to the state. Thus, this entails an acknowledgement that one must understand both the actors' agency and how other actors and processes are shaping the actor's state proximity. When speaking of actors, thereby, it is of great importance to have an in-depth look at a specific time period, as all the meanings and relations between the actor categories shift across time, necessitating arch-ival research.

Second, with privateering being a speciality of this analogy, a macro-his-torical process focus means to enquire into privateering over the long term. I am interested in not only how privateering becomes possible but also what impact it has on the longer term evolution of security policy. This leads to the identification of path-dependent policy choices and an analysis of their im-pact on the relations to and evolution of other actors.

Third, one of the key issues in cybersecurity politics is that much of cyber-space is produced, maintained, and used by private actors. Thus, one of my focuses in the historical research is on how different actors' naval security became an affair of the state (or not). How did the actors of interest (pirates, privateers, and mercantile companies) contribute to or prevent making naval security a state task? What resistance was there? How did it tie in with the strategies of the respective actors?

Thus, I apply these three focuses in the secondary and archival research. Together, they enable a rich macro-historical picture of how shifts between non- and semi-state actors and the state took place across time and to context-ualize, as well as historically reflect on, the current period in cybersecurity in a way that would not be possible without such a historical investigation.

Overall, the historical analogy enables learning more about the structure of relations between different actors working together with or against states in cyber(in-)security. It recognizes a prima facie analogical nature of the at-tempts of states to extend their influence over cyberspace through cooper-ation and competition with, or toleration of, other actors. Through exploring this historical analogy, I will work against the trend in cyber(in-)security to concentrate too much on current events and to treat cyber(in-)security as a new, distinct type of problem.

To do that, we will have to step deeply into naval history and gain a his-torical awareness of the concurrent actors on the sea to explain how priva-teering existed between the late 16th to the mid-19th century and eventually became extinct, a period also referred to as the 'age of sail'. We will look at dif-ferent constellations of mercantile companies, privateers, and pirates at three different points in time. Periodization is necessary to develop an in-depth understanding of the interrelationships between these actors and the state in the respective time period based on archival materials. This serves as a process of alienation from today's state-centric discourse. I am interested in how the different actor categories are mobilized in different time periods and ordered within a larger frame of authority amongst different polities. Such a serial synchronic investigation can capture the disruptive potential of a historical transfer of concepts, namely, to see with a macro-historical view into the constitution of the cyber mercantile companies, privateers, and pirates.

Roadmap: Cyber Mercantile Companies, Privateers, and Pirates in the 21st Century

The book is organised in four parts covering eight chapters. The four parts reflect the overall organization of the study. This first part contains this introduction followed by a discussion of the research strategy for evaluating the analogy. Together, they are meant to give an in-depth understanding of the study at hand.

Chapter 2 outlines the strategy for evaluating the claim, that by looking at the historical dynamics of another ungoverned space—the sea—one can learn some of the contemporary dynamics associated with state, semi-state, and non-state actors. Consequently, Chapter 2 explains how to use a historical analogy for research and how the specific analogy is used. It also introduces the necessary conceptual tooling to categorize the actors: for example, a spectrum of state proximity ranging from state actors to non-state actors to classify mercantile companies, privateers, and pirates. This classification is then used to identify cooperative and conflictive cases, some of which will be looked at in detail in later empirical chapters. Finally, Chapter 2 explains the three macro-historical focuses that will be used to analyse the actors over time and to identify the main analytical lines of enquiry with which to make the analogical claims that the book advances.

The second part, containing Chapters 3–5, covers the history of the main actors on the sea and in cyberspace and distils the main insights of the historical research. This results in locating the analogy in time and setting up the analytical lines of enquiry for applying the historical insights to the modern actors.

Chapter 3 offers a historical narrative investigating navies, mercantile companies, privateers, and pirates from the late 16th to mid-19th century focusing on Britain. Thereby, the focus lies on the interaction between different authorities and the actors in question. Integrating the knowledge from primary and secondary sources, the chapter highlights the evolution of the challenges associated with the different actors. It illustrates the challenges and relationships between the different actors in three different time periods. The time periods include late 16th-century Elizabethan privateering; a late 17th-century account of pirates, privateers, and the East India Company; and the abolition of privateering in 1856.[25]

Chapter 4 offers a short narrative history of cyber(in-)security drawn from secondary sources to establish the types of interactions between the main stakeholders of cyberspace, namely states, corporations, and users. The chapter introduces examples of cooperative and competing aspects of cyber(in-)security between the different stakeholders. With increasing interconnectivity, technology and telecommunication companies' roles in the protection of societal networks and end-user data have become more prominent. Whilst states have acknowledged the challenges arising from cyber(in-)security and tried to address them, they faced both defensive and offensive interests. The defensive interest acknowledged companies' increasingly important roles and made them key stakeholders in the protection of critical infrastructure. The offensive interests, rooted in signals intelligence, led to an investment by states in exploiting cyber insecurity to further their national goals.

Chapter 5 presents the analytical payoff of the historical analysis and develops the thinking tools for analysis in Chapters 6 and 7. Having observed both naval and cyber histories, Chapter 5 first assesses the general comparability of the two domains. Then the focus is on integrating the historical insights gathered into the conceptualization of the different actors, especially with regard to their proximity to the state. This chapter takes stock of how actors are rendered proximate to a state, how the interests in privateering evolved and transformed across time, how longevity and path dependencies are associated with privateering as a policy choice, and how the understanding of mercantile companies can explain the state's interest in security and stability on the seas. Based on the historical insights, the chapter also argues that the mid-19th century period can be ruled out as a possible analogue, as several of the key features defining the period are absent in cyber(in-) security. This sets up the analytical lines of enquiry with which to investigate the modern equivalents to the maritime actors, in analogy to the late 16th- and late 17th-century periods.

The third part follows these lines of enquiry in modern-day empirical cases in two chapters. It shows, what new understandings are possible when applying this analogy to cyber(in-)security. Chapter 6 uses the analogy to pirates and privateers to better understand the governmental response by

Estonia in 2007 and to analyse the cooperation of Russian cybercrime and the Russian government. It argues that the existence of untransparent relationships allow governments to strategically associate activities to other states. Cybercriminals thereby behave similarly to pirates and privateers by sometimes collaborating with states in exchange for the states' ignorance about their criminal enterprises. Chapter 6 then analyses three criminal court cases of Russian hackers which document the usefulness of the cyber pirate and privateer in understanding the government-criminal nexus. Special focus will lie on the longevity and path dependencies such historical privateering set-ups have shown and analyse how they may be present in the modern-day cases.

Chapter 7 focuses on the usefulness of analogies to mercantile companies to understand cooperative and conflictive interests between states and companies in the present era. It does so by using three cases. The attacks against Google in 2009 suggests that some corporations are powerful enough to play in the leagues of states. Their policies resemble the mercantile companies' policies of the past; their dilemmas are analogous. Thereby, their relations to states, both cooperative and conflictive ones, are interlinked. The case of the attacks against Sony Pictures Entertainment in 2014/2015 contrasts with the Google case because of a different U.S. attitude towards protecting the private company from a 'state-sponsored' attack. Finally, the case of signals intelligence, with the cooperation between large technology companies and Five-Eyes signals intelligence agencies, focuses on the cooperative aspects of such relationships and uncovers some further dynamics between companies and states.

The final part, the conclusion, summarizes the arguments made and takes stock of the book's contributions to international relations thinking and cyber(in-)security research. It addresses the issue of what the research community and policymakers can learn from the investigation of this analogy, especially how semi-state actors were historically and contemporarily linked to understandings of statehood, sovereignty, and the legitimacy of the state. It highlights this murky intersection of state, semi-state, and non-state actors and identifies avenues for future research.

2

Using a Historical Analogy as a
Research Strategy

What is an analogy? How does one use a historical analogy for research? And how does this book investigate pirates, privateers, and mercantile companies using such a research strategy? This chapter provides answers. I explain the status of the knowledge claims made, argue why disrupting the current discourse with a historical analogy can be theoretically and empirically productive, and set up the main conceptual toolkit to pursue the specific historical analogical research strategy employed in this book.

Thereby, applying an analogy destabilizes the meanings of both the source and the target of the analogy. For example, researching the privateer considering the modern-day phenomenon changes the enquiry into the past as well as the understanding of the modern form of privateering. The analogy to the historical security dynamics on the sea, thus, suggests a holistic argument, which puts the phenomenon of interest in a larger context and has the potential to capture changing arrangements of state-society-economy relations over time.

For the analysis, concepts describing the interactions between diverse actors are needed. In this respect, I explore two types of questions. First, I analyse whether the historical claim that mercantile companies, privateers, and pirates were connected can reveal connections between otherwise seemingly distinct phenomena in cyber(in-)security. The resulting analysis contributes to a better understanding of the political constitution of cyber(in-)security. Second, I assess, if the collaborative and confrontational arrangements between state and semi-state actors, captured by the analogy, can illuminate the security dynamics introduced by the blurring of lines between these actors. For example, an enquiry into the incentives of how policymakers deal with the modern-day equivalent of a privateer uncovers the intended and unintended consequences such close relationships entail and the degree to which they are comparable. To explore these two questions, I interrogate the conflicting and cooperative endeavours

Semi-State Actors in Cybersecurity. Florian J. Egloff, Oxford University Press. © Florian J. Egloff 2022.
DOI: 10.1093/oso/9780197579275.003.0002

between the different actors and employ a macro-historical process perspective to analyse the actors across time.

The first part of this chapter discusses how to use a historical analogy for research purposes. I then turn to how the specific analogy of privateering and cyber(in-)security are used in policymaking and research and the approach to analogical reasoning this book undertakes. The analysis shows that, in contrast to much of the literature, the book does more than analogize one point in time; it looks at how the actors and their relationships evolved across time, following a pragmatist stance of analogical research.

To sharpen the research focus, the chapter introduces state proximity as a conceptual lens and uses it to elaborate a baseline understanding of the different actors. It categorizes them into state, semi-state, and non-state actors, whilst recognizing that the boundaries between them are fluid. These conceptual typologies are used to set up a framework for selecting the modern cases. The framework encompasses the cooperative and conflictive relationships between state, semi-state, and non-state actors and enables a mapping of major cyber(in-)security cases.

Finally, the chapter closes by combining the focus on state proximity with the interest in the specific historical analogical analysis. To capture the evolution of state proximity of the actors and its implications for security and policy across time, I adopt a macro-historical process perspective and identify three focuses for the historical research. As a whole, the chapter explains the analogical research strategy employed in the ensuing chapters.

How to Use Analogies for Research

An analogy can be defined as a 'correspondence or resemblance between things, as a basis for reasoning or argumentation'.[1] Much of human thought is based on analogical reasoning. Analogies differ from metaphors in the degree to which they are specified. Analogies are argued in much more detail than metaphors. Analogies can thus be considered a specific form of metaphor. Cognitive psychologists argue that analogies and metaphors make up the fundamental building blocks of our thinking.[2] Since research findings indicate that our thinking is structured by conceptual metaphors, the use of metaphors in an academic process has to be explained.[3] Many scientific theories are based on underlying metaphors. For example, Theodore L. Brown explains in his book *Making Truth*:

The models and theories that scientists use to explain their observations are metaphorical constructs. To understand how science works and to account for its success, we have no need for the proposition that scientists have unmediated access to the world 'as it really is'. We have no grounds for believing that there exist objective, mind-independent truths awaiting discovery. Rather, statements we regard as truths about the world are the product of human reasoning.[4]

He then goes on to explain this statement by using various examples from chemistry, physics, and biology. Metaphors hold together research programmes and define theories. For example, thinking of the state as an individual, mirroring the qualities of human nature, has influenced much of international relations (IR) theory. However, holding onto the same metaphors can lead to theoretical stagnation and can be constraining.[5] For example, famous quantum physicists David Bohm and F. David Peat argued that had 19th-century physicists been able to think of a particle as a wave, a breakthrough in quantum physics could have occurred much earlier. The fundamental building blocks of mathematics would have been available, but holding onto seeing the world as either a particle or a wave limited the realm of the possible. Thus, they argue for a greater inclusion of creativity in the scientific process. They speculate:

It would be better to regard scientists, in the case of interpretations, as being somewhat like artists who produce quite different paintings of the same sitter. Each theory will be capable of giving a unique insight which is aesthetically satisfying, to a given person, in some ways and not in others. Some interpretations may show creative originality while others may be mediocre. Yet none give the final 'truth' about the subject.[6]

This quote mirrors an argument Ron Deibert makes when he explains how 'large-scale conceptual revolutions are driven by the creative use of metaphors, by novel redescriptions of the present that help shake us free from the current dogma and stale vocabulary that has us intellectually stifled'.[7]

New metaphors can be disruptive. They change the fundamental assumptions about a subject. They 'often ask us to project one system on to another sort of terrain entirely . . . . The metaphor highlights certain unpleasant and perhaps controversial features of both subjects; the features become the more prominent for their being parallel'.[8] In this process, neither the source nor the target of the metaphor stays constant. Rather, sometimes called the interaction view of metaphors, it is widely acknowledged that metaphors change both the understanding of the source and the target of the metaphor.[9] The analogy explored in this book is a case of such a new metaphor. Thinking of the modern-day equivalents of mercantile companies, privateers, and pirates offers a conceptual space to disrupt traditional notions of state and non-state actors. Thus, the evaluation of the analogy does not only capture how it can order empirical phenomena but also how far it is useful in enabling a more nuanced understanding of state–non-state actor relationships.

In IR, research on metaphors and analogies is relatively sparse. Michael P. Marks's contributions on metaphors and Richard Little's contribution on the balance of power as a metaphor in IR are notable exceptions.[10] Both note that the use of metaphors in IR is abundant and that the re-examination of forgotten metaphors is an important endeavour for the discipline. They also point out that studying the metaphors used by theoreticians can be problematic as they reflect the academic community's own understanding of how the world works and not necessarily the experiences of the subjects. This critique places them on the understanding (i.e. hermeneutical) side of IR research.[11] As a consequence, Marks highlights that 'scholars who invoke a metaphor must therefore ensure that there is corresponding comprehension of those who have lived experiences of that which the metaphor invokes'.[12]

This also connects to the post-positivist commitment of the inseparability of the researcher and the subject. Even if we acknowledge mind-independent information, 'there is no mind-independent way of *thinking about it*'.[13] As mentioned, a metaphor used in IR theory is the state understood as a human being. Other examples in IR theory are states as billiard balls or containers;, power understood as a balancing act; nuclear deterrence strategy as a game of chicken; and levels of analysis used for horizontal abstraction layers between domestic, state-level, and system-level politics. Far from being value neutral, these metaphors do not arise out of a thought vacuum. They are shaped by the experiences and value commitments of the researchers as well as the surrounding discourses in which they are deployed. With this in mind, the next section turns to the specific historical analogy at hand and explains, how this book uses the analogy as a research strategy.

How Does This Book Use the Specific Historical Analogy as a Research Strategy?

This book evaluates the analogy of the historical security dynamics on the sea to cyber(in-)security. The cyber(in-)security discourse is open for ideas and framings to compete in capturing different aspects of the security challenges. The assessment of an analogy, purporting a holistic understanding of the phenomena, probes to what extent it can render political interactions between a mercantile company, privateer, and pirate intelligible and thereby offer a language with which to capture the political effects of such a structure.[14] This is based on an understanding of partial truth claims: there is a 'real' world out there, but we have no mind-independent way of accessing it. The way we speak about the world matters and has significant implications on what is rendered possible. For example, the framing of the cyber(in-)security problem, with reference to the historical analogy of actors on the sea, has the potential of destabilizing the fiction of a clean state and non-state dichotomy. This productive opening up of a conceptual space will be used to develop conceptual thinking tools that can then be applied to cybersecurity. The analogy will then be applied to evaluate how such an application is useful in capturing empirical phenomena and how it changes our understanding of cyber(in-)security.[15] Thus, the aim is to explore how the conceptual understanding of the actors and their relations to the state, which are built during the historical enquiry, generate new understandings of the contemporary cases.[16] This newly generated understanding can then be used in further problem-solving oriented research.[17]

The historical analogy is interesting epistemologically. It constitutes the cyber(in-)security challenge by recourse to an older world. As Robert W. Cox writes of critical theory, it calls institutions and power relations into question: 'the critical approach leads towards the construction of the larger picture of the whole of which the initially contemplated part is just one component, and seeks to understand the processes of change in which both parts and whole are involved'.[18] This strand of theorizing was subsequently picked up in the 1990s critical security studies literature with an aim to denaturalize power structures through historicizing and questioning. Thus, the analysis will tease out the potential as well as the detriments of constituting the cyber(in-)security challenge in terms of the historical naval security challenge. The structure of the cyber(in-)security challenge is questioned, with particular focus on how some actors are rendered state or non-state and how they interact with the state.[19] Through so doing, the book illuminates grey spaces of political action and renders them intelligible.

Since multiple epistemological types of analyses are possible, it is pertinent to point out what this book is setting out to do. First, one can distinguish between using an analogy as a thinking tool for scholarship versus analysing the use of an analogy by policymakers. Whilst both are valuable endeavours, this book is doing the former, not the latter. Second, to agree on the status of the knowledge produced by the book, the epistemological stance needs to be further specified. Following Kornprobst, the next few paragraphs present the positivist, post-structuralist, and pragmatist account of the status of analogies, and then it is decided to follow a pragmatist stance of truth.

Positivists use historical analogies to 'describe, explain and predict' an objective reality.[20] They believe that an application of the correct methods and research design leads to the discovery of truth. This causes several problems when using historical analogies in a positivist research design. First, an analogical comparison necessarily involves two very different situations that are not strictly comparable, and second, the data relied on is often produced by actors that do not share a positivist rule-set for producing the facts.[21] This is problematic as, for the positivist, the true historical fact is the basis on which to build the analogy.

Post-structuralists do not have this problem, though they face other challenges. For them, the main thrust of enquiry lies in the deconstruction of dominant discourses, often using genealogy to do so. Genealogical accounts, thereby, use analogies as 'tools for denaturalizing discursive constructs'.[22] For post-structuralists, analogies remain solely tools to denaturalize. As they are tools for critique, they cannot ever produce an alternative constructive account of the world.[23]

Pragmatists share the rejection of an objective truth with post-structuralists but see the purpose of research as generating useful knowledge.[24] Hence, to pragmatists, analogies can be used to increase our understanding of the world. Truth claims, thereby, are partial to the assent of the stakeholders in open debate. The way to agree on whether analogies are leading or misleading is by debate and adjudication by peers. To the degree that they are accepted by peers, the truth claims constitute working truths, which are 'always provisional'.[25] This matches the understanding put forward in this book.

Finally, historical analogies can be evaluated by their use as first- or second-order constructs.[26] The evaluation of a first-order construct looks at the appropriateness of the analogy by comparing its empirical applicability with the historian's working truths. The evaluation of a second-order construct refers to the political function of labelling two things as analogues (e.g. comparing a politician to Hitler). The two functions are not fully separable in practice, though some applications of analogies invoke stronger political functions than others.

This book focuses on the evaluation of the first-order construct and pursues this in two steps, namely enquiring both about its empirical applicability and about how it changes our understanding of cyber(in-)security. The empirical claim is an analytical judgement on the comparability of the historical and modern political contestations, building on working truths generated by historians as well as archival work. The claim of changing, or disrupting our understanding, is a normative claim, arguing that due to the application of the analogy, we can better understand a part of cyber(in-)security.

The distinctive benefit of such an approach is that it enables the conceptual foundations for a study of security arrangements in which a private actor's relationship with a state is co-constitutive of the actor type. Thus, the book explores the usefulness of the analogy in terms of its ability to capture the political processes that associate an actor with the state. Considering the actor categories of the analogy as morally neutral ensures that the security dynamics can be captured as reflexive practices giving rise to security dilemmas. Critical reflection, therefore, enables one to capture the performative aspect of calling an activity a 'state-sponsored' act. Analysing this process with reference to the historical cases allows one to evaluate whether the phenomena in question are comparable. The book does not try to demonstrate whether 'real' privateers exist. Rather, it shows, how historical comparisons elucidate the security dynamics of specific cases and contexts. Thus, I will follow a pragmatist methodological approach to exploring the utility of the analogy.

The Analogy to Privateering in the Literature

Before further refining the research strategy, I will briefly explore how the analogy to privateering is currently represented in the literature and explain why the analogy to privateering is fruitful to explore further. A group of scholars researched the governing metaphors of cyber(in-)security and argued against the dominant Cold War metaphor. Others suggested different analogies.[27] For example, Betz and Stevens assess a range of spatial and biological analogies in use. They find that the application of the analogies clearly serves some productive purpose, whilst the wholesale application of them is probably misleading.[28] A number of alternative analogies could have been evaluated (see Table 2.1).

The analogy to privateering merits further investigation. Whilst other analogies have become common when describing digital phenomena of insecurity (e.g. viruses), privateering was offered on the international stage as a way of vocalizing the international conflict-dimension of digital activity. The domain analogy used by the U.S. Department of Defense privileges the strategic military dimension (also in terms of budgetary implications), and the Wild West, Pearl Harbor, and cyber 9/11 analogies are U.S. specific.[29] The global commons analogy is, in some ways, the underlying analogy to privateering, as policymakers today often mention the sea as a paradigmatic case for global commons.[30] Privateering is thus a specific way of operating in such a space, specifically as a form of producing security (or insecurity, depending on the perspective). The privateering analogy lays its emphasis on the actors possessing the capabilities to act and those authorizing the use of such capabilities in a commonly used space. The analogy investigated is used in the policymaking discourse, with little regard for its appropriate historical embeddedness—perhaps deliberately so.[31] Given these characteristics, it merits further enquiry. The research journey in this book is to go back to history, enquire what the historical political contentions surrounding the use of privateers and their interactions with pirates and mercantile companies were, and approach the modern environment with a refined understanding.

Until now, no one has undertaken extensive research on whether this analogy can be supported considering the privateers' historical contemporaries,

Table 2.1 Alternative analogies of cyberspace

Analogies	Used by
Domain (e.g. space, air, sea, land)	Throughout militaries (originally U.S. DoD)
Public health, particular focus on immunology & epidemiology	Throughout computer science (e.g. virus, infection, etc.)
American Wild West	Anecdotal use in U.S. intelligence community, use in some policy reports
Global commons, especially comparing to the sea, including privateering	Foreign Office use; often also navy officer's use
Event-based analogies (cyber Pearl Harbor, cyber 9/11)	U.S. politicians

namely mercantile companies, and pirates. However, to build on previous research, the previously existing arguments shall be discussed.

In 2006, after offering a short historical overview, John Laprise developed the ideas of the French late 19th-century *Jeune Ecole* regarding the war on commerce, using the *guerre de course* in analogy to cyberspace. He suggested that cyberspace offers strategic advantages of dependency to the United States: 'just as it was impossible to cease trading with the British Empire during the nineteenth century, it is difficult for a nation to forego trade with the U.S. today as the economic costs are too high'.[32] Following this, Laprise focused on the tactical parallels between possible cyberspace strategic doctrines and sea power doctrines, including decisive battle, siege, sea control, sea denial, and commerce warfare. He developed the analogy of commerce warfare to cyberspace concluding that the 'U.S. is in a position similar to that of Great Britain during the nineteenth century'.[33] Although a remarkable contribution to strategic discourse, his perspective is focused on cyber warfare and strategic thinking at the turn of the 19th century. In contrast, this book aims to engage in a more holistic use of the analogy, following the development of privateering throughout history and finding reference points that connect to the situation in cyber(in-)security.

In 2013, Michael Lesk published an article focusing on the difficulties introduced when using privateers. He argued against the enthusiasm of a subset of U.S. policymakers for so called 'active defence' of the private sector.[34] While agreeing with Lesk about the policy recommendations, it is worth exploring whether the analogy employed reflects the broader reality of today's cyberspace, rather than 'just' a policy option.

Robert Axelrod and Peter W. Singer & Allan Friedman mentioned the analogy briefly.[35] Having mentioned the analogy in a blog post in 2011, Singer and Friedman come closest to making a similar argument as pursued in this book, namely exploring the analogy by analysing the privateers and pirates concurrently.[36] However, their focus lies mainly on the policies adopted after the War of 1812.[37] In addition, their brief treatment allows for little in-depth research on the actual pirates, privateers, and mercantile companies. Rather, they used the analogy as one of many ways of analysing cyberspace.

Finally, there have been some contributions in the legal, information security, and policy realm. In the legal realm, scholars explored letters of marque and the law of piracy as potential legal instruments to address cyber(in-)security.[38] In information security and policy, some analogies of navies, privateers, and pirates to cyber(in-)security were made at conferences and in blog posts.[39] However, no one presented the in-depth research neces-sary in order to evaluate the analogy.

This book remedies that gap. Through undertaking the secondary and archival research necessary to understand the lifeworld of the main actors at different points in time, it can contextualize and refine our understanding of the current interactions between the cyber actors and the broader trans-formations of international politics in our time. This goes far beyond existing analyses by not only analogizing one point in history but also by developing a broader understanding of the evolution of pirates, privateering, and mercan-tile companies. This perspective highlights how certain solutions were ren-dered possible over time. It both shows the commonalities and contingencies of each realm and allows for a more nuanced understanding of the domain.

A 'Use with Care' Warning

Before turning to the systematic approach embarked on, a 'use with care' warning is in order. Historical analogies are tricky beasts. They have great potential to enlighten novel subjects but are just as often used for political purposes.[40] Both functions are inherent elements of any historical analogy, though with some analogies one function is more pronounced than with others. With regard to the analogy studied, this poses some hazards. To miti-gate those, a 'use with care' warning for three specific aspects is issued. It in-cludes the risk of further militarizing the discourse on cyber(in-)security, the risk of advocating empire, and the risky temptation of assuming that history can be used to predict the future.[41]

The analogy considers cyberspace with relation to another relatively aggressive and militarized discourse, namely that of naval (in-)security between the late 16th and mid-19th centuries.[42] Whilst it is useful for generating insights in the analysis of the current politics of cybersecurity, for policymakers, civilian analogies may be more productive in creating oppor-tunities for dialogue and cooperative solutions. Other, more peaceful, analo-gies could be more desirable in the context of a multilateral forum to reshape the perception of the cyber(in-)security problem and to extend the possible range of solutions. After all, the technologies we develop and integrate into our lives are a function of our political values and principles—as such we ought to treat the politics of cyber(in-)security inherently as a deliberation about human security, accountable practices, and limits of power.[43]

A superficial reading of the analogy could entail advocating for empire, including all its oppressive and dominating aspects, as a solution to the security problems of cyberspace today. After all, when privateering was abolished in 1856, the Royal Navy was the dominating naval power. To make this explicit upfront: the book will not advocate this pathway as a desirable solution for cyber(in-)security. Furthermore, the analytical judgements arrived at in Chapter 5 will clarify why this is also not a feasible solution.

Finally, historical experience does not guarantee a parallel course of events today. Just as policymakers in the past were making decisions in the face of uncertainty, knowledge of the past should not lead the scholar into the misguided belief that history will repeat itself. When considering the insights from the analogy to mercantile companies, privateers, and pirates, policies for the 21st century must take into account the idiosyncrasies of today's political landscape. The 21st century offers some new opportunities, which can and should be embraced by policymakers. Thus, whilst the book does put forward the analogy as a diagnostic tool to identify and interpret novel problems, it refrains from advocating the analogy as a prescriptive tool for following historically selected solutions.

Systematic Approach: State Proximity as a Conceptual Lens

When starting to conceptualize the interactions between our actors of interest and the state, it is useful to examine how others have dealt with the same problem in the literature. For example, the literature on violent non-state actors, with few exceptions, uses typologies to conceptualize the different actors captured under the armed non-state actor umbrella.[44] Whilst building the typologies as heuristic devices, the empirical cases usually blur these types when examining a specific actor. Furthermore, the entanglement of these actors with states has been identified as a field for further research. Clearly, the cyber actors of interest in this book are neither necessarily violent nor armed in the traditional sense.[45] However, the type of analysis employed by scholars studying violent non-state actors can aid the conceptualization of the actors observed in cyberspace, not least because similar incentive structures can apply to states.

Two focuses of analysis are of interest. First, the evaluation of the analogy to mercantile companies, privateers, and pirates focuses on the holistic analytic task of identifying connections between phenomena otherwise seen as distinct in cyberspace. Thus, an answer must be given as to whether the analogy is applicable to groups as diverse as cyber commands, technology companies, hackers, and cybercriminals. Can a spectrum of analysis of cyber influence and conflict bring them together? Second, like the research on armed non-state actors, I focus on typologies of cyber phenomena to identify specific ways in which the different types of actors interact. The focus is on whether the collaboration and confrontation between the different actors can be usefully captured by the analogy. The analysis of the interactions between state, semi-state, and non-state actors will uncover the security dynamics at play. For example, the collaborative aspects between companies and governmental security institutions may uncover insights into the dynamics of company and state security. Similarly, the confrontational aspects between the modern companies and states can capture corporate powers and weaknesses when interacting with multiple states at once.

To support the analysis of these two focuses, a spectrum of state proximity will be used to refine the concepts of the mercantile company, privateer, and the pirate. As an anchoring point, this also includes navies (i.e. state actor). Thereby, state proximity is understood as how closely an actor collaborates with the organs of a state. This conceptualization mirrors Ersel Aydinli's understanding of 'distance from the state'.[46] Thinking of the level of autonomy from the state as a matter of degree acknowledges the difficulty of classifying an actor as non-state. The state closeness of actors on this spectrum can be understood to be coalescing, analogous to the colours on a colour spectrum. Whilst the different colours on a colour spectrum are clearly recognizable, the boundaries of one to the other are fluid. However, it is clear that on the one end we have non-state actors and on the other end we have state actors. We are interested in the middle between them, the semi-state actors.

This basic framework of state proximity can now be refined with the concepts of the actors developed in this book. Each actor type—pirate, privateer, and mercantile company—captures a specific type of relationship, but the way that it can manifest itself is manifold. I will revisit the conceptualization of actors in Chapter 5, after having done the historical work. The historical research presented in Chapters 3 and 4 will sharpen our understanding of how the mercantile company, the privateer, and the pirate are different with respect to their relations to the state. This will provide the baseline for the application of the analogy to the cyber actors. Thus, the idea here is not to come up with one definition of the ideal types. Rather, the intent is to explore the different manifestations of the concepts that provide a rich understanding of the family of cases that are referred to as mercantile companies, privateers, and pirates. With this repertoire of historical constellations of state proximity, the full strength of the analogy can be assessed. The historical examples can expand the contemporary realm of how the different actor constellations may fit together to form a holistic realm. In a second step, based on the state proximity framework, both cooperative and conflictive types of interaction between the actors can be looked at. Attention is paid to extracting common challenges from the different constellations between the different actors.

Three Actor Types: State, Semi-State, and Non-State Actors

The basic conceptual understanding of the naval actors of interest provides a good starting point for applying the framework of state proximity. Although *navy* can sometimes be used as a term indicating the ships of a particular maritime institution (e.g. the merchant navy), in this book, it denotes a state institution.

There is no consensus definition of a *mercantile company*. Rather, they are defined inductively by referring to examples, such as the chartered companies operating predominantly out of European states. A prominent chartered company is the British East India Company which was founded in 1600. Such companies are characterized here as semi-state actors due to their strong relationships both with their home states and with the foreign territories they operate within.[47] They are not classified as non-state actors due to their intimate relationship with a particular home state. We will observe this relationship in-depth in later chapters. Suffice it to say that this relationship creates severe national security challenges for foreign states dealing with such actors. They are not classified as state actors as they are not formally integrated in the state organs and as they have special relationships with foreign polities also. The reason for classifying the mercantile company and the privateer as semi-state actors is to acknowledge their relationship to the state as qualitatively different enough to merit further inspection. Briefly summarized, the concept of the mercantile company captures the political aspects of private sector foundations of cyberspace. It recognizes that unlike many security challenges that are becoming more privatized (e.g. through private security and military companies), in cybersecurity, we start out with private security being the norm.

The term *privateer* denotes a privately owned vessel that operates against an enemy with the licence or commission of a government in times of war.[48] Compared with that, a *pirate* is 'a person who plunders or robs from ships, esp. at sea; a person who commits or practises piracy'. But also 'a person who goes about in search of plunder; a freebooter, a marauder; a raider, a plunderer, a despoiler'.[49] The privateer differs from the pirate because the actions of the privateer are committed under the authority of a state. Privateers are classified as semi-state actors, whilst pirates are considered non-state actors. Pirates are considered non-state actors, as they work outside the state system, sometimes even rejecting the state's authority to govern them. However, in specific cases, they may be found to be more closely affiliated with a state, which would merit treating them as semi-state actors.

Introducing the concept of a *privateer* offers a perspective on how to understand states' motivations for using private actors for political goals. There is a variety of such actors contemporarily and their numbers are growing. The concept of the pirate illuminates how the blurred lines between state support and tolerance can introduce challenges and opportunities into the relations between states.

Table 1.1 shows how the equivalent actors in cyberspace can be categorized alongside the same spectrum of state proximity as on the sea. For an actor to be categorized as a state actor, it must be part of the state's organs or in direct support thereof. They should be distinguished from semi-state actors, which are in a close relationship with one particular state (which I refer to here as their 'home' state), and sometimes advance this state's interests but are not organizationally integrated into state functions. They also stand in a special relationship with foreign states, in that they sometimes collaborate and compete also with foreign states, sometimes independently of their 'home' state. Non-state actors are actors whose interests lie outside the formal activities of a state, who might even reject the state's authority to govern their activities. Nevertheless, they may sometimes be in complicated relations to states, enabling each other to pursue their interests. Overall, only those actors are of interest that directly interfere with another group's or individual's security interests.

This conceptual understanding of mapping state proximity based on the collaboration with the state is extended, with regard to mercantile companies, in a functional mapping of state-like agency (see Figure 2.1). Thus, a feature of mercantile companies is that they not only collaborate intimately with particular states (state proximity), but that they are also functionally set-up as a state-like actor (i.e. some of their behaviour and organizational structure looks and acts similar to a state). Hence, whilst some smaller companies may have the same state proximity in their collaborations with a state, they are not classified as mercantile companies functionally.

These conceptual understandings provide a perspective with which to analyse the different actors in cyberspace. Each concept provides a distinct way in which the respective actor is connected to the state. Importantly, the concepts do not carry an inherent moral value. The concepts of the navy, mercantile company, privateer, and pirates are understood as concepts that, by themselves, are morally empty. This also reflects the historical understanding of them: some viewed privateers as heroes, others thought of them as criminals.

The three categories of actors, developed based on the state-proximity framework, can be used to analyse the interactions between them. To do that, I will expand an argument about two concurrent states of nature, eloquently laid out by Lucas Kello.[50] The argument tries to capture the increasingly

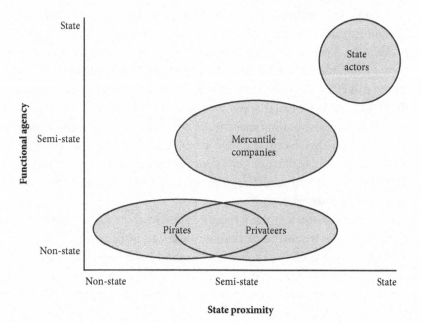

Figure 2.1 Spectrum of state proximity versus functional agency

diverse stakeholder landscape in international politics beyond states. One state of nature, the one very familiar to the international relations scholar, consists of states acting amongst one another under the condition of anarchy. The state versus state interactions in cyberspace can thereby potentially benefit from the web of norms that governs the relations between states. The other state of nature consists of non-traditional actors competing with one another in a global system, with actors that do not necessarily strive for statehood, but they are not under direct control of states. It is in the cases where these two states of nature converge and collide that the experience of the mercantile companies, privateers, and pirates may illuminate some of the security dynamics at play in the international politics cyber(in-)security.

Whilst the old state of nature (state vs. state) exists, cyber(in-)security has accentuated a new state of nature involving non- and semi-state actors. This global state of nature can be analysed using the state/semi-state/non-state framework, both for when the actors' interests collide and for when they converge. With respect to when they collide the question arises: when are the respective actors attackers and when are they victims?

When mapping some prolific cyber incidents onto the categories identified (see Table 2.2), a clearer picture of the complexity of responding to cyber operations starts to emerge. Each of these categories of constellations involves different challenges for the attacked party. For example, in the cyber operation against Estonia in 2007, all the signs pointed to Russian patriotic hackers attacking the Estonian infrastructure. How should a state handle such a situation? In another case, Sony Pictures Entertainment (SPE) was attacked in 2014, allegedly by the North Korean government, so how should the U.S. government react? Some of these constellations will be looked at in more detail in the following chapters. By doing in-depth research on some of these cases and thereby contributing to building knowledge about how states reacted in particular situations, the book refines the knowledge on how these constellations provide analytical leverage to better understand the security dynamics of cyberspace.

With respect to when the interests of the different actors converge, the question is, who is demanding assistance and who is supplying it?

Mapping some of the prolific cooperation cases onto the matrix (see Table 2.3) captures the constellations that are difficult to explain in a traditional state versus state framework. For example, the cooperation between technology or telecommunication service providers and states needs to be carefully researched. Similarly, the cooperation between cybercriminals and

Table 2.2 Collision of interests between state, semi-state, and non-state actors

		Victims		
	Actor types	*State*	*Semi-state*	*Non-state*
Attackers	*State*	Moonlight Maze GhostNet Stuxnet Red October	NSA/Huawei PLA /Google, Lockheed (e.g. Titan Rain, Operation Aurora) RU/Ukrainian power grid	PLA/Tibetan activists (GhostNet) NK/SPE RU/TV 5 monde
	Semi-state	Patriotic hackers/Estonia Iranian hackers/ Saudi Aramco (Shamoon)		Russian hackers/ JPMorgan Chase Iran/Sands Casino cybercrime
	Non-state	Activist hackers/ NK ISIS/ STRATCOM	ISIS/AP Phineas Fisher/ HackingTeam & Gamma International	cybercrime Anonymous/ Scientology Ashley Madison

Source: Previously published in Florian J. Egloff, 'Cybersecurity and the Age of Privateering', in *Understanding Cyberconflict: Fourteen Analogies*, ed. George Perkovich and Ariel E. Levite (Washington DC: Georgetown University Press, 2017), 231–47.

Table 2.3 Convergence of interests between state, semi-state, and non-state actors

		Supply of cooperation		
	Actor types	*State*	*Semi-state*	*Non-state*
Demand for cooperation	*State*	Five-Eyes	USA/PRISM companies CN/Huawei, Boyusec RU/Patriotic hackers, Enfer	Iran/hackers Russia/ cybercrime U.S./Hector Gonzalez
	Semi-state	Google/U.S. (Operation Aurora) Huawei/U.K.		
	Non-state	SPE/U.S. Cybercrime/Russia		Wikileaks/ Anonymous

Source: Previously published in Florian J. Egloff, 'Cybersecurity and the Age of Privateering', in *Understanding Cyberconflict: Fourteen Analogies*, ed. George Perkovich and Ariel E. Levite (Washington DC: Georgetown University Press, 2017), 231–47.

states is of interest. As in the case of the collision model, some of the constellations will be researched in-depth in this book to build a better understanding
of the choices made by the actors. In both models, there are constellations
that indicate the presence of dynamics of an old state versus state type of
interaction as well as those of a new type of state of nature.

With this in mind, we can now revisit the case selection. The purpose of
the case studies are (a) to analyse to what extent there is evidence of effects of
the presence of the actors of interest in the cyber(in-)security cases and (b) to
elucidate how the historical cases can aid our understanding of the security
challenges modern-day cyber mercantile companies, cyber privateers, and
cyber pirates introduce.

The two matrices identified a range of cases with both converging and
conflicting interest. Five of those cases will be analysed as single case studies
in Chapters 6 and 7 (see Tables 2.4 and 2.5). This allows for an assessment of
the degree to which the analogy can shed light on the differing types of constellations. Whilst the spectrum of state proximity is the focal point of the
analysis of all cases, specific claims are evaluated in the different cases. Each
of those cases highlights key aspects of how the analogy can be applied and
how such an application of the concepts of a mercantile company, privateers,
and pirates changes our understanding of cyber(in-)security.

The cases were selected to best evaluate the conceptual applicability of the
analogy.[51] Due to the book's interest in the state's relationships to different
actors, only cases in which a state is involved, excluding those in which both

Table 2.4 Collision of interests between state, semi-state, and non-state actors
(selected cases)

	Actor types	State	Semi-state	Non-state
			Victims	
Attackers	State		China/Google (Operation Aurora) (Chapter 7, Case 1)	North Korea/ SPE (Chapter 7, Case 2)
	Semi-state	Patriotic hackers/ Estonia (Chapter 6, Case 1)		Russian cyber criminals/ U.S. businesses (Chapter 6, Case 2)
	Non-state	Activist hackers/ North Korea (Chapter 7, Case 2)		

Table 2.5 Convergence of interests between state, semi-state, and non-state actors (selected cases)

	Actor types	Supply of cooperation		
		State	*Semi-state*	*Non-state*
Demand for cooperation	*State*		RU/Patriotic hackers (Chapter 6; Cases 1+2) USA/PRISM companies (Chapter 7, Case 3)	Russia/ Cybercrime (Chapter 6, Cases 1+2)
	Semi-state	Google/U.S. (Operation Aurora) (Chapter 7, Case 1)		
	Non-state	Cybercrime/RU (Chapter 6; Case 2) SPE/U.S. (Chapter 7, Case 2)		

semi- and non-state actors only attack each other and those in which states attack other states. This choice is driven by the motivation of this book, namely, to research unconventional yet important actors and their connections to states in cyber(in-)security. From this subset, important cases in the subject under investigation were chosen. They all contain key actors and events that significantly shaped the history of global cyber(in-)security.[52] Two cases are used to evaluate the insights gained from historical pirates and privateers, namely (a) the cyberattacks against Estonia in 2007 and (b) the criminal-political nexus of Russian cybercrime. Three cases highlight the conflicting and cooperative relations between cyber mercantile companies and states: (a) the intrusions into Google in 2009/10, [53] (b) the attack against SPE in 2014/15, and (c) the cooperation between large technology companies with Five-Eyes signals intelligence agencies, particularly those of the United States and the United Kingdom.

How to Proceed from Here: A Focus on Macro-Historical Processes

Having introduced the spectrum of state proximity, it is worth reflecting a final time on what type of, and how exactly, the application of a historical analogy can produce knowledge in cybersecurity. As introduced earlier, the analogy is applied with a dual focus, empirical and normative. That is not yet sufficiently narrow to guide archival work. Thus, narrowing the focus on state proximity of the main actors was necessary. I still need to clarify how exactly I want to investigate state proximity in the past and present. In the specific application of the analogy, I am not just interested in the state proximity of the main actors at one point in time; rather, I want to observe how the actor constellations changed over time. I call this a focus on the interactive macro-historical processes that shape and are being shaped by the actor constellations in place. What do I mean by that?

First, if one wants to focus on actors' state proximity over time, the question shifts from 'how is this actor related to the state?' to 'how is this actor both rendering itself and being rendered as (not) proximate to a state over time?' Thus, in an interactive macro-historical process view, one must pay close attention to both the actors' agency and how other actors and processes shape the actors' state proximity. Note that this entails sensitivity to what type of polities existed at the relevant historical period and how they are linked to one another.[54] Thus, recalling the early modern focus, the reconfiguration of these actors to one another can also shed light on how it contributes to or works against the emergence of state sovereignty. Researching these configurations in-depth in three historical time periods, as well as in the present, enables a concrete understanding of the comparability of the different actor constellations. This will develop a sensitivity to processes of authorization, for example, when interrogating the boundaries of someone successfully claiming to be a privateer and how those limits are established between different actors. Hence, one focus will be on the representation of actors' connections to the state over time.

Second, with privateering being a speciality of this analogy, a macro-historical process focus means to look at not only how privateering became possible but also what impact it had on the longer term evolution of a state's security policy. Thus, the macro-historical focus engenders sensitivity to path-dependent policy choices and their impact on the relations to and evolution of other actors. I am thus interested in what privateering represented as an element of security policy in each of the historical time periods and how this element interacted with the other actors.

Third, one of the key issues in cybersecurity politics is that much of cyberspace is produced, maintained, and used by private actors. The security role of the state is still up for political debate.[55] Thus, one of the focuses in the historical research is how different actors' naval security became an affair of the state. How did the actors of interest (pirates, privateers, and mercantile companies) contribute to or prevent making naval security a state task? What resistance was there? How did it tie in with the strategies of the respective actors? Paying close attention to these questions in the different historical time periods allows me to distil which constellations the current cyber(in-) security challenge is best compared with. It also reveals the diverse public-private relations that contemporarily exist in different parts of the world and how those different conceptions lead to security challenges internationally.

Thus, these three focuses were applied in the secondary and archival research that followed. Together, they enable a rich macro-historical picture of how shifts between private actors (economic and societal) and the state took place across time and to contextualize, as well as historically reflect on, the current period in cybersecurity in a way that is not possible without such a historical analogy. The result of this research, that is, how this took place on the seas, where we stand in cyberspace, and how this can be compared with one another, is what will be reported on in the following part. Thereby, the subsequent two chapters (Chapters 3 and 4) are written in a historical mode, reporting on the historical research. Chapter 5 then compares the two domains and discusses the main analytical insights before applying the analogy to the modern cyber actors.

HISTORIES OF THE SEA AND CYBERSPACE, COMPARISON, AND LOCATING THE ANALOGY IN TIME

3

A History of the Loosely Governed Seas between the 16th and 19th Centuries

From the Age of Privateering to Its Abolition

This chapter discusses the main historical trends and characteristics of navies, mercantile companies, privateers, and pirates from the 16th to the 19th
century to set up the analogy to contemporary problems of cyber(in-)se-
curity. The chapter defines the historical bounds of the analogy and identifies different constellations between the actors investigated in three historical
cases: an account of late 16th-century Elizabethan privateering; the interaction between mercantile company, privateers, and pirates in the late 17th
century; and the abolition of privateering in the mid-19th century.[1]

The chapter focuses on how non- and semi-state actors, with the capacity to deploy violence at sea, were interacting with one another and with
states. I argue that non- and semi-state actors had different options for collaboration at different points in time: whilst violence at sea was a relatively
state-independent activity in the 16th century, the late 17th century shows an
increased ambition for state control of semi- and non-state actors deploying
violence at sea. This changed the operating environment and realms of possibilities for these actors. Some chose to capitalize on the state's willingness to
claim authority over their domain of action, whilst others chose to resist it.
The mid-19th-century period features states as actors, who dictated the permissible activities at sea and abolished privateering in the Paris Declaration
Respecting Maritime Law of 1856. The historical research and the detailed
analysis of different periods show that mercantile companies, privateers, and
pirates were operating in a volatile environment. Their proximity to a state
depended on the context. Non- and semi-state actors' selective representation of their relationships to a state is of particular interest in this book as it
provides a baseline for the comparison to today's actors' representations of
their links to states. Consequently, special attention is paid to it, and it will be
further discussed in the following chapters.

Semi-State Actors in Cybersecurity. Florian J. Egloff, Oxford University Press. © Florian J. Egloff 2022.
DOI: 10.1093/oso/9780197579275.003.0003

Before embarking upon the historical analysis, a reflection on sources used by the secondary literature is in order. The book engages in archival historical analysis in particular with regard to the British history of interaction with mercantile companies, privateers, and pirates. The history of British naval engagement between the 16th and 19th centuries profits from the primary source records of the Admiralty at the National Archives, the East India Company records at the British Library, and individual collections of papers held by the Royal Navy and other archives, such as, for example, the Bodleian Special Collections.

Collections of printed source documents also exist, for example, coverage of Elizabethan privateering compiled by the Hakluyt Society. Some historians have looked at French, Spanish, Dutch, and Portuguese archives to inform their analysis of the British experience. Comparatively little work, however, utilizes documents from Indian, Chinese, Indonesian, or Latin American sources. This means that much of the engagement with the historical record reflects a European within empire and between empire discourse and does not account for a potentially significantly different, non-European experience. However, sometimes non-European experiences are reflected in letters and orders received sent by extra-European writers, for example, the Indian Imperial Mughal Court's correspondence with the East India Company. For the specific cases examined in this chapter, the research strategy entailed the use of archival resources, which contributes to a deeper understanding of the narratives constructed both by actors at the time and is contextualized by the secondary literature.

This chapter proceeds by providing some historical background on piracy and privateering and introducing the three cases. This is followed by an analysis of the constellations of actors in three historical contexts: the late 16th century, the late 17th century, and the mid-19th century.

Historical Background

Between the 13th and mid-19th centuries, privateering was an established state practice. Privateers, privately owned vessels that operated against an enemy with the licence or commission of the government in times of war, would be used to attack the enemy's trade. In peacetime, the practice of reprisal represented the means to seek redress against the harm suffered at the hands of another nation's ships at sea. A *letter of marque* allowed merchants to attack any ship of the offending nation until they found something of equal value to their loss (in later periods, letters of marque allowed the holder to participate in naval war and take as many prizes as they wanted).

In the 15th and 16th centuries, several developments concurrently led to an increase in European exploitation of the sea, with the Portuguese and the Spanish leading the way. Shipping and military technology advanced, so that long-distance sailing and war-fighting possibilities became more viable. At the same time, a will to explore, proselytize, and conquer led the seafarers into new territories.[2] Financed by investing parties expecting lucrative returns and backed by their respective sovereigns to attack both colonial locals and rivals, privateers represented an early means of colonial expansion.

In the early 16th century, Spain and Portugal were competing for territory. The world of exploration and religious conquest brought with it territorial claims. In early colonial fashion, the two powers settled on a deal dividing the world into two colonial spheres of influence. Spain received the territory west of the 46°W Meridian (up to the 146°E Meridian) and south of the Tropic of Cancer, whereas all territory in the east was claimed by Portugal.[3] Portugal would henceforth claim control of the southern Atlantic and Indian Oceans, whilst Spain expanded into the Americas and the Pacific. This splitting up of the territory is an important antecedent for the maritime imperial practice later named 'no peace beyond-the-line' agreement. The agreement divided the affairs of European imperial states into European international relations and colonial affairs, where a formal state of war or peace did not exist.

By 1580, the Iberian Union unified the Portuguese and Spanish Crowns, leaving Spain the dominant power ruling the sea. By that time, other European powers (e.g. the Dutch and the English, and, from the 17th century onwards, the French) were competing with Spain. They did not accept Spain's sovereignty claims of the sea on paper. Rather they challenged Spain's interpretation of sovereign claims by arguing that there must be a degree of effective control to be able to assert a sovereign claim.[4] Following the no peace beyond-the-line logic, England, France, and the United Provinces engaged abundantly in privateering south of the Tropic of Cancer. From the late 16th century onwards, rather than claiming whole oceans, the different navies and merchant companies struggled for control—not of whole oceans—but of specific sea lanes.

By the end of the 16th century, the era of the mercantile companies had begun. Private stock companies enabled states access to risk-taking and capital, particularly those states that did not have the resources to invest and sustain the imperial expansion. The companies had to look after themselves but were granted privileges in return. Mercantile companies operated according to their own international policies. They made deals with other companies or sovereigns, or were at war with them, engaging in open warfare, piracy, and privateering—sometimes independently and against the interests of their home states. At the time, merchants had to provide their own protection. Even in the Narrow Seas (the English Channel and the southern North Sea[5]), the Elizabethan Royal Navy did not yet provide protection for them.[6]

Since the book is interested in the interaction between the different actors, it is pertinent to briefly survey the literature on causes of piracy and its relationship to states. This analysis clarifies how piracy can be connected to other forms of raiding at sea. In an excellent literature review, historian David J. Starkey points to a variety of economic, political, and social arguments as causes of piracy.[7] Ranging from the deficiencies of trading markets, to entrepreneurial opportunities in areas of limited policing and legal enforcement, to the oversupply of labour after wars ended, many a historian concluded that there are economic reasons that caused piracy.[8]

However, some also purport political causes of piracy. For example, according to Anne Pérotin-Dumon, pirates are the product of political will and the policies of empires. They occur in two cases, namely, (a) when empires extend their hegemony over areas where they were previously weak, or (b) when there is a conflict between an established and a new political entity.[9] In both cases, the political challenge over the authority of determining who is allowed to trade, and under what circumstances, renders certain existing behaviour as illegitimate. For example, in the case of the East India Company, the monopolization of the East India trade rendered other often smaller merchants, who had been active in the same trade routes, as illegitimate interlopers. In her study of the legal history of piracy, Lauren Benton details that whilst piracy rhetorically was framed as an offence against humanity, the treatment of it was often as a 'crime under municipal law in which subjects ignored the terms of their commissions or failed to comply with requirements that they bring captured ships to vice-admiralty courts for adjudication.'[10] Explaining the anti-piracy measures, Pérotin-Dumon concludes that increasingly 'merchants laid down their weapons and accepted that the state would protect their business in exchange for regulating and taxing it. There would have been no 'suppression of piracy' without this change in relationship between merchant and the state.'[11] This conclusion mirrors Robert C. Ritchie's analysis, who identifies the double shift of merchants increasingly relying on 'order and regularity' and the administrative apparatus of the state valuing 'routine and discipline'.[12]

In Thomson's reading, the practice of privateering represented an attempt to control and bring non-state violence under the authority of the state. She reads pirates as an unintended consequence from the reliance of the state on privateers. Sometimes they were used as a resource by states, sometimes pirate practices could be read as political struggles against the authority of the state to control non-state violence. Over time, the pirates' existence transformed from being an outflow of state policy to a mix of unintended consequences of the use of privateers and active political resistance.[13]

Different pirates had different relationships with states. Mark Shirk offers a useful four-way classification of different narratives of piratical violence: entrant, resource, revisionist, and criminal.[14] Entrant violence constitutes piracy as a threat to the power of a particular state. The resource perspective casts piratical violence as something to be used by the state, reinforcing the current practices and norms. Revisionist narratives see piratical violence as a 'threat to the system as a whole as it exists in a particular time and place'.[15] Finally, criminal narratives render piratical violence as something outside the state but not as a threat to the sovereignty of the state. Hence, Thomson's account can be read as a transformation of the piratical threat narratives from resource to revisionist and criminal violence.

One could also construe the presence of pirates as a side effect of the absence of sovereignty on the seas. However, as Benton convincingly argues, the absence of sovereignty on the seas is an outcome of a political process rather than a forgone conclusion. The legal development across different regions allows one to trace the more and less effective control different empires had over their colonies. Benton highlights the difference between the emerging Atlantic system of prize courts (initiated in the 17th century) and the India trade, which was predominantly regulated through inter-imperial policies between the land-based Mughal Empire and the trading companies (who were perceived as extensions of European powers).[16] Benton notes the contrast between an imagined territorial claim on a map and differing degrees of control in practice:

> In both the real and imagined legal order, ships and their captains moved as delegated legal authorities along intersecting paths, extending corridors of control, in turn weakly or strongly associated with jurisdiction, into an inter-imperial space that could not be owned but could be dominated.[17]

Hence, she emphasizes the Europeans' view that law travels with the captains of the ships, that sovereigns extend their rule over the actions taken abroad.

Finally, besides the economic and political causes of piracy, Starkey also highlighted the historians' conjectures for social drivers of piracy.[18] Some mariners found personal freedom in pirate communities. Some pirate communities were characterized as more egalitarian and structured with a different set of social norms. Accounts of female pirates, black slaves, and gay men all speak to a set of political and social motivating reasons for becoming a pirate.[19]

The remainder of this naval historical analysis will proceed along three cases. Each case will highlight a particular historical constellation amongst actors of interest to this book. The first case is an account of late 16th-century Elizabethan privateering.[20] The time was selected based on secondary literature, which identifies the late Tudor period as one of the most significant phases of licensed private naval warfare in English naval history, particularly for reprisals and early forms of privateering.[21] The case offers an account of a queen that could not afford to finance naval operations on her own. In that situation, she shared risks and returns with influential investors (including her lord admiral), who had a motive in profiting from the war against Spain (some merchants were compensating for the loss of the Spanish trade due to the war). Spain and, due to the Iberian Union, Portugal represented the largest naval power of the era, with the United Provinces being strong investors into naval capacity. England had small, and mostly private, naval capacities. The accounts from an era of conquest and bullion describe raids motivated by a mix of adventurism, a will to proselytize, and profit seeking. In the Elizabethan period, pirates were not that different from any other seafaring undertaking, as deep-sea seafaring embodied a spirit of predation. The no peace beyond-the-line agreement of the European powers rendered deep-sea raiding a policy option between war and peace. Occurring at an important time for the understanding of sovereignty, the flurry of privateering triggered a legal discussion about the distinction between piracy and privateering, which would prove important for the understanding of sovereign responsibility.

Before turning to the late 17th-century case, a note on the use of the word 'privateering' is required. Most scholars (including the author) refer to the actions in this late Tudor age analytically as privateering, as it forms what would, by the mid-17th century, be called privateering. This is strictly speaking an anachronism—in Elizabethan times it would have been referred to as general reprisals, authorized by the issuance of a letter of marque and reprisal or just a letter of marque.[22] For terminological ease, I will use 'privateering' throughout.

The late 17th-century case offers an account of a government divided.[23] The time period was selected as it represents a key turning point for the understandings of piracy, a shift in the function of the navy, a shift in the interest in predation towards an interest in trade, and involves all the particular actors of interest in this book: mercantile companies, privateers, and pirates.[24] Whilst France was the wealthiest and dominant power of the time, England had become much stronger in commerce, financially, and was capitalizing on its geographic position.[25] A stronger Royal Navy, not least due to the administrative body strengthened in the 17th century, could be used to protect the sovereign's interests. Some investment parties were corporatized into formal mercantile companies, who had a strong stake in protecting their monopoly over certain sea lanes and ports. This is important conceptually, as they grew into large political actors with their own sets of interests and capabilities to deploy violence, sometimes in competition with state actors. Other investment parties, as in the case of Captain Kidd, financed privateering raids that sometimes ended up at odds with the government's policies. In a mercantile era, the domination of trade was the political goal, and taxation of trade was the new source of revenue for the state. Increasingly, pirates became a nuisance and interfered with the globalizing trade relations between empires. A redefinition of the pirate and a concurrent shift of the line between the state and the empire enabled the British state to address piracy.

Finally, the mid-19th century case about the abolition of privateering, accounting for the situation of a dominant power, will be analysed.[26] The case was selected due to its importance in the history of privateering.[27] It represents a major change in a multi-century development of practices around the legitimacy of privateering, and it shows how actors' interests in the governance and stability of a commonly used space changed over time. At the time, Britain operated by far the strongest navy which protected its global colonial interests.[28] By the early 19th century, an increased interest in the protection of property at sea rendered the business of pirates increasingly dangerous. Multi-state efforts to eradicate pirates were undertaken. Mercantile companies retained their trading functions, but the state had taken over the political administrative aspects of territorial control and foreign policy. Industrializing Britain promoted a free-trade agenda, which dove-tailed with its global interests of exploiting profits made through trade. In such a position, privateering became a strategically dangerous and an ideologically unviable option. Therefore, Britain had an interest in denying other states this option.

Elizabethan Privateering

In English history, privateering is best known by the acts of the Elizabethan Sea Dogs. The voyages of Sir John Hawkins, Sir Francis Drake, and Sir Walter Raleigh not only brought wealth to themselves and their investors but also inspired subsequent generations of English singers and playwrights. Besides their voyages against the Spanish in the New World, English privateers formed a key part in the still fledgling Royal Navy. The Crown invested into privateers, outfitted them with official protection duties for the state, and thus directed their efforts. Booty remained a significant motivation, as it spurred private interests to 'share expense of the venture and partly because it might repay the queen's own outlay'.[29] The English also used the skills and experience of the privateers, gained in attacking commerce abroad, for the defence of the home country.[30] For example, Sir Francis Drake and Sir John Hawkins served in the Royal Navy to fight against the Spanish Armada. Thus, privateering was used to augment national strength through military means.

Control over privateers was exerted through the admiralty, who tried to regulate the number of sailors involved in privateering and the targets that would be attacked by the issuance of privateering licenses. For example, it issued bonds outlining the expected behaviour of the privateers, that is, the procedures that should be followed (e.g. pay the tenth to the lord admiral or not to attack French ships).[31] However, effective control was not guaranteed. At the end of the 16th century, the admiralty was weak. This weakness was rooted in an understanding that the admiralty was 'at once a department of state under the authority of the Crown and a private province of liberty of the Lord Admiral'.[32] The lord admiral's private profit out of his public function led to a loss of authority of the admiralty.[33] This is reflected, for example, by the judgements made by the High Court of the Admiralty being overturned by political interference on the part of the Privy Council.[34]

During the Anglo-Spanish War in the late 16th century, many merchants engaged in privateering to redress harm suffered by the Spanish.

For example, members of the Levant and Barbary companies could 'find in privateering an appropriate substitute for and supplement to their normal dealings. Inevitably their appetite grew with what it fed on, and privateering reinforced both their power and their ambition to penetrate an enemy's colonial trade'.[35] Hence, with trade disrupted, the merchants and seamen had a strong incentive to engage in privateering. The result of the privateering was 'a transformation of the English merchant fleet, and of the London merchant class, who owned so large a share of it'.[36]

Naval historian Nicholas A. M. Rodger sums up the alliance between the royal household and private interests:

> This uniquely Elizabethan hybrid war effort, which made up for some of the weakness of royal finances by invoking private investment, was partly based on the long-standing pirate traditions of England in general, and the West Country in particular. The crown co-opted . . . seamen capable of oceanic naval warfare—but the more it encouraged and depended on them, the less it controlled them. In peacetime, the crown frequently regarded piracy as a local problem for shipowners to sort out for themselves. In wartime, the patriotic pirate who only attacked foreigners could be sure of having public opinion on his side, whatever the diplomatic damage done by plundering neutrals.[37]

Not only professionals engaged in attacking foreign commerce. Many amateur seamen engaged in naval predation too. It presented a possibility to gain some income for a poorer part of Elizabethan society. Andrews concludes that the best the government could hope to achieve was to 'direct the force of this popular movement against the queen's enemies'.[38]

During the early years of James I's reign, the admiralty tried to reassert its authority. However, some privateers were hard to control. For example, problems arose when, after being knighted for his services to the court, the notorious privateer Sir Walter Raleigh did not stop looting, even after the peace treaty between James I and His Most Catholic Majesty, Philipp III.[39] Finally, James I had Raleigh executed. This episode is a case in point for one of the problems that some scholars argue contributed to the abolition of privateering (i.e. the difficulty of controlling privateers).[40]

The technical innovations in naval warfare in the 16th century made invasion of a well-defended island more difficult. For the English, this 'meant that national defence could be organised more cheaply around a fleet which could also be used for offensive operations at long distance'.[41] However, the capacity for strategic action at sea was still very limited by the small size of the fleet.[42]

The longer wars lasted, the more privateering was professionalized and institutionalized. At the end of wars, privateers were either integrated into the navy, worked on merchant ships, or became pirates.[43] The line between privateering and pirating was blurred. As Fernand Braudel noted, pirates could serve as a 'substitute for declared war'.[44]

Much discussion in Europe about piracy revolved around the North African Barbary corsairs, who frequently crossed the boundaries between privateering and piracy.[45] The legal history of piracy in this particular time is instructive.[46] Legal scholar Alfred Rubin explains that, in the late 16th century, Alberico Gentili understood piracy as the 'taking of foreign life or property not authorized by a sovereign'.[47] A professor and advocate of the Spanish in England, Gentili switched opinions on the legitimacy of the Barbary corsairs several times during his career.[48] Before him, Jean Bodin had argued that the Barbary pirates, despite their criminal conduct, became lawful due to the Ottoman sultan's sovereign authorization, conferring lawful combatant status upon them.[49] Thus, Bodin's sovereignty-based argument reflected the legal distinction between privateering and piracy made at the time.[50] It put much emphasis on the necessary existence of a recognized, lawful sovereign, in absence of which, acts at sea could be labelled piratical. Strategically, this was of interest, as it gave sovereigns large flexibility in framing activity as piratical. For example, when convenient, states could not recognize the Barbary states as sovereign and hence deny any activity to be lawful privateering. The Spanish, Portuguese, and Italians, who suffered most from the Barbary threat, were especially interested in this.[51] Much of the debate at the time concerned the status of the United Provinces.[52] Gentili accepted Bodin's argument about the Barbary corsairs being sovereigns but argued that, under the law of nations, they did not wage war for a just cause but only for private gain, like pirates.[53] He considered pirates to be enemies of civilisation, 'who broke off every bond with society of mankind as a whole and should be considered as common criminals, not lawful belligerents'.[54]

Contrary to that, Alfred Rubin contends, Hugo Grotius understood pirates as 'individuals whose primary object was plunder regardless of place'.[55] The pirate offended humanity, as commerce and property were parts of fundamental human nature.[56] Hence, the status of the Barbary corsairs was not directly impacted by their sovereignty claim to the Ottomans but by whether their acts were self-interested acts against property (as opposed to political struggles for a community). To back up his points, Grotius also observed that historically there were several instances of pirate communities turning into lawful sovereigns.[57] He looked to the ancient law of nations for justification of the Barbary corsairs. He argued that, just as the Romans had extended the right to enslavement and *postliminy* not only to Romans themselves but also to 'free and independent peoples', who had no relationship to Rome, the same should be applied to the Barbary corsairs.[58] The argument between Gentili and Grotius reflects the struggles between the European nations at the time, who each tried to find justifications for their actions against or in cooperation with pirates and privateers, and, in the case of the United Provinces, argue for the existence of its own sovereignty.

Even though England profited from privateering, both by disrupting enemy commerce and as a source of income, privateering also brought disadvantages. It was a lucrative undertaking for the sailors. Serving on a privateer was associated with better food, and the individual seaman took a higher share in the prizes than in the Royal Navy. Consequently, many of the most able seamen served as privateers not as sailors in the navy. Over time, the Royal Navy addressed the competition for skill by impressment (forcing sailors to join the navy) and improving working conditions on royal vessels. Privateering also fostered a relative state of lawlessness, incentivising corrupt practices and generally undermined the sovereign's power and authority.[59]

Privateering as a strategy of war could distract from the more formal naval efforts of building the Royal Navy. Indeed, the Elizabethan navy consisted of men who had 'grown up in the school of oceanic trade and plunder and remained promoters and leaders of the privateering war'.[60] These interests were so strong that they delayed the formation of a formal state navy.[61]

This late 16th-century Elizabethan privateering case depicts a weak state, which was not yet administratively integrated. The admiralty was serving both a public and private function. There were wide freedoms for the privateering parties to undertake deep-sea raiding, as long as the targets were politically favourable. Privateering transformed the London merchant class, as the joint investment (and risk-sharing) into privateering was an appreciated way of profit-making during times of conflict. However, when the war with Spain ended, a generation of privateers was still trying to capitalize on their tried and tested skills.

Whilst the late 16th-century case illuminated the constellation between the sovereign, merchants, and privateers, the 17th-century case will introduce the interaction between the most prominent English mercantile company, the East India Company, and pirates.

Late 17th Century: The East India Company and Piracy

During the second part of the 17th century, the status of privateers changed. The no peace beyond-the-line practice became untenable, not least due to an expanded and regularized trade network of different states. In the mid-17th century, the Spanish claims of jurisdiction over the sea collapsed completely with the recognition of Dutch and English overseas territories.[62] The European imperial states expanded their purview of international relations and gradually integrated their colonial relations into rule-based European politics.[63] This rendered the chaotic and ambiguous use of privateers/pirates beyond-the-line increasingly untenable.

A tightening of control over privateering and a war on pirates were the results. However, that is not to say that privateering stopped. French privateers (*corsairs* and *filibustiers*) became increasingly active. While English privateers were used as a tool of influence alongside the growing navy, the corsairs were used as a primary tool of naval warfare (*guerre de course*).[64] For France, corsairs provided an ideal weapon against the English, who, comparatively, relied more on foreign trade.[65] However, this emphasis on the *guerre de course*, which was supported by the profiting investment circles, shifted the (limited) funds and efforts away from building a more formal naval capacity.[66]

During the 17th century trade expanded massively. Whilst early 16th-century English efforts were based on emulating the Spanish model of expansion with the aim of gaining bullion, during the 17th century English ambitions transformed towards inner-imperial trade. The Navigation Acts of 1651 forced all English colonial trade to be carried by English vessels, which resulted in tensions with other countries (e.g. Anglo-Dutch wars), but it also had the effect of strengthening English mercantile interests. Still mercantile in nature, but focused on making England the profiting trading centre, this transition resulted in the growing importance of merchant interests in English political life.[67]

Philip J. Stern made an excellent case about how to understand the East India Company, which was founded in 1600, on its own terms: as a corporation with political, economic, and social effects.[68] He persuasively argued that understanding the company as an own body politic, recovering the political programmes and ideas from the correspondence of its officers, allows for an assessment of the company that goes beyond a mere 'quasi-state' actor. Consequently, he calls it a 'company-state'.[69] This insight is important: the historiography of the English state formation does point to a diverse set of coexisting political corporations—the state being just one of them—at the end of the 17th century. Whilst the absolutist vision of the hierarchical state existed at that point in time, it was exactly that—a vision and not reality.[70]

As such, it is important to understand the company as a polity of an own kind, co-inhabiting an early modern world of multiple types of polities. The company was itself a political player in different other political systems (e.g. Mughal Aurangzeb's Court). It did assume sovereign-like functions abroad. For example, it had the right to raise an army and to declare war. Thomson read these practices through a state-formation lens: 'at the heart of these practices was the state-building process. To attain wealth and power promised by overseas expansion, states empowered nonstate actors to exercise violence' as the states' capabilities were insufficient or too constrained.[71]

However, this claim assumes that the English 'state' was already formed to a degree where it could 'empower' a semi-state actor. At least for the early period of the East India Company (i.e. in the 17th century), the company had its own body politic. Whilst the English state granted the company charters, they were 'often more tenuous claims on [rather] than authoritative dispensations of authority'.[72]

Thus, the East India Company operated in multiple spaces of political authority: it secured an authority to trade both from the English Crown and from the Mughal emperor, formally submitting to both. In the Mughal empire, it inserted itself into the local political fabric, submitting to local rule to be allowed to trade. By submitting to the Mughal as 'exotic vassals', and thereby confirming his authority to rule universally, the European mercantile companies strengthened the Mughal's power.[73] The Europeans profited thereby from the 'relative indifference of the Asian empires to maritime affairs'.[74] In smaller island polities in Southeast Asia, local rulers used 'stranger king' norms to accept companies as foreign suzerains, using it 'as a means of strengthening their own authority'.[75]

Thus, when it suited the company, it used its position as a group of 'mere merchants', who were only interested in peaceful trade.[76] Nevertheless, the company operated its own foreign policy, made deals with other companies or states, or was at war with them, engaging in open warfare, piracy, and privateering, sometimes independently and against the interests of the home state.[77] For a long time, the mercantile companies ruled vast territories. It is important to highlight the political economy of this: in a mercantilist economy, the political and the economic were not functionally differentiated. John Anderson wrote that 'the term *mercantilist* reflects the symbiotic alliance between the state and the commercial interests in pursuit of power and wealth at the expense of other states'.[78] The use of violence allowed mercantile companies to establish trade monopolies. In Britain, a slow process of incorporation merged the company and the state and eventually rendered the company commercial.[79]

Scholars have struggled to classify the various surges of piracy into defined periods. However, they agree that one peak in piratical activities occurred in the Indian Ocean in the mid-1690s, which triggered a reconfiguration of English policy towards piracy with important impacts on the Golden Age of piracy (1716–1726).[80] The policy change was partially the result of a joint interest between the East India Company and the English government. And it is in this mid-1690s period that I will illuminate the interdependence of piracy with the mercantile interests and state power as exercised by the Royal Navy using the case of Captain Kidd.

By the end of the 17th century, the English imperial state depended on stability. The merchants were interested in monopoly profits and depended on stable trade routes, whilst the enlarged administrative apparatus valued 'routine and discipline'.[81] Specifically the East India Company wanted a kind of *imperium*[82] over the trade to the East Indies: it wanted to control all Englishmen and the ships passing across specific sea lanes, requiring passes from the company. It also wanted authority over some coastal territory and people in the East Indies.[83] It was dissatisfied with English interlopers (i.e. traders that did not respect its monopoly). While pirates did not pose a concern to the East India Company itself, it saw them as an extreme form of interloper. Politically, the company used the fight against pirates to advocate for its authority to control trade more generally. Hence, the fight against piracy became a 'claim to be able to draw fundamental distinction between just and unjust violence, public and private right, and honourable and dishonourable behaviour at sea'.[84]

The last decade of the 17th century was financially, economically, and politically challenging for the East India Company: English exports were down, and the Whig rise in Parliament led to a challenge of the company's monopoly. At the same time, piracy was flourishing. Many pirates originated from North America, where they set out 'under cover of privateering against France, and with the discreet encouragement of Whig political interests in London'.[85] English pirates, did not refrain from attacking ships of local rulers in the colonies.[86] In India, after a piratical attack by Henry Avery on a Mughal pilgrim ship, the Mughal forced the Dutch, French, and English to provide protection from English-speaking pirates on the pilgrimage and to reimburse the losses suffered by threatening to shut down their trade.[87] The Dutch fuelled the Mughal's perception that all pirates were English by ordering 'their officials to send any captured English pirates to Surat for delivery to the governor'.[88]

In 1695, Captain William Kidd was engaged as a privateer and was issued a letter of marque to attack French vessels and pirates.[89] His backers were powerful Whig lords that expected a financial profit from the undertaking. Kidd left England as part of the English anti-piracy policy. However, it was during the years that Kidd was away, fuelled by the impact of the piratical exploits of Captain Henry Avery, that the English government policy changed. Kidd's actions were qualified under a different political climate then when he had left.

Kidd's attack on the *Quedah Merchant* was particularly significant for his future prosecution.[90] Kidd attacked an Armenian merchant, flying 'French Colours with a design to decoy',[91] which carried goods that belonged to Abdul Ghaffur, who was close to the Mughal Aurangzeb's Court. This had a direct impact on the East India Company trade. The company was forced to provide convoy protection to the Mughal's ships going forward.[92] The company reported on Kidd's activities in detail and pushed for a prosecution in London.[93] Their lobbying paid off: Whitehall first requested more intelligence about the pirates and later issued the long sought-after commission to fight pirates in the East Indies.[94] Whitehall informed Mr Blackbourn, secretary to the East India Company, on 21 November 1698: 'If there be anything more that the company judges proper to be done for vindicating the honour of the nation against the calumnies raised in India, and for the security of the factories there, I desire you will let me know it'.[95] The prosecution impacted the Whig lords, who dropped their support for the mission to forgo any additional embarrassment. Captain Kidd tried to prove his innocence. However, two French passes were key to his defence strategy, which went missing before his trial.[96] Captain Kidd, without help from his political supporters, faced trial and was hung a pirate.[97]

The case of Captain Kidd is interesting for two reasons. First, it is an example of how enforcement could be tightened when raids of ships 'threatened the interests of powerful merchants'.[98] Exceeding a commission did not consistently lead to the prosecution as pirates. To the contrary, attacks against traders of rivals were often strategically ignored.[99] Second, the time period encapsulates both the expansion of the capabilities of the Royal Navy and an expansion of piracy.[100] It demonstrates how the East India Company, facing a political standoff abroad, was able to use piracy as a political opportunity to gain the government's support for the company's ambition to control the English subjects in the East Indies more generally. It used the negotiation with the Mughal Court around the protection of his ships to create leverage over the Mughal. For example, it argued that to provide adequate protection, the Mughal's ships needed company passes, lest they be mistaken as pirates.[101]

Raiders naturally tried to avoid capture and disposed of raided goods outside of the official prize courts. However, attacks against commerce were often justified by the use of different flags and commissions. Captains had elaborate defence strategies. As Benton notes:

> They [the mariners defined as pirates by their enemies] offered creative interpretations of the terms of their commissions, purchased or falsified commissions, feigned ignorance of peace treaties and carried multiple flags and sets of papers—all strategies claiming the legitimacy of their actions based on the sponsorship of particular sovereigns.[102]

The self-identification of raiders as pirates (e.g. by raising the black flag) was the exception rather than the rule. The pirates of the late Golden Age were an exception, in that some actively rejected the English state. This is substantively different, for example, from Henry Avery who self-identified as an 'Englishmen's friend'.[103]

In the 18th and early 19th centuries the British state responded with a comprehensive set of policies, for example, offering incentives to pirates (including amnesties), implementing legal reform in the colonies to prevent offering a market to pirated goods, and sending the Royal Navy to destroy pirates' home bases.[104] Increasingly, reprisals were settled diplomatically.[105] This differentiation of policies between piracy and privateering has to be analysed in light of the increasing power of navies supported by a thickening administrative body, the integration of privateering in a strategy of naval warfare, and the decreasing usefulness of pirates due to their negative impact on trade.[106] This increasing naval and administrative capability of the state, at the same time as trade networks got thicker, made pirates more of a nuisance and raised the chances of action against them.

The navy had grown during wartime and merchants demanded protection. In return, the state levied taxes, which would stay around in peacetime.[107] This mirrors the state-building by war-making argument as told by historical sociologists such as Charles Tilly.[108] However, Shirk reads the English state's measures introduced against piracy of the Golden Age as a realignment of the empire and the state.[109] Much like Stern analyses the East India Company as a company-state, Shirk reads early 18th-century England as a state-empire hybrid polity. He observes that pirates forced a redrawing of boundaries between the state and empire. Changes in law, making piracy a universal crime, was a redrawing of what piracy meant.[110] 'Pirates were legally extricated from the state and citizenry, an effective declaration that England would not be offended if an English pirate met justice in France.'[111]

Together with the changes in law, England instituted a new legal process. Instead of London or local colonial courts, pirates would now be tried by English Vice-Admiralty courts, presided by English judges, directly in the colonies. This resolved the tension of local courts being too close to the pirates versus London being too far away to have meaningful influence. It also enabled a standardization of policy across the colonies. Two additional measures reinforced this redrawing of boundaries. A tightening of control over the colonies via the appointment and replacement of governors willing to fight pirates. Furthermore, a strong anti-piracy propaganda campaign constructed a narrative of pirates being the outcasts of society, thereby strongly differentiating the colonists from the pirate. All three measures, the legal measures, the appointment of adequate personnel, and the propaganda campaign contributed to bringing the colonies closer to the English state, thereby redrawing the boundary between the empire and the state.

Shirk also highlights the shift towards the collaboration between European states against pirates in a 'recognition that the enemies to trade were no longer other states, as had been the case in the 17th century, but were instead non-state actors like pirates. It was in every trading state's interest to eradicate piracy and protect trade.'[112] Thus, the term *hostes humani generis* (enemies of mankind) was transformed in use to label the outcast, the ones outside the society of states, who could not be legitimate combatants, and were therefore enemies of all. As the legal scholar Christian Wolff noted in the mid-18th century: those who engage in unjustified war, who transgress the law of humanity, and seek war as an end in itself cannot be said to wage war, but to practice brigandage, and are to be compared to robbers whose malice extends to the farthest limit. Therefore the right to punish them belongs to all nations, and by this right they can remove from their midst those fierce monsters of the human kind.[113]

This distinct late 17th-century/early 18th-century shift marked a move away from the legitimate state-sponsored piracy towards universal jurisdiction.[114] Universal jurisdiction implied that states could prosecute each other's nationals for crimes of piracy committed on the high seas. An example is renowned English pirate Captain Edward Lowe, who was hung in Martinique by the French, without any intervention by the British.[115] Pirates, thus, could not rely on state protection anymore.

The reinterpretation of the purview of European international relations to include the imperial world can thus be read as making possible the reinterpretation of piratical violence at sea. Whilst the Spanish governments once claimed vast parts of the oceans as their territory, in effect, by the early 18th century the disputes (e.g. between the English and the Spanish in the 1730s) were mostly about the degree of control over sea lanes, no longer about the distinction of piracy and privateering. Questions of dispute were, for example, whether a government may search the ships connecting a foreign colony to its home state, or to what degree neutral trade could be interdicted if they carried enemy goods not acquired from the enemy.[116] These were questions that would rise to central importance in the debate on the abolition of privateering.

The Abolition of Privateering in the Mid-19th Century

British privateering flourished during the wars of the 18th century.[117] For example, to incentivize privateers in the War of the Spanish Succession, Queen Anne passed an English Prize Act that allowed privateers to retain all profits and introduced a bounty for prisoners taken.[118] By 1744, George II pardoned prisoners who volunteered to serve as privateers. In 1756, Britain introduced a policy that encouraged privateers to attack neutral ships trading French colonial goods (i.e. Dutch ships).[119] This spurred so much interest in privateering that the maritime insurer Lloyd's filed a complaint with the government. The government responded by announcing a minimum vessel size, which raised the entry requirement for active privateers.[120]

In maritime warfare, one important figure for the navy's mobilization potential was the total number of able seamen. More than in land combat, naval capacity directly relied on a set of specialized maritime skills and expertise.[121] Thus, a standard assumption was that countries with larger merchant fleets could draw on a larger number of able seamen. Wartime demand usually exceeded peacetime supply.[122] At the beginning of a conflict, however, it was the speed of mobilization that determined who could project naval power quickly. For example, in the 18th century, the French 'système des classes . . . could recruit men up to a certain level of manpower, faster than the British practice of bounties backed by the press', and hence France had an advantage at the beginning of the mobilization.[123] However, due to the larger total number of skilled seamen, the British would enjoy an advantage in the later stages of mobilization.

British policy towards neutral ships was not well received by the Russians. In 1780, Catherine II reacted by enacting the Free Ships Free Goods policy, which allowed neutrals to trade with nations at war (excluding contraband), to denounce ineffective blockades, and to defend this policy by force if necessary (the so-called Armed Neutrality). Other neutrals agreed with Russia. The renewal of this agreement in 1800 led to a convention between England and Russia in 1801, in which Russia gave up the Free Ships Free Goods policy in return for immunity from search by privateers.[124]

By the end of the 18th century, it was mostly the United States (in the War for U.S. Independence) and France (in the French Revolution and later in the Napoleonic wars) that employed privateers against Britain. Thus, privateering had 'evolved into a weapon of the weak against the strong'. However, 'it was invented and encouraged by the "strong" states of Europe, whose naval power was largely an outgrowth of privateering'.[125]

Britain operated by far the strongest navy which protected its global colonial interests. By the early 19th century, the strong interests in the protection of property at sea rendered the business of pirates increasingly dangerous. After the Congress of Vienna in 1815, multi-state efforts to eradicate pirates were undertaken.[126] Mercantile companies retained their trading functions, but the state had taken over the political administrative aspects of territorial control and foreign policy. Industrializing Britain promoted a free-trade agenda, which dove-tailed with its global interests of exploiting profits made through trade. In such a position, privateering became a strategically dangerous and ideologically unviable option. As a consequence, Britain had an interest in denying other states this option.

For the duration of the Crimean War, France and Britain agreed to extend the Free Ships Free Goods policy to the neutral powers.[127] In 1854, the United States launched a diplomatic offensive to try to persuade the European countries to settle this principle contractually. Britain, however, knowing that it would be difficult to revert to its former policy after the war, wanted something in return: the abolition of privateering. Lord Clarendon highlighted this difficulty of reverting back in his opening words in a letter to Prime Minister Palmerston on 6 April 1856: 'It is quite clear that we can never again reestablish our ancient doctrines respecting neutrals, and that we must in any future war adhere to the exception to our rule which we admitted at the beginning of the present war, under pain of having all mankind against us'.[128] He then proposed the tactic of at least getting something in return (the abolition of privateering), and links this as a direct response to U.S. maritime policy.[129]

The interest in this was both ideological and strategic.[130] Ideologically, some members of the liberal elite were appalled by the crude method of warfare. Strategically, Britain's naval commerce had become very large. In addition, the large merchant navy of the United States posed a risk even to the country with the largest navy in the world. Lecturing Lord Clarendon in a letter, Prime Minister Palmerston wrote on the 5 April 1856:

> Privateering is a Practice most inconvenient to the Power which has the largest number of merchant men at sea, and the least useful to the Power which has the largest War Navy. England is that Power and we should therefore willingly agree to abolish that Practice in regard to all Powers which would enter into the same Engagement towards us.[131]

Considering the possible instability of the Anglo-French alliance, a U.S.-French alliance would have posed a direct risk to Britain's survival, a scenario feared by Britain. In contrast, the United States relied on being able to transform its considerable number of merchant cruisers into weapons of warfare and lobbied for its own proposal in European capitals.[132]

Meeting for a settlement of the Crimean War in Paris in 1856, the Congress of Paris decided to resolve some other questions of concern. France seized the opportunity to press for establishment of the Free Ships Free Goods policy as international law, proposing to concede to the British demand to abolish privateering.[133] Both France and Britain had not engaged in privateering since the Napoleonic wars, and besides Britain, France held the largest navy.

As this policy option was evaluated in the context of a new U.S. proposal to protect private property at sea, Britain felt compelled to act. Prussia, having evaluated its policy options in an earlier U.S. proposal, was now ready to support the British proposal.

The declaration was passed, and, in an invention of international public law, it was agreed that it would be widely circulated so that as many powers as possible could comply with it.[134] Most powers happily acceded as Britain, the predominant sea power, was finally ready to support a practice protecting neutral commerce. This agreement, however, left the U.S. out. Since there was a consensus among the parties of the declaration that no port may receive privateers, privateering was made practically impossible. A privateer would have to return to his home state to sell his prizes. During the U.S. Civil War, the northern states enquired about signing the Declaration of Paris to prevent the southern states from using privateers against commerce. At that time, though, the two parties were already in a state of belligerency, thereby losing the justification to sign away rights for the other party.

In summary, this chapter has given an account of the different constellations and framings between the major actors involved in the provision of historical naval (in-)security. The chapter offered a historical narrative of mercantile companies, privateers, and pirates with an emphasis on their relations with states. Being intrigued by the speciality of privateers and their peculiar connection to states, we followed this changing institution of privateering between the late 16th to the mid-19th centuries and identified three different constellations of non- and semi-state actors at different points in time. The late 16th-century offered insights into the early modern world of overlapping sovereignties and a chaotic interplay of personal ambition and political state projects, in a world in which states were still weak. The Crown, the admiralty, and early mercantile companies all contributed to a system of contested and blurred boundaries between pirates and privateers. England's situation as a small competitor, spurred by the willingness to emulate Spain's and Portugal's successes in conquest and bullion, generated a flurry of private and semi-state initiatives. Formal naval capacities were in their infancy and were used both for personal and political gains, and the no peace beyond-the-line agreement still separated the colonial sphere from European international relations.

The late 17th-century period showed a world in flux. Imperial lines were redrawn, navies bolstered and given extensive responsibilities, privateers controlled more tightly, and pirates hunted. Strengthened commerce, through mercantile companies, left England stronger financially and opened possibilities for a more developed administrative state body and a bolstered Royal Navy.

Finally, the mid-19th-century case about the abolition of privateering showed the situation of a dominant power. At the time, Britain operated by far the strongest navy which protected its global colonial interests. By the early 19th century, an increased interest in the protection of property at sea rendered the business of pirates increasingly dangerous. Multi-state efforts to eradicate pirates were undertaken. Mercantile companies retained their trading functions, but the state had taken over the political administrative aspects of territorial control and foreign policy. Industrializing Britain promoted a free-trade agenda, which aligned with its global interests of exploiting profits made through trade. In such a position, privateering became a strategically dangerous and an ideologically unviable option. The chapter showed how Britain went about to deny other states this option.

4

A Brief History of Cyberspace

Origins and Development of (In-)Security in Cyberspace

Having identified the challenges that existed between pirates, privateers, and mercantile companies in three different historical contexts raises the question of which time period or constellation of actors the present-day situation can be usefully analogized to. To that end, this chapter reviews the history of cyber(in-)security to identify the structure of relations between some of the main actors. It features a short history of cyber(in-)security drawn from secondary sources and highlights the interaction between state security interests, global technology companies and internet providers, and users in the development of cyber(in-)security. It traces how cyber(in-)security was shaped and perceived by these different actors.

The chapter finds that corporations' role in providing cybersecurity grew more important and complex over time. They had cooperative and conflictive interests with other actors, including states. Explaining the challenge of signals intelligence in a digital era, I trace how cyber(in-)security became a topic of interest for states and how they sought strategies to expand their influence both overtly and covertly. I thus identify the main structures of interaction between the modern actors of interest, which will be analysed in-depth in the subsequent chapters. In Chapter 5, I will then identify which periods in the age of sail can be most fruitfully compared to the actors in the contemporary context of cyber(in-)security.

Compared to the history of privateering, the history of cyberspace and its security challenges is relatively short. This chapter highlights the emergence of different actors and their interactions with the government in the cyber domain to gain a historical understanding of the problems of cyber(in-)security from different actors' perspectives. Three perspectives are integrated into a narrative history of cyber(in-)security: governments, large technology and telecommunication companies, and users. This means we will touch on diverse aspects such as end-user perspectives, critical infrastructure, interstate espionage, and surveillance. The governmental perspective highlights how

Semi-State Actors in Cybersecurity. Florian J. Egloff, Oxford University Press. © Florian J. Egloff 2022.
DOI: 10.1093/oso/9780197579275.003.0004

cyber(in-)security is at once an opportunity and a challenge to governments. Touching on many high-profile incidents, I argue to really understand the governmental perspective, one has to understand cyber(in-)security's historical embedding in signals intelligence. For this reason, digital network intelligence as a challenge is explained, and it is argued that it is one of the drivers of collaboration between governments and the large technology and telecommunication companies. The corporate perspective focuses on the emergence of companies as early investors that exploit opportunities, take risks, and pioneer new markets. Their converging and conflicting interests with other actors will be highlighted. Important cases of such interactions lay the foundation for the in-depth empirical analysis in Chapter 7. For example, a constellation, in which a state actor compromised the network of a large technology company, Google, in 2010 highlights the complex problems arising from non- and semi-state agency. Finally, the user perspective highlights how individuals have been neglected parties when it comes to cybersecurity.

The research of the historical actors on the sea has highlighted the importance of state and private interaction in exploiting the opportunities offered by oceanic travel and predation. The state facilitation and enablement of privateering and mercantile companies transformed the mercantile class in London. Similarly, cyberspace, and especially the internet, expanded rapidly as a result of commercialization and advances in personal computing, particularly from the early 1990s onwards. The internet—enabled by government-funded technology, the liberalization of telecommunications markets, and, at first, a mainly government and academically used internetwork—was quickly utilized and expanded by companies.

Different actors have shaped the trajectory of the development and the norms associated with cyberspace. Early proponents, mainly from the United States, focused on an open, unregulated network. With the expansion of the network, states started to realize the vulnerabilities that became apparent when analysing the relatively unchecked interconnectivity with the rest of the world. Alongside the increase of a technically literate user base, attacks arose. At first, Computer Emergency Response Teams (CERTs) were formed (e.g. Carnegie Mellon University's CERT/CC in 1988) to respond to the technical challenges of the growing number of threats. CERTs started cooperating internationally by sharing data about vulnerabilities and attacks.[1] While performing the same basic defensive functions, however, the diversity of national political systems and practices created challenges for cooperation.[2]

Whilst the whole internet economy was largely a private endeavour, cybersecurity in particular was and is provided by private actors. With increased end-user connectivity, the role of companies in the protection of consumers grew more important and complex. Companies have also reacted to the insecurities demonstrated by the various viruses and worms circulating in the 1990s and early 2000s. For example, Bill Gates, who was the CEO of Microsoft at the time, announced trustworthy computing as the number one priority for the company in 2002. He outlined a ten-year vision of computing becoming an 'integral and indispensable part of almost everything we do'.[3] Consequently, security needed to be integrated from the ground up. His vision though, of computing being as reliable and risk free as using electricity or water, has not become reality. Rather, security for consumers was delivered in a piecemeal fashion, as a patchwork between fundamental improvements in operating systems and protection using cloud services. Consumers were taught to use anti-virus products (which increased the visibility of customer data by security vendors) and to choose strong passwords for authentication. Both have turned out to be ineffective against increasingly skilful and complex attacks. After the end of the millennium dot-com boom, the market consolidated and a few winners emerged: Microsoft, Apple, and later Google provided the largest share of endpoint operating systems, while Google, Amazon, and later Facebook offered the largest share of online services. Consumers' security would henceforth be directly impacted by the business decisions made by those companies. A few large telecommunication companies that provided international distribution of internet traffic (examples are Alcatel-Lucent, AT&T, British Telecom, Cable & Wireless, Deutsche Telekom, Level 3, Telefónica, Verizon, and Vodafone) were less overt but equally important in terms of access to data flows. Many were formerly state-owned telecommunication and telegraph companies that had been privatized during the second half of the 20th century. The networking equipment was provided by a few large hardware manufacturers (e.g. Cisco, Huawei, Juniper Networks, and ZTE). With increasing interconnectivity, technology and telecommunication companies became important players in the protection of key societal functions.

States labelled the providers of these key societal functions as critical infrastructure (mid-1990s onwards). The realization that the interconnectivity of critical infrastructures posed new risks to national security drove two different state responses.[4] First, since the infrastructures were mostly owned by the private sector, increasing collaboration between the government and corporations became a necessity. In the United States, various iterations of cybersecurity policies would pick up on that need, including public-private partnerships, information-sharing centres, as well as government-provided intrusion prevention capabilities. Second, militaries and intelligence agencies anticipated the increasing role that the control of, and attacks against, networks would play in their respective future operating environments. Consequently, the U.S. military developed its policy of information warfare of the early 1990s into a fully operational cyber command structure (U.S. CYBERCOM).

Growing out of the capabilities of traditional signals intelligence (SIGINT), many states have teams working on ways to exploit cyberspace for their own interests. The foreign intelligence value of the internet was highlighted in a U.S. counterintelligence operation codenamed 'Moonlight Maze'.[5] The operation was mounted in 1998 and investigated a set of intrusions that were traced back to 1996 and were targeting key military, government, and academic systems. At the time, the intrusions were traced back to Russia. However, the espionage campaign never stopped, and some of the attack infrastructure remained technically linkable to attacks occurring up to the present day.[6]

Whilst the increasing use of computers would eventually offer vast opportunities for spying, it was first perceived a challenge to SIGINT agencies due to the increasing use of fibre-optics and the wide availability of encryption. Progress in cryptographic research meant that not just states, but also citizens and businesses, could use strong cryptography to protect the confidentiality of their messages. For example, the software Pretty Good Privacy (PGP) developed by Phil Zimmermann in 1991 made public-key cryptography available to everyone. Starting in 1999, U.S. General Michael Hayden embarked with the National Security Agency (NSA) to 'tackle the internet'.[7] Similarly, the British signals intelligence agency (GCHQ) invested in a modernization programme. The 11 September 2001 terrorist attacks against the United States transformed the political climate, which made money and extended operational powers available to intelligence agencies. For example, on 4 October 2001 President George W. Bush authorized a metadata- and content-collection programme as a direct response to 9/11.[8] In addition, signals intelligence agencies were tasked to support the military campaigns in Afghanistan and later in Iraq, which gave their capabilities added political impact.

As more of their targets used the internet, during the first decade of the 21st century, the signals intelligence cooperation between the U.S., U.K., Canada, Australia, and New Zealand (called Five-Eyes) significantly expanded their use of the internet for data collection.[9] In a similar fashion, many advanced industrialized nations have given their defence and intelligence agencies a large role in exploiting the vulnerabilities of increasingly networked societies.

At the same time, SIGINT agencies were tasked to also take a defensive role. Intelligence historian Richard J. Aldrich noted: 'GCHQ did not like this, since it resurrected the familiar dilemma of "offence versus defence" in the realm of code-breaking, but in a much more unmanageable form'.[10] The agencies were asked to brief private sector entities on good practices of computer security, including how to use strong cryptography to protect against online threats. This sat strangely with agencies that had tried to prevent the spread of strong cryptography to other countries—in part by undermining cryptographic products—for decades.[11]

However, several large espionage campaigns uncovered in the last two decades contributed to the perception that a stronger defence against cyber threats was necessary. Just as the Moonlight Maze investigation showed that (presumably) Russian agencies were using the internet to spy on U.S. technologies, a set of intrusions code-named 'Titan Rain' (later renamed Byzantine Hades) at the U.S. Department of Defence labs, NASA, and defence contractors revealed (presumably) Chinese spying since early 2003.[12] To the Five-Eyes governments these intrusions demonstrated that their defence industrial base was a prime target for Chinese espionage. By the end of 2007, it was clear to the signals intelligence agencies that more had to be done against cyber espionage. The U.K.'s domestic intelligence agency, the security service (MI5), even went as far as writing a letter to 300 chief executives warning about Chinese electronic espionage.[13]

In 2007 the distributed-denial-of-service (DDoS) attacks against Estonian institutions, in the wake of the political decision to move a Red Army Second World War memorial outside the centre of Tallinn, raised cyber operations as a means of influencing the politics of a foreign country to the attention of Western politicians. Whilst the attacks were unsophisticated, the policy community learned that cyber operations had become a means of influencing a country's domestic policies.[14] Whilst not providing conclusive evidence, Estonian politicians were quick to point to Russia as the sponsor of the attacks. The attacks against Estonia will later feature in a case study, as they reflect the politicization of cyber actions. In close analogy to pirates and privateers, the case study will focus on the competing narratives portraying the attackers either as state-sponsored hackers or as independent patriotic hackers.

The espionage campaigns of the early days of the internet were not perceived to impact the individual's security directly. However, this was different for groups perceived as a threat to a state's security. In 2009, a report named *GhostNet* on an espionage operation was released by the Information Warfare Monitor, a partnership between the Citizen Lab (University of Toronto) and SecDev Group (think tank).[15] *GhostNet* revealed a sustained espionage operation against the embassies of various countries, including the offices of the Dalai Lama and many Tibetan activists. Starting with reports on *GhostNet*, the cyber(in-)security community regularly produced intelligence reports, highlighting the activities of threat actors targeting specific industries, groups, or countries. This is indicative of a peculiarity of cyber(in-)security: most of the defensive (and some offensive) work is undertaken by private actors.

One of the most interesting early interactions between a large technology company and a state-level attacker were the intrusions into Google, which were revealed to the public in January 2010. The campaign, including at least 34 different targets across the technology, finance, and defence sectors, was labelled as *Operation Aurora*. This operation will later feature in a case study to look at the interactions between a large technology company and (at least) two governments (the U.S. and China).

In mid-2010, the most sophisticated intrusion to date became known: Stuxnet. Stuxnet was found to be a state-directed malware attack against an Iranian nuclear enrichment facility. Whilst uncertainty about the strategic intent of the attackers remains, the technical effects of the malware are known. The malware was traced back to a joint operation between the United States and Israel, with other (some perhaps still unknown) states supplying key parts of the operation.[16] Since then, other state-directed campaigns have been uncovered with differing degrees of confidence in their attribution to a particular state.[17] Having first taken note of the importance of cyber operations in influencing policy covertly in Estonia in 2007, Stuxnet added impetus to the development of national cybersecurity strategies in many countries.[18] For example, Iran also developed its offensive cyber capabilities. By 2012, NSA analysts assessed, based on signals intelligence, that

Iran reacted to (presumably subsequent) Western activities against its nuclear sector by conducting DDoS attacks on U.S. financial institutions.[19] The U.S. later indicted seven Iranian nationals, who worked for private security companies, allegedly on behalf of one of the Iranian intelligence services.[20] They were accused of hacking U.S. financial institutions between December 2011 and May 2013.

In 2013, NSA contractor Edward Snowden leaked documents to journalists that shed light on the covert offensive and defensive initiatives of the Five-Eye signals intelligence cooperation. A subset of those documents was published by various media organizations (henceforth referred to as the Snowden archives). The Snowden archives offer valuable insights about the interactions between large technology companies and signals intelligence agencies.

In 2014, the U.S. government formally indicted five Chinese People's Liberation Army officers for having committed commercial espionage. At the same time, it prosecuted Su Bin, a Chinese businessman, who aided two China-based hackers to exfiltrate sensitive data from defence contractors. Importantly, the court documents gave some idea of the financial dimension such an operation takes on. They revealed that an operation against the plans for a C-17 transport plane cost 3.5 million Renminbi (ca. £350,000) in 2011 and up to 6.8 million Renminbi (ca. £660,000) for previous operations and infrastructure set-up.[21]

In 2014–2015 the public posting of documents acquired by hacking two private companies, Gamma International (summer 2014) and Hacking Team (summer 2015), allowed researchers to gain a deeper insight into the international market for interception and surveillance tools. Meanwhile, data breaches have continued to make headlines. For states, one of the most notable was the U.S. Office of Personal Management breach, which led to the exfiltration of the national security relevant SF86-Questionnaires (security clearance background information) for 21.5 million individuals. Private sector analysts attributed this to a Chinese intelligence operation. However, no official (i.e. government-issued) conclusion was proffered supporting this claim at the time, though unofficially, the U.S. government supported the conclusion.[22]

In 2016–2018 several high-profile cybersecurity incidents captured the attention of political leaders. Amongst them were the intrusions into the Democratic National Committee (DNC) in 2015–2016 and the subsequent use of the data in influence operations in the U.S. elections. 2017 brought with it two destructive campaigns that spread globally, labelled WannaCry and NotPetya. Both included, though the latter did not spread predominantly via, leaked NSA exploits and resulted in tremendous damage and affected numerous governments, firms, and individuals worldwide. NotPetya, originally inserted into the Ukrainian tax accounting software MeDoc, viscerally reminded the world of the global access a well-placed intrusion into the software supply chain can bring. Not that the cybersecurity community needed reminding: in April 2017 a collaborative private sector landmark report named *Operation Cloud Hopper* detailed how Chinese-state hackers used supply-chain access to managed security service providers to further their (commercial) espionage.[23] In 2020 this would become prescient as the popular network management platform Orion by SolarWinds was found to be used to gain access to a variety of government and corporate customers, including several agencies of the U.S. government.

To better understand the connection between the large technology companies and intelligence services, a short explanation of modern-day signals intelligence regarding digital network exploitation is in order.[24] First, one differentiates the collection of data in transit versus data at rest. The collection of data in transit is sometimes referred to as 'upstream' (or 'midpoint') collection. Upstream collection can happen at any point in the internet infrastructure (data cables, switches, routers, internet exchange points, etc.). Most of this infrastructure is owned and maintained by private companies. If a SIGINT agency wants to collect traffic, it needs to access this infrastructure. It can do so overtly, for example through collaborating with an internet service provider, or covertly, for example by installing malware in a backbone network router.[25] The other large digital network exploitation category is the collection of data at rest (i.e. stored data), sometimes referred to as 'downstream' (or 'endpoint') collection. This can also be achieved overtly, for example with the cooperation of an email provider, or covertly, for example by installing malware on a target's smartphone. These relationships will later be analysed in the case studies on modern-day mercantile companies.

Today, cybersecurity is still provided as an afterthought: most computing and networking equipment is not designed with security as a design goal. The cybersecurity of an individual user relies on the user's safe usage practices—an assumption that frequently breaks down and is exploited by cybercriminals.[26] Most users have to rely on large companies being incentivized to deliver services securely for them. As witnessed by several large data breaches and the regular catastrophic vulnerabilities reported, this is not a safe assumption. Companies are not largely held accountable for how much insecurity they generate in the digital ecosystem, which, in economic terms, creates large negative externalities. Companies have increased their investments in cybersecurity, but there is great variance across different sectors of the economy. At the same time, states have increased their investment in cybersecurity. However, one should note, states include money spent on offensive capabilities as cybersecurity investments. Thus, states too are in part incentivized to retain some digital insecurity.[27]

This short overview of the history of cyber(in-)security shows the constellations between the main actors. It has introduced examples of cooperative and competing aspects of cyber(in-)security between different stakeholders. With increasing interconnectivity, technology and telecommunication companies' roles in the protection of societal networks and end-user data have become more prominent. Whilst states have acknowledged the challenges arising from cyber(in-)security and tried to address them, they faced both defensive and offensive interests. The defensive interest acknowledged companies' increasingly important roles and made them key stakeholders in the protection of critical infrastructure. The offensive interests, rooted in signals intelligence, led to an investment by states in exploiting cyber insecurity to further their national goals.

This chapter presented a historical account of cyberspace to uncover the different constellations and framings between the major actors involved in the provision of cyber(in-)security, focusing on the three perspectives of users, technology corporations, and states. This analysis will now be integrated in the following Chapter 5, which will assess the general comparability of the two domains, the sea and cyberspace, and discuss the analytical value of the historical insights that can then be applied in modern case studies.

5

The Sea and Cyberspace

Comparison and Analytical Lines of Enquiry

This chapter integrates the insights gained from the two historical chapters, specifically, how the different actors were interacting among one another, into the conceptualization for the different actors. It will provide an answer to the question, which of the three historical periods examined in the age of sail can be best applied to cybersecurity? The chapter argues against the 19th-century case as a useful analogue and recommends the late 16th and late 17th centuries as closer approximations to current trends. In so doing, we can further specify the scope for a more focused analysis of the modern-day case studies in the ensuing two chapters.

The chapter first assesses the general comparability of the two domains, the sea between the late 16th and mid-19th centuries and cyberspace. The analysis concludes that there are many shared characteristics of insecurity observed in both domains, and, whilst the differences do not alter the fundamental structure of the insecurity problem, they do change our assessment of the expected speed of interaction, the range of possible potential policy solutions, and our expectations of the stability of insecurity reproduced across time.

I then move to a discussion of the historical findings considering the spectrum of state proximity, clarifying the differing types of relationships of the actors with the state and among one another, and building on the richness of the different historical constellations encountered. Using the three interactive macro-historical focuses outlined in Chapter 2, in the historical research, special attention was paid to uncovering how the actors are rendering themselves (or are being rendered) proximate to the state, how privateering impacted the longer term evolution of security policy, and how naval security became an affair of the state. This chapter reports on the results of these focuses, including the narratives of piracy, the evolution and transformation of interests in privateering, longevity and path dependency,

Semi-State Actors in Cybersecurity. Florian J. Egloff, Oxford University Press. © Florian J. Egloff 2022.
DOI: 10.1093/oso/9780197579275.003.0005

the evolution of mercantile companies, and the abolition of privateering. Each of them is discussed, their impact on the conceptualization of each actor evaluated, and the security dynamics between the actors analysed in a section of this chapter.

Briefly summarized up front, the chapter finds that the nuances of the connection to the state are usefully captured in the different narratives of piracy. Accordingly, it integrates the narrative conceptualization of the relationships between pirates and states from the study of pirates for a modern analysis. Furthermore, I find that the actors' goals changed over time. Whilst early expansion was enabled by adventurism, the will to proselytize, predation, and the growing interest in trade during the 17th century created incentives for stability. Concurrently, having taxed the expansion of seafaring, governments had more resources to build dedicated state capabilities. This has implications on the structure of the analogy. To usefully locate the cyber(in-)security challenge in time, the characterization of the environment as exploratory and predatory or more trade-like is of importance. Furthermore, the notion of pirates as enemies of mankind is of importance for the comparison of cybercriminals to pirates. On this basis, the chapter argues against the 19th-century case as a useful analogue, as both the absence of the state as the provider of security and the lack of a clear dominant state in cyberspace indicate severe differences. This narrows down the scope of the analogy and sets up the three claims made in the next two chapters, where I will use these insights for analysing mercantile companies, privateers, and pirates based on the understandings built from the late 16th- and the 17th-century cases, to investigate their utility in understanding actors in cyber(in-)security.

The chapter concludes with proposing such a way to study the cyber pirates, privateers, and mercantile companies following three main lines of inquiry. First, the background of the history of contestations in piracy and privateering sets out a pathway to better understand how state proximity, as well as the ambiguity thereof, was a political play used strategically by both attackers and defenders. Second, the longevity and path dependencies of historical privateering set-ups suggest a focus of the enquiry on the constancy, as well as the long-term risks and rewards, of state collaboration with cybercriminals. Finally, the mercantile company lens suggests focusing on how cooperative and conflictive relations of large technology companies to states and their practices of self-protection influence cyber(in-)security.

A Comparison of the Two Domains: The Sea and Cyberspace

Having assessed the history between the different actors in both domains, a number of similarities and differences between the sea and cyberspace can be identified (see elements of comparison in Table 5.1).

Here I will discuss these similarities and differences and assess their impact on the further analogical research (see detailed comparison in Table 5.2). Naturally, specific characteristics are always only similar or different to some degree: the categorizations are thus to be read as 'more similar than different' and 'more different than similar'.

Geography

To the degree that the sea and cyberspace are interpreted as geographic realms of action, they form similar operating domains. For centuries, naval forces have tried to control specific sea lanes. Similarly, in cyberspace, geographic access to specific communication choke points represents an advantage for the host country. However, one geographic difference is the actors that have access to the domain in the first place and their potential reach: land-locked countries never represented major naval forces, whereas all countries have access to most of cyberspace now.

Table 5.1 Elements of comparison between the sea and cyberspace

Similarities	Differences
• Geography	• Actors' exposure to physical sanctions
• Costs of offensive and defensive capabilities	• Pace of technological change and diffusion of knowledge
• Public-private divide of capabilities	• International society and institutions
• Difficulty of attribution	• Stability of domain characteristics
• Dependence of actors on the domain	

Cost of offensive capabilities and defensive capabilities

The cost of entry for offensive naval capabilities in the age of sail stand in direct relationship to the cost of defensive capabilities. In naval history, the cost of offensive and defensive capabilities varied across time. At first, the entry-level offensive costs were low, mainly due to the low protection of ships, and amounted to outfitting a merchant ship with arms. Success rested on the size of the boat and the skill level of the labour force. Over time, this changed, as more ships were protected by an accompanying private force or dedicated state navies that started to provide convoy duty. Navies were an expensive investment by states, which, over time, raised the entry level for persistent offensive success.[1] Furthermore, certain sea lanes were protected by companies who held a monopoly for trading in the area. In cyberspace, the cost of entry for offensive capabilities is still relatively low, in part due to weak defensive postures and in part due to the lack of incentives to build secure systems. Persistent offensive success rests mainly on skilled labour and protected network access, both factors a moderately well-resourced actor can provide.[2] The cost of defending cyberspace at a national scale is not yet determinable, as states have neither taken responsibility nor demonstrated success at defending national assets in cyberspace. For companies, both on the seas and in cyberspace, investments in defensive measures are part of the operating cost and risk structure considered when relying on cyberspace.

Public-private divide of capabilities

In the period of naval history observed, the nature and affiliation of the actors deploying offensive and defensive capabilities varied across time. They started out as small and with largely private crews, then grew into larger and distributed private capabilities. Concurrently, larger public capabilities (i.e. deployed in furtherance of the state) were built. For a long time, skills for deploying force rested in semi-state (companies, privateers, some pirates) and non-state (some pirates) hands.

In cyberspace, we are witnessing a similar development. Offensive and defensive capabilities started out small and private and have only recently transformed into larger and distributed private (defensive and offensive) and public capabilities (mostly offensive). There is still a lack of public capability

to protect. Skills for deploying security practices and insecurity are distributed among many actors.

Difficulty of attribution

Attribution represents a challenge both on the seas and in cyberspace,
though the nature of the problem is slightly different. On the seas, it was
a non-trivial task for a captain of a ship to determine the association of
another ship with a particular political entity. Several signs were used as
markers for belonging, though many were subject to forgery. First, ships
regularly carried multiple flags as defensive and offensive measures. Thus,
when encountering an English vessel, a French crew might decide to hoist
a Dutch (false) flag to confuse the origin of the attack. Second, some captains carried several letters of marque, selectively producing the one allowing the capture of a particular ship when challenged to do so. Third, the
crews operating the ships were quite diverse, including many nationalities
and languages. Finally, the verification mechanisms for the defenders were
poor. Inter-imperial networks of information were slow and subject to political influence.

Today, the problem of attribution has arisen in cyberspace. The problem of
attribution in cyberspace can be split into three challenges.[3] First, one must
match the experienced attacks to a particular source of computers. Second,
one must associate the actions of those machines to a human agent (individual or group). Third, one must ask, which political actor (individual or
group) is associated with the behaviour (i.e. who is responsible for the actions of the individual/group that undertook the attacks)? Every step requires a different set of expertise and sources of information. And for each
step, the attackers can undertake efforts to shape the attribution process of
the defender. Hence, the attackers can still use 'false-flag' attacks (i.e. try to
mimic the attacking profile of a different state).[4] They can mask the origins of
the attacks by operating out of a different location. And, more importantly,
it is still very difficult to reliably ascertain an attacker's sponsors. Conversely,
it is also very difficult to persistently run offensive operations and mask one's
sponsors. Time can aid the defender here: mistakes become visible in hind-
sight; actions associable to political sponsors. Defenders who choose to invest in attribution capabilities upfront will have an advantage when having to
attribute particular cyber operations.[5]

Dependence of actors on the domain

The dependence of the different actors on the seas in the observed period increased drastically. Whilst England had been a seafaring nation, the relative dependence on trade in terms of its share of the economy multiplied. Similarly, most states are growing increasingly dependent on cyberspace, both economically and societally, as evidenced by data measuring the integration of networked computing into modern economies.

Actors' exposure to physical sanctions

A major difference between attacking in the two domains is the physicality of the attacker. On the seas, attackers had to expose themselves to the defender physically, thereby risking their lives. In cyberspace, attackers often can operate remotely, far away from the defender. This lowers the risk profile experienced by the attacker and potentially aggravates incentives to offensively use insecurity in cyberspace.

Pace of technological change and diffusion of knowledge

In the early modern system, both the pace of technological change and diffusion of knowledge was slow. Ship designs took a long time to be copied, emulated, and tested. It took even longer for a dominant form of naval administration to form. Whilst different countries may have tried to copy the leading country's model of success, they did not succeed (e.g. England copying Spain). Rather, it took an extensive time of exploration and experimentation until the imperial-trade model took hold. In today's time, particularly with regard to operating in cyberspace, the pace of technological change is high and knowledge spreads rapidly, both about the technologies and designs used and about the administrative structures in place. For example, after the U.S. launched a dedicated cyber command in 2009, within a short time span, a flurry of countries modelled their own cyber commands on the U.S. design. I would thus expect any international process analogized to happen in a compressed time span.[6]

International society and institutions

A difference between the naval history of the seas and cyberspace is the nature of international society and depth of international institutions. In the periods of naval history covered, international society is thin and globally fragmented according to competing imperial realms. It covers a period of European international relations expanding in depth and geographic scope, often by the force of arms, with many rules and principles of naval practice that were still unsettled. By comparison, today's international society is more global (including some globally shared norms, such as those in the Geneva Conventions) and international laws and institutions are more robust. For example, 193 countries are permanently represented at the United Nations in New York.[7] However, in cyberspace, international consensus on acceptable behaviour is still very limited and norms globally adhered to are few. The lack of shared norms in cyberspace increases the risk of misunderstanding and escalation. Despite that though, given the depth of relations between countries in many other areas today, it is unlikely that actors are settling for very hostile options lightly.

Stability of domain characteristics

Whilst technologies of operating on the seas have changed, the sea itself has not.[8] Contrary to that, cyberspace is an artificial domain. As a living technology, it is always evolving. Consequently, this also means that the characteristics of cyberspace are changeable. This has important implications on the analogical logic applied here. As the historical chapters laid out, the current-day analogy assesses a similarity with regard to the impact of distributed, private capabilities can have on actors in the same domain. This rests on two assumptions: reachability within the network (packets can traverse the domain relatively unhindered), and decentralized control (most control lies in the endpoints). A fundamental technology change affecting these two assumptions would consequently also demand a re-evaluation of the applicability of the analogy. However, a fundamental technology change is, at the time of this writing, not expected. Whilst some networks may become less reachable, a complete overhaul of the engineering of cyberspace would require a massive technology investment, which is currently unlikely to be in any actor's interest.

Table 5.2 A comparison of two domains: the sea and cyberspace

Aspects	Sea (16th –19th centuries)	Cyberspace
Geography	Strategic sea lanes, limited number of countries (access to the seas)	Strategic communication points, potentially larger number of countries (access to cyberspace)
Cost of offensive capabilities	Varies across time. *Offensive capabilities*: first low costs due to low protection (mainly skilled labour and access to a ship). Later higher barrier	*Offensive capabilities*: relatively low due to weak protection (mainly skilled labour and protected network access)
Cost of defensive capabilities	Expensive (national), part of the operating costs/risks (company)	Not determined yet (national), part of the operating costs/ risks (company)
Public-private divide of capabilities	Varied across time. From small and private, to large and distributed private capabilities, to large and public capabilities. For a long time, skills for deploying force rested in semi-state hands	From small and private, to large and distributed private capabilities. There is a lack of public capability to protect. Skills for deploying force rest in semi-state hands
Difficulty of attribution	Problematic (multiple flags, letters of marque, diverse crews)	Problematic (false-flag attacks, masking of origins, ambiguous sponsors)
Dependence of actors on the domain	Increased over time	Increases over time
Actors' exposure to physical sanctions	Attackers physically expose themselves to the defender	Attackers work remotely
Pace of technological change and diffusion of knowledge	Slow change and slow diffusion of knowledge	Fast change and rapid diffusion of knowledge
International society and institutions	Thin and globally fragmented (empires)	Thicker and more globally shared
Stability of domain characteristics	Stable (the sea does not change)	Evolving (the characteristics of fundamental domain are changeable)

White = More similar than different; Grey = More different than similar

This first part assessed the general comparability of the two domains, the sea between the late 16th and mid-19th centuries and cyberspace. I argued that some characteristics of the problem of insecurity in the domains are very similar and enable a useful comparison.[9] The discussion of differences resulted in an appreciation of where difference in security dynamics and policy solutions may be expected. The decreased physical risk to the attacker, the more rapid diffusion of knowledge, and increased pace of technological change point to a more aggravated problem of insecurity and a faster changing interaction between the actors. Denser international society and institutions, though still sparse in the cyber domain, allow for a broader range of solutions to the insecurities experienced in cyberspace than on the seas. Finally, the possibility of a change in the fundamental characteristics of cyberspace, though unlikely, makes the specific problem of insecurity studied potentially transformable.

Thus, there are many shared characteristics of insecurity observed in both domains, and, whilst the differences do not alter the fundamental structure of the insecurity problem, they do change our assessment of the expected speed of interaction, the range of possible potential policy solutions, and our expectations of the stability of insecurity reproduced across time.

Assessing the Historical Insights and Developing Analytical Lines of Enquiry

Having discussed the major similarities and differences of the domains, in this section I will take stock of the insights gained through the historical research. Recall the three focuses applied in the historical research: how an actor is rendering itself and being rendered as proximate to a state over time, how privateering became possible and its impact on the longer term evolution of security policy, and how the contestations and interactions between the actors shaped the security tasks of the state. Applying these three focuses, I identified five insights in studying the history of the different actors that will be discussed in turn: the narratives of piracy, the evolution and transformation of interests in privateering, longevity and path dependency, the evolution of mercantile companies, and the abolition of privateering. I will then decide how to apply them to cybersecurity in the third part of this book.

Narratives of piracy

The identification of political narratives of piracy enables a useful clustering of the interactions between pirates and the other actors of their time.[10] The entrant, resource, revisionist, and criminal narratives all offer a particular type of framing the relationships between states and pirates. Rather than looking at the motivations of the actors, the analysis focuses on how a particular piratical episode is rendered a matter of state concern. For example, in the case of Captain Kidd, those in power had no interest in the attacks he led against the *Quedah Merchant*. Rather, the political blowback (via the East India Company) led them to declare his action as piratical. These categorically different ways of shaping the associations to the state are one tool to better understand the proximity to the state.

Similarly, in the cyber(in-)security context, different narratives compete in classifying different incidents. Some attackers are classified as purely criminal, a nuisance, but not a fundamental challenge or threat. Other attackers are labelled state-supported criminals, constructing a resource narrative of hacking. An example would be parts of the Russian-speaking cybercriminal underground; its size and existence often associated with tolerance by the Russian state. The Russian political cybercriminal nexus will form part of the next chapter's empirical investigation. Yet other attackers are labelled revisionist, threatening the fundamental state system. Examples were certain hacktivist groups (e.g. some offshoots of Anonymous) that promote an anarchist political vision of the future. Finally, some portrayals of other attackers' actions could be labelled as entrant narratives. Examples are the politically motivated hacks by the Palestinian and Kurdish hacking collectives; their hacking undertaken as measures of pursuing the objective to establish their own state.

Evolution and transformation of interests in privateering

The analysis of privateering showed an evolution of interests in privateering across different time periods. Whilst in the 16th century privateering was a method of warfare and conquest, the growing interest in stability of trade relations from the mid-17th century onwards made privateering a more complicated policy choice. The mercantile companies' growing trade network, as well as the increasing revenues generated from that, raised the potential costs of employing privateers. In addition, the growing navies offered new alternative naval strategies. Both elements point to changing interests of globalizing trading conglomerates and states over time. In addition, dedicated state capacity is to be analysed as both enabled by successful trade (source of income, knowledge, and skill sets for the state) and as a guarantor of continuing stable trade.

In cyber(in-)security, a similar question around transformation of interests can be posed. Are we still in an era of conquest, in which the hostile appropriation of data is seen as a method for advancing the actors' interests? Are there actors that promote a strong interest in the stability of relations in cyber(in-)security and others that do not? Some observers argue that regarding the Chinese interest in intellectual property theft, a similar transformation of interests can be observed. Whilst intellectual property theft may be a useful strategy to avoid investment cost in catching up technologically, in the long run participation in the global market may incentivize the possibility to defend one's own intellectual property against other countries' abuse.[11] Furthermore, cyber(in-)security and the use of private actors by states is changing as many states invest in dedicated offensive capabilities. Different models of acquiring capabilities are used, some relying on state-controlled contractors, on forms of national service, or on the supply chain in a grey market. The opportunities and risks associated with the use of privateers can hence be observed in cyber(in-)security. Examples are the lack of control, the inability to clearly classify attacks, and the government-private sector competition for skills.

Longevity and path dependency

When researching naval history in the age of sail, one quickly learns to appreciate the dependencies of naval capacity on specialized skills and supply chains, and one gains an awareness of career paths and personal investments. Especially with deep-sea privateering, the range of skills; personal bets; social relationships; and the size of ships, armament, and investment communities all highlight the depth institutionalized privateering can have. This has direct implications on the analysis of privateering as a government policy: there is a stickiness to this policy.[12] Once privateering is institutionalized as a form of living, switching from such a policy is associated with friction. Specialized labour is asked to leave the only job it trained for. Powerful investors, having gained lucrative returns, are asked not to continue seeking those returns. Ships outfitted for deep-sea raiding are to be repurposed. The protection offered by outfitting trading companies with privateering licenses has to be considered. Furthermore, there are effects on other policy choices.

The investment in this form of force directly affects the building of state capacity. For example, Elizabethan privateering brought with it incentives for state officials to become invested in gaining private returns. For sailors, serving on a privateer often meant better living conditions on the ship as well as a larger share of the booty. However, naval history also demonstrates the absolute dependency of any navy on specialized expertise. In the different time periods, the differing amounts a government could spend on retaining dedicated personnel for a state navy also impacted the attractiveness of allowing a private capacity to be financed—even if that choice introduced additional political risk.

In cyber(in-)security, some of these dependencies seem present. As a domain that relies on a set of highly marketable and specialized skill sets, different countries have taken different approaches to incentivize such specialized labour to become active in their interests. A specialty of this domain is that private actors take on defensive and offensive roles. Even states hire private actors for both tasks. Thereby, private industry can attract talent with large salaries and very flexible working conditions, whereas states continue to struggle to retain talent and frequently have to resort to rehiring former staff as consultants/contractors. The interdependencies among policy choices made, career paths chosen, and the friction resulting from the competition for talent significantly shapes cyber(in-)security and—as the subsequent chapters will show—merits further investigation.

Mercantile companies: from early investor to reaping the benefits of monopoly

One interesting phenomenon to observe is the degree of independent agency exerted by the mercantile companies and their framing the proximity to states. Depending on the audience, the companies chose to represent their affiliation and status differently. In some relationships, for example with the Indian Mughal, the East India Company chose to represent itself as a mere merchant, whereas to the English Crown and merchants, it self-identified as the sovereign over the English people in the East Indies.

The East India Company's constitution in the 17th century shaped the development of both empire and private property. The freedom to trade, enabled by the Crown, allowed for a rapid global expansion. Trade became both a source of revenue and influence for the state. The early investor in global exploration and conquest was increasingly interested in reaping the benefits of monopoly by protecting its network of trade relations from other entrants. Besides the corporate policies with the Mughal Empire, where it competed for trade routes and products, making the affairs of the company a matter of the home state was one way of protecting its interests. The East India Company contributed to the rise of the commercial reason of the state, as exemplified in the period of mercantilism.

In cyber(in-)security, there is a different starting point. Ideologically starting in a neoliberal market environment, many of the (predominantly) U.S. technology companies, that fundamentally shaped the commercialization of cyberspace, did not start out with close government interaction. However, the government enabled and facilitated their expansion, for example, by supporting the commercialization of internet exchange points and by not imposing software liability. As the companies' reach grew, they gained more weight in influencing the political process and lobbying the government to support their interests. In the reverse, as more people started using the companies' products and services, the state also became more interested in the activities of the companies. As introduced in Chapter 2 and substantiated in the historical narrative of cyberspace, this could lead to both cooperative and conflictive outcomes.

One insight from the historical research was to interpret the analogues of companies as their own body politic.[13] Just as the East India Company heeded its own political ambitions, so do many modern technology companies. For example, Larry Page and Sergey Brin—the founders of Google—have a vision of Google's role in the world: organizing the world's information. The specific ways of doing this sketches out a political vision of what they consider a better world. Similarly, when Apple challenged the FBI in court over the phone of a deceased terrorist in 2016, Tim Cook, Apple's CEO, claimed the authority to advocate on behalf of millions of Apple users. By doing so, the company uncovered the diverging interpretations of *security*: one defined by a national government, the other by a multinational company.

Abolition of privateering

The case of the abolition of privateering raises multiple points of insight. From a constellation of actors' point of view, this case could be read as a situation in which a dominant power was able to lock in its interests when it was willing to trade off something in return. It showed that not all great powers were needed to force a global change in behaviour. This was in part due to the network effect of privateering: it was only beneficial if you could turn the spoils gained into durable assets. However, the abolition treaty prevented treaty members from offering privateers access to their ports. The applicability of the analogy to the mid-19th century to the cyber realm is questionable for two reasons. First, there is today no comparable dominant power that can control cyberspace to the degree Britain was able to influence the activities on the seas in the mid-19th century. Despite the United States' superiority in other realms of power, in cyberspace it is more equal to other powers, such as China and Russia, than in any other domain. Second, the analogy would suggest that the still limited state capabilities and willingness to intervene in the cyber domain on behalf of other actors rules out the analogy to the mid-19th century. States currently do not routinely provide protection for their companies and citizens in cyberspace. In naval history, a key turning point was the early 18th century, when Britain's interests shifted to stable trade, protected by a strong navy and a more 'coherent involvement of the state in the country's commercial affairs'.[14] Whilst the dependency on cyberspace keeps rising, and states are investing in dedicated cyber capabilities, the following chapters will build on the claim that current cyber(in-) security practices are best analogized to the pre-18th-century history of sail.

How do these insights impact the conceptualization of state proximity?

The narratives of piracy arguments have offered one way of interrogating the construction of a criminal or state-supported actor. Whilst early narratives casted pirates as resources to the state, later pirates were represented as non-state actors in the extreme form, their sheer existence representing a threat to the state system (e.g. as *hostes humani generis*). The agnostic nature of researching incidents of 'hacking', and then observing how different actors render them criminal or political in particular constellations, offers a methodologically and theoretically robust way of analysing the comparability between the historical and modern-day political contestations. It impacts the spectrum of state proximity insofar as it offers a richer set of categories to be compared, instead of just casting all pirates as 'non-state' actors. In Chapter 6, the Estonia case will show that by analysing these contestations in cyber(in-)

security with the background of the history of contestations in piracy and privateering in mind, we better understand how state proximity is a political play used strategically by both attackers and defenders, and how this can change our understanding of attribution.

The history of privateers has shown that they need to be closely observed with regard to their impact on the mercantile companies' interests. The expansion of global trade and thereby also the exposure of assets and markets overseas, feature large in the debates around the use of privateers. Furthermore, the incentives of using privateers and the interaction with (the lack of) formal state capacity will continue to be of interest for the analysis of the modern cases. In addition, the interaction between privateers and pirates has shown multiple constellations: privateers as former pirates, privateers as pirate hunters, and privateers as pirates. Coupled with the narratives of piracy, this encourages a focus on the state-criminal nexus. In Chapter 6, in addition to making an argument about state proximity and attribution in the Estonia case, three court cases against Russian cyber criminals will be used to further the claim that the understanding of the longevity and path dependencies of historical privateering set-ups can refine our understanding of the constancy, as well as the long-term risks and rewards, of state collaboration with cybercriminals. Furthermore, it can refine our understanding of the difficulty to exit a policy of a political cybercriminal nexus. We will see that the analogy is uniquely placed to make these long-term observations.

The history of the East India Company suggests their (state-enabled) freedom of action was made possible by a relatively weak state, which sought to access capital it would not otherwise have had access to.[15] In this sense, the mercantile company could be reduced as a state strategy. However, the historical analysis has offered episodes of independent agency beyond the English state and, indeed, went as far as introducing the company-state. This analysis substantiated the conceptual imaginary of sometimes cooperative and sometimes conflictive interests. The analysis of cyber(in-)security in the modern context has sketched out the constellation between the modern actors. It focused on states, technology corporations, and users' conceptions of security and how they are represented in the present context. An introduction to the modern-day signals intelligence environment introduced cooperative and competitive interests between state agencies and corporations. Rather than being, as in the physical domain, the provider of security for users and corporations, the state in cyber(in-)security is just one among many players. Its ability to provide any meaningful security beyond its own institutions has yet to be proven. No clear rules of interaction amongst the players have been established.[16] Hence, this further supports the claim of not analogizing the security situation with the mid-19th century case, where many rules of interaction on the high seas were established.

Contrary to some pirates, the existence of the East India Company itself did not challenge the existence of the state. Nevertheless, it is possible to analyse companies with the same lenses: how does a company become close to the state? How does it establish independence? Does the state protect the company or does it protect itself? As an empirical question, the spectrum of state proximity can be left open. One can observe the positioning of a multinational company towards other actors only in concrete instances. In Chapter 7, three cases will analyse these questions and further the claim that by treating large technology companies as political actors as their own kind, the mercantile company lens can sharpen the focus on how cooperative and conflictive relations to states and practices of self-protection influence cyber(in-)security. It can refine our understanding of the role companies play in providing cyber(in-)security.

This chapter discussed the insights from the historical research which I will apply to cyber pirates, cyber privateers, and cyber mercantile companies in the next part. It uses empirical cases to evaluate the applicability and the utility of the analogy in changing our understanding of the security dynamics between the different actors in cyber(in-)security. While Chapter 6 will apply the understanding of the privateer and pirate to contemporary cases, Chapter 7 will evaluate the usefulness of analogies to mercantile companies to better understand cooperative and conflictive interests between states and large technology companies.

APPLYING THE ANALOGY
TO CYBERSECURITY

6

Cyber Pirates and Privateers

State Proxies, Criminals, and Independent Patriotic Hackers

Many states are currently building capacities to conduct offensive and defensive cyber operations. States' growing capacities are augmented by the expertise and experience of private actors. In this chapter, the alignment between Russian cybercriminal networks and Russian state interests will be documented. The chapter analogizes the relationship between Russian cybercrime and the Russian state to historical privateers and pirates and draws insights based on the type of relationship found and the political strategies used to interact with such actors. The case studies in this chapter show the merit of drawing on the historical experience with late 16th- and 17th-century pirates and privateers.

The interests of skilled personnel and governments can overlap in three main ways. First, instead of recruiting personnel for governmental positions, many governments rely on the support of private personnel. Countries rely on a form of national service (e.g. formalized cyber militias), the use of contractors to draw on key capabilities (e.g. experienced operators, developers, etc.), or the use of a range of services offered by the cybercriminal underground, as part of the toolset for state exploitation of the cyber realm.

Second, there is the phenomenon of so-called patriotic hackers. Working in the political and economic interest of a country, patriotic hackers have been active in many highly visible cases ranging from the attacks by Russian hackers on Estonia in 2007 and on Georgia in 2008, to the attacks by Chinese and U.S. hackers in 1999 and 2001, and to those by the Syrian Electronic Army.

Third, criminal intelligence collection efforts have also been mounted. These are less evident than the highly visible and clearly politically motivated attacks. The influence and direction of criminal activity is multilayered, ranging from discretionary enforcement, based on the selected targets, to the way in which cybercriminals have become active in Russian political

Semi-State Actors in Cybersecurity. Florian J. Egloff, Oxford University Press. © Florian J. Egloff 2022.
DOI: 10.1093/oso/9780197579275.003.0006

interests, sometimes with hints of coercion.[1] Empirical evidence, however, is usually incomplete and open to interpretation. Tacit support is sometimes inferred by the absence of cooperation between governments to prosecute identified criminals in the presence of a mutual legal assistance treaty (MLAT).

The first part of this chapter shows how the historical strategies used to connect an act of piracy to a government are implemented today to transform an act of hacking into an act of state-sponsored hacking, using the case of the cyberattacks against Estonia. The analysis of this case shows how the Estonian and Russian leadership acted before, during, and after the crisis between the two countries in 2007. Using the insights of the different historical narratives of piracy, I trace the narratives that each government constructs regarding the proximity to the state of the attackers. The narratives of piracy observed in the historical chapter showed that states used different narratives to construct piracy, including as a threat or as a resource. The historical case of Captain Kidd has shown that governments have agency in the framing of the state association. The contemporary case of Estonia will unveil how the Estonian leadership rhetorically connected the cyber incidents with the Russian government, whilst the Russian government introduced distance between its officials and the hackers. The case emphasizes that governments make political choices about whether to treat a specific instance of hacking as political or criminal. The case closes with a discussion of the resulting strategic ambiguity that uncertainty about the attacker's proximity to the state introduces. It argues that the perception of collaboration raises the stakes of non-involvement and increases the escalatory potential.

In the second part of the chapter, the analysis of three different criminal cases against Russians will lead to a discussion, based on the insights of privateers and pirates, about the risks and opportunities associated with the closeness between cybercrime and politics. Specifically, the analysis focuses on the longevity and path dependencies that a reliance on privateers and pirates brought historically and probes the extent to which they are visible in the cases observed today. Three different contemporary associations to the state are examined. First, the case of a politically supported cyber pirate shows that like pre-18th-century pirates, cybercriminals are not treated as enemies of mankind. There is not a common understanding among states that cybercrime represents an evil that has to be addressed jointly. The second case of a cyber pirate and cyber privateer identifies the existence of a deal for political cover for some of cybercrime. As in the case of early

17th-century piracy, the case highlights both the provision of a safe harbour and the indications of political profit from the criminal enterprise itself. The signalling of the acceptance of cybercrime brings with it the risks of self-reinforcing tendencies. Finally, the third case features a cyber privateering setup. It analogizes the problems of control of late 16th-century privateers with those evidenced in contemporary case and shows that similar risks manifest itself in this case. In close analogy to the historical risks, a Russian contemporary's assessment of the risks of institutionalization of the cyber privateering set-up is examined. The case study finishes with the analysis of the effects this has on recruitment and capability building and an assessment of how the analogy to privateering can offer insights into the political constitution of cyber(in-)security.

The chapter concludes that the constellations of actors analysed in this chapter, with regard to their state proximity, are most comparable to the late 16th- and early 17th-century pirates and privateers. Based on this analysis, the conclusion advances two claims. First, we can better understand the label of state sponsorship when reading the association to the state as a narrative constructed by the different stakeholders involved. As the Estonia case shows, multiple narratives can coexist. Public and private attribution should be distinguished. In doing so, we can better understand the political contestation of public attribution claims. The public attribution claim is a strongly political choice about how to frame the relations of the attacker and the entity that the state blames. Introducing this distinction leads to a better understanding of the politics of attribution. Overall, I will show that governments can derive political benefits from managing the proximity of the relationship, but the same relationship also offers adversaries opportunities to assign blame for actions by semi-state actors to the (supposedly) sponsoring government. This is closely congruent with the way governments have managed their relationship with privateers in the past. Hence, drawing on this analogy explains framing and changes in attribution strategies that a focus on technical evidence alone would fail to capture.

Second, the longevity and path dependencies of historical privateering set-ups refine our understanding of the constancy and the long-term risks and rewards of state collaboration with cybercriminals. The identification of both drivers and feedback loops, characteristic of such path-dependent choices, refines our understanding of the difficulty to exit a policy of political cybercriminal nexus. This offers a conceptual explanation of the stability of politically constituted cyber(in-)security in the domain of political cybercriminal interaction. The analogy is uniquely placed to make this long-term observation.

I will end the chapter with a reflection on the differences observed between the historical and the contemporary semi-state actors. In particular, I will highlight the type of currency that flows between privateers and governments (not just money, but also information), the uncertainty about the magnitude of the problem, and the increased regulatory and coercive capacity of the state today.

The 2007 Cyberattacks in Estonia: Examining Public Attribution and Ambiguity

The case of the 2007 cyberattacks in Estonia interrogates the competing narratives that rendered the attacks as 'state sponsored' or 'patriotic'. It integrates different political perspectives of the same events. To do so, research was undertaken to access these different narratives. Primarily, Estonian and Russian official statements and press reporting was relied upon. Research was performed—where necessary—with the aid of GoogleTranslate, an online tool that allows for the translation of text and entire websites. Imperfect though it may be, it allowed for a deeper penetration into the meaning-making processes of both governments.[2]

In 2007, the moving of the Bronze Soldier, a Soviet Second World War memorial, built next to war graves in 1947, led to political controversy (see Figure 6.1 for a case overview). Given the tense relations between ethnic Estonians and Estonian Russians, the moving of the statue led to two days of riots in Tallinn, protests in front of the Estonian embassy in Moscow, and cyberattacks against Estonian public and private networks.[3] The handling of these incidents by the Estonian government, specifically regarding the cyberattacks, are of interest to this case study.

Specifically, the analogy to piracy and privateering is used with regard to the governmental construction of state proximity of the attackers. The different narratives of the Russian and the Estonian governments represent different categories of framing the same activity. Their strategies resemble the different narratives of piracy that historically either legitimized or delegitimized pirates. Uncovering the construction of state-sponsored cyberattackers versus the patriotic undertakings of fervent cyber patriots allows for the drawing of parallels to historic narratives of piracy.

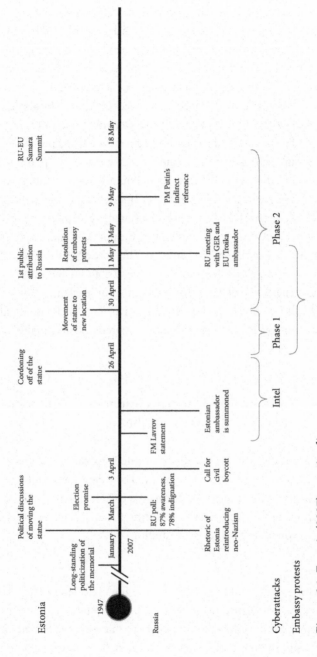

Figure 6.1 Estonia (2007) case timeline

To summarize the argument in the Estonia case succinctly upfront: the analogy to privateering and pirates helps us better understand how state association gets established. The case mirrors a historical debate about whether and how the actions of individuals on the high seas can be attributed to a sovereign. Recall from Chapter 3 that whilst Grotius insisted on a matter of substance, Gentili advocated for a solution of political convenience. The case of Estonia shows elements of both. The Estonian government used the narrative of state-sponsored attackers to its political convenience, but it did so by arguing that it possessed the evidence to back up its claims. The argument for the attribution in this case is similar to privateering, as the government attributed the actions of a small group of hackers to the state. The case shows the political agency of government leadership in the discourse about the state proximity of the attacker. The Russian state denied sponsorship but was content with the patriotic actions of their citizens. Thus, the privateering analogy helps us understand the political nature of attribution by highlighting the political choice a government has in framing the association of an attacker. Thus, the discussion of attribution here will go beyond getting towards a 'correct' attribution and rather focus on the political contestation of particular public attribution claims.

The case will first cover the Estonian narrative, then the Russian narrative, and conclude in how the analogy aids our interpretation and analysis of attribution in this case.

Estonian official narrative: crisis response and the politics of (public) attribution

This first part of the case study will set out the Estonian official narrative. It starts with an overview of the crisis, followed by a detailing of the cyber (and non-cyber) actions that took place during the 2007 incident. I will then cover the attributions of the cyber incidents during the crisis and end this section with a discussion of the politics of attribution.

Overview
The Estonian government knew that the moving of the statue would be controversial. Whilst to many Estonian Russians the statue signified the Red Army's contribution to the end of fascism, to many ethnic Estonians it signified the begin of an era of Soviet occupation. The statue came to signify

two different readings of history and, consequently a conflict of identities. This conflict was fuelled by exchanges between Russian and Estonian politicians.[4] The Estonian election in March 2007 further politicized the marker of the war graves. After the election of the reform party's Andrus Ansip, who had promised to move the statue before 9 May 2007, the Memorial Day of the end of the Second World War, he did not wait long with delivering said promise.[5] Cordoning off for the excavation of the war graves on 26 April 2007 was met with two nights of riots on the streets of Tallinn. Not having anticipated the extent of violent resistance, an emergency meeting of the Estonian government decided to move the statue in the morning hours of 27 April 2007. Heavy police reinforcements brought the situation in Tallinn under control with hundreds of arrests, dozens injured, and one permanent resident of Estonia, who also held Russian citizenship, dead. On 30 April 2007, the government moved the statue to its current-day location in the military cemetery in Tallinn.

The cyberattacks 27 April–18 May 2007
The cyberattacks started on 27 April 2007 and were resumed sporadically with different intensities and durations up to the 18 May 2007. They took place in two phases. The first phase could be called 'online protest'. It represented unprofessional and disorganized attacks and lasted until 29 April 2007. The second phase could be labelled 'organized attack'. It was much more professional and coordinated.[6] Several layers of attacks were observed, including the probing of infrastructure and the subsequent adaption to the targets accordingly. They consisted mostly of distributed denial of service (DDoS) attacks, but also of 'website defacements, DNS server attacks, mass e-mail, and comment spam'.[7]

The Estonian Computer Emergency Response Team (CERT) and internationally connected private sector entities had about two weeks of warning before the attacks started.[8] The warnings came in the form of reports on Russian-language forums inciting attacks on Estonian public and private entities (with instructions) and in the form of network probes to gauge the network capacities. Whilst the online protest phase (27–29 April 2007) resembled an unorganized group of people performing simple DDoS attacks, the organized attack phase (30 April–18 May) relied on hired botnets, displayed more coordination, and demonstrated more adaptable targeting.

The concurrent demonstrations in front of the Estonian embassy in Moscow

From the 27 April 2007 onwards, young demonstrators, including members of the patriotic, nationalist youth group Nashi, set up camp in front of the Estonian embassy in Moscow, harassing embassy staff and demanding the Estonian ambassador leave the country. In the process, the Estonian flag was torn down, eggs were thrown, and Estonians were labelled fascists. The Estonian government protested with the Russian Foreign Ministry and discussed their concerns bilaterally and multilaterally with European countries. Eventually, upon intervention of the European Union, represented by the German presidency, on 3 May 2007 a deal was struck: the Estonian Foreign Ministry agreed for the ambassador Marina Kaljurand to leave Moscow for a 'vacation' and the Russian government agreed to end the protests.[9] The correlation of this deal and the protesters packing up and leaving was read, by some observers, to indicate a coordination between the Russian government and the organizers of the protests.[10]

Estonian government attribution during the crisis

The Estonian government first informed the public about the cyberattacks on the night of 28 April 2007 and warned about the possibility of spreading misinformation.[11] On the next day, Estonia's CERT informed that the cyberattacks came 'from abroad'.[12] On 1 May 2007, the minister of foreign affairs, Urmas Paet, released a statement that opened:

> The European Union is under attack, as Russia is attacking Estonia. . . . IP addresses have helped to identify that the cyber terrorists' attacks against the Internet pages of Estonian government agencies and the Office of the President have originated from specific computers and persons in Russian government agencies, including the administration of the President of the Russian Federation. . . . . I affirm to you that we have sufficient material to prove our accusations.[13]

He also accused the Russian embassy staff of having met the organizers of the riots before they took place, the demonstrators in front of the Estonian embassy of being paid by the Kremlin, and the Russian TV-media campaign lying to their viewers about the actions of the Estonian police forces.

This governmental shaping of the narrative is important. By claiming attribution to the Russian government, he labelled the cyberattacks as deliberate political acts between the two countries and assigned responsibility for the actions to the Russian state.[14]

The next day, the Estonian President Toomas Hendrik Ilves weighed in. He addressed Russia directly:

> Finally, I turn to Russia, Estonia's neighbour, with a clear message—try to remain civilised! It is not customary in Europe to demand the resignation of the democratically elected government of another sovereign country. It is not customary in Europe to use computers belonging to public institutions for cyber attacks against another country's public institutions. In Europe, as well as in the rest of the civilised world, it is not considered possible to violate the Vienna Convention when an embassy of a small enough country is concerned. It is customary in Europe that differences . . . are solved by diplomats and politicians, not on the streets or by computer attacks.[15]

In this message, Ilves again highlighted Russia's governmental responsibility of the cyberattacks and engaged in a civilizational discourse, casting Russia's behaviour as outside of Europe and outside of the 'civilized world'. On the 3 May 2007, President Ilves's office released a summary of a phone call with U.S. Secretary of State Condolezza Rice. The summary claimed that Secretary Rice called the pressure against the Estonian state unacceptable. It also mentioned the attribution of the cyberattacks to Russia. The attribution to Russia, however, was not part of the statement attributed to the secretary in the summary; rather, it formed context offered by President Ilves's office.[16]

On 11 May 2007 Estonian Minister Urmas Paet addressed the Council of Europe and repeated:

> We analyse the logs of these ongoing actions. However, there is already clear evidence that these attacks are well-coordinated and a significant amount of them originate from Russia. (Russian government agencies have also been involved in cyber attacks against Estonia.)[17]

Urmas Paet's formulation also found its way into a European Parliament resolution of 24 May 2007 on Estonia:

> Whereas systematic cyber attacks have been organised, mostly from outside Estonia, in an attempt to block official communication lines and Estonian administration websites; whereas those attacks have come from

Russian administration IP addresses, and whereas intensive propaganda attacks have continued via the Internet and mobile telephone messages calling for armed resistance and further violence.[18]

It is notable, that in the European Union's statement, only the fact of Russian administration IP addresses is mentioned, and those are not further politically attributed to the Russian government. For good reason: IP addresses are not strong evidence of responsibility of any actor. By June 2007, the Estonian Defence Minister Jaak Aaviksoo also chose not to attribute the attacks anymore but focused on what to do about them. In his remarks, he analogized cyberspace to the sea and looked to the Declaration against Privateering of 1856 for inspiration.[19] Finally, in September, Aaviksoo adjusted the government's claim of incontrovertible evidence in an interview with the Estonian TV Channel Kanal 2: 'Of course, at the moment, I cannot state for certain that the cyber attacks were managed by the Kremlin, or other Russian government agencies'.[20] Still today, the government of Estonia does not formally uphold its claims of state responsibility. Recalling the situation in 2007, Marina Kaljurand, the Estonian ambassador to Moscow in 2007, explains:

> There was no direct evidence linking the attacks to the Russian state, but there was enough circumstantial evidence to conclude that these attacks were carried out with the knowledge and support of the Russian state.[21]

The politics of attribution
The Estonian case illustrates how politics shaped attribution. During the heat of the crisis, the political decision was made to publicly attribute the cyberattacks to the Russian government. The case can be reinterpreted using the analogy to privateering and pirates to better understand how state association gets established. The case mirrors a historical debate (as introduced in Chapter 3) about whether and how the actions of individuals on the high seas can be attributed to a sovereign. The debate included both a discussion on whether the sovereign could legitimize the otherwise criminal actions undertaken by individuals at sea (i.e. by issuing privateering licences) as well as the nature of that sovereign. In the late 16th century, Gentili understood piracy as 'any taking of foreign life or property not authorized by a sovereign'.[22] This highlighted the necessary existence of a recognized, lawful sovereign, in absence of which, acts at sea could be labelled piratical. Contrary

to that Grotius argued, that pirates could be identified as 'individuals whose primary object was plunder regardless of place'.[23] Whereas Grotius's approach was based on the intent of the group, Gentili's realist approach rested on 'political decisions of the decision-makers in each society as to what labelling system would best suit their needs, and achieved the legal and political results they preferred as a result of their choice of labels'.[24] The difference in the Estonian case is that, historically, states would often have been incentivized to call their attackers pirates to be able to take drastic measures against them. However, when convenient, some also associated piratical actions to states. An example of this was raised in the historical Chapter 3: the Indian Mughal chose to associate piratical acts committed by English-speaking pirates to the English Crown and hold the East India Company responsible for them, despite the company's innocence with regard to sponsorship pirates. This enabled the Mughal Empire to force the company to provide protection for the Mughal's ships. The opposite case was also highlighted in the historical investigation. In the case of Captain Kidd, the English government chose to deny state sponsorship for the actions undertaken, also to mend relations with the Mughal Court. Thus, to better understand governments' agency in framing state proximity of the attackers, one can analogize to the history of pirates and privateers in the 17th century.

Of course, Estonia was in a very different position than the Mughal Empire. Nevertheless, it effectively used the public attribution to Russia to rally support for the government's position in the European institutions (EU, Council of Europe), in NATO, and bilaterally between countries.[25] President Ilves's invocation of the civilizational discourse is also similar to the historical imperial discourse, as it draws boundaries between the civilized world—and what would in the colonial context have been called the 'barbarians'. Once the crisis was over, the government became more cautious and retracted the accusations, still implying state sponsorship, but not openly accusing the Russian government.

It is likely that the retraction came about due to the lack of conclusive evidence. The Estonian government had publicly attributed the attacks, despite not having any conclusive evidence of Russian state sponsorship at that time. For example, Estonia's CERT privately informed U.S. officials before 18 May 2007 that 'there is still no smoking gun that links the attacks to Moscow'.[26] A post-crisis assessment by the U.S. embassy summarizes the Estonian internal position, relying on Mikhel Tammet, the Estonian Ministry of Defence's (MoD) director for communications and IT. He stated:

> Looking at the patterns of the attacks, it is clear that there was a small, core of individuals who intended to launch their attack on May 9 . . . but when the MOD announced its plans to move the Bronze Soldier on April 27, they moved up their plans to try to link the attacks with the monument's removal. . . . You don't expect spontaneous, populist cyber attacks to have a pre-determined list of targets and precise dates and times for coordinated attacks.[27]

The government of Estonia's assessment was based on the level of organization, coordination, and timing of the attacks as well as their sophistication. Furthermore, the government repeatedly asked the *cui bono* question (i.e. who profits?). Interestingly, whilst Estonian analysts pointed to the sophistication of the attackers (e.g. having shut down a key router) in a debriefing reported by the U.S. embassy, they pointed out how much worse the attack could have been. For example, Rain Ottis 'noted had the attacks specifically targeted Estonia's key servers and routers, they could have shut down Estonia's entire cyber infrastructure.[28] Hence, the dual claims of sophistication on the one hand, but not so sophisticated as to target the 'key servers and routers' on the other hand, raise the question whether not having shut down the entire infrastructure was due to a lack of target intelligence by the attackers, a more limited strategic aim, or due to a lack of sophistication on the attackers' side.

In 2007, Russia had one of the most competent hacker scenes worldwide. Operating within an environment of widespread corruption, as long as cybercriminals stayed out of attacking Russian interests, they could operate relatively safely.[29] The types of cybercrime ranged from intellectual property thefts, extortion, financial fraud, spam, to service-oriented models such as DDoS for hire or criminal infrastructure provision.[30] Some of these services were offered by the same groups. For example, spammers may own botnets that they rent out for use by third parties.[31]

Political DDoS and website defacement were nothing new in Russia in 2007.[32] Especially if targeting a website of politically undesired groups (e.g. Chechen rebels), attackers could rely on not being prosecuted. Examples go as far back as 1999, when the Chechen website Kavkaz.org was first attacked.[33] This type of hacking made the news in 2002. When Siberian hackers attacked the website anew, the local Federal Security Service (FSB) office was quoted as appreciating this type of action as a legitimate expression of its citizens.[34] Later, hackers started to target opposition websites, like the National Bolshevik Party, Garry Kasparov, and newspapers (e.g. the *Kommersant*) and radio stations (e.g. Echo Moskvy).[35] State support is usually inferred and cannot be proven. Exceptions exist, as evidenced in the Duma certificate issued to a hacker on behalf of the right-wing extremist party LDPR Deputy Kuryanovich in March 2006.[36] At the time, the hacking of targets within the broad political directive of the Russian government was not seen as to entail personal risk of prosecution. Rather, one could be acknowledged as a patriotic hacker.[37]

In 2007, the Estonian government chose to associate the behaviour of a small group of actors, which used a known political practice in Russia, with the Russian government. Later, the accusation of state complicity would be upheld only informally (i.e. in public discourse but not in diplomatic affairs), due to not honouring a mutual legal assistance treaty.[38] Politically, the Estonian government thereby chose to raise behaviour that it could have labelled as criminal, or political activism, to an interstate political level. Whilst the attacks were taxing on a highly internet-dependent country, the Estonian government used its representation of the sophistication of the attacks to rally political support among its Western partners and cast Russia as the 'uncivilized' aggressor. Thereby, it succeeded in raising some support in NATO and in the EU.

Russian narrative: a demonizing discourse

The Russian state did not stay silent during this crisis. Rather, already in January 2007, the Russian Federation Council voiced its discontent with Estonian domestic actions by classifying the Estonian government policies as a step towards legalizing neo-Nazism in Europe.[39]

Strong public sentiments towards the Estonian plans were present throughout the Russian population. Polled on the 3–4 March 2007, 87% people had heard about the Estonian government's plans of moving the statue, 78% reported to feel a sense of indignation towards them, and 90% of the polled population thought the Russian government should do something about it, although opinions varied on the extent of such measures.[40]

At the beginning of April, Russia's First Deputy Prime Minister Sergei Ivanov called for a civil boycott of Estonia's products.[41] On 18 April 2007, Foreign Minister Sergei Lavrov called the planned Estonian actions 'blasphemous—an outrage upon the memory of those who liberated Europe from the fascists'.[42] On 23 April 2007, Russia summoned the Estonian ambassador and issued a diplomatic note protesting the exhumation of the soldiers and the move of the statue—actions which, according to the Russian Foreign Ministry, would review the role of Russia in the victory over fascism in World War II.[43] The Russian Foreign Ministry held on to that narrative, highlighting the desecration of soldiers' graves as rewriting World War II history, and labelled the protesters in front of the Estonian embassy as citizens protesting the mockery of sacred sites and the cruelty of the Estonian police.[44] It also criticized the treatment of the Russian minority in Estonia, specifically the non-issuance of passports. The Russian government made an appeal to the European Union, Organization for Security and Co-operation in Europe (OSCE), and expressed support for its statements trough the Commonwealth of Independent States (CIS). Sergei Lavrov also wrote a letter to major European governments outlining the Russian position and detailing the expectations of the European partners to act.[45] In his Great Patriotic War memorial speech, Russian President Vladimir Putin mentioned Estonia indirectly:

> Those who attempt today to belittle this invaluable experience and defile the monuments to the heroes of this war are insulting their own people and spreading enmity and new distrust between countries and peoples.[46]

Dmitry Peskov, spokesman for the Russian government, denied Russian involvement in the cyberattacks and warned 'the Estonia side has to be extremely careful when making accusations'.[47]

What emerges from this narrative is a climate, within which patriotic hackers may have been at work. The Russian official bodies outlined an interest of the Russian state against the removal of the monument. By doing so, the government supported a narrative with a clearly identifiable opponent (the Estonian government), victims (the Russian people), and a call for political action (e.g. civil boycott). In such an environment, similar to the ones during previous political DDoS activities, it is likely that Russian pro-government hackers took it upon themselves to attack the Estonian infrastructure. Indeed, a leader of the Transnistrian regional section of Nashi, the pro-nationalist youth movement, did take credit for the attacks in 2007. This was corroborated later by the U.S. National Security Agency and a Russian Duma member.[48] This could still be consistent with the Estonian MoD's (private) assessment that DDoS attacks were planned for the 9 May 2007 anyway.

The connection to the Russian government, however, is tenuous at best. No evidence directly linking the government to the attacks was ever published. Rather, the hacking activity and the demonstrations in Moscow were kept at arm's length from the state. In that respect, it is interesting that it was the youth section of Nashi in Transnistria: given its special international status, it adds another layer of deniability, which could at the same time indicate deliberation and planning.

Re-assessing Estonia 2007: pirates, privateers, or something else entirely?

This case illustrates how a government engaged in a narrative of state sponsorship and used it strategically to lobby for political support from its allies. Estonia claimed Russian-government involvement during the crisis and signalled willingness to present evidence for the claim. Private diplomatic conversations with U.S. officials, however, reveal that the technical evidence was insufficient. Hence, political attribution was used as a rhetoric strategy to shift the blame on the Russian government. The Estonian government struggled to defend their attribution claim.[49] This was further complicated because the construction of a cyberattack as an active attack against a country was still a novel discursive space to occupy.[50] NATO and the EU did come to the aid of the Estonian republic, but their messaging to Russia highlighted upholding the Vienna Conventions, thereby referring to the Moscow embassy incidents, rather than acting based on Estonia's attribution claim.

To draw direct parallels to history: the blurred lines between piracy and privateering had been classified by some historians as a substitute for open warfare. The official denials of support were a predictable feature of that form of conflict. What is surprising, and what deserves further study, are the dynamics that lead states to challenge these denials. In the case of Estonia, a mix of a sense of national emergency due to the realization of vulnerability and the spotting of a policy opportunity seems to have given rise to the challenge. Just as the Mughal Empire chose to blame the English Crown for the actions of English-speaking pirates attacking the Mughal's ships, the Estonian government chose to blame the Russian government for the cyberattacks against the Estonian institutions.

This highlights a new element to the literature on attribution.[51] Scholars have pointed out the element of uncertainty and the political judgement that an attribution claim is made under.[52] For example, Rid and Buchanan label attribution as 'being what states make of it' and point out the uncertainties that arise in making strategic attributions under time 'pressure'.[53] However, their focus lies on there being a 'correct' attribution, and time pressure leading to the possibility of getting it wrong.[54] Whilst their scholarly contribution is very valuable, it does not shed any light into the political contestation of the specific public attribution claims. Clement Guitton paid more attention to this public contestation by casting attribution as a 'game to convince an audience', which depends on trust and authority of the entity making the claims.[55] Herb Lin built on this analysis by including the specific standards of evidence required to convince different audiences, modelled on different domestic and international legal standards.[56] Thus, I extend Guitton's and Lin's analyses by identifying these public claims as inherently political choices about how to frame the relations between the attacker and the entity that the state chooses to blame. Timo Steffens touched on this when discussing public attribution as an element of political strategy, demanding that each public attribution judgement be tailored to achieve a specific goal, be audience specific, and be communicated with a certain quality.[57] According to him, protection, justice, diplomacy and politics, and—for companies—reputation are such high-level goals that can motivate an entity to attribute publicly.

In contrast to much of the previous scholarship, the focus in this case study on how state-sponsorship attribution is attained has brought to the fore the significant agency that a government has when making those attribution claims in public. Hence, applying the historical analogy of piracy and privateering to the situation in Estonia fostered a conceptual advancement in the analysis of attribution into three elements: not only is it a political judgement to attribute the cyberattacks to the Russian government (i.e. privately answering the question, 'who is responsible?'), something I called elsewhere the sense-making process of attribution.[58] But also it is a political judgement whether to disclose any attribution judgements publicly (i.e. answering the question, 'should we publicly blame someone?'), a process I refer to as the meaning-making part of attribution.[59] And above all, and that was shown in this case study, it is a political judgement about how exactly to frame such a judgement in public. The meaning-making efforts of the defending entity are especially powerful, given the absence of authoritative third-party analyses.[60] The analysis of the Estonian case study suggests that the resource-based state-sponsorship attribution narrative was used, at least in part, as a policy opportunity to rally international support.

The analysis of the different narratives presented by different stakeholders in the Estonia case illustrates a similarity to historical piracy. The government being attacked gets to frame its response. It may choose to frame the attack as a criminal act and use its criminal justice system to respond. Or it may choose, as in the case of Estonia, to react politically, and, by associating the hacking with a political actor, such as a government, raise the hacking to an interstate incident. These differing narratives open different paths for political resolution or escalation of a cyber incident. Thereby, the specific framing may sometimes not be aimed at the attacker, but rather influenced by other goals, such as building a coalition against an attacker, convincing a domestic public, or trying to shape operational space by offering an interpretation the desired rules of the 'game' (i.e. by publicizing those activities that contravene such rules).[61]

It is specifically relevant for international relations that the government is making this political choice. As experience with cyber operations (and campaigns) grows, the palette of policy responses becomes more nuanced. In a long and drawn out process the community of states build a repertoire of practices that may ensue after a suffered cyber incident. As the very early case of Estonia shows, the decisions taken by governments are made under uncertainty about both the identity and the exact motivation of the opponent. This makes the response particularly difficult.[62]

One of the interesting implications of the perceived convergence of interests between Russian cybercrime and the Russian state is how this assessment complicates statecraft for other actors. One of the fundamental judgements state defenders must undertake is how closely the attacker is associated with a state. The analytic judgement has implications not only for the (legal) assessment of state responsibility but also informs whether the particular attack can be read as a signalling component of a particular state's leadership.[63] Hence, the blurring of the official state-led operations and criminal undertakings introduces strategic ambiguity, which offers advantages and disadvantages.

The effect in the Estonia case was carefully assessed. The ambiguity of sponsorship enabled Russia to publicly talk about the Estonian situation, without having to take responsibility for the actions happening on the internet. At the same time, the ambiguity also enabled the Estonian government to blame the Russian government for the cyberattacks, without providing any evidence. In the Estonian case, the political interests of Russia were signalled long in advance. Hence, even if the government of Russia was not directly responsible for the disruptive activities undertaken on the internet against Estonia, Estonia could assume that the Russian government was not going to do anything to stop them.

However, in other cases, where the overlap of interests is less clear, the picture grows much murkier. Consider this example from the former head of U.S. counterintelligence, Joel Brenner, in *International Security*:

> When Russian intruders penetrated JPMorgan Chase Bank's computer system in 2014 during tensions over Ukraine, no one could tell President Barack Obama whether Russian President Vladimir Putin was sending repercussions, and Chase's vulnerability was there for all to see. When evaluating his options, could the president ignore the possibility that exercising one of them carried the palpable risk that a major U.S. bank could be taken down? . . . The incident demonstrates the way in which a critical vulnerability in the civilian economy could constrain the exercise of national power, including military power, in a crisis.[64]

Today we know that two Israeli and one U.S. citizen conducted the intrusions into JPMorgan Chase and other U.S. financial institutions. It looks like there was no Russian state involvement—in December 2016 the American agreed to voluntarily terminate his stay in Russia and face charges in the United States.[65]

This situation raises two challenges. To start with, uncertainty about the actors' links to the state can be a source of power. If the U.S. leadership really did not know the true source and link to the Russian state, this could have had a positive impact on the success of Russian actions in the Ukraine, as a concurrent undermining of the U.S. financial institutions could have raised the stakes of policy action against Russian interests. In addition, the uncertainty about the links can create long-term advantages for the Russian state, as it can try to use the existence of 'patriotic hackers' as a front for state-led operations to gain plausible deniability.

However, the flipside of this reveals a challenge in the cyber offensive space. Using cyberattacks for signalling purposes is still an underdeveloped practice and the risk of miscalculation and misinterpretation is high.[66] As a direct consequence of the assumed convergence of interests between the Russian state and Russian cybercriminals, the risk that a criminal action may send a signal, when none was intended, increases the escalatory potential.

To sum up: the Estonia case can be reinterpreted with the aid of the analogy to privateering and pirates. To start with, the case can be better understood with the background of how state association was established for historical actors on the high seas. Whilst Grotius insisted on a matter of substance, Gentili advocated for a solution of political convenience. The case of Estonia showed elements of both. The Estonian government used the narrative of state-sponsored attackers to its political convenience, but it did so by arguing that it possessed the evidence to back up its claims. Furthermore, by choosing to construct the attackers as resources of the state in its narrative, Estonia made a political choice to raise the cyberattacks to the interstate level. This focus on political agency of the defender adds a new element into our understanding of public attribution. Finally, similar to state collaborations with pirates, the perceived blurring of state and criminal interests highlighted opportunities and difficulties such strategic ambiguity introduces both for the perceived attacker and the defender.

Evidence of the State-Criminal Nexus: The Cases of Seleznev, Bogachev, and Dokuchaev et al.

Whilst the book does not aim to establish if the Russian state actively supported, instigated, directed, or steered the attacks against Estonia, the evidence documenting the relationships between Russian cybercriminals (unconnected to the Estonia case) and organs of the state has changed significantly since 2007. Fifteen years later, the uncertainty about cooperation between cybercriminals and the Russian state has been somewhat dispelled. Official Russian policy still grants hackers great leeway in being active outside of Russia and in the direction of its general interests. Here is a quote by Vladimir Putin, made in June 2017, when the Russian president was questioned by the media about Russia's role in interfering in the 2016 U.S. election:

> Hackers are free spirited people, like artists. If they are in a good mood in the morning, they wake up and paint. It is the same for hackers. They wake up today, they read that something is happening in inter-state relations, and if they are patriotically minded—they start making their contributions which are right, from their point of view—to the fight against those who say bad things about Russia. Is that possible? Theoretically, it is possible.[67]

His romanticising of patriotically minded hackers reinforces the top-level political cover for hackers becoming active in Russian interests and reveals the strategic use of patriotic hackers as a front to establish plausible deniability.[68] Research has uncovered several sub-pockets of the cybercriminal underworld that could not continue to exist were there not, at least tacit, support from state officials.[69] Many analysts have pointed to the political enablement of Russian and Eastern European cybercrime. Supporting evidence for this is the way cybercriminals have become active in Russian political interests and engage in selective targeting, deliberately avoiding touching on Russian law enforcement interests.[70] Tacit support by a government is also inferred by the absence of honouring a mutual legal assistance treaty or by the leaking of information to cybercriminals. Strong evidence, however, is hard to establish in this area of investigation. In addition, there is some evidence of high-profile arrests of Russian cybercriminals by the Russian police. Examples are the 2015 arrests of hackers associated with the Dyre Trojan or the 2016 arrests of the criminal group named 'Lurk'.[71]

In this second part, the risks and opportunities associated with the closeness between cybercrime and politics will be explored further. The analysis will build on the insights, including the risks and opportunities, of the historical chapter that highlighted the longevity and path dependencies that a reliance on privateers and pirates brought.

Three cybercriminal cases shed more light onto the pirate/privateer aspect of this state-criminal nexus. First, the case of Roman Seleznev highlights the political rift between Russia and the United States when it comes to the prosecution of their nationals. This establishes, on the one hand, that we are clearly not in an age in which cybercriminals are accepted as *hostes humani generis* (i.e. enemies of mankind). On the other hand, it shows a case, where Russia voices a public intent to prosecute cybercriminals but prefers to do so in its own courts. Second, the case of Evgeniy Bogachev substantiates another type of state proximity a cybercriminal could have with a state, namely guaranteeing a safe operating base in return for information leveraged through the cybercriminal enterprise. The cases of Seleznev and Bogachev highlight the institutionalized toleration of cyber piratical enterprises. Whilst the cases of Seleznev and Bogachev most closely resemble cases of piracy, the third case (Dokuchaev et al.) documents a joint operation between government officials and Russian hackers that closely resembles privateering-like structures. The analysis shows that the risk of not exerting control over the historical privateer also manifested itself in this contemporary case.[72]

Roman Seleznev—a politically supported cyber pirate

Discussing Roman Seleznev,[73] a career cybercriminal and son of a member of the Russian Duma, the U.S. government alleged that

> federal agents eventually developed evidence that Roman Seleznev, the son of a Russian politician, was the true identity behind nCuX. On May 19, 2009, agents with the Secret Service and the FBI met with representatives of the Russian Federal Security Service (FSB) in Moscow, and presented substantial evidence of defendant's computer hacking activities including his credit card hacking and other computer crimes. U.S. law enforcement provided the FSB with defendant's online alias names and information that they believed nCuX's true name was Roman Seleznev of Vladivostok, Russia. The agents' attempt at international coordination backfired. Just one month later, on June 21, 2009, nCuX notified his co-conspirators on multiple criminal forums that he was going out of business. Shortly after that, nCuX completely disappeared from the internet.
>
> As U.S. Probation noted, the information that U.S. law enforcement was investigating Seleznev 'clearly got back to Mr. Seleznev'. Indeed, Seleznev had his own contacts inside the FSB. In chat messages between Seleznev and an associate from 2008, Seleznev stated that he had obtained protection through the law enforcement contacts in the computer crime squad of the FSB. Later, in 2010, Seleznev told another associate that the FSB knew his identity and was working with the FBI.[74]

This U.S. official narrative of a backchannel relationship with the FSB, reinforced by the connections of his father, leads to a picture of state complicity. Reinforcing this impression, but with a different narrative, is the way the Russian state took an interest in the case. Foreign Minister Sergei Lavrov raised the U.S. practice to arrest Russian criminals worldwide in an interview in 2016:

> The Americans, for example, literally 'steal' our people in violation of the laws of the countries on whose soil these abductions take place. This was the case of Viktor Bout, Konstantin Yaroshenko, Roman Seleznev and dozens of other people 'snatched' from Europe and other countries.
>
> But I am sure that this work will bring results, and indeed, we are already starting to see the fruits. If some cyber criminal is arrested, we would be the

last to try to protect him. After all, these people steal money in Russia and abroad. But he [Roman Seleznev] should be put on trial here.[75]

Furthermore, the Russian Foreign Ministry labelled his arrest a 'kidnapping' and criticized the sentence of 27 years in prison.[76] Hence, the Russian government claimed that whilst cybercriminals are to be prosecuted, if they are Russian, they should be prosecuted by Russia.

Remarkably, in this case we have an account of Roman Seleznev himself. He summarized his life story in a handwritten letter, testifying on his behalf (see Figure 6.2).

In the letter, he claimed, in broken English, that in 2009, when his wife and daughter were away on holiday that

> robbers suddenly show up in my home, our apartment. I was home. The robbers torture to me all night. They take all password from computer, laptop, money and everything of any value. . . . The robbers knew I was doing wrong so they believe to never get caught. . . . I was in fear and I take my family move to another country for our security.[77]

He claimed that this was the time he announced to his cybercriminal associates that he would exit the business.

The letter is part of his criminal defence materials. Hence, one can expect him to present only facts that shed a positive light on his motivation and character. Equally, one would not expect him to bring up cooperation with the FSB (at least in publicly available court transcripts) for fear of potential negative consequences. Rather, he mentioned that a robbery significantly altered the course of his life. Naturally, no corroborating evidence is expected to exist when a cybercriminal is robbed alone in his apartment. However, what this establishes is a timeline that matches the assistant U.S. attorney's claims. This means something triggered Seleznev to leave his apartment, and, together with his wife and his 1-year-old child, move to Indonesia (a country without an extradition treaty to the U.S.) and announce to his collaborators that he was leaving the world of cybercrime.[78] Whether the FBI is right in asserting collusion between the FSB and Seleznev, or whether, as Seleznev's account seems to imply, he underwent a violent form of persuasion is unclear. We will probably never know for certain what happened.

However, the Seleznev case establishes the politicization of cybercrime between Russia and the United States. Roman Seleznev, with a father in the

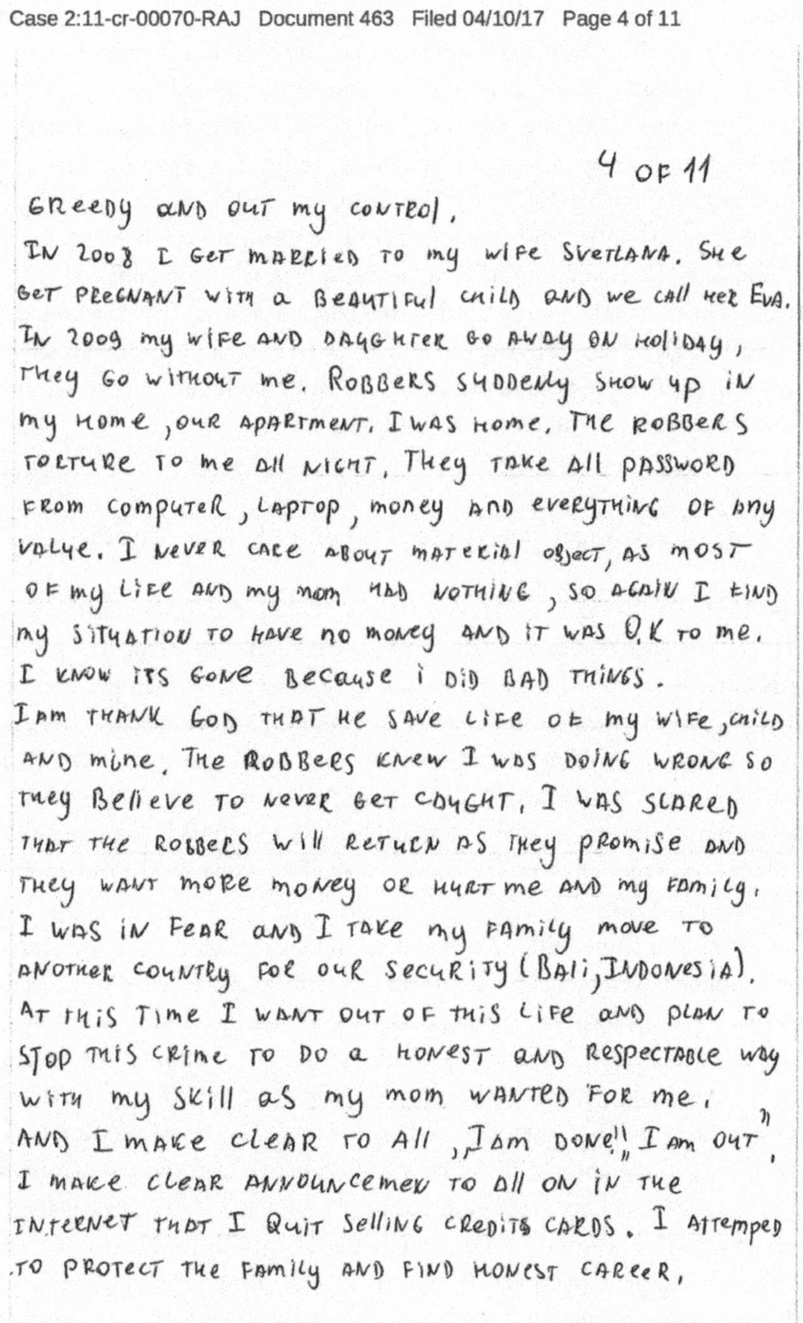

Case 2:11-cr-00070-RAJ Document 463 Filed 04/10/17 Page 4 of 11

4 OF 11

GREEDY AND OUT MY CONTROL.
IN 2008 I GET MARRIED TO MY WIFE SVETLANA. SHE GET PREGNANT WITH A BEAUTIFUL CHILD AND WE CALL HER EVA.
IN 2009 MY WIFE AND DAUGHTER GO AWAY ON HOLIDAY, THEY GO WITHOUT ME. ROBBERS SUDDENLY SHOW UP IN MY HOME, OUR APARTMENT. I WAS HOME. THE ROBBERS TORTURE TO ME ALL NIGHT, THEY TAKE ALL PASSWORD FROM COMPUTER, LAPTOP, MONEY AND EVERYTHING OF ANY VALUE. I NEVER CARE ABOUT MATERIAL OBJECT, AS MOST OF MY LIFE AND MY MOM HAD NOTHING, SO AGAIN I FIND MY SITUATION TO HAVE NO MONEY AND IT WAS O.K TO ME.
I KNOW ITS GONE BECAUSE I DID BAD THINGS.
I AM THANK GOD THAT HE SAVE LIFE OF MY WIFE, CHILD AND MINE. THE ROBBERS KNEW I WAS DOING WRONG SO THEY BELIEVE TO NEVER GET CAUGHT. I WAS SCARED THAT THE ROBBERS WILL RETURN AS THEY PROMISE AND THEY WANT MORE MONEY OR HURT ME AND MY FAMILY.
I WAS IN FEAR AND I TAKE MY FAMILY MOVE TO ANOTHER COUNTRY FOR OUR SECURITY (BALI, INDONESIA).
AT THIS TIME I WANT OUT OF THIS LIFE AND PLAN TO STOP THIS CRIME TO DO A HONEST AND RESPECTABLE WAY WITH MY SKILL AS MY MOM WANTED FOR ME.
AND I MAKE CLEAR TO ALL „I AM DONE!" I AM OUT",
I MAKE CLEAR ANNOUNCEMEN TO ALL ON IN THE INTERNET THAT I QUIT SELLING CREDITS CARDS. I ATTEMPED TO PROTECT THE FAMILY AND FIND HONEST CAREER,

Figure 6.2 Extract of Roman Seleznev's handwritten testimony

Source: United States of America V. Roman V. Seleznev, CR11-0070RAJLetter. Document Nr. 463, p. 4 (2017).

Russian parliament, has the political support of the Russian government. Even though the Russian government may have wanted to stop his criminal activities as well, it was not prepared to let the United States prosecute him. This substantiates the fact that the United States and Russia, at least in the Seleznev case, do not accept each other's judicial processes to prosecute their own nationals involved in cybercrime. As was laid out more fully in the historical chapter, privateering was only abolished once there was international agreement among states to prosecute pirates of any nationality and treat them as enemies of mankind (*hostes humani generis*). This happened in the early 18th century. Hence, this case gives an indication that, with regard to the analogy to pirates and privateers, the situation found in cybercrime is better analogized to situations pre-18th century.

Evgeniy Bogachev—a cyber pirate and cyber privateer

The United States did not let the claims of state-criminal collaborations rest on just that one case. Rather, it brought several cases against prolific Russian cybercriminals. The analysis of Elizabethan privateering has shown that a political-criminal nexus spurs self-reinforcing tendencies. The case against Evgeniy Mikhailovich Bogachev, one of the creators of the ZeuS trojan, perhaps the most notorious online banking trojan, shows the longevity and depth the special relationship with the Russian state entails.[79] This case is of particular importance, as Bogachev is one of the most-wanted cybercriminals worldwide.

Despite the United States' detailed criminal case against the individual, he continues to enjoy his freedom. His last known address was in the Black Sea resort Anapa, Russia. Having exhausted all legal measures to prosecute Bogachev, the U.S. instituted a $3 million bounty for information leading to Bogachev's arrest.[80] The absence of an official criminal case in Russia against Bogachev is substantial evidence of the existence of political cover for him. The evidence detailing cooperation between Russian state organs and Bogachev is further substantiated by private researchers' investigations. For example, in a joint presentation at Blackhat 2015 by Michael Sandee (Fox-IT), Tillmann Werner (Crowdstrike), and Elliott Peterson (U.S. FBI), the researchers detailed the workings of a variant of ZeuS called Gameover Zeus.[81] Both the presentation and the associated whitepaper detailed 'a much lesser known side' of ZeuS, namely 'its use for espionage'.[82] The researchers discovered subparts of the botnet searching computers for files with specific words (e.g. top secret) and email addresses (e.g. of intelligence agencies) in the respective languages in Georgia, Turkey, and the Ukraine.[83]

The precise nature of the relationship between Bogachev and the Russian state is not publicly documented. However, the appearance of political cover confirms the long-standing impression of analysts that as long as cybercriminals in Russia seek their targets outside of the Russian state's interests, and as long as they provide some form of collaboration, when asked or coerced to do so, they remain beyond the U.S. criminal justice system's reach.[84] Whilst Seleznev's case could be regarded as a special case, due to his parliamentary connection, Bogachev's case indicates a deeper connection between cybercrime and the government. The governmental willingness not to prosecute the worldwide most-wanted cybercriminal sends a signal to the rest of the Russian cybercriminal community; namely, the Russian government is willing to tolerate certain cybercriminal activities. The specifics of that collaboration, however, remain shrouded in secrecy.[85]

What one can surmise, though, is that Bogachev was able to run his criminal enterprise for years with his base in Russia even though the Russian authorities knew about it. In terms of state proximity, this indicates, at the very least, a similar structure as a pirate port that is willing to tolerate the lucrative activities undertaken by the hackers. Depending on the exact arrangements, the structure could also resemble privateering (i.e. the state profiting directly from the enterprise in the form of information or money). Both have precedent in the history of piracy and privateering. As the historical chapter showed, once such a structure is in place, it can instigate self-reinforcing tendencies. Officials that profit from the set-up politically lobby for it to persist. As other criminals learn of the opportunity to seek political cover, the network of criminal-government interactions grows. A self-stabilizing feedback loop thus reinforces the tendencies that keep the privateering set-up. Because a change in policy against cybercriminals is associated with much friction, the likelihood of a government undertaking one decreases.

Dokuchaev et al.—a modern-day privateering set-up

Both Seleznev's and Bogachev's cases of collaboration with the state ultimately rested on, even if available in significant quantities, circumstantial public evidence. This changed in 2017, when the U.S. chose to indict the

FSB officers, Dmitry Aleksandrovich Dokuchaev and Igor Anatolyevich Sushchin, and career cybercriminals, Alexsey Alexseyevich Belan and Karim Baratov, for hacking Yahoo Inc. and other webmail providers between 2014 and 2016.[86] They charged the four men with a flurry of offences, including conspiracy to commit economic espionage, theft of trade secrets, and a range of U.S. Computer Fraud and Abuse Act offences. The interesting aspect of this indictment is the level of detail it reveals about the collaboration between criminal hackers and FSB officers, working for the FSB Center for Information Security. The U.S. Justice Department expressed its discontent, as the FSB Center for Information Security also serves as the FBI's 'main point of contact in Moscow on cybercrime matters'.[87]

The indictment lays out in detail how the four men conspired to hack Yahoo and profit from it. The theft of Yahoo's source code of its authentication system and user database enabled the attackers to impersonate any of 500 million Yahoo accounts. The targets included U.S. users affiliated with

> webmail providers and cloud computing companies, whose account contents could facilitate unauthorized access to other victim accounts; Russian journalists and politicians critical of the Russian government; Russian citizens and government officials; former officials from countries bordering Russia; and U.S. government officials, including cyber security, diplomatic, military, and White House personnel.[88]

Further targets included personnel of financial and transportation companies. Specific examples of cooperation were given. On the FSB's side this included the target selection by the FSB officers, the tasking and payment of Baratov by Dokuchaev, and the provision of 'intelligence information that would have helped him [Belan] avoid detection by law enforcement, including information regarding FSB investigations of computer hacking and FSB techniques for identifying criminal hackers'.[89]

The FBI had issued an Interpol red notice (arrest alert) for Belan in 2012. He had escaped a European arrest in 2013 and subsequently travelled to Russia. The 2017 indictment frames this as 'rather than arrest him, however, the FSB officers used him'.[90] Belan certainly proved to be a capable asset; he established covert access to the Yahoo network.[91] However, Belan did not use that access only for the purposes of exfiltrating information for the FSB, but he also used it for personal gain. This included collecting credit card information, gift card information, contact information for spam campaigns, and the alteration of some Yahoo servers to promote a specific online pharmacy website. The scheme involved routing traffic from English-language users searching for erectile dysfunction medications through one of Belan's servers, which in turn sent them to an online pharmacy site that paid kickbacks to the traffic originator.[92]

No information about the financial arrangements between the FSB and Belan are known. When returning to Russia in 2013, he would have been in a very weak position (being wanted by the FBI). From the level of detail provided otherwise in the indictment, it is at least conceivable that the deal involved Belan avoiding arrest for his hacking (criminal and otherwise) and in return providing his services to the two FSB officers. Of course, there is no indication of how voluntary such an agreement might have been on Belan's part.

As part of the same scheme, the two FSB officers had further directed Karim Baratov to hack non-Yahoo webmail accounts (e.g. 50 Gmail accounts).[93] Compared with the operation with Belan, these webmail hacking assignments were more transactional in nature. The FSB officers would task Baratov with a specific email address, which he would then acquire the credentials for (usually through spear-phishing). In return, the FSB paid him around $100 per account.[94]

Unfortunately for the conspiracy, Baratov kept a large online footprint. He marketed his services online on various websites, kept an active social media profile, and used his substantial income on luxury cars.[95] Living in Canada, and as the only member of the conspiracy outside of Russia, the 22-year-old was arrested by the Canadian police in March 2017.

In public hearings, former FBI Director James Comey pointed to this indictment as an example of Russian state-criminal collaboration:

> They have a relationship that's often difficult to define with criminals and that the Yahoo hack's actually an example of that. You had some of the Russia's greatest criminal hackers and intelligence agency hackers working together.[96]

However, many questions about that collaboration are still unresolved. For example, why the FSB officers were briefing Belan on the FSB techniques for identifying hackers, or why the FSB officers also instructed Baratov to hack accounts of Russian webmail providers, despite the FSB being able to access those based on Russian legislation, or why Dokuchaev used a Yahoo account to communicate with Baratov, despite the U.S. government's access to U.S.-based communications service providers.[97] The data that would answer these questions lies outside the spectrum of the feasible for the current research. At this stage, there is at least doubt about whether the two FSB officers were operating the entire mission on the official books of the FSB.

This case, however, substantiates the privateering-like structure that shapes Russian cybercrime and parts of the Russian government tasked with investigating cybercrime. Dokuchaev et al. suggests that collaborating with hackers that also engage in criminal activity entails similar risks as were identified in the collaborations with privateers in the Elizabethan age. For example, the Russian model of enlisting criminal hackers carries considerable risks for the Russian leadership. Some of those risks are very similar to the ones that existed for states employing privateers. When commenting on the Elizabethan privateers, historian Paul Kennedy pointed out that the privateers were 'prone to alter carefully formulated plans in favour of rash enterprises and all too easily tempted by the prospect of plunder and glory into forgetting the national strategy'.[98] As an example, he mentioned Sir Francis Drake's attack on the *Rosario*, abandoning the chase of the Armada.[99] The similarities with the Dokuchaev et al. case are significant: by using the access to Yahoo's network to enrich himself, Belan was risking the exposure of an operation with potentially significant intelligence value for the Russian Federation.

Ruslan Stoyanov, a well-respected cybersecurity expert working for Kaspersky and former investigator for the Moscow cybercrime unit, was arrested for high treason in Russia in December 2016, and he described these risks further. In letters given to the press, he warned that Russian cybercriminals, fostered by the state, could eventually turn against Russian interests. Because any investigation would implicate Russian officials politically, this would lead to nightmare scenarios.[100]

To the extent that his account is deemed credible, this further highlights the institutionalization of the collaboration between criminals and state officials.[101] This was similar to the arrangement in British colonies, where the economic base would be significantly dependent on the piratical trade. When Britain decided to counter this in the early 18th century, it took major efforts by London to crack down on governors and implement law enforcement and justice reforms to eradicate piracy. As described in the historical part, this included the replacement of personnel and a central administration of court cases against pirates, as some of the colonial courts were compromised.

Similarly, Stoyanov pointed out that if the experts working on cybercrime investigations are also collaborating with cybercriminal groups, it is going to be very difficult for the Russian state to reverse this policy.

The analogy to privateering suggests that competition for skilled personnel is persistent and that it influences the way a formal state capacity can be developed. Several accounts substantiate that Russia hires skilled hackers from the criminal scene, sometimes under threat of a court case.[102] Indeed, Dmitry Dokuchaev, one of the indicted FSB officers, was also a criminal hacker in the past and, according to some reports, started working for the FSB after having been caught in the mid-2000s.[103] One risk of this is that they not only supply their services to the state but also continue to rely on their criminal income on the side, like in the case of Belan. Further risk is taken on, in that criminal operators, especially those having been able to operate in relative freedom from law enforcement, do not necessarily bring the same strict awareness of operational security with them. An early example of such low operational security was seen in Canada's ability to attribute cyber intrusions to Russia's intelligence services, due to personal use of operational infrastructure, and the infection of the malware development team with crimeware.[104]

For the state, relying on cybercriminals is not only a risk. It also brings benefits. First, the criminal ecosystem finances technical innovation itself, which offers a financial advantage to countries that can draw on such criminally financed technical innovation. In countries without such collaborations, the offensive capability market has to be paid for solely by the state. Second, a deep pool in technical know-how and operational experience is one of the great advantages of having a mature cybercrime market. The risk of the criminal market turning against the state is—at least partially—mitigated if the criminals are responsive to Russia's political ambitions.

The interpretation offered, of a (at least partially) loyal and politically steered cybercriminal underground, also fits within the larger pluralistic authoritarian Russian political context, in which officials not only profit financially from their official position, but can call upon private resources to aid the survival and furtherance of the state.[105] Since the state gets to regulate what is a legitimate business practice, special types of offensive cyber(in-)security contracting services may also be legitimized. For example, one report details a Russian cybersecurity firm supplying offensive cyber capabilities and access to Russian intelligence, drawing on its access and knowledge gained from its international client base in selling defensive cybersecurity services.[106]

This collaboration offers some appreciation for the various ways states have tried to work with skilled personnel (be it militias, volunteers, public-private partnerships, contractors, or army personnel). The risk of policy-makers profiting financially from cybersecurity policies is always linked to this. Further research could highlight why some governments seem to en-able economic and commercial espionage. Also, the job prospects of pol-icymakers and key cybersecurity personnel once they leave governmental employment should be more carefully evaluated. Parties that invested in his-torical privateering offer one possible understanding as to how governments are persuaded to sanction policies from which both officials and private cor-porations can profit. For example, one argument put forward by critics of historical privateering was that commerce raiding diluted the state's efforts to build an effective state-owned naval warfare capability. At least with re-gards to the situation in Russia, the politics-cybercrime nexus seems to have fostered a skilled cadre of professionals that supply their services both to the state and to further their own financial interests, generating similar inter-national political conflicts and institutionalized incentive structures as in the late 16th and early 17th centuries. That is not to say that the Russian gov-ernment does not possess advanced state dedicated capabilities—it does.[107] However, it has, in part, relied on criminal know-how to supply state-owned capabilities and has relied on the relationships detailed here.

This conceptual explanation extends the current literature on the political constitution of cyber(in-)security. Current studies of the political constitu-tion of cyber(in-)security often frame the different actors as threat sources (intelligence agencies, criminals, terrorists, etc.), without analysing their reconstitution across time and space. One exception is the theorization of politically constituted cyber(in-)security with the aid of the security di-lemma.[108] However, the argument made thus far solely rests on analysing the security between states, with other actors only complicating the state-driven analysis.[109] Going beyond this, Lucas Kello included non-state actors into his theorization of the impact of what he calls the 'cyber revolution' on the international system.[110] His theorization acknowledged the importance of including unconventional actors into the analysis, including true non-state actors (or non-state actors of the purest form), which want to change the fun-damental framework of the international system. However, the semi-state actors discussed in this book are not treated separately. Rather, Kello's con-ceptualization splits the actors into two categories, private and state actors, with only a brief discussion of four degrees of closeness to the state that they might have.[111] The limitation of Kello's two-part categorization is shown, for example, in the categorization of Saudi Aramco as a private actor, whilst categorizing Huawei as part of a state.[112] This shows that, even for a theorist who puts much emphasis on non-state action in cyberspace, the bifurcation of actors into state and non-state can hinder a more nuanced analysis of their relationships. This book thus refines the analysis by going beyond the bifurcation and provides a coherent answer to the presence and type of relations to the state of non- and semi-state actors.

To achieve this, the case study has extended the realm of analysis beyond states by analysing the stability of cyber(in-)security through the political-criminal nexus in Russia. Using the analogy to privateering, I have probed the presence of both the drivers and feedback loops that are characteristic of the path-dependent strategic choice associated with privateering and thereby offered a conceptual explanation of the stability of politically consti-tuted cyber(in-)security in the cases observed.

Conclusions and Implications

The analogy to pirates and privateers has enabled the focus on the spectrum of state proximity, as well as the specific analytic approaches, through which the state–non-state actor relationships were analysed. The case of Estonia in 2007 showed how an attacked government had significant influence on shaping the public narrative of the state proximity of the attackers. Just as his-torically the Mughal Empire, attacked by pirates, used a state-sponsorship at-tribution to shift the blame politically onto the English Crown, the Estonian government faced choices about how to frame the responsibility and nature of the cyberattacks in the public narrative.

Rather than just being an analytic puzzle or political judgement about who is attacking, the framing of the response entails political choices about the narrative being presented by the government. Much like in the cases of piracy and privateering, the government gets to choose when and how to associate an action to a government in public or when to strategically ignore such links. Analysing the Estonian and Russian narratives illustrated the usefulness of empirically applying the analogy to privateering and pirates. The application highlighted the multiplicity of Estonian and Russian narra-tives and showed the resulting strategic ambiguity that uncertainty about the attacker's proximity to the state introduces. This uncertainty is important for international relations, as the perception of collaboration raises the stakes of non-involvement and escalatory potential.

The application of the analogy in the case of Estonia also changed our understanding of cyber(in-)security. First, reading the contestation of public and private attribution as taking place in a similarly contested space as the one from which the definition of pirate and privateer emerged refocuses our attention onto the political contestations about what is deemed acceptable, and consequently unacceptable, in the use and toleration of cyber means. It foregrounds the international competition in constituting an act of hacking in a frame, thereby stabilizing a particular interpretation of legitimacy and statecraft. In so doing, the privateering/piracy analogy improves our understanding of the international politics of public attribution. Second, reading the case as a case of piracy/privateering highlights the governmental choices in framing the actor. It starts with an act of hacking and observes governments define the figure that attacks ('state-sponsored hackers' vs. 'patriotic hackers'). This lens is important in understanding the politically constructed nature of 'state-sponsorship' in particular situations. The application of the analogy to pirates and privateers enabled a conceptual advancement in the analysis of 'state-sponsored' hackers. Thus, the application of the analogy led to the development of a new conceptual element in attribution, namely by adding nuance to the analysis of the political choice about what public attribution claim is made.

The analysis of the three criminal cases showed three differing types of relationships to the state. Seleznev as a hacker with political cover through his personal relationships, Bogachev as a hacker that likely paid his dues to the state in the form of information, and Dokuchaev et al. as a direct (official or non-official) collaboration of government employees and hackers. The analysis of Elizabethan privateering shed light onto the problems and opportunities for statecraft such collaborations entail. Whilst the Estonia case highlighted (a) the political choice of public attribution and (b) the introduction of strategic ambiguity and its effects, the examination of the criminal cases unveiled (c) the depth such collaborations entail (longevity, institutionalization, path dependency, and lack of control), and (d) their effects on recruitment and capability building.

The application of the analogy to analyse the relationship between the state and hackers in the three criminal cases has changed the understanding of cyber(in-)security in two ways. First, applying a framework of institutionalized privateering to the modern cases identifies some of the possible drivers reconstituting the cyber privateering relationships. Specifically, personal investments, political structures, and financial and informational profits must be accounted for. The personal investments into offensive techniques of insecurity, the toleration of crime by the state, and the financial and informational advantages gained are all drivers to keep the privateering relationship in place.

Second, the introduction of a long-term perspective is a unique advantage òf applying this historical analogy. Given that there is a relatively short history in cyber(in-)security to draw on, historical observations are often not made. Looking at cyber(in-)security through the analogy to a process that developed over centuries opens the perspective to recognize elements of path dependencies. It allows for the observation of the longitudinal effects of political interaction that would not otherwise be visible. It could be suggested that the cybercrime-political nexus could have been studied from a criminological perspective, leaving out the analogy entirely. Two arguments speak against this. First, researching it through the privateering/pirate lenses recognizes the fluidity of the legitimacy created by the state. By anchoring the analysis in a historical process, in this case state consolidation of authority and responsibility to protect commerce, important elements of the constitution of political authority are brought into scope. Second, by using the analogy, questions about the politicized nature of cybercrime can be asked that cybercrime researchers today usually bracket.[113] Using the analogy thus enables an enquiry that would not otherwise have been made.

The empirical analysis of analogical relationships of pirates and privateers has shown that, while there are significant similarities, there are also notable differences. For example, first, the remuneration of state officials when tolerating pirates/privateers is not solely in the form of money, it may also be in the form of information. This potentially changes the logic of the collaboration relationships since not all targets are of equal interest.

Second, the magnitude of the problem is uncertain and the interaction with the state is less globally accepted. At the height of state-directed privateering and collaboration with pirates, the collaboration, in the form of letters of marque or agreements with pirates, was highly structured and widely known. Even foreign captains recognized the validity of privateering licenses and knew that Barbary pirates would not attack amicable polities. This is certainly not the case today. As introduced at the beginning of this chapter, the models of developing and integrating private capacity differ across countries, with different political contexts determining the boundaries of acceptable collaboration. There is no generic analogue of a letter of marque that applies across all the different contexts of cybercrime. However, the analysis was able to show how similar international political contestations are occurring with regard to state, semi-state, and non-state actor collaboration.

A third notable difference is that the regulatory and coercive capacities of the contemporary state organs in all the states observed (Estonia, Russia, United States) differ in quality from the historical cases analogized. The governments today have a much stronger claim on regulating their citizen's behaviour than in the late 16th century when sovereignty was still divided among many different polities. Furthermore, the states also differ from the 16th- and 17th-century polities with regard to their possibilities of mobilizing citizens based on patriotic and nationalist agendas. Whilst the analogy holds that the current Russian government's nationalist agenda provides the analogical modern cyber pirates and privateers legitimacy, the level of control exercised by the government is judged to be qualitatively greater than of Queen Elizabeth over her pirates and privateers.

In conclusion, the analytic lens uncovering the narratives deployed by officials regarding cybercrime shows that the activity is still highly politicized. Comparing this to piracy, it is similar—with some caveats—to the early 17th century, when different states were profiting from pirate bases, using them as trading hubs, and as means for undertaking undeclared warfare. As outlined in the historical chapter, the lines between pirates and privateers were blurred.

State efforts to build dedicated cyber capabilities, and thereby draw on private personnel with significant experience and skills, show similarities to the early investments in the late 16th century, when some states transitioned from the use of privateers to professional navies. In naval warfare, this transition over time reduced the interest in the use of private actors. Judging by this process, globally speaking, state actors' cyber capacities are in their infancy. The historical analysis has shown that once a state had opted to collaborate with pirates and privateers, this type of use of force became institutionalized over time. It unleashed a range of incentives to reproduce that model of collaboration, which in turn raised the difficulty to turn away from it. It can thus be labelled as a strategic choice that brings path dependencies. It created a new set of strategic problems, some of which this chapter found to be present today through the collaboration between cybercriminals and the Russian government.

Lastly, the analysis of the legal cases shows an emerging discourse around regulating the activity undertaken in cyberspace. In the absence of legal enforcement against cybercriminals in Russia, the United States has started a global enforcement campaign against Russian cybercriminals. Whilst this is effective against the cybercriminals that travel to zones, where the U.S. can bring its pressure to bear, individuals such as Bogachev or Belan stay out of reach. The analogy to the regulation of piracy would suggest that regional enforcement regimes may take hold. Piracy was dealt with differently in the Atlantic prize court system than in the Indian Ocean inter-imperial system.[114] Whilst the Atlantic system was mainly based on colonial enforcement, and thus depended on inner-imperial management, in the Indian Ocean, mercantile companies had a large role to play negotiating the inter-imperial legal systems. Indeed, the digital crimes and safety units of some of the larger technology companies may be playing similar roles today—managing the careful balance between the different legal regimes and zones of enforcement. If history were a guide, it could be expected that the large technology companies become equal political actors involved in the negotiation between the different great powers. The next chapter will thus focus on the insights generated by the analogy to mercantile companies.

7

Cyber Mercantile Companies

Conflict and Cooperation

Mercantile companies once ruled vast territories. They were in constant political struggles with different states to defend their authority, to govern their activities, and to expand their markets. There is no genealogically traceable line between the mercantile companies of the past and today's large technology companies. Notions of sovereignty in the international system today are fundamentally different from the ones in the early modern period when multiple types of sovereigns populated the system. However, today's large technology companies hold vast influence and power over the way information is generated, transmitted, stored, accessed, and deleted. Some of them functionally resemble a state-like actor, incorporating teams of diplomatic staff across the world and managing assets larger than many a state's gross domestic product. Some have even gone as far to suggest new rules for states (see e.g. Microsoft's Digital Geneva conventions proposal). Some states have reciprocated the state-like interaction that the large technology companies seek. In some countries, their CEOs are received with state honours. Denmark has even instituted a technology ambassador, recognizing that many of the technology companies 'have a much greater degree of influence than most nations'.[1]

As introduced in Chapter 2, the functional resemblance to a state is different to the spectrum of state proximity. The large technology companies can be functionally state-like, and closely aligned with a particular state's interests (e.g. this appears to be the case with Huawei and China), or they can be further removed in terms of state proximity, frequently opposing their home state's political leaders (e.g. Apple denying the FBI help accessing a dead terrorist's iPhone). So far, we have not witnessed a cyber mercantile company that consistently rejects the state framework (like a true non-state actor would).[2] As with the preceding chapter, this chapter looks at how such state proximity is established in practice and how it creates complications and opportunities for the different actors involved.

Semi-State Actors in Cybersecurity. Florian J. Egloff, Oxford University Press. © Florian J. Egloff 2022. DOI: 10.1093/oso/9780197579275.003.0007

A further difference in today's mercantile companies is that there are many more of them. Historically, there were only a few mercantile companies, whereas now there are numerous ones, spanning different domains. Since this book focuses on cyber(in-)security specifically, it only looks at mercantile companies in the cyber domain. It thus makes a sectoral distinction that did not exist historically. However, the distinction is reasonable and appropriate, as the security challenges introduced by state collaborations and confrontations with, for example, large energy companies may differ in nature.

This chapter shows how the role mercantile companies played in the early modern system, and their interactions with pirates, privateers, and navies can be used to gain a better understanding of today's large technology companies' roles and their relationships to the analogical cyber navies, privateers, and pirates.[3] I argue that the mercantile company lens can aid the understanding of how cooperative and conflictive relations to states, as well as practices of self-protection, influence cyber(in-)security. By doing so, we can further refine our understanding of the role companies play in providing cyber(in-)security. The chapter develops this argument by applying the analogy in three ways.

One focus is on the protection of a company's assets from threats propagated through cyberspace. The historical shift from self-provided protection to more reliance on state resources informs the analysis of the shift witnessed in the protection from threats in cyberspace. This includes an analysis of corporate offensive action (i.e. hacking-back), which is an authority that mercantile companies possessed historically, and one that leads to considerable policy debate in today's context.

A second area of comparison is the competition for skilled personnel between mercantile companies and states. The competition emerges due to skilled personnel being the key enabler and constraint of capacity in both cyberspace and historical maritime defence and offence. The focus on mercantile companies captures the converging and competing interests in the absorption of such capacity.

Finally, this chapter analyses the overlapping interest between states and mercantile companies in the pursuit of their business. In the historical case, mercantile companies were a form of gaining influence and power over large parts of the world that a state-driven expansion would not have achieved on its own.[4] Analogically, in today's context, the large technology companies provide states with access to data, which the state on its own likely could not have collected.

The analysis will unfold in three case studies. Each case highlights a different constellation between states and companies. While the first case features Google, a modern mercantile company, the second case looks at the U.S. government's reaction to the attacks against Sony Pictures Entertainment (SPE), which is functionally not a state-like actor in the domain of cyber(in-)security. The two cases allow for an analysis comparing and contrasting both the actions of the different types of companies and the actors involved in their defence. Finally, while the first two cases look at aspects of conflict, a third case of cooperation between modern mercantile companies and signals intelligence agencies highlights the cooperative aspect of the coexistence of mercantile companies and states. Before continuing with the Google case, in the following paragraphs I will provide a short overview of each case.

First, I will focus on Operation Aurora (2009/10), a conflict between a state, China, and a modern mercantile company, Google. How the company uses its own resources to fend off what it perceives to be an attack by another state is of specific interest. The case highlights the political debate about who is responsible to protect the company. Not having been protected by a state, Google subsequently fortified its own security posture. This in turn sheds light on the recruiting problems unleashed by companies' demand for the best security engineers. The special case of Google also engages in the debate on hacking-back and raises the question whether a company should be allowed to pursue offensive actions for defensive purposes. The discussion of the authority to act is then linked to mercantile companies and privateers.

The second part highlights the conflict between a state, North Korea, and a company, SPE. As opposed to the Google case, SPE is a much weaker actor in terms of its cyber capacity and business model and cannot usefully be classified as a cyber mercantile company. However, in contrast to the Google case, the SPE case shows how the U.S. government actively assumes defensive responsibilities on behalf of the company. The empirical application of the historical analogy contributes to the analysis by identifying a shift in the interpretation of the authority and responsibility to defend private actors in cyberspace, just as happened in the late 17th century on the seas. Furthermore, the case links the analysis to the previous chapter's focus on the topic of authority and control over cyber pirates when discussing how the U.S. government's silence on the activity of independent hacking collectives can be read as a tacit endorsement of their actions.

Whilst the first two cases mainly focus on the conflictive interaction between a state and a company, the third case focuses on the cooperation between large technology companies and states for the purposes of signals intelligence. It draws attention to the cooperative aspects of such relationships and thereby enables an analysis of the opportunities and challenges that state proximity introduces. The case analogizes the modern mercantile companies to the historical ones of the 17th century, who pursued expansionary policies and displayed independent agency both towards their home government and abroad.

This chapter concludes that treating large technology companies as mercantile companies changes our understanding of cyber(in-)security by bringing into scope their imperial practices of expansion, which come through submission to other jurisdictions, integration into other systems, and renegotiation of responsibilities and control. Consequently, this chapter closes with a discussion of the shared interests in terms of access to data, the still expansionary corporate policies, and the shared interest in stability.

Operation Aurora: A Mercantile Company Responds

The case study of Operation Aurora highlights the relationship between one of the largest companies in the world, Google, and the two largest state powers in the world, the U.S. and China (see Figure 7.1 for an overview). If the analogy to mercantile companies can enlighten the politics of cyber(in-) security, then one would expect the politics of mercantile companies to come to the fore in this case. The case study first lays out the three different narratives offered by the three actors. The study then identifies analogical features to a mercantile company, which include the independent representation of itself towards both the home and foreign government, the independent capability and will to defend itself, and the competition for key personnel with the state's analogy of a navy. The analysis closes with a discussion of the hacking-back debate.

Google's narrative

In mid-December 2009, Google's security team discovered traces of a cyber intrusion on their internal networks.[5] Someone had searched for multiple Chinese names on the internal legal discovery portal. When checking in with

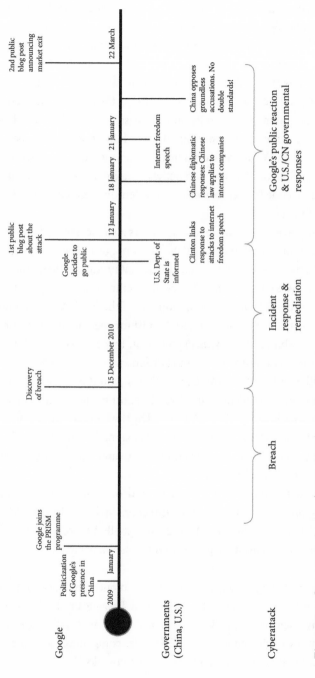

Figure 7.1 Operation Aurora (2009–2010) case timeline

the employee from whom the search requests had supposedly originated, she denied having made the queries.[6] A long search for the intruders ensued, in which co-founder of Google, Sergey Brin, personally got involved.[7] A team of security experts traced the intruders' footprints back to the original breach—a Google China employee had been spear-phished in a MSN chat message with a link to a photo-sharing site that exploited a zero-day vulnerability in Internet Explorer.[8] From there, the intruders moved laterally into Google's core network. In its public messaging, Google would later emphasize the intruder's interest in identifying human rights activists, such as Tibetan activists. What one would hear less about, but what must have been a major security concern for Google, was the intruders' successful exfiltration of source code (Gaia), as well as their demonstrated intent to find code-signing certificates.[9]

According to Bruce Schneier the intruders also accessed a database for law enforcement and intelligence, which raised major concerns for U.S. intelligence officials.[10] Several Snowden documents indicate that, since January 2009, Google was part of a surveillance programme called PRISM.[11] As part of this programme, authorized by Section 702 of the FISA Amendments Act of 2008, Google had to provide data to the FBI for specific selectors. According to Ellen Nakashima of the *Washington Post*, this database, holding the surveillance orders, as well as FISA court orders, was hacked as well.[12] Knowing the surveillance targets of the United States would be greatly beneficial to Chinese counterintelligence and directly contrary to the national security and intelligence investigations conducted by the United States. Confirmation of the motivation of the intruders was also signalled by Microsoft, another target of the same campaign, although they later retracted the statements given by one of their directors.[13]

Google swiftly undertook efforts to find out who was targeting them. A *Washington Post* article claims the intruders had been in Google's systems for at least a year.[14] The *New York Times* labelled Google's investigation a 'counteroffensive'. It quotes a government consultant saying:

It [Google] managed to gain access to a computer in Taiwan that it suspected of being the source of the attacks. Peering inside that machine, company engineers actually saw evidence of the aftermath of the attacks, not only at Google, but also at least 33 other companies, including Adobe Systems, Northrop Grumman and Juniper Networks.[15]

In other words, Google gained access to one of the servers involved in the operation of the campaign. This is significant, as few companies acknowledge accessing computers outside their corporate network in public, preferring not to open themselves up to legal risk.[16]

By 'early January' Google's investigation had 'conclusively confirmed the origin and scale of the attack'.[17] 'Over the course of Google's investigation, it gathered sufficient evidence to know that the Chinese government or its agents were behind the attack'.[18] Later, Sergey Brin, co-founder of Google, would be issued a temporary security clearance by the U.S. government and was briefed on the specific unit of the Chinese People's Liberation Army that conducted the cyberespionage operation.[19] Brin, who was leading the investigatory team, wanted to publicize the findings and stop implementing the Chinese censorship requests as a reaction.

This reopened a debate amongst the executive management over whether Google should operate in China at all.[20] Brin had long objected to operating in China and thereby accept having to implement the governmental censorship practices.[21] In 2009, China had tightened its censorship practices around several of Google's products and had put pressure on Google to remove its link to Google.com, allowing Chinese internet users access to an uncensored version of Google.[22] Brin decided the hacking went too far. In his own words:

> The hacking attacks were the straw that broke the camel's back. There were several aspects there: the attack directly on Google, which we believe was an attempt to gain access to Gmail accounts of Chinese human rights activists. But there is also a broader pattern we then discovered of simply the surveillance of human rights activists.[23]

Others, such as Eric Schmidt, the chairman of Google, argued that through being present locally, Google would have the chance to inform on the questionable practices applied by other search providers and provide greater access to information to Chinese users.[24] Larry Page, the second co-founder, had shared Eric Schmidt's view when entering the Chinese market in 2006, but by early 2010, considering the newly discovered behaviour, changed his mind. 'The behaviour we were seeing was evil, he [Larry] told Eric, and wasn't going to stop; in fact, the harassment would likely get worse'.[25] The founders 'no longer felt that our [Google's] presence in the market was helping change government censorship practices, and didn't want to participate in any way in that censorship'.[26]

Google's management took the decision to stop censoring its search results on Google.cn and to publicize the findings about the cyber operation. The management knew that this would most likely result in Google's market exit from China. Describing the decision, Eric Schmidt and Jonathan Rosenberg wrote:

> The majority sided with Sergey, who believed that the Chinese government would eventually change their behaviour because their current model would not be sustainable, leaving the door open at some point in the future for Google to reenter the market.[27]

On 12 January 2010, David Drummond, Google's chief legal officer, posted a blog post, thereby implementing Google's decision.[28] The blog post informed the public about the cyber operation but stopped short of publicly accusing the Chinese government. Instead, Google detailed the targeting (intellectual property, Chinese human rights activists) and pointed interested parties 'wanting to learn about these kinds of attacks' to a section in the 2009 annual report of the U.S.-China Economic and Security Review Commission, which detailed the Chinese intelligence activities targeting Chinese dissidents abroad.[29] Google also linked to an 88-page Northrop Grumman report, prepared for said Commission, detailing the capability of the People's Republic of China (PRC) to 'conduct Cyber Warfare and Computer Network Exploitation'.[30] Furthermore, it linked to the operation GhostNet report, one of the first public APT-reports detailing espionage practices against Tibetan activists, as well as to one of the report's co-authors', Nart Villeneuve's, blog.[31]

Three months later, after unsuccessful discussions with the Chinese government about offering uncensored search results, Google announced that it would redirect all search traffic from China to their Hong Kong–based site Google.com.hk, ceasing its operations in mainland China.[32] This meant that from now on, Google would no longer self-censor their search results; rather, the search results would be censored by the technical censorship implemented at the internet service provider level on behalf of the Chinese government.[33]

The U.S. government's narrative

In the first week of January 2010, Secretary of State Hilary Clinton attended a dinner with various leaders from the information technology sector. All the publicly available information indicates that she had not yet been briefed on the Google investigation. Rather, the U.S. State Department was briefed on Google's decision to publicly accuse China of spying on 11 January 2010, one day after the decision had been taken in Google's executive management team, and a day before Google went public.[34] On the day of Google's announcement, Secretary Clinton issued a press release:

> We have been briefed by Google on these allegations, which raise very serious concerns and questions. We look to the Chinese government for an explanation. The ability to operate with confidence in cyberspace is critical in a modern society and economy. I will be giving an address next week on the centrality of internet freedom in the 21st century, and we will have further comment on this matter as the facts become clear.[35]

In so doing, Hilary Clinton tied Google's going public to a policy speech on internet freedom that had been in the planning since at least December 2009.[36] In the week leading up to the secretary's internet freedom speech, the U.S. State Department highlighted the strong, mature bilateral relationship with China. They indicated that it was a serious issue and that they expected China to explain.[37] Within that timeframe, various meetings between U.S. and PRC diplomats took place to discuss the issue.

Then, on 21 January 2010, Hilary Clinton delivered her policy speech on internet freedom. She addressed internet censorship and turned to Google's situation:

> Increasingly, U.S. companies are making the issue of internet and information freedom a greater consideration in their business decisions. I hope that their competitors and foreign governments will pay close attention to this trend. The most recent situation involving Google has attracted a great deal of interest. And we look to the Chinese authorities to conduct a thorough review of the cyber intrusions that led Google to make its announcement. And we also look for that investigation and its results to be transparent.

The internet has already been a source of tremendous progress in China, and it is fabulous. There are so many people in China now online. But countries that restrict free access to information or violate the basic rights of internet users risk walling themselves off from the progress of the next century. Now, the United States and China have different views on this issue, and we intend to address those differences candidly and consistently in the context of our positive, cooperative, and comprehensive relationship.

Now, ultimately, this issue isn't just about information freedom; it is about what kind of world we want and what kind of world we will inhabit. It's about whether we live on a planet with one internet, one global community, and a common body of knowledge that benefits and unites us all, or a fragmented planet in which access to information and opportunity is dependent on where you live and the whims of censors.[38]

Hence, she strongly reiterated Google's call against censorship. In the same speech, she highlighted that the State Department was supporting tools to circumvent censorship: 'Both the American people and nations that censor the internet should understand that our government is committed to helping promote internet freedom'.[39]

The American national security establishment was also interested in the intrusion campaign. Following the discovery of the attacks, Google reached out to the National Security Agency (NSA). A former White House official told journalist Michael Joseph Gross:

After Google got hacked, they called the N.S.A. in and said, 'You were supposed to protect us from this!' The N.S.A. guys just about fell out of their chairs. They could not believe how naïve the Google guys had been.[40]

The anecdote captures the uncertainty about the distribution of responsibilities around the protection of networks against state-directed adversaries. The roles and responsibilities were uncertain.[41] This uncertainty was fostered by the ongoing political battle over authorities (who protects whom from whom?), approaches (market based vs. regulatory vs. law enforcement), and budgetary implications (which agency gets how much of the cybersecurity budget).

The NSA drafted a cooperative research and development agreement.[42] Under such an agreement, Google could share the details of the cyber intrusion with NSA, whilst the NSA could aid Google with its expertise in information assurance and up-to-date threat intelligence. The company would also profit from the NSA's evaluation of their hardware and software. In addition, according to Shane Harris, as part of the agreement, Google provided information about traffic on its networks and let the NSA analyse past intrusions.[43] Whilst reports indicate that Google came to terms with the NSA, Google 'without any guarantees about the scope of the investigation, denied access' to the FBI.[44]

China's reaction

Whilst the U.S. launch of the internet freedom agenda was not necessarily coordinated with Google, it sure looked like it from a Chinese perspective. To better understand the Chinese action and reaction, some context on the Chinese information security perspective is required. Between 2006 and 2009, the percentage of Chinese citizens using the internet almost tripled.[45] The Chinese government saw the internet not only as a possibility for sustaining economic growth 'but also [as] a major threat to domestic stability and regime legitimacy'.[46] To mitigate these threats, the Chinese government used the monitoring of the internet to identify discontent and corruption. It also played an active part in shaping the online conversations on social media to guide public opinion.[47] Thus, Chinese state leaders perceived the unguided expression on an open internet as a potential threat to regime legitimacy and domestic stability and undertook measures for state control. Hence, information security in the Chinese sense encompassed not only the integrity of computer systems and networks but also a broader understanding of government control of the information content.[48] In this understanding, censorship was considered a matter of state security to fight, in the words of the Chinese state ideology, the three evils and five poisons.[49]

The Chinese government had applied pressure on Google to be more responsive to its censorship requests throughout 2009. Now, the company publicly levied spying charges against the Chinese government, followed by an official statement by the U.S. State Department connecting its own statement with an upcoming policy speech on internet freedom.

The Chinese initial official reaction was to deny any hacking charges, stating 'Chinese laws strictly prohibit cyber crimes'.[50] Up to that point, companies targeted by Chinese espionage campaigns kept quiet about it, often fearing that the disclosure would bring bad publicity and unnecessary legal risks. Hence, one can assume that the forceful reaction by Google came as a surprise to the Chinese leadership. That is not to say that Google had not contemplated exiting the Chinese market before.[51] Rather, the Chinese government could not have anticipated that Google would publicize this incident and that it would come in conjunction with a U.S. foreign policy initiative.

In the days after Google's publication, Chinese officials met with U.S. diplomats and explained the Chinese position.[52] After the U.S. internet freedom speech, Chinese Vice Foreign Minister He Yafei warned: 'The Google case should not be linked with relations between the two governments and countries; otherwise, it's an over-interpretation'.[53] Noting the differences in messaging between their working-level partners and the vice foreign minister, the U.S. embassy concluded that this suggested 'that the negative reaction to the speech originated at higher levels in the foreign policy hierarchy'.[54]

The next day, the Chinese government reacted to Secretary Clinton's speech by urging the 'U.S. to stop accusations on so-called Internet freedom'.[55] The article claimed that besides the targeting of Google, the Chinese search engine Baidu.com had suffered the worst attack to date on 12 January (the day of Google's publication).[56] A commentary published by the official Chinese news agency Xinhua sent a strong message: 'Don't impose double standards on "internet freedom" '.[57] It referenced the U.S. measures to control activities on the internet and its own activities in cyber warfare. It claimed: 'It is quite hypocritical to point one's finger at others without proper justification while managing to strengthen one's own cyber warfare capacity'.[58] On 25 January, a Chinese government spokesperson issued the official denial of government involvement:

> Accusation that the Chinese government participated in [a] cyber attack, either in an explicit or inexplicit way, is groundless and aims to denigrate China. We [are] firmly opposed to that.[59]

Meanwhile, the U.S. embassy in Beijing informed the U.S. government that one of their well-placed contacts claimed the cyber operation against Google were 'coordinated at the State Council Information Office with the oversight of [two named] Standing Committee members'.[60] The embassy staff noted that it was yet unclear whether the Chinese president and premier minister had been aware of the intrusions before Google going public.

The reaction of a mercantile company?

Three aspects of this case are of special interest. The first is Google's fight against the Chinese government. From the documentation of the case, it is clear that Google's leadership decided to exit the Chinese market as a response to the cyber operation. This section analyses how this compares to a mercantile company's policies. Two further aspects are particularly relevant for our interest in cyber mercantile companies and will be discussed later in the chapter; namely, the competition to hire the best security professionals, and what the *New York Times* labelled the 'counteroffensive' undertaken by Google.

Google acted decisively by combining a business decision with publicly taking on the Chinese government. Google knew that this would have political and commercial implications. It tried to motivate other U.S. technology companies to support their stance—but to no avail. One can draw the analogy to the political and economic competition between the different mercantile companies. As shown in the historical chapter, mercantile companies would not be afraid to lobby the Mughal Court against other companies' interests. Contemporaneous examples are plentiful. For example, Steve Ballmer, then Microsoft's CEO, commented that Google's decision was an irrational business decision. He cited oil imports from Saudi Arabia that were ethically acceptable, despite the country's abhorrent human rights record.[61] This was followed by Bill Gates informing the U.S. public on *Good Morning America* that 'Chinese efforts to censor the Internet have been very limited. It's easy to go around it, and so I think keeping the Internet thriving there is very important'.[62] In a different interview, he claimed that Google essentially pulled a publicity stunt: 'They've done nothing and gotten a lot of credit for it'.[63] He added: 'If Google ever chooses to pull out of the United States, then I'd give them credit'.[64] Two days later, Ballmer followed up his earlier comments over the Microsoft PR channels. The message read that Microsoft supported internet freedom, but 'our business must respect the laws of China. That's true for every company doing business in countries around the world: we are subject to local laws'.[65]

Google's Sergey Brin voiced staunch criticism of Microsoft: 'I'm very disappointed for them [Microsoft] in particular. . . . As I understand, they have effectively no market share—so they essentially spoke against freedom of speech and human rights simply in order to contradict Google'.[66] Of course, Microsoft's statements at times of crisis were not just against Google but can also be read as aiming to strengthen Microsoft's position with the Chinese government.

To better understand this situation, the 17th-century mercantile companies are particularly instructive, as they, too, operated in multiple spaces of political authority. As detailed in the historical chapter, in the East India Company's case, the company secured an authority to trade both from the English Crown and the Mughal emperor, formally submitting to both. In the Mughal Empire, it inserted itself into the local political fabric by adopting local practices. It had to submit to local rule to be allowed to trade. By submitting to the Mughal as 'exotic vassals' and thereby confirming his authority to rule universally, the mercantile companies strengthened the emperor's power.[67] In smaller island polities in Southeast Asia, local rulers used 'stranger king' norms to accept companies as foreign suzerains, using it 'as a means of strengthening their own authority'.[68] Observing the modern case, Google's executive team's confrontational response to the Chinese government clearly falls outside the spectrum of submission. Google chose to independently interpret the security needs of its Chinese users and considered the Chinese government a threat to them. This open challenge to the Chinese government's interpretation of how to govern their information space undermined the government's claim to authority. Other companies' leaders, such as Microsoft's Bill Gates, did exactly the opposite. They had long-standing policies of submitting themselves to local power structures, thereby confirming the government's authority to rule.[69] In China, internet companies had to integrate themselves into the Chinese system of rule, for example by signing the 'Public Pledge of Self-Regulation and Professional Ethics for China's Internet Industry'.[70]

Google picked a fight with the Chinese government and lost. The Chinese asserted their sovereign right to enforce their laws the way they chose. A realist scholar may read this as the absence of important agency on Google's part, reflecting a broader state-centric trend. It was not Google's reaction, either, that was highlighted in the Chinese response; rather, it was the concern that Google and the U.S. government decided to jointly implement the 'internet freedom' policy. The fact that Microsoft executives distanced themselves from Google's response shortly after Hilary Clinton's internet freedom policy speech could also be read in that light. Microsoft did not want to become associated with Google's confrontational response. However, to discount Google's response as irrelevant would be missing the security dynamics that are particular to this large economic and political actor. Google chose to react politically to the cyber intrusion. Instead of keeping quiet, Google chose to publicly reveal the details of the intrusion, only stopping short of directly calling the Chinese government responsible. As seen in the previous chapter, this element of public attribution is political in nature.[71] Instead of opening a criminal investigation, Google's executive team chose to respond on their own. This is crucial, as it differentiates a private company from a mercantile company. The mercantile company perceives itself to be important enough to act independently on the stage of international politics. Hence, it does not rely on a single state or state institutions to defend its interests. Rather, it asserts its interests with its own capabilities. It represents itself differently towards various governments and finds political accommodation with them, sometimes by submission, sometimes by confrontation. Two implications follow from Google's response to the intrusions: a heightened competition for security personnel, and a debate about hacking-back.

Google undervalued the importance of ensuring their own security. Whether one believes Google's alleged reaction to having been caught unawares and about whether the NSA would protect them, Google retrospectively invested in hiring more security staff. Michael Joseph Gross reports:

> Caught unawares and shorthanded, the company made a list of the world's top security professionals, and Brin personally called to offer them jobs— with $100,000 signing bonuses for some, according to one person who received such an offer—and quickly built Google's small, pre-Aurora security operation into a group of more than 200.[72]

Today, Google runs one of the most respected security teams worldwide, counting more than 500 employees.[73] The competition for talent between large corporations and governments in cyber(in-)security is acute. Whilst industry's big attractions are the financial incentives, workplace environments, and engagement with the security community, the government offers mission motivation and the ability to make offensive actions legal. Google expanded its efforts to protect users against state-sponsored attacks and notify users when they have identified a specific state-sponsored threat. This mirrors the early expansionary years of activity on the seas. Just like on the seas, users of cyberspace were largely left to protect themselves. In the absence of a state capacity and/or willingness to provide redress, users have to rely on their own abilities to withstand threats propagating through cyberspace. In such an environment, defensive and offensive skills are sought by a variety of actors. Just as mercantile companies in the early 17th century could not rely on the Royal Navy to protect their trade, and hence armed their merchant navies and sometimes sought protection from specialized private men-of-war, large companies today are able to attract some of the most skilled cyber(in-)security experts in the industry.

Google reacted by going on the offensive. They accessed one of the operation's servers (presumably a command-and-control server) in Taiwan. This is of interest, as it would be—if it were done without authorization by the respective agencies and asset owners—a violation of both the U.S. Computer Fraud and Abuse Act and the Taiwanese Criminal Code. The decision of the company to investigate themselves and its reluctance to have the FBI on its premises closely resemble some of the elements of the corporate-state we have seen in the era of mercantile companies. Google did talk to NSA but was disappointed with the lack of protection they provided. There was a negotiation between the NSA and Google about what kind of information exchange there would be. The accounts of that exchange described this as a contract negotiation and not a hierarchical act of authority.[74]

The account of the corporate offensive operation raises the question about the extent to which companies can protect themselves against state-directed attacks and about whether private actors should be engaged in state-sanctioned hacking-back.[75] Hacking-back, as used in this book, means reactive offensive actions undertaken for, from the defender's perspective, a defensive purpose and excludes self-initiated (i.e. not responsive) offensive actions.[76] It is worth delving into the risks introduced when companies are seen to be engaged in state-sanctioned hacking-back a bit more deeply and use the analogy to privateering to do so.

Whether a private company can defend itself from a state-directed intrusion depends on the intent and capacity of the attacking state and the defensive capabilities of the company. If a company with a high cybersecurity maturity is a generic target, it may be able to dissuade an attacker by making itself a hard target. However, when private companies are the direct target of a motivated, well-resourced state attacker, their defensive capabilities will not deter the attacker. It is worth reflecting on what the aims of hacking-back may be for a private company.[77] Is it to impose costs on the attacker? Is it to help attribution of the cyber operation to a particular actor? Is it to research the motivation of the adversary? Given the uncertainty about the ramifications of any offensive or retaliatory actions against an attacker, it is unclear to what extent private actors would deem such actions to be in their interests. In the United States, the government tries to dissuade corporate hacking-back by claiming that it is illegal under the Computer Fraud and Abuse Act and highlighting the danger of escalation against unknown adversaries.[78]

However, the Google Operation Aurora case gives an indication about why a company might want to hack-back: to gather information about the intent and scope of an intrusion. Having access to a command-and-control server also has the potential to allow a more fine-grained analysis of the origin of the intrusion. Such hack-backs could also be used to identify and aid further victims, improve defensive capabilities, and, potentially, stop further distribution of malicious software.[79]

As most companies do not necessarily possess the skill sets for offensive actions, one could expect them to hire the skill sets privately.[80] Indeed some evidence of offensive skill set for hire has surfaced over the last few years. An investigation by the Toronto-based Citizen Lab, for example, has surfaced an Indian contractor, aliased Dark Basin, attacking targets worldwide, seemingly for corporate backers.[81] This resembles the private men-of-war that were hired by mercantile companies to protect their ships and trade routes and attack hostile targets. Such offensive action incurs many risks for both the company and the state that would be, or could at least be seen to be, sanctioning the hacking-back operation. Three risks are worth highlighting here: an increased risk of unnecessary escalation, the potential for reprisal, and setting an international norm that may be strategically destabilizing.

First, a company may overstep its defensive aims and be tempted to profit from their offensive undertaking. This is not without historical precedent. Historically, privateers were hard to control. They regularly overstepped their commissions, especially when it was in the interest of their sponsors' government. Such overstepping was highlighted in the previous chapter in the case of Belan's use of his access against Yahoo for private purposes. It is likely that companies who hack-back also face situations with such adverse incentives.

Even if it is assumed, for the sake of argument, that the private sector could perform cyber operations with a high degree of discrimination and proportionality and it is stipulated that the corporate sponsors weigh the potential blowback carefully against their business interests, in such a case, offensive actions still constitute a means of engaging in conflict. Which countries should a country be willing to issue hacking-back licenses against? Such a licensing would surely be seen as a hostile act by the receiving party. Recall also the difficulty of precise attribution, which makes issuing a license, depending on the attribution capabilities of the issuing country, a highly risky affair.

Once the private sector engages in these limited offensive operations, at some point, they may be discovered. A foreign government will be informed that part of their supply chain suffered an intrusion. Will the targets recognize the attackers and their intentions? A capable adversary may trace the intrusion back to the attacking country. Distinguishing between a company working for evidence gathering for another company and one working for the government will be hard, particularly as both may be customers of the same offensive contractor. As argued in the previous chapter, this can be an advantage for a state that intends to use strategic ambiguity to its advantage. However, as this policy would further cloud the government's intent, it would compound problems for cyber defence. Given the possibility of a worst-case analysis by the defender, hacking-back magnifies the risk of unintentionally setting off an escalatory spiral.[82]

Second, intentionally breaching foreign domestic law brings risks upon the hackers, their corporate sponsors, and, if done at scale, their government. Under domestic law, the injured party may have a legitimate criminal case to pursue in court. The full range of consequences for people engaging in hacking-back, as well as potentially their sponsors, are unclear, but among other things, some restrictions on their ability to engage in international travel unless they are willing to stand trial abroad might be expected.

But there are further countermeasures that might be taken against hackers—reprisals. The injured party could appeal to their own government to seek retribution. A country that adopts a policy of hacking-back needs to be prepared to accept intrusions sponsored by other countries' companies. In such a system, each country is their own arbiter of whether their claims are legitimate—recall, for example, the analysis of the competing narratives deployed by the Russian and Estonian governments in Chapter 6. Furthermore, retribution may not be restricted to cyberspace. Rather, having sponsored a cyber intrusion, company assets residing in the country that was targeted may suddenly be exposed to legal and political risk abroad. Other countries may also choose to broaden the definition of whom to take reprisal against. After all, historically, privateering was a tool to seek redress against harm suffered by another national. What restricts a foreign power to take a more expansive definition of privateering?

Finally, Once hacking-back is established as a legitimate course of action in the cyber realm, the question then arises, who profits most from such a regime? Historically, privateering was the policy tool of the challengers, not the incumbent great power. The power with the largest trade interests had the most to lose. By the end of the 18th century, when Britain became the dominant naval and trading power, it was France and the United States that relied heavily on privateers. As seen in the historical chapter, Britain took the threat of U.S. privateering so seriously that it struck a deal with most other naval powers to abolish privateering in 1856. Recalling the quotation from Chapter 3, England's Prime Minister Lord Palmerston summed up the logic as follows:

> Privateering is a Practice most inconvenient to the Power which has the largest number of merchant men at sea, and the least useful to the Power which has the largest War Navy. England is that Power and we should therefore willingly agree to abolish that Practice in regard to all Powers which would enter into the same Engagement towards us.[83]

As laid out in the analysis in the historical chapter, no power today holds the same dominant position as Britain did in the 19th century. Hence, multiple powers may opt for a policy of hacking-back, potentially endangering user trust in the viability of a global digital system. The analogy to privateering suggests that the states most likely to adopt such a strategy would be those that do not yet have a large state-owned offensive cyber capacity and thereby rely on private sector capacities as their only option for hacking-back, or those that use privateers as a strategy to deliberately increase the difficulty of disambiguation between government and private, offensive actions. Among corporations, the historical analogy to mercantile companies would suggest that their modern analogues, the largest technology companies, are the likeliest candidates to seek strategies to enhance their defences by incorporating reactive offensive measures if the states they are operating within are unwilling to enforce the law against it.

To sum up, treating Google as a mercantile company in the Aurora case focuses the attention on the politicized aspects of the crisis and its further implications. It draws out how the Chinese perceived close state proximity between Google and the United States government, whilst Google had a self-perception of political and economic agency that was further removed from the government. This was reflected in Google's refusal to let the FBI investigate; rather, it chose to cooperate with NSA on a contractual basis. Furthermore, in strong resemblance to the mercantile companies of the past, Google tried to fend off the cyber operation of a foreign state actor by accessing the servers in a different country and by extensively recruiting security experts.

Both elements have the potential to trigger similar effects present in the naval security in the 17th century. Then, the British East India Company competed with the navy for personnel and organized its owns protection force to fend off foreign ships and protect its sea lanes. Both then and now, this introduces interaction effects with states. The offensive actions in other state's jurisdictions increase the risk of escalation, invite the potential for reprisal, and could set an international norm that may be strategically destabilizing.

Sony Pictures Entertainment (2014): The Interplay of Governments, a Private Company, and Independent Hackers

The analysis of the attack against Sony Pictures Entertainment (SPE) in 2014 reveals several characteristics of the dynamics among actors with various types of state proximity. It details a (non-mercantile) company that was attacked by a state actor. The case examines governmental responsibility to protect companies that cannot protect themselves. The case contrasts the Google case by showing how the U.S. government was involved in the response to the attacks against SPE. The response to the attack also highlights the management of independent hackers responding in concert with the government. The case study is structured into a case overview (for a visual overview see Figure 7.2) followed by an analysis of how the different actors used their capabilities against one another. It will then discuss how strategic ambiguity can be advantageous not only to the attacker and but also to the defender. The case closes with the finding that the SPE case may mark a transition in the protection of private companies in cyberspace from self-provided towards a more public form of protection.

Case overview

On 21 November 2014, SPE received a warning 'to behave wisely' by email.[84] On 24 November 2014, a wiper malware was activated on a large part of SPE's infrastructure, crippling the company's ability to continue their work. The malware issued a warning that company documents would be released if demands were not met by 11:00 at night. Having let that deadline pass,

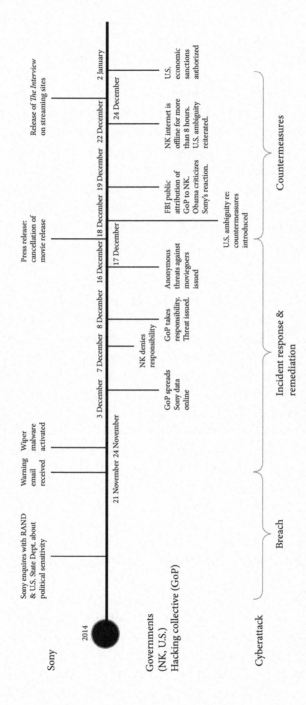

Figure 7.2 Sony Pictures Entertainment (2014) case timeline

the group Guardians of Peace (GoP) published several movies, SPE internal documents, and email archives of SPE executives over the next month. Given the upcoming release date of the movie *The Interview,* speculations about possible North Korean connections were raised. North Korea reacted by issuing a press statement denying responsibility but praising the attacking group for their actions and condemning SPE for producing a film 'abetting a terrorist act'.[85] This was followed by a statement by GOP on 8 December 2014, which directly connected the showing of a movie to their actions. It demanded that SPE should 'stop immediately showing the movie of terrorism which can break the regional peace and cause the War!'[86] Lacking any indications of cancelling the movie, it was a threat of terrorist attacks against moviegoers issued on 16 December 2014 that changed the dynamic. Despite the U.S. Department of Homeland Security's claim of having no intelligence about a plot against movie theatres, many movie theatres opted-out of showing the movie.[87] The next day SPE issued a press statement cancelling the release, which had been scheduled for Christmas day. On 18 December 2014, the White House announced it was considering a proportional response.[88] On 19 December 2014, the FBI attributed the GOP's actions to the North Korean government.[89] The same day, U.S. President Obama criticized SPE's decision.[90] SPE then prepared to release the movie online, and several theatres opted to show it on Christmas day. On 22 December 2014, North Korea's internet went offline multiple times, including an eight-hour timeslot.[91]

On 2 January 2015, President Obama authorized the U.S. treasury to impose economic sanctions on North Korea.[92] Sony estimated the remediation efforts to have cost about US$41 million, with the total costs incurred by the corporation estimated at US$80 million.[93] Much later, in 2018, the U.S. reinforced its attribution to North Korea by releasing a detailed-rich criminal complaint of a North Korean citizen.[94]

How did different stakeholders use their cyber capabilities?

The SPE case is a good example of the interaction between different types of state and non-state actors. It highlights how not only attackers but also defenders deliberately introduce strategic ambiguity to sow doubt about their relationships to other actors and the authorship of actions taken. Following the case time line, the events can be abstracted as follows. SPE, an actor not allied with a particular state, was attacked by an entity with unclear relations to a state. The attacker attempted to coerce SPE's leadership into forgoing the publication of a movie but failed in the first instance. Hence, it raised the pressure and strategically published material gained through a cyber intrusion, which raised the interest of the media in SPE's activities. SPE hired Mandiant, a firm with significant cyber capabilities, including many ex-government employees (i.e. a semi-state actor). The media speculated that this attack was state sponsored. North Korea reacted to the media and denied any involvement but endorsed the attack. At this point, the convergence of interests between the attacker (GOP) and the North Korean state was a fact. This raised profile captured the interest of the U.S. government; the FBI and NSA got involved (both state actors). The veracity of the terror threat could not be established, but the U.S. government reacted in an official capacity (DHS statement). By this time, the U.S. intelligence community and its international partners had concluded that the GOP could be attributed to the North Korean government.[95] Thus, the U.S. government prepared a reaction strategy, including publicly attributing the attacks, reaching out to the Chinese about discussing countermeasures, weighing options for proportional cyber responses, and assessing sanction options.

The most interesting aspect for the discussion of the interaction between different types of actors is the ambiguity the U.S. government introduced about whether they would use an offensive cyber response. In a press briefing on 18 December 2014, the White House spokesperson informed the public about the deliberations regarding the proportional response:

> I wouldn't speculate at this point about the range of options that are currently under consideration. I also wouldn't commit at this point to at some point being entirely transparent about what that response is. . . .
>
> I don't anticipate that we'll be in a position where we're going to be able to be completely forthcoming about every single element of the response that has been decided upon.[96]

On the day of and the day after the network outages in North Korea, the State Department held press briefings:

> We are considering a range of options in response. We aren't going to discuss publicly operational details about the possible response options or comment on those kind of reports in any way except to say that as we implement our responses, some will be seen, some may not be seen.[97]

[after several questions whether the U.S. took North Korea offline]

> Well, there's a range of options. I don't think I want to put anything on the table or off the table at this point, but that's—there're obviously financial options. But again, I'm not ruling anything in or out from a policy perspective. There are a range of both seen and unseen options that we have, though. And if we ever have anything to outline publicly, we will do so.[98]

Whilst the media wondered whether the U.S. government had performed a distributed denial of service (DDoS) attack, other experts pointed to activist chatter that detailed how such an attack could be performed.[99] Two specific points are noteworthy about the interaction between different actors. First, the U.S. government made a policy choice not to publicly clarify whether it had taken down the North Korean networks. Second, when activists incited others to DDoS the North Korean networks, the U.S. government did not publicly distance itself from these incitements. Both points are important when considering the strategic impact of the response. Tying this back to the privateers and pirates, the U.S. government's silence in this case could be read as a signal to activists that it does not consider their activities worth prosecuting or dissuading (despite the publicly announced intent to disrupt someone else's computing networks).

As introduced in Chapter 6, introducing ambiguity over the authorship of an action can be a strategic choice. What the SPE case adds is that this is true not only for the attacking side but also for the defending side. On the attacking side, North Korea never took credit for the GOP's attacks. This left the onus of attribution on the defenders' side. When the FBI first attributed the attacks to North Korea, there was significant backlash from various experts. They received so much disputation that FBI Director James Comey released more details to back up their attribution claim, and Director of National Intelligence James Clapper named General Kim Yong-Chol, the director of the North Korean Reconnaissance General Bureau, as ultimately responsible for giving the go-ahead for the cyberattack against SPE.[100]

However, the U.S. government also inserted ambiguity into their response. They left no doubt that some responses would be unseen but did not discuss whether that would include the DDoS attack. By creating that ambiguity, the U.S. engaged in the same strategy as other actors, leaving open the speculation of why North Korea's internet went down that day. Indirectly, this encouraged the activists, who had incited attacking North Korea, to react the same way in future cyber crises.

Some commentators thought the White House distanced itself from the attacks with the announcement of sanctions on 2 January 2015: 'As the President has said, our response to North Korea's attack against Sony Pictures Entertainment will be proportional, and will take place at a time and in a manner of our choosing. Today's actions are the first aspect of our response'.[101] Those observers read the use of 'first aspect' as signalling the commencement of the official reaction, thereby negating taking responsibility for North Korea's network outage.

However, North Korea publicly blamed their network outage on the United States. The state newspaper reported that 'the U.S., a big country, started disturbing the internet operation of major media of the DPRK, not knowing shame like children playing a tag'.[102] Investigatory reporting by the *New York Times* at the time, and supported in follow-up articles years later, attributed North Korea's internet outage to the Chinese government.[103] For example, an article in December 2016 noted: 'the Chinese even cooperated, briefly cutting off the North's internet connections'.[104]

What features of this case are analogous to mercantile companies, privateers, and pirates?

The SPE case raises questions pertaining to a longer term impact about the responsibilities of responding to cyberattacks: who must respond? When does the state become active? The SPE case highlights a state taking public responsibility of the security of a company hosted in its country. The U.S. government publicly attributed the attacks to North Korea—only a month after the destructive attacks against SPE. This was an unprecedented move. The U.S. government opted to take public political steps to seek retribution for a specific cyberattack.

This stands in stark contrast to the reaction to the Chinese cyberespionage operation against Google four years earlier. In the 2010 Aurora case, the U.S. government commented on the intrusion but did not respond confrontationally. It allowed the Chinese government to save face by referring to it as cyber intrusions that needed a transparent investigation from the Chinese government's side. Whilst it politically rallied on the side of Google, the U.S. government did not officially oppose the Chinese government.

Similarly, in the summer of 2014, the U.S. government had opted to publicly address Chinese cyberattacks against U.S. companies by publicly indicting five People's Liberation Army (PLA) officers for committing commercial espionage.[105] However, they did not launch economic sanctions against China. Rather, the U.S. used the criminal proceedings, as well as the threat of sanctions, as a diplomatic pressure point.

One of the fundamental differences driving the U.S. reaction may have been the strategic intent of the two cyber operations. Whilst Chinese economic espionage threatened the economic well-being of the United States, U.S. leadership discussed the attacks against SPE as a threat to freedom of expression, one of the cherished political values in the United States.[106] NSA Director Admiral Mike Rogers and commander of U.S. Cyber Command summarized his viewpoint of the SPE attack as follows: 'Sony had in some ways encapsulated everything we had seen before. Theft of intellectual property, theft of personally identifiable information, destructive activity, the use of a nation state to use cyber as a coercive tool'. He argued, first, that the government could not ignore it, second, that it must publicly attribute the attack to the threat actor, and, third, that the unintended consequences of doing nothing would be too great. The government worried about sending a permissive signal to other actors (i.e. a non-response would encourage more action). Finally, Rogers was also concerned about the signal sent to the private sector:

> If you're in the private sector, you're a company, you're being—you [are] receiving this attention from another nation state in this case and if the government is not going to do anything, what does this drive the private sector to? Do we start to get under the hack back? Do you get into cyber mercenaries? Do you get into this idea that the private sector believes well if I can't count on the government then I'm going to have to do this myself?[107]

To prevent such a world, he believed that the government was right to take responsibility of the response to the SPE situation. Rogers's highlighting of this point is significant because the need for protection was deemed so high that the governmental actor in charge felt compelled to take action lest the private sector armed itself. Or, read differently, the self-perceived governmental capability by the commander of the U.S. Cyber Command was mature enough that he deemed it appropriate to be used for public response. Precisely what was driving his interpretation, the quality of the threat, or the possibility for response remains unclear. The SPE case marked a transition—the protection and response shift from being provided entirely privately to a more public and political form. In naval history, this mirrors the shift towards navies taking over the protection functions to stabilize trading operations at sea. As was detailed in Chapter 3, in Britain, this happened in the early 18th century when the admiralty and the navy had become a fully-fledged administrative body with the capacity to sustain a fleet roaming the seas worldwide and over some significant amount of time.[108] The Royal Navy's counter-piracy operations in the 1720s could be interpreted as early indicators of this larger process towards the public protection of trade.[109]

In addition to the difference in strategic intent, the difference in time and actors further complicates ascertaining what generated the different outcomes in the Google and SPE cases. Whilst the descriptive case of transition in the supply of protection indicates a difference in time as important, there are also some significant differences between the actors. In contrast to Google, no one expected SPE to be able to respond to a state-driven cyberattack. To the contrary, other subsidiaries of Sony had been the target of cyber operations before and were known to be poorly defended targets. Thus, having the U.S. government accused the North Korean state was a convenient way to shift the blame away from its own responsibility and its inadequate security practices.[110] In contrast to Google, which had an incentive to stay at arm's length from the U.S. government, there was no risk to SPE to be perceived as an arm of the U.S. government. The market of SPE films and other U.S. products in North Korea was small. Hence, there was also not much to lose economically from antagonizing the North Korean government. Thus, it was politically much easier for the U.S. government to involve itself in the response to the attacks against SPE publicly. The issue of public protection for private companies raises questions to consider for further research. In which situations should a state take on a protective role for a foreign subsidiary abroad? How would a home state provide assistance, and how would that involve the local state? To take the SPE example: what would it have looked like if Japan had sent its government response teams to aid Sony? Would the U.S. government have been comfortable with a foreign state providing assistance? What would the scenarios look like if the local (host) government disagrees?

Another element that can be analogized to situations involving pirates and privateers is the calculated strategic ambiguity on both the attackers' and defenders' side. As laid out here, no state ever took credit for the attacks sponsored by North Korea or for the network outages in North Korea.

North Korea's creation of the hacker group the 'Guardians of Peace' introduced an element of deniability to the attack against SPE. This left the onus of public attribution on the defender. This was similar in piratical attacks undertaken by sailors of a specific country. If no one is physically caught, despite the knowledge of who might have been involved, the country itself can deny having authorized the mission whilst agreeing with its result. This raises the question about when a country would publicly claim responsibility. In Elizabethan times, the queen's control of the privateers was very limited. Actions by English sailors abroad could thus often not be directly attributed to a command given by the Crown. Nevertheless, this did not stop the queen from claiming victory in successful operations to bolster her domestic claim of authority, whilst denying involvement or even denouncing the activities in the event of failure. In the case of North Korea, the house of Kim was in a very different position. Contrary to the domestic politics of Queen Elizabeth, who struggled to assert her claim of authority over the operations of the men at sea, Kim's claim to power and control of the operation was not endangered through the mission. On the contrary, given the dictatorial rule in North Korea, claiming that the attacks were 'a righteous deed of the supporters and sympathizers with the DPRK in response to its appeal' and informing the U.S. that 'there are a great number of supporters and sympathizers with the DPRK all over the world as well as the "champions of peace" who attacked the SONY Pictures' may be proof enough for Kim Jong-un's domestic base to claim success in this operation.[111] After all, North Koreans were able to strike the U.S. in its homeland and punish the company who, in the regime's eyes, disrespected its rightful leader.

By its ambiguous messaging about the network outage in North Korea, the U.S. government engaged in the same tactic as North Korea, leaving the attribution open to the victim state. Furthermore, by not discouraging activists from counter-attacking North Korea, it left the possibility open for a non-state-sponsored counter-attack. Silence during a crisis could be regarded as tacit support. This has implications. In naval history, there is a long history of coastal communities engaging in predation at sea. Depending on the strength of the authority of the state, their actions could be rendered legitimate or illegitimate politically, and depending on the capabilities of the state to enforce their authority, their actions could also be controlled. As detailed in the historical Chapter 3, the English state's authority and ability to control actions at sea grew over time. In cyberspace, there is a similar phenomenon with regards to the authority and capacity to control 'coastal' communities, that is, communities harbouring the skilled workforce that can deploy offensive capability through cyberspace. Thus, silence about offensive actions initiated independently by the citizenry weakens a state's claim of control of the activities resulting from its territory. As discussed, this can be beneficial if, by having such activist chatter, the response benefits from the same ambiguity as North Korea used in the attack.

To sum up: the analysis of the attack against SPE revealed several characteristics of the different actors. Most fundamentally, it contrasted the arm's length U.S. governmental response in the Aurora case with the interventionist response in the attacks in the Sony case. Differences were observed in the perceived governmental responsibility to protect a company that could not protect itself. In contrast to the Google case, the SPE case shows how the U.S. government actively deemed the protection of the company as part of its responsibility, while also attempting to prevent corporations from arming themselves. In addition, the response to the attack raised the question of managing independent hackers, who called for a retaliatory strike on North Korea. The case highlighted that strategic ambiguity can be a choice, both on the attacker's and the defender's side, involving similar situations as when, historically, pirates became active in a state's interest.

Signals Intelligence: Cooperative Cyber Mercantile Companies

Whilst the Google and SPE cases focused mostly on the conflict between a government and a corporate actor, this final case study will look at the cooperation between mercantile companies and signals intelligence agencies. Chapter 4 introduced the basics of modern signals intelligence (SIGINT) with regard to digital network intelligence. This case study will zoom in on one aspect of SIGINT, namely, its access to digital information with the cooperation of technology companies. The case will highlight the advantage of an indigenous technology sector to modern signals intelligence and explore how aligning interests between companies and states can be better understood using the concept of the mercantile company.

This case starts with an overview of the modern SIGINT environment with regard to digital data. Two specific instances of collaboration are focused on: sharing data between service providers and governments, and the efforts to weaken encryption standards, both in the context of the Five-Eyes, particularly the United States and the United Kingdom. These two instances of collaboration are of interest, as they are especially well-documented, both with technical and documentary evidence, a rare occurrence in the field of signals intelligence.[112] The shared interest between businesses and governments will be discussed, particularly data collection and storage. To close, an analysis of which historical period the constellation of actors and interests encountered in the signals intelligence space can be best analogized to will be offered.

To appreciate the global importance of the U.S. technology sector, some numbers are illustrative. Apple, Microsoft, Alphabet (formerly Google), Amazon, and Facebook are all in the top ten of the world's largest digital companies—in descending order.[113] All were founded and are headquartered in the United States. In 2019, 4 billion people had internet access globally.[114] A large percentage of those users use services provided by these U.S. technology companies. For example, about half of the global internet users have a Facebook account, and a third use their Facebook account daily.[115] Just under a third of all global users have a Gmail account they use at least once per month (for further statistics see Table 7.1).[116] There are over 1.4 billion Apple devices used globally, with at least 588 million users.[117]

This global user base creates large traffic volumes, most of which is routed through North America. This is represented in global network connectivity, which is still heavily focused on North America.

Table 7.1 Number of users of selected large U.S. technology companies

U.S. tech companies (selected)	Amount of users
Facebook	2.45 billion people, 1.62 billion users per day[a]
Alphabet (formerly Google)	Over 1.5 billion Gmail users per month[b]
Microsoft	1.2 billion office users[c]
Yahoo	1 billion monthly active users[d]
Apple	588 million users (estimate)[e]

Notes:

[a] Facebook, 'Facebook Reports Third Quarter 2019 Results'.

[b] Miller, 'Gmail Now Has 1 Billion Monthly Active Users'.

[c] Microsoft, 'Microsoft by the Numbers', 2016, https://perma.cc/R5X5-CH2S.

[d] BBC, ' "One Billion' Affected by Yahoo Hack', 15 December 2016, https://perma.cc/J566-AJEV.

[e] Leswing, 'Investors Are Overlooking Apple's Next $50 Billion Business'.

In 2015, 83% of used interregional bandwidth was connected to the United States and Canada (and as you can see from the Figure 7.3, the situation has not changed drastically up to 2020).[118] A large part of that bandwidth was used by content providers, such as Google, Facebook, Amazon, and Microsoft, who have become major customers of intercontinental traffic for their internal networks.[119] In 2015, for example, 64% of the transatlantic capacity was used by private networks, and about a third of new capacity is deployed directly by content providers.[120] As reported in 2020, content providers' private network continue to have significant impact on traditional backbone network operators, allowing them to shift their capacity to other locations.[121]

For SIGINT agencies, such large traffic flows pose both an interesting target and a challenge. The Snowden archives have documented the efforts that the Five-Eyes intelligence-sharing partnership spends on accessing these global data flows. Because of the large data flows through the Five-Eyes, and their overseas territories, a significant share of the data can potentially be accessed in their domestic jurisdictions.

The easiest way to gain state access is to compel companies, who handle or own the data, to cooperate. Then director of the U.S. Central Intelligence Agency Michael Hayden described the situation in 2006 in a U.S. Senate Committee Hearing:

> Because of the nature of global communications, we are playing with a tremendous home field advantage and we need to exploit this edge. We also need to protect this edge and those who provide it.[122]

Recalling Palmerston's quote on shaping the law of the seas around norms from which Britain would profit the most, the imperial analogues are noteworthy. In Hayden's view, the nature of global communications was such that the powers who have the best access to the companies supplying global communications gain an advantage. That power, in 2006, was the United States. Thus, Hayden was protecting America's edge. In subsequent legislation, the U.S. Congress followed that logic. It enabled the collection of information from U.S. service providers first in the Protect America Act of 2007 and later in enacting the Foreign Intelligence Surveillance Act Amendments Act of 2008 (FAA). Under FAA Sec.702(h)(1), U.S. electronic communication service providers are compelled to provide the government secret assistance in the acquisition of information on non-U.S. persons located outside the

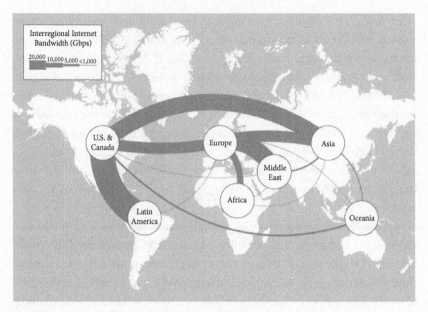

Figure 7.3 Interregional internet bandwidth 2020

Source: Global Internet Geography Report. Global Internet Research Service, TeleGeography, 2020, www.telegeography.com.

Note: Bandwidth is a good proxy for overall traffic. It correlates with pricing, which correlates with total traffic (also due to least-cost-routing algorithms used by telecommunication companies).

United States. They provide assistance both for access to the raw data flow (upstream collection) and to their customers' account data through a programme named PRISM.

The Snowden archives reveal how the U.S. government has compelled various U.S. service providers to cooperate (see Figure 7.4[123]). The PRISM programme gives the NSA (via the FBI) access to internet records stored by service providers (see Figure 7.5[124]). The degree of willingness to cooperate on the service providers' part is unclear and will be discussed later.

Why is this important? The NSA strategy for 2012–2016 referenced the characterization of the current environment as a 'golden age of SIGINT'.[125] The spread of internet technology has made more data accessible about more people than ever before. However, there is a clear trend towards a higher share of the total traffic being encrypted.[126] According to the U.S. director of National Intelligence, the Sowden disclosures had significantly accelerated the trend towards universal encryption.[127] This trend has two consequences.

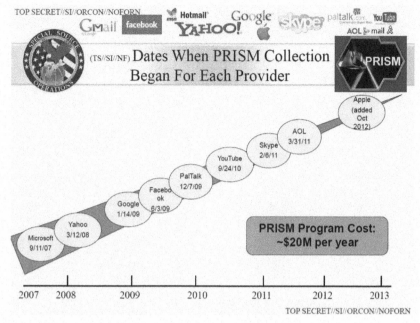

Figure 7.4 Dates of enrolment into the PRISM programme

Source: Slide from the presentation entitled 'PRISM/US-984XN Overview or the SIGAD Used Most in NSA Reporting Overview', National Security Agency: *Washington Post*, 6 June 2013 (dated April 2013).

First, access to content and metadata directly provided by service providers becomes more valuable. This increasing valuation of the PRISM programme was already reflected in the Snowden archives. For example, PRISM was the most cited signals intelligence source contributing to the U.S. president's daily brief in 2012.[128] The programme is used across various targets derived from NSA's strategic mission list.[129]

Second, the NSA adopted countering 'the challenge of ubiquitous, strong, commercial network encryption' into its strategy.[130] Note: the US intelligence community had been trying to undermine the encryption gear of its targets already during the Cold War—and was successful. In one of the largest operations, it took over ownership, together with the German foreign intelligence service, of one of the larger exporters of encryption technology, Crypto AG.[131] However, in the internet era, times had changed: encryption technology became implementable in software and ubiquitous in use. Thus, in part, to make up the loss of its bulk interception capacity (due to loss of visibility and diversification of traffic), the

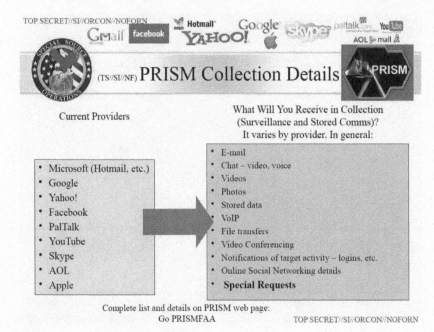

Figure 7.5 PRISM collection details

Source: Slide from the presentation entitled 'PRISM/US-984XN Overview or the SIGAD Used Most in NSA Reporting Overview', National Security Agency: *Washington Post*, 6 June 2013 (dated April 2013).

NSA invested in undermining the encryption systems, as well as broadened its capacity to infect midpoints (i.e. networking gear) and endpoints (end-user devices and servers). In its 2013 budget request, the NSA requested US$250 million for a project labelled 'SIGINT Enabling'. It was described as the following:

> The SIGINT Enabling Project actively engages the US and foreign IT industries to covertly influence and/or overtly leverage their commercial products' designs. These design changes make the systems in question exploitable through SIGINT collection (e.g. Endpoint, MidPoint, etc.) with foreknowledge of the modification. To the consumer and other adversaries, however, the systems' security remains intact. In this way, the SIGINT Enabling approach uses commercial technology and insight to manage the increasing cost and technical challenges of discovering and successfully exploiting systems of interest within the ever-more integrated and security-focused global communications environment.[132]

Among other things, the project suggested (1) to 'influence policies, standards and specification for commercial public key technologies,' (2) to 'shape the worldwide commercial cryptography marketplace to make it more tractable to advanced cryptanalytic capabilities being developed by NSA/CSS' and to 'insert vulnerabilities into commercial encryption systems,' and (3) to collect data 'via cooperative network carriers'.[133] Several instances of how such efforts were successful have been uncovered since 2013, although not all of them have been attributed to the NSA. The following paragraphs explain how this three-step process was likely implemented in collaboration with key U.S. telecommunications and technology companies.

First, the initial reporting on the efforts to undermine encryption standards in a standard issued by the United States National Institute for Standards and Technology (NIST) in 2006 pointed to a dual elliptic curve pseudorandom number generator (named Dual_EC_DRBG). The *New York Times*, *ProPublica*, and *The Guardian* reported jointly:

> Classified N.S.A. memos appear to confirm that the fatal weakness, discovered by two Microsoft cryptographers in 2007, was engineered by the agency. The N.S.A. wrote the standard and aggressively pushed it on the international group, privately calling the effort 'a challenge in finesse'. 'Eventually, N.S.A. became the sole editor,' the memo says.[134]

Whilst the potential of a backdoor was highlighted in 2007, after this new reporting, the exploitability of the weakness in applied cryptographic products (specific Transport Layer Security [TLS] implementations) was demonstrated.[135] Subsequent research into the emergence of this backdoor tied the origin to the NSA.[136]

Second, upon the recommendation of NIST, the backdoored algorithm was implemented by various products providing TLS encryption. In December 2013, Joseph Menn, a Reuters journalist with extensive experience reporting on cyber(in-)security matters, reported on a contract between the NSA and RSA, a major U.S. encryption and network security provider. Menn claimed that 'RSA received $10 million in a deal that set the NSA formula as the preferred, or default, method for number generation in the BSafe software, according to two sources familiar with the contract'.[137] The US$10 million would have been a significant source of revenue for the small BSafe part of the company in 2006. Though spending much money on signals intelligence, US$10 million for one contract was, in 2006, also a significant expenditure for the NSA—their total budget request in SIGINT enabling projects in 2013 was US$250 million.

RSA adopted the Dual EC DRBG in its BSafe suite even before NIST had approved it but emphasized never to have 'entered into any contract . . . with the intention of weakening RSA's products'.[138] In a context in which many other companies who demonstrably did collaborate with the NSA issued similar denials, the veracity of RSA's statement is hard to assess. The details of the contract are unknown, and we do not know how much RSA knew about the backdoor. However, there would have been good reasons for RSA to be more critical of the standard, particularly after the research findings presented by Shumow and Ferguson in 2007.[139] RSA's implementation, combined with NIST's recommendation of using the NSA-provided mathematical points for government certification, created a powerful incentive to adopt this default setting in the corporate world.[140]

Thus, RSA was not the only company impacted by this backdoor. Juniper Networks, another large U.S. computer security company producing corporate network equipment adopted the Dual EC DRBG in 2008. However, in Juniper's case, it was not the adoption of this backdoor that led to the exploitability of their product (which included Virtual Private Network [VPN] functionality). Rather, research undertaken by Checkoway et al. traced a series of changes in the Juniper implementation in 2008 as giving rise to the possibility of exploiting the Dual EC DRBG vulnerability.[141] Interestingly, in Juniper's case, an unknown attacker modified the backdoor in 2012, as disclosed by Juniper in December 2015 (Ben Buchanan quotes two unnamed private sector individuals attributing this change to 'Chinese hackers', Bloomberg named the group to be APT5 based on an internal Juniper document).[142] U.S. Director of National Intelligence James Clapper mentioned this unauthorized change in the source code in his worldwide threat assessment in February 2016, thereby highlighting the danger of such backdoors being abused by a third-party attacker.[143]

Finally, in a third step, the NSA was able to profit from this weakness by spying on global internet traffic. The U.S. ensured this through partnerships, both with other countries' governments and corporations. Partnerships with global telecommunications providers represent 'a large portion' of the NSA Special Source Collection team.[144] For example, AT&T's 'extreme willingness to help' allows elaborate on-the-net operations and integration of active-passive SIGINT.[145]

To summarize this three-step process: first, the U.S. was able to influence cryptographic standards both through its participation in the standards creation process (through NIST) and through contractual agreements with companies (e.g. by allegedly paying RSA for adopting the backdoored random number generator). Second, standard adoption was encouraged through making the backdoor a requirement for getting federal certification and, potentially, through influencing the implementation of it in large network equipment (in the case of Juniper). Third, the exploitation of the backdoor only worked by having global network traffic visibility, and such visibility is enabled in large part through corporate partnerships.

A close look at the Snowden archives reveals that some companies were displaying a much closer degree of cooperation with the state than others. For example, AT&T and Verizon stand out as having NSA's monitoring tightly integrated into their systems.[146] Similarly, in the United Kingdom, BT and Cable&Wireless (a subsidiary of Vodafone since 2012) stand out as having close collaboration with the British signals intelligence agency GCHQ.[147]

The revealed collaborations caused significant media coverage, with many media outlets acting very surprised about the interaction between government and businesses. Had analysts taken the analogy to mercantile companies as a lens of analysis, the surprise would have been unwarranted. To a historically informed analyst, these government-industry partnerships are unsurprising. Many large U.S. telecommunications companies have an institutionalized relationship with the U.S. government. For example, for much of the 20th century, AT&T had held a government-sanctioned monopoly over telephone communications in the United States.[148] The signals intelligence integration of telegraph, telephone, and later internet traffic can be traced back at least to the Second World War. In project Shamrock, after the end of the Second World War, the U.S. government (first the military, later the NSA) sought the cooperation of commercial communications companies.[149] Through this, it secured access to international communications routed over these commercial circuits.[150] Uncovered through an intelligence scandal in the 1970s, involving the NSA spying on Americans, U.S. Congress then passed the Foreign Intelligence Surveillance Act (FISA), creating a court regulating spying by the NSA on people in the United States and American citizens worldwide. According to the counsel of the investigative committee, the companies acted 'out of patriotic reasons' and never received compensation.[151]

Since then, much has changed. However, as detailed in Chapter 4, after 9/11, many companies once again started to cooperate with the U.S. government to enable it to spy on foreign communications.[152] Intelligence historian James Bamford notes: 'By the late fall of 2001, [NSA Director] Hayden succeeded in gaining the secret cooperation of nearly all of the nation's telecommunications giants for his warrantless eavesdropping program,' but this time the NSA paid for the access.[153]

Whilst the U.S. has an advantage in terms of access to service providers (e.g. Alphabet, Amazon, Apple, Facebook, Microsoft, etc.), due to its geographic reach and its historical imperial efforts to shape the global telegraph routes, the United Kingdom has an advantage in terms of access to diverse cable traffic.[154] Cable&Wireless, which emerged out of the imperial network of the telegraph and wireless companies, has a long history of working with the British state (it was both nationalized and privatized in the 20th century).[155] Intelligence historian Richard Aldrich traces the 'tradition of handing over all its [Cable&Wireless'] cable traffic to GCHQ' back to the First World War.[156] According to the BBC's national security correspondent, Gordon Corera, the cooperation between telecommunication companies and the British state was formalized under Section 94 of the 1984 Telecommunications Act.[157] The vast scale of GCHQ's internet traffic interception, with the aid of telecommunications companies, was revealed before the Snowden documents. However, the Snowden archives substantiated the scale of interception further with specific evidence.[158] By 2010, GCHQ claimed to have the 'biggest internet access in the Five Eyes'.[159] GCHQ had also become the biggest real-time storage unit of internet traffic. By 2012, Tempora, GCHQ's internet buffer capability, stored three days of preselected full internet traffic and roughly 30 days of internet metadata.[160] The investment in the Mastering the Internet programme had paid off. GCHQ was providing a capability that outmatched the NSA's storage, and it was trying to keep it that way.[161]

An alignment of corporate and state interests

Up to this point, my analysis of signals intelligence collaboration was at looked via the state—collaborations with large corporations give the state access to information it would not otherwise have access to. The analysis will now turn to examine the comparison to mercantile companies.

The strongest contribution of the concept of the mercantile company is in the management of the relationships to states from the perspective of the companies. The Five-Eyes were aware of the sensitivity of their partnerships. The briefing on cryptanalytic capabilities against network security technologies highlighted that the capabilities 'require a long lead time', 'are very fragile', and, 'if lost, may never be regained'.[162] They include 'CNE, interdiction, industry relationships, collaboration with other IC entities, and advanced mathematical techniques'.[163]

Bruce Schneier, an applied cryptography expert and industry insider, highlighted the mutually constitutive aspects of the political and economic goals:

> Corporate surveillance and government surveillance aren't separate. They're intertwined; the two support each other. It's a public-private partnership that spans the world. This isn't a formal agreement; it's more an alliance of interests. Although it isn't absolute, it's become a de facto reality, with many powerful stakeholders supporting its perpetuation. And though Snowden's revelations about NSA surveillance have caused rifts in the partnership ... it's still strong.[164]

The quote highlights the mercantile aspects of the relationship. Many of the technology companies' business models are built on having interconnected and data-rich business relationships with their consumers. These business relationships generate a large amount of fine-grained data about individual users' lives, which often translates into a better experience for the customer. In their role as security guarantors, governments find these data an attractive target. This case study exemplifies this.

The interest of governments in access to data also stabilizes the viability of the business models.[165] An example of this is the internet freedom agenda that includes not only the freedom of people to connect to the internet but also the freedom from taxation on data and the freedom to move data into different geographical spaces. From the perspective of a mercantile company, lack of taxation and the freedom to move the data lowers transaction costs (i.e. makes it more profitable), whilst, from the perspective of the state, it facilitates overt (as in disclosed to the company) access to the data of the companies' global user base.

However, the analysis of this case study would be insufficient if businesses only featured as long arms of the state. Rather, the lens of the mercantile company allows for the discovery of aspects that exemplify independent agency. For example, the historical East India Company had its own foreign policy with different countries, quite apart from the official government policy in the state of its headquarters. Similarly, in the case of government access to data, companies had independent agency as to the extent of the cooperation they would venture into. They were aware of the sensitivity surrounding their cooperation. Evidence points to some companies being very cooperative with the U.S. government in the response against terrorism after 9/11. Some observers label this cooperation as 'patriotic'.[166]

In the wake of the Snowden disclosures, several companies displayed public outrage at the practices that were uncovered. This can be partially explained as a market strategy. Clearly, many technology companies are competing in the global marketspace and are therefore dependent on international users' trust. Hence, public voicing of their outrage served to work towards the recovery of such trust.

The newly declassified documents after the Snowden revelations allow for a more detailed look into how individual companies cooperated. Yahoo, for example, objected to the initial cooperation order under Protect America Act of 2007.[167] Yahoo's objections are significant. The representations made to the Foreign Surveillance Court of Review consisted of Yahoo claiming that they were being asked 'to participate in surveillance that we [Yahoo] believe violates the Constitution of the United States'.[168] One can speculate about the motivation Yahoo had. But it is significant that they raised concerns about the constitutionality and tried to resist the government's broad interpretation of the governing statute. Yahoo raised its customers' Fourth Amendment concerns—in a secret setting—one in which they could not anticipate a direct publicity benefit from their objection. This rules out a publicity objective. To date, only Yahoo's objections are a matter of public record. It seems likely that, had other large technology companies objected, they too would have had an incentive to appeal to the Foreign Intelligence Surveillance Court for declassification. No such proceedings are currently known.

From early investor to reaping the benefits of monopoly

As outlined in the history chapter, mercantile companies exerted independent agency when framing proximity to the state. Depending on the audience, companies chose to represent their affiliation and status differently. Both in the Aurora and the SIGINT-cooperation cases, similarities to this historic behaviour can be seen. The companies observed chose to represent themselves in different ways in the U.S. and abroad. State proximity of the companies was found to be empirically variable and not uniform across all global technology companies. In the Aurora case, Google thought it was protected by state resources, although it was not. This can be read as a judgement about state proximity from Google's side. In the analysis of SIGINT cooperation, some companies represented themselves as publicly distant when they were privately collaborating with the state.

Amazon, Apple, Google, Facebook, and Microsoft were all founded in the last 50 years. In that time, they have developed from small start-ups into large multinational companies that try to defend their, in some areas monopolistic, market positions. The case study showed that a large share of the global user base generates data within those five companies. Currently, there is a battle for authority between states and companies on who gets access to that data and through what processes access can be gained.[169] The SIGINT case has shown a settlement within the United States starting in the early 2000s, in which companies give the government access to their data for national security purposes. However, they did so in the expectation that the collaboration would stay a secret. In a post-Snowden environment, such collaboration is much harder to sustain. Thus, technology companies have a large interest in publicly distancing themselves from the government to protect their global markets.

From predation to interest in stability

The history chapter captured an important shift from an interest in maritime predation to an interest in trade relations. In the late 17th century, maritime violence still played a large role, but the uncontrolled nature of piracy increasingly became a nuisance to both the state and mercantile companies. Analogizing this process, the modern mercantile companies have not made their own cyber(in-)security affairs of the state. As seen in the case of Google, rather than gaining protection from state resources, the company opted to reinforce its security team. In the case of the SIGINT cooperation, the state profited from access to the data of the companies.

With regard to the historical analogy, this confirms the time period for analogical reasoning in the 17th century when companies were still protecting themselves by investing in protection fleets; although, they also had significant shared interests with their imperial home states. However, in the 17th century, predation and expansion were still major interests of the mercantile companies. They were still capturing new markets by making deals with other sovereigns or by capturing territory by force. Similar interests can be seen today, for example, with regard to the Chinese market, where the biggest companies in the world all have a major stake in expanding their market positions there. As happened historically, the companies chose specific strategies to integrate themselves in the Chinese market. For example, Apple, who strenuously fought the U.S. government against being compelled to provide aid in accessing a dead terrorist's phone, agreed to store Chinese users' data within China and to remove VPN applications, which allowed users to access the internet past the Chinese censorship authorities, from the Chinese AppStore.[170] A political reading of the largest technology companies' interaction with different states has foregrounded varying practices when it comes to providing access to data and thereby has improved our understanding of these companies as political actors of an own kind.

Conclusions and Implications

This chapter applied the conceptual toolkit to probe how it contributes to an understanding of the modern-day mercantile company, and how it changes our understanding of cyber(in-)security. Thereby, I left state proximity as something to be defined, rather than something that is assumed, and detailed the conflicting and cooperative relationships between the different actor types.

The case of the cyberespionage operation against Google has identified the political discourse around the responsibility to protect companies in cyberspace. The analogy to a mercantile company has been applied in multiple ways. The focus on state proximity aided understanding the political conflicts that arose in the Aurora case. It identified the simultaneous conflicts between Google and the Chinese government and the tensions resulting from the perceived proximity to the U.S. government. Furthermore, the case highlighted challenges in recruitment and the risks of corporate offensive cyber operations as analogical to the situations encountered in the 17th century. Importantly, the Google case highlighted how political ideals sometimes shape international corporate actions. Google's reaction in the Aurora case could not be understood without recourse to the political convictions of its founders and managers, especially Sergey Brin's. Being in a powerful position to both lead the operational response and influence the business strategy, it was his conviction against censorship that led to a confrontational response. Thus, using the concept of a cyber mercantile company improved our understanding of Google's actions.

The case of SPE contrasted the Google case. SPE relied on the U.S. government to respond to the attacks against it. Whilst the cases are not completely comparable due to the different nature of the cyber operations (espionage vs. coercion), the different attitudes of both the companies and the U.S. government surrounding the protection of the companies were stark. Whilst the company, SPE, was able to use the state affiliation of the attacker as a claim to absolve itself of the responsibility for its insecure systems, the U.S. government worried about the impact on companies if it was seen not to be protecting them. Linking the case to the discussions in the previous chapter, the case also identified the strategic use of ambiguity by not only attackers but also defenders with regard to their collaboration with non-state actors and the authorship of actions taken.

Finally, in the case of SIGINT cooperation between the large technology companies and the Five-Eyes signals intelligence partnership, the analogy to the mercantile companies was used to better understand the overlapping interest in the fine-grained data and the interest in corporate expansion. Both elements suggested that the analogy is best suited to comparing modern technology companies to 17th-century mercantile companies. Whilst the companies display independent agency regarding their protection and, due to their still expansionary policies, with regard to their representations to various governments, their shared interest with states in terms of access to data introduces a cooperative element to their relationships.

CONCLUSION

Conclusion

This book explored the role of semi-state actors with varying degrees of state proximity in cyber(in-)security. I examined how the historical analogy to mercantile companies, privateers, and pirates can be applied to better understand the analogical actors' links to states in the contemporary cyber domain. The book has advanced the theoretical claim that actors in cyber(in-)security are increasingly exerting agency beyond the control of states and, in so doing, are affecting the security and insecurity of citizens. Whilst this could lead theorists to focus on the radical challengers of the state, the interest of this book is on those actors who collaborate and compete with states at the same time. Their activities, both when cooperating and conflicting with state agendas, are of such importance to cyber(in-)security more broadly that they merit independent study.

The book took a historical perspective that analogizes the modern actors to those of a different domain; specifically, that of the sea in the age of sail between the late 16th and mid-19th centuries. In so doing, the preceding chapters applied the historical analogy to mercantile companies, privateers, and pirates to better understand the roles of semi-state actors with varying degrees of state proximity in cyber(in-)security and explored how such application changes our understanding of cyber(in-)security. Two main research outcomes were attained. Empirically, I showed the degree to which we can usefully analogize the security dynamics on the seas between the late 16th and mid-19th centuries to the dynamics witnessed in cyberspace today. I found that the security dynamics amongst 17th-century naval actors are most helpful to better understand today's cyber(-in)security. Conceptually, I clarified how mercantile companies, privateers, and pirates as thinking tools can disrupt our current understanding of, and generate insights for, cyber(in-)security in areas such as attribution, the constitution of insecurity over time, and the cooperative and competitive dynamics of cyber mercantile companies.

This concluding chapter takes stock of these main insights and assesses their broader implications for the study of international relations. I start by

Semi-State Actors in Cybersecurity. Florian J. Egloff, Oxford University Press. © Florian J. Egloff 2022.
DOI: 10.1093/oso/9780197579275.003.0008

revisiting the main historical analogical claim and then discuss the implications for international security of the three main claims advanced. The book concludes with a discussion of semi-state actors, sovereignty, and the legitimacy of the state and offers an outlook on the further study of non- and semi-state actors in cyber(in-)security and beyond.

Anchoring the Historical Analogy in Time

Chapter 2 laid out the research strategy and set up the conceptual lens on state proximity and the macro-historical process focus. The state-proximity lens suggested to view state-proximity as a continuum, enabling a broad categorization of actors into state, semi-state, and non-state actors. Thereby, mercantile companies were found to be a special type of semi-state actor due to their functional agency that, in some respects, resembles a quasi-sovereign.

The focus on interactive macro-historical processes led to three specific ways of investigating the actors in history. First, as I was interested in state proximity of the actors over time, the question of interest was on how an actor renders itself and is being rendered as proximate to the state. This enabled a sensitivity to processes of authorization, for example, when interrogating the boundaries of someone successfully claiming to be a privateer and how those limits are established between different actors.

Second, with privateering being a speciality of this analogy, a macro-historical process focus meant to enquire into privateering over the long term. This led to the identification of path-dependent policy choices and an analysis of their impact on the relations to and evolution of other actors.

Third, one of the key issues in cybersecurity politics is that much of cyberspace is produced, maintained, and used by private actors. Thus, one of my focuses in the historical research was on how different actors' naval security became an affair of the state (or not), recognizing the fluidity of the legitimacy of the state. How did the actors of interest (pirates, privateers, and mercantile companies) contribute to or prevent making naval security a state task? What resistance was there? How did it tie in with the strategies of the respective actors? Paying close attention to these questions in the different historical time periods allowed me to distil constellations the current cyber(in-)security challenge is best compared with. It also meant to acknowledge the diverse public-private relations that contemporarily exist in different parts of the world, and how those different conceptions lead to security challenges internationally. These three focuses enabled a rich macro-historical picture of how shifts in and between the actor categories of private actors (economic and societal) and the state took place across time. Further, it enabled to contextualize, as well as historically reflect on, the current period in cybersecurity in a way that would not have been possible without such a historical investigation.

Chapter 3 investigated mercantile companies, privateers, and pirates in the context of naval history. Being intrigued by the speciality of privateers and their peculiar connection to states, this historical investigation focused on the changing institution of privateering between the late 16th to the mid-19th centuries. It identified the different constellations of non- and semi-state actors in three different time periods.

The book then briefly explored the history of cyber(in-)security (Chapter 4). Chapter 5 expanded the purview of the analysis to comparing both domains—the sea in the age of sail and cyberspace. Both fundamental similarities and differences of the two domains impact the analogy. Whilst the book shows the merit of the insights that can be generated due to the similarities, the differences contextualize and situate the scope of the analogy. Some differences introduce more rapid interactions between the actors and aggravate the problem of insecurity. In contrast, an increasingly integrated international society and global institutions potentially soften the impact of insecurities by expanding the range of solutions available between states (remember: reprisal was an action of last resort, a breakdown of diplomacy).

Based on the historical comparison of both domains, Chapter 5 found that the late 16th- and late 17th-century periods are superior analogues to cyber(in-)security than the mid-19th-century period. Just like in late 17th century, in cyber(in-)security, despite the investment in state-owned cyber capacities, they are still in their infancy, and their responsibilities for the protection of private cyber assets are still nascent.

Consequently, Chapter 6 and Chapter 7 explored the comparison of cyber pirates, privateers, and mercantile companies to their historical late 16th- and late 17th-century analogues. In a detailed empirical and conceptual application of the analogy, these chapters advanced three main claims about how best to apply cyber pirates, privateers, and mercantile companies to semi- and non-state actors in cyber(in-)security and explore how this changes our understanding of cyber(in-)security. I will now reassess the insights and discuss their implications.

Cyber Pirates and Privateers: Narratives of State Proximity, Attribution, and Emerging Shared Understandings of State Sponsorship

First, the analogical analysis of the contestations in cyber(in-)security with the contestations of piracy and privateering improved our understanding of how state proximity is used politically by attackers and defenders. The application of the analogy to pirates and privateers in the case of Estonia showed that both the attacking and defending governments had significant influence in shaping the public narrative of state proximity. In other words: one person's pirate is another person's privateer. The discursive framing thereby resembled the contestations in the 17th century when lines between privateering and pirates were still blurred. Both offensive and defensive parties had possibilities in legitimizing certain kinds of violence and delegitimising others, and sometimes made a sovereign responsible for the actions of a third party, as evidenced in the case of Captain Kidd and the Mughal emperor's dealings with English piracy.

The contemporary analysis highlighted the multiplicity of Estonian and Russian narratives and showed the resulting strategic ambiguity that uncertainty about the attacker's proximity to the state introduced. The narrative interpretation of the pirate further improved our understanding of the multiplicity of connections to states that illegal hackers may have.

The application of the analogy in the case of Estonia also changed our understanding of cyber(in-)security. By focusing the analysis on public and private attribution it conceptually advanced the analysis of 'state-sponsored' hackers.

The implications of this claim for the analysis of international security are twofold. For one, it encourages a shift of the analysis of attribution in cyber(in-)security from a factual analysis (i.e. is attribution possible and if so how?) to an analysis of the political drivers of public attribution (i.e. what logic drives a government's decision-making to frame its attribution claims?). The book established that the presence of ambiguity in international cyber conflicts leaves large leeway for both defenders and attackers to use it as a political opportunity. In stark difference to the literature on attribution, which mainly highlights the attribution as a problem for defenders in cybersecurity, this perspective illuminates the political opportunities brought by it. Due to the difficulty to attribute, defenders have a large political spectrum to interpret and give meaning to the specific cyber incidents and use it for domestic and international political purposes. Further research should thus analyse the international and domestic drivers of the specific attribution claims advanced.[1] For example: what strategic logics do policymakers apply? And, of special relevance to the international relations analyst, to what degree are international political concerns present in those strategic logics? Regarding the attackers' behaviour, one can note, that non-attribution is not always the goal of a cyber operation. Rather, implausible deniability may represent the new norm, enabling the attacker to contest the attribution claims made by the defenders whilst shirking the political responsibility.[2]

As a second implication, the analogical comparison also highlighted the long process of contestations sovereigns had over the international status, legitimacy, and responsibility of privateers and pirates. Importantly, the formation of these relationships also implicated the formation of statehood, highlighting the fluidity of the legitimacy of the state, but also the stability of some political spaces. The reflection on these processes, using the narratives of piracy as an interpretation aid, led to a better understanding of the type of political processes we are currently going through. The historical analogy suggests that differing interpretations over the legality and responsibility for actions are likely to persist for some time. Whilst the analogical structures to regional regimes of enforcement may form and strengthen (e.g. through the Budapest Convention on Cybercrime in analogy to the Atlantic system of Prize Courts), a global order in analogy to Britain's 19th-century rule of the sea is neither desirable nor in sight. As an implication, the fragmentation into regional structures may be more than a temporary transition period, but rather go together with the move towards a more multipolar international political order.

Further research could also investigate responsibilities arising from specific types of cyber operations. Are there clusters of reactions from states and other actors that are stabilizing the expectations of responses from particular actors after different types of cyber operations? In analogy to the historical crystallization of the pirate and the privateer in the late 17th century, the indications to look for would be increasing agreement on the types of operations deemed attacks against all. For the state system, the UN Open Ended Working Group's (OEWG) 2021 consensus report reaffirming the 2015 UN Group of Governmental Experts (GGE) recommendations shows that some possibilities of such normative consensus is possible, though few norms are universally operative.[3] Perhaps as a consequence of the slow speed of multilateral progress, some states have started to act in coalition to condemn specific operations and assign blame for them on governments (e.g. to North Korea in the case of WannaCry, or to Russia in the case of NotPetya). Such coordinated behaviour may ultimately lead to normative rough consensus on which operations are deemed 'offences against humanity'. This could, for example, be offences that endanger the stability and trust in the very mechanisms that make cyberspace work[4] (a notion that was included in the 2021 UN OEWG report), offences that indiscriminately create effects in global systems (for example destructive worms like NotPetya), or attacks that generate significant negative effects for all of humanity (e.g. attacks against vaccine research during a global pandemic). Just like human espionage is tolerated in the world of states, cyberespionage is here to stay. It is unlikely that any normative consensus against the principle of cyberespionage will emerge. Rather, if cyberespionage is to be reined in normatively at all, it will be the manner of operation (e.g. in the risk mitigations employed).

The global responses thereby are not left only to states. Interesting normative movements also come from cyber mercantile companies, whose reactions to specific operations allow researchers to chart the normative expectations that companies hold towards particular actors in cyberspace.[5] Such normative reactions also show the self-interpretation of these semi-state actors. An example is Microsoft's proposal for a digital Geneva Convention, which seems to show that Microsoft sees themselves as a legitimate steward of a conversation of what states at large ought (not) to be doing. As seen in the history of privateering, a mercantile company's interpretation of piratical action can significantly influence government policy. Further research should thus also pay close attention to their interpretations, as mercantile companies from different parts of the world may find agreement on normative expectations before states do, a route that the Swiss foreign ministry seems to be pursuing in their initiative entitled Geneva Dialogue.

If one accepts this first conclusion, then it has further consequences of how political efforts need to be expended: rather than trying to raise 'accountability' through being more public about a particular attacker's actions, policymakers will need to take a much more comprehensive approach to addressing a particular country's on- and offline actions. The focus on 'cyber' actions in this case obscures the activity's embeddedness in a larger strategic and political context. Thus, rather than trying to shape the 'cyber' actions of a particular state, policymakers will need to build regions that not only align in their interpretations of how to govern cross-border digital offences but also integrate these with market and political logics. Remember: the contestations about regulating privateering and piracy also did not only concern what was permissible at sea. Rather, the contestations also reflected the political struggles about the status and responsibility of the sovereigns (states and mercantile companies). Thus, on the one hand, if it is a political choice to leave cybersecurity to be addressed by cyber mercantile companies, then they need to be held accountable for providing this security. If, on the other hand, states want to assume responsibility for certain aspects of security, then they need to adequately address the (domestic and international) processes of legitimization and authorization they are going to require to step into that role. This will not be a harmonious effort, with lots of parties disagreeing. However, considering the cyber history, each large-scale political incident has changed the political space, slowly advancing the political contestations about responsibility. As an observer, I can counsel that each incident is at once a challenge and an opportunity, not just in the relationship between the attacker and defenders but also, in offering a possibility to reintroduce oneself as an actor assuming responsibility for wider public goods, be that as an international organisation, state, a cyber mercantile company, or even a privateer.

Cyber Privateers: Longevity and Its Effects on State-Capability Building

A second main claim of this book concerns the longevity and path dependencies of historical privateering set ups. They refined our understanding of the constancy and the long-term risks and rewards of state collaboration with cybercriminals. The application of the analogy in three criminal cases highlighted the depth of state-criminal collaborations in terms of their longevity, institutionalization, path dependency, and lack of control. The cases also discussed the secondary effects on recruitment and capability building.

By identifying the drivers stabilizing insecurity across time, this analysis refined our understanding of the difficulty to exit a policy of political cyber-criminal collaboration. The analogy was uniquely placed to make this long-term observation. Partially as a result of the short and patchy availability of cyber(in-)security history, many analyses focus on the newness of cyber(in-)security. In contrast, the analogical claim put forward highlighted the constancy of one aspect of cyber(in-)security studied.

This finding has important implications for the analysis of agency in international security. The analysis of longevity and depth of privateering structures suggests a prolonged period of blurred lines between state, semi-state, and non-state actors. This is an outflow of the two domains' chief characteristic: the availability of skilled personnel is one key constraint driving—both defensive and offensive—capability. Hence, the question that presents itself to all the actors in this space is how to motivate skilled personnel to become active in the respective actor's interest. Thereby, privateering, as a hybrid form of agency, is a particular type of incentive structure, in which one actor (the sovereign/the state/the mercantile company) tries to channel the self-interested capacities to become active in their interest.

The longevity that this entails is of interest for the assessment of cyber(in-)security in the long run. The analogy suggests that states that opt for a privateering structure are likely to experience a lock-in effect, in which a policy change against privateering is associated with much friction (from within parts of the government, the profiting ventures, and the privateers themselves). Due to such lock ins, governments experiencing them will have an interest in legitimizing their own approach internationally, lending further support to the blurred boundaries between governments and semi- and non-state actors. Thus, the clarification between cybercrime and state-supported hacking is unlikely to originate from governments locked in a privateering-like structure.

Since there is overlap in the recruitment of skilled personnel between normal trade and security structures, some interaction between the two is also to be expected. Regions that do not possess enough economic opportunities for skilled personnel can thus be expected to have a higher chance for pirate/privateering-like structures to emerge than regions where the normal economy can absorb skilled personnel. Such interaction was a feature of historical privateering. There was an interaction effect with trade and with piracy both regionally and temporally. Regionally, certain areas that did not generate much economic surplus made a living off piracy (e.g. the buccaneer communities, the Barbary states). Temporally, in times of conflict, trade could absorb less personnel, and a higher share was employed in the navy and privateering business. After conflicts ended, and trade picked up again, some went back to trading, whereas others sought their luck as pirates. Analogizing this situation to Russia in the mid-2000s, one could expect a higher share of highly skilled personnel to have sought their luck within the privateering part of the economy than if Russia had had a strongly growing digital economy offering globally competitive salaries.

To understand the further implications of this conclusion, one can relax the focus on cyber criminality and include other forms of contracting relationships into the purview, particularly those in which private outfits mainly work (offensively) for a state and (defensively) for cyber mercantile companies. In this case, we encounter two issues: a further muddying of private sector-government relationships and political contestations over private offensive authority. The first issue arises from the collaboration states seek to work with skilled personnel (be it militias, volunteers, public-private partnerships, contractors, or army personnel). That skilled personnel may have ample economic opportunity to work in the private sector, potentially selling back their services to the state. The risk of policymakers profiting financially from cybersecurity policies is always linked to this: the job prospects of policymakers and key cybersecurity personnel once they leave governmental employment should be more carefully evaluated. Parties that invested into historical privateering offer one possible understanding as to how governments are persuaded to sanction policies from which both officials and private corporations can profit. Historically, relying too much on privateering-like structures has led to arguments about diluting the state's efforts to build an effective state-owned capability. Thus, in particular in countries like the United States, where contractors in the national security space are the norm and not the exception, an assessment of the long-term effects of the diffusion of skills and capabilities into the private sector is needed. One concern to look at, for example, is how this (perhaps inadvertently) legitimates targeting the U.S. private cybersecurity companies, as it remains unclear to foreign states which companies directly contribute to U.S. government offensive and defensive capabilities. An example of this could, for example, be the targeting of FireEye's red-team tools in the supply chain–based intrusion campaign leveraging SolarWinds in 2020. Particularly actors that rely on privateering-like structures for their offensive capability may be more inclined to mirror image and expect a company with large government contracts, like FireEye, to also be in the business of supplying offensive capability development.[6]

The second issue, contestations over private offensive authority, connects to the literature on private violence. This literature has added the context of the interconnection of state development and normative shifts that have—in Western states—produced a monopoly of violence. The cases of cyber pirates and cyber privateers have contributed to this discussion by demonstrating the absence of a monopoly of offensive action in cyberspace. As previously detailed, offensive action in cyberspace is undertaken by many different types of actors. In the offensive space, different states seem to have varying tolerances for employing non-nationals for generating state used capabilities.[7] Further research could focus on which factors shape a state's willingness to collaborate with foreign actors in the cyber offensive space, and whether this correlates with a collaboration with non-nationals outside of the cyber domain.

The discussion hacking-back has also raised the question about state control over the cyber domain. In the absence of government ability or willingness to protect private actors, some private companies are using offensive measures for their own protection. In the United States, this has led to a policy discussion about legalizing limited offensive measures undertaken by companies, thereby legitimizing a practice that some private actors are already engaged in.[8] More hack-for-hire organizations, such as the Indian outfit aliased Dark Basin, are bound to form as offensive skills proliferate.[9] Theoretically, this strengthens the argument that multiple loyalties and authorities coexist and that states are currently not controlling offensive action in the cyber domain. From a state perspective, this is an unwise situation to tolerate, as it undermines the legitimacy of the state. Thereby, legitimizing private hacking(-back) without state control is, in my view, doomed to fail. As this book has shown at length, the co-presence of private reprisal and international trade makes for a very hostile environment indeed, potentially leading to a downturn in economic activity. Thus, especially for countries deeply embedded in the international trading system, it is a strategically unwise idea. Furthermore, besides the strategic downsides of legitimizing such a practice, it also unlikely to lead to long-term results both for the state and for the private entities. To briefly restate the argument for both actors here: the risk for the state is that it loses control over who will be 'hacked-back' and thereby accumulates risk in other sectors experiencing reprisals by the attacked country. The risk for the private entity is that it may not have the context whom it is dealing with, inviting further attacks on itself. For the vast majority of corporations, it remains unclear what commercial sense, beyond a feeling of having 'retaliated', such hack-back is supposed to serve, as it is unlikely to dissuade attackers from pursuing their aims through a counter-offensive. Only few cyber mercantile companies thereby will have, what international relations would call, escalation dominance over a subpart of the offensive actors. Instead, my counsel is to motivate states to assume both those duties and risks.

Moreover, states could go further to regulate this offensive market. Evidence of abuse of commercially supplied offensive cyber capabilities is growing. As of now, states seem to be the main buyers of those capabilities. Perhaps, just as states, industry, and civil society came together to generate the Montreux Document (and triggering the following International Code of Conduct as well as the International Code of Conduct Association) to clarify the responsibilities of Private and Military Security Companies (PMSCs), the offensive security supplier market seems ripe for a similar initiative.

Cyber Mercantile Companies: From Strategies of Expansion to Strategies of Monopoly

The third main claim of the book is that the application of the analogy to mercantile companies has sharpened the focus on how their cooperative and conflictive relations to states, and practices of self-protection, influence cyber(in-)security. The historical investigation identified strategies of expansion and monopolization, examined how companies used their state association strategically, and selectively framed this association depending on their relationships with other states. Thus, whilst at-home mercantile companies were perceived as a specific type of domestic polity, abroad they chose self-representations ranging from mere traders to sovereigns.

In the contemporary analysis of the Google and Sony Pictures Entertainment (SPE) cases, the book used the focus area of self-protection of private companies and analogized it to the transformation in the protection offered by the English state starting in the late 17th century. The Google case detailed how a private company retaliated against a government. In the case of SPE, it used the publicity generated by a state actor to distract from its inability to defend itself. By 2014, the U.S. government had built up capabilities and evolved its understanding of its public duty to protect the private sector from specific threats. Historically, the form of shared rule between the sovereign and the companies licensed by the sovereign shifted over time. Thus, the reading of this process as a process of state transformation generated insights for the way the state accommodates and integrates other powerful actors domestically and expands its influence abroad.

The third case, focusing on signals intelligence (SIGINT), explored how cyber mercantile companies provide states with access to data, which the state, on its own, could not have collected. The SIGINT case thus analogized the cyber mercantile companies to the historical ones of the 17th century, who pursued expansionary policies and displayed independent agency both towards their home government and abroad. States thereby create an enabling environment for the mercantile companies to flourish. Their relationship represents a symbiotic alliance between different types of polities.

This third claim changes our understanding of cyber(in-)security in treating large technology companies as international political actors of an own kind. Using the mercantile company lens drew out imperial practices of expansion, reflected in their submission to other rulers, the integration into other systems, and the renegotiation of responsibilities and control at home.

The mercantile company lens impacts our assessment of international security. Due to the importance of the private sector in both owning and securing the cyber domain, the private sector's prominence in the political debate of cyber(in-)security is ensured. The politicization of cyber(in-)security moved the debate, first, from entirely private decisions about corporate and individual insecurity to a public debate about wider insecurities generated by the cyber domain. In a second step, there is now a further politicization from the public sphere towards the governmental sphere, contesting the extent of state authority and responsibility in protecting private assets.

Cyber mercantile companies are key political actors, not just domestically, but internationally, as they can authoritatively contribute to such political contentions, due to their multi-jurisdictional spread, large size, and technical competency. Their alliances and conflicts with states vary across time. As seen in the historical analogy, the expansionist phase of the mercantile companies was followed by a monopolistic phase of consolidation. The cyber domain is still expanding. The analogy suggests that cyber mercantile companies are in the latter part of the expansionist phase. Thus, I would still expect cyber mercantile companies to have a major stake in gaining access to new markets and to embedding themselves into local systems of rule. The more infrastructure and services are provided by cyber mercantile companies, the more they will use their political power to advocate for their authority in making autonomous security claims to defend their monopolistic enterprises. At the same time, as the connectivity of societies deepens, the common stake in higher levels of security generated by companies also rises. Thus, in a global trading system, the incentives for more cooperative, jurisdictionally compatible solutions, could also be expected to rise.

Conversely, from a state perspective, as the dependence on cyber mercantile companies becomes more apparent, difficult national security challenges present themselves, with limited durable solutions available.

The current debate around 5G telecommunication networks and its supply chain illustrate that well. The overlap of the political challenge posed by a rising, state-capitalist-oriented and increasingly authoritarian China, the economics of the technology with Huawei being a cheap and capable supplier, and the context of a liberalized telecommunications market in Western democracies make the rollout of 5G a particularly vexing national security challenge. Thereby, the political conflict between the United States and China has already accelerated efforts to unbundle technology supply chains. The U.S. export control measures targeting Huawei may delay Huawei's roll-out of 5G but also predictably accelerates the Chinese efforts to reduce dependence of the Chinese ICT sector on U.S. software and hardware. A complex interplay between politics and economics, addressing particularly these cyber mercantile companies, is here to stay.

There are two elements in addressing these problem complexes: one is the overarching requirement to have a long-term strategy of how to manage and develop the political relationships to other states, especially a rising China and a United States in a multipolarizing world. In this context, cyber(in-)security is just one of many aspects of an overall relationship. Perhaps, the level of hostile activity in the cyber area, including privateering against a specific other power, can be seen as a temperature measurement of latent political conflict, which states are currently unwilling to go to war over but are not able to resolve diplomatically. Thereby, the unlikely but important national security risks emanating from embedding a foreign mercantile company into one's critical national infrastructure concern mostly the war scenario. In particular, they concern the impacts that would arise when the possibility of war rises, and one has to expect as a consequence that at the outset of conflict the telecommunications networks may become unavailable.

The other overarching national security judgement is how to manage the risk of the political relationships deteriorating faster than dependencies can be reduced. Thus, one requires pragmatic policies to address the supply-chain challenges. One pertains to reducing the dependency on any one cyber mercantile company. An enabling solution reducing dependency (i.e. lock in) is mandating interoperability of suppliers in the same sector, so that the cost of switching is reduced. The goal is to build a common set of standards and incentivize knowledge and production capacities in various parts of the world, so that access to technology is not used as political leverage. Another way to address dependency is to only create dependencies commensurate with the rest of the economic and political context, that is, if one is going to build dependencies, ensure the counterparty also carries value and risk from that dependency. Indeed, some of the data localisation requirements could be read that way: states are starting to force companies to at least have some assets within geographical borders, thereby giving them something to hold at risk.

Overall, the risk of further technological and political fragmentation is a challenge not just for states wanting to interact with both China and the United States but also for the mercantile companies wanting to be able to sell to as many markets as possible. To preserve their long-term room for man-oeuvre, they would be well advised to advocate a strategic policy of enabling neutral, open, interoperable, transparent, and secure technology stacks. Coupled with a commitment to strong data protection, the European states may be well placed to lead such an effort.

Semi-State Actors, Sovereignty, and the Legitimacy of the State

In the introduction, I raised the debate about the status of cyber(in-)security in international relations and its relationship to semi- and non-state actors. The insights generated can directly speak to the arguments about whether cyber(in-)security presents a fundamental challenge to the system of states or whether it is much ado about nothing. The challenger side argues that technological progress has changed the opportunities for revolutionary states and non-state actors to such a degree that systemic and systems change became more likely.[10] On the other side, the sceptics of the 'cyber revolution' hold that technological change has empowered states—the traditional mas-ters of the international system—to an even greater degree, reinforcing the state-centric paradigms of international relations.[11]

Both sides find merit for their claims in the empirical observation of the politics of cyber(in-)security today. Not submitting to either side of the de-bate fully, the semi-state lens has shed light onto the interaction of unconven-tional actors with states, without a need for an ex-ante theorization of either their revolutionary capacity or their insignificance. Rather, and this was the pathway chosen here, the intellectual merit lies in the middle of these two options. Neither demonstrating the insignificance of non-state actors nor the underlining of the novel revolutionary political actor attaining primacy in the international system was the main interest, but the semi-state actors both collaborating and competing with states.

This is important, as there is still a lack of knowledge and concepts describing a domain in which much of the offensive and defensive security is still largely privatized. Thus, delivering accessible and poignant conceptual tools to better understand recent and future developments is a key contribution of the book.

The semi-state actor concept enables nuance when it comes to analysing power dynamics between different states and cyber mercantile companies and privateers. State proximity as the relevant classifier brings mercantile companies and privateers in the same semi-state actor category. State proximity is crucial, as it allows for the conceptual classification of actors that coexist alongside states but are distinct from those that actively threaten the state system. Some of the actors observed profit from their state proximity by gaining stable operating conditions. Whilst the state cannot fully control them, it is able to shape the boundaries of the activities undertaken. Thus, state proximity is an important characteristic when theorizing a hacker's ability to generate independent effects over time.

State-like functional agency thereby differentiates between the two semi-state actor types: the mercantile company and the privateer. While a mercantile company in some respects acts as a semi-sovereign (or company-state), privateers are fully dependent on the grey space being made available to them by larger political actors. Taken together, the concept of a mercantile company provides a historically informed lens into how sovereign actions change over time, how states adapt and are shaped by domestic and foreign power-houses cyber mercantile companies represent. And in reverse: it provides a more thorough lens to look at state use of cyber mercantile companies than, for example, a 'proxy' lens could have given us. It is precisely this symbiotic nature involving both conflict and alignment of interest at the same time that generates the added value of the historical perspective. Through it we recognise, it is not just the state that shapes mercantile companies, but mercantile companies that shape the state, including its state-society relations. Thus, the political contentions of what sovereignty and statehood means, what states' roles are, and the what the semi-state actors' roles are, are not just a historical phenomenon but fundamentally characterize the political contentions we see today.

As an example, the pirate/privateer distinction, as well as the politics that historically informed it, enable a superior understanding of the rhetoric states employ when publicly attributing state-sponsored intrusions. The book has shown that using an awareness of such historical actors and their links to private offensive and defensive capacities to understand the narratives constructed generates a novel understanding of cyber(in-)security. I encourage scholars to use such insights to generate new knowledge, for example about the current politics of public attribution.[12]

The insights also have implications for the neo-medievalist literature as well as Joseph Nye's treatment of non-state actors in the cyber domain. The book contributes to Hedley Bull's notion of new medievalism in that it takes historical redescription seriously.[13] Thus, it brought to the fore a new conceptual toolset and language to address the state–semi-state linkages. The analysis undertaken allows for a reassessment the restoration of private violence, the analogy of multinational companies to the East India Company, and the effects of a unified technology across the planet. Hedley Bull concluded that private violence was mainly motivated by a longing for statehood. Without judging whether this is the case today, the phenomena observed in this book are certainly not classified as a struggle for statehood.[14] Neither the hackers who attacked Estonia nor the cyber operation against Yahoo can be read as a claim for independent statehood. Rather, criminal and political motivations overlap. They are more complicated phenomena that can be interpreted under the wider category of political conflict but would be missed in a purely state-centric analysis.

Bull's contention that the ability of states to deny multinational corporations' access, or restrict their activities, was still found to be valid for large states. The Aurora case confirmed China's ability to deny access to a very large corporation. Further research could consider whether and how smaller states can restrict their activities in the same way. However, the claim that, for the running of their operations, multinational corporations are dependent on security provided by states, is invalidated with respect to the cyber domain's mercantile companies. Up to the time of writing, states have not (comprehensively) provided security: the SPE case being the exception rather than the rule, and even there, it is at least debatable whether the government response instilled more trust in government or rather further eroded the legitimacy of government as a useful actor for private sector defence. Most large technology companies still provide their own cybersecurity. What is more, the provision of cybersecurity to individuals is also predominantly in corporate hands.

Finally, the impact of a unified technology on political integration is still unclear. The technology companies observed in this book have their own audiences: they are authorities of their own kind. It is yet unclear to what degree their security claims will continue to clash with governments' security claims or whether durable settlements between them will be found. At least for the time being, there are contentions about who is the right authority to protect private assets in the cyber domain. For states to hold a legitimate claim to the governance of security in cyberspace, they need to be perceived as adding value to the security provision. The political challenge is significant, particularly if done whilst at the same time expanding the offensive operational remit of the state. This is a space where much policy innovation, pragmatism, and humility are needed.

Nye's work on power diffusion provided a theoretical motivation to analyse 'non-state' actors more closely. The research of the analogy both evaluates a claim made by Nye and provides greater detail to how non- and semi-state actors are linked to states. The book provided evidence that in the cyber domain, non- and semi-state actors can exert significant influence over international events, as evidenced in the case of Estonia.

I showed how particular semi-actors are linked to states. Nye argued that cyberspace alters state sovereignty, just as town markets changed sovereignty in feudal times. In Nye's words, cyberspace creates 'new wealth, new coalitions, and new attitudes'.[15] The book detailed this change. It brought forth actors that share the stage with states and change them. The pirate, privateer, and mercantile company lenses developed allowed for a detailed discussion about how they feature in the international debate of legitimate cyber actions and how they change particular states. Recall, the contention about the state connection of the pirate in the early 17th century was precisely such a process. The (sometimes weak) sovereignty claims of different sovereigns (e.g. the United Provinces or the Barbary pirates) were politically debated with regard to their ability to sponsor privateers. In this process of contention, the definition of the privateer and pirate changed, as well the authority claim of what it means to be a sovereign state. Thus, the legal and political rendering of violence at sea served as a point of contention for elaborating broader changes in the interpretation of state sovereignty.

Today, the legal and political cyber pirates and privateers serve a similar, yet also a slightly different, function. Whilst some states use semi- and non-state actors as resources, others are in the process of trying to impose costs on such usages. The construction of particular narratives about how to govern transborder hacking, be they cybercriminal or state-sponsored political hacking narratives, reflects different political judgements about the usefulness of keeping non-state originated acts of hacking at a distance or drawing them into the realm of state versus state interaction (i.e. politicizing them internationally). Thus, the difference with the debates about the legitimacy of pirates and privateers in the early 17th century is that today's debate is about the status of the actors and the responsibilities of the sovereigns, whilst the fundamental sovereignty claim of states is not called into question (i.e. no state uses cyber to defend its claim of being a sovereign state).

Some states were found to be severely affected by such unconventional actors. In the case of Estonia in 2007, it found itself on the receiving end of an attack conducted largely by non- and semi-state actors. Yet, the Estonian government brought a state responsibility claim against Russia. On the opposite side, Russia's President Putin implied uncontrollability of hackers, thereby trying to absolve the state from responsibility. Thus, this shows, not only a world of unconventional actors colliding with certain states but also, increasingly, these actors being a point of contention in interstate interactions.

What is even more poignant, with regard to Nye's town markets, is that the analysis of cyber mercantile companies has brought to the fore new wealth, with new coalitions, and new attitudes. Thus, each cyber mercantile company has emerged in a particular political context and is positioning itself with differing degrees of state proximity. The current international political contention about how to get cyber mercantile companies to cooperate more closely with states or keep foreign mercantile companies from gaining too much influence over one's own society and networks shows the power such companies hold. If they were not as powerful, states would just legislate their preferred solution. Rather, some governments struggle to convince their citizens, who, in the case of the large consumer-facing technology companies, have a personal relationship to these companies that governments are not making cyberspace more insecure through their actions. Thus, at least in some states, governments have not attained the legitimacy to decide on the politicised issue of cyber(in-)security.

The book then assessed an argument about the two global realms of action in the cyber domain: an international set of relations between states and global interactions between various types of actors, including not only states but also global companies and transnational groups with the capability of carrying out independent offensive actions.[16] The two conceptual realms were found to be interacting. This book went beyond the two-part categorization between private and state actors to capture the phenomena of interest. Rather, the semi-state actors observed are of such importance to understanding cyber(in-)security that a more nuanced conceptual framework, based on the spectrum of state proximity, enabled the capturing of the diversity of relations to states.

The actors observed have considerable power in influencing their relationships to states. Sometimes they take actions that are impossible for states to ignore so that their actions become a matter of the state. States then decide on how to interpret their actions, sometimes raising them into the realm of interstate relations. The risks emanating from this clash between the two worlds are plentiful—some of them were detailed in the empirical chapters. However, what the analogy also showed was that these actors also serve as transmission belts for interstate relations. A mercantile company, not formally a part of a state's organs, can generate a wealth of interaction between the host government and the home government. They need not be conflictual—mercantile companies can also act as stabilizing forces. To the degree that we can read technology companies as such transmission belts, they strengthen Joseph Nye's claim of the transformation of states themselves and challenge the utility of the conceptual distinction between the two international realms. When these semi-state actors possess the authority over managing their own security judgements (both offensively and defensively), they start performing important functions in the international (state) system. Cyber mercantile companies claims about proper state conduct thus show how they see themselves as legitimate stakeholders to shape the debate of sovereign responsibility. To the degree that this leads to change of states' conduct, they are indeed the new wealth that has built new coalitions and as a result changed states. Future research could thus further unravel the conceptual and theoretical conundrums that this empirical analysis of the transformation of sovereignty has offered.

Bringing the Claims Together

The claims advanced in this book give a deep insight into the global politics of cyber(in-)security. We have seen that those politics look most similar to the macro-historical processes observed in the 17th century, when state structures were growing and governments of the day had to cope with the newly formed powerhouses called mercantile companies. Over the time span of two centuries, thereby, the mercantile companies grew and gradually became more integrated into state structures. Thereby, these semi-state actors carried important weight in the discourse on what sovereignty and statehood means. Through this grappling between these semi-state actors and states, responsibilities for naval security gradually became an affair of the state.

Similarly, today the technology industry is undergoing a process of re-negotiating authorities over the control of data and over the adjudication of just and unjust action in cyberspace. In so doing, it is inextricably linked to money and power. Their negotiations with both home governments and governments abroad shows the careful balance they must strike between appearing as 'mere merchants' in some spaces, whilst using their positions of power as quasi-sovereigns in others. Sovereignty claims about who controls action in cyberspace are contested; security provision for actors in cyberspace is still mainly a private affair. Cyber mercantile companies are actively claiming semi-state actor roles, shaping the still fluid political spaces, thereby contributing to a contestation around what statehood means in the digital realm.

The case studies gave some insight into how much power is diffused when considering offensive cyber action: highly skilled smaller actors can still produce significant effects.

Pirates and privateers were the pioneers of their time. Through their experimenting, they shaped the outcome of how a global empire was experienced, both by the dominators and by the dominated. However, as the history of Captain Kidd showed, pirates' and privateers' powers were limited. They were powerful in that they were the masters of their profession, quick to find investors and allies, and often acting in conjunction with politicians and large companies. However, their power was limited, as the boundaries over the legitimacy of their actions were often policed by others, masters of more powerful interests than their own. Thus, narratives of how to interpret their actions were, in a large part, shaped by governments and mercantile companies, who were able to police the boundaries of who gets to be labelled an 'enemy of mankind' and who will become a hero of the state.

Today, these opportunities and risks are present again. Hackers, the masters of the new technologies of insecurity in cyberspace, have found allies in governments and investors. The expansion of global technology companies has once again brought opportunities and risks to companies and individuals involved. Thereby, some governments have opted to attract talent in giving them relatively free rein in earning an income derived from their offensive skills—outside of performing their duties for the state. Historically, this led to a lock-in effect in policymaking, where moving away from such a system is much harder than entering it. Consequently, I would expect to see similar path dependencies to be operative today, some of the indications of which having been documented in this book.

As a result of the alliance between companies and states, however, civil society worldwide has suffered, particularly parts of it that were already weak and oppressed.[17] Just as mercantile companies of the past had a vast influence over how the process of expansion took place, and whose power structures they reinforced or challenged, today's cyber mercantile companies have a major moral stake in guiding the spread of technology worldwide and how its insecurities are used and abused for processes of influence and control. As seen in the historical chapter, the reconfiguration of the state-economy relationships is not a unidirectional process. Mercantile companies can make themselves heard in the corridors of state power, their choices over shaping the technological and social spaces thereby reflecting both the opportunities and limits of state reach. Indeed, we once again see how mercantile companies become active in enabling and constraining the offensive actions of others. For example, Microsoft, Google, and Facebook all have reported on their efforts to counter adversarial activity using their platforms, both by states and by cyber privateers.[18] In some ways, their influence is even more foundational than on the seas: in cyberspace the cyber mercantile companies are increasingly the terrain through which cyber operations take place. As such, the companies own part of the responsibility for the dire effects such operations can have on people worldwide.[19]

Emerging Trends and Outlook

We are currently witnessing a double transformation of cyberspace. First, the strategic use of cyberspace by states is growing rapidly, driven by the potential for the advantage it promises. Second, cyberspace itself is growing rapidly in terms of both users and devices, rendering societies more interconnected than ever before, and magnifying the impact that fundamental insecurities of digital products and services have on individuals, companies, and states. The combination of these two transformations renders the problems of insecurity in cyberspace more acute.

The analogy establishes grounds for both optimism and pessimism. On the pessimistic side, structural insecurity abounds. The pirate and privateer phenomena were observed to have inherent drivers stabilizing their own existence. Change should not be expected to come swiftly. Similarly, cyber mercantile companies are renegotiating their rights and responsibilities, with potentially large consequences for individual users. As shown in the Google and SIGINT cases, the cyber mercantile companies are pushing their own political agendas and are not shying away from offensively defending their interests or collaborating with states when deemed necessary. Through insecure products and services, cyber mercantile companies continue to produce fundamental insecurity in societies, with no clear legal or political accountability in sight. Finally, the actions of cyber mercantile companies remain relatively opaque to observers outside of them.

On the optimistic side, while the age of pirates and privateers may adequately capture some of the (in-)security dynamics present in the current environment, this need not be the future. Countervailing trends exist. Cybersecurity is becoming more important to all stakeholders. Even actors profiting from the cyber *insecurity* of their adversaries have a growing interest in more defensible cyber infrastructures and platforms. And, whilst investments in personnel and changes of incentive structures to build more secure products and services will offer the best long-term hope for a more secure environment, in their absences in the short and medium term, actors' investments into better technologies can spread swiftly and improve security for all.

The cyber mercantile companies need not be a menace either. Their inventions and investments make the world more globally connected; their existence in-between the world of states opens spaces for change in the international political system. Examples might be their political resistance to excessive government surveillance or their insistence on globally compatible jurisdictional solutions to cyberspace, curtailing some states' extraterritorial ambitions. Furthermore, some cyber mercantile companies' investments into privacy-preserving communication technologies, in practice, may protect some of the fundamental human rights more effectively than the UN Declaration of Human Rights.

States remain the main actors in the cyber domain, but they share this domain with others, including the semi-state actors observed in this book. The common practice of labelling them 'non-state' actors obscures their interlinkages with the current international political system. This book offered a new way to witness the transformation of the current international political system by zooming in on these linkages and introducing the concept of the semi-state actors. By doing so, it enlightened the international political contentions about state-sponsored actors, the political reconstitution of the state-criminal nexus in cybercrime, and cyber mercantile companies' role in and contribution to the international politics of cyber(in-)security.

A Note on Sources

The research uses Wikileaks and the Snowden Archives as archival sources.

Wikileaks Archives

Out of the Wikleaks archives, the Wikileaks Public Library of U.S. Diplomacy and the Sony Archives are used. A subset known as 'Cablegate' are used from the former. Chelsea Manning is the source of 'Cablegate,' that leaked circa 250,000 U.S. State Department cables to Wikileaks. Most of these documents fall within the time span between 2004 and 2010 and represent a sub-sample of the total U.S. diplomatic cables sent in that period (2.4 million).[1] They only encompass those diplomatic cables marked SIPDIS (i.e. the ones deemed worthy to be shared with users of SIPRNET, a classified network for sharing secret information mainly with Department of Defense users).[2] Independent statistical analysis, based on the message resource numbers of the cables, corroborates the witness statements given at Manning's trial and increases confidence in this assessment.[3] Since the analysis performed in this book uses these documents as evidence, the caveat of other diplomatic reporting possibly outlining a different narrative exists. However, where a narrative persists throughout multiple documents from various embassies, it is unlikely that the narrower distribution channel's narrative (e.g. State Department internal) would completely diverge. The authenticity of the documents is to be judged as high. Not a single case of forgery has been reported in that data set, and the U.S. government prosecuted Chelsea Manning for the release of the documents, confirming the authenticity of at least some of the documents. The original dataset was redacted by Wikileaks. Following the release of the decryption key in 2011, the unredacted data set is now available for research. Comparison of the two data sets for the documents used has indicated that the redactions solely concerned people who may have been at risk from the publication of the documents. This increases the confidence in the authenticity of the archive, as no political censorship was found.

The following documents from the Wikileaks Public Library of U.S. Diplomacy are cited in this book:

Estonia: Demonstrators Quit Estonian Embassy as Ambassador Returns to Tallinn, 4 May 2007, Diplomatic cable from the U.S. Embassy in Moscow, No. 07MOSCOW2065_a, Wikileaks Public Library of U.S. Diplomacy, Wikileaks, https://perma.cc/LHZ5-GCFP.

Estonia's Cyber Attacks: Lessons Learned, 6 June 2007, Diplomatic cable from the U.S. Embassy in Tallinn, No. 07TALLINN374_a, Wikileaks Public Library of U.S. Diplomacy, Wikileaks, https://perma.cc/3ABQ-6J7D.

Estonia's Cyber Attacks: World's First Virtual Attack against Nation State, 4 June 2007, Diplomatic cable from the U.S. Embassy in Tallinn, No. 07TALLINN366_a, Wikileaks Public Library of U.S. Diplomacy, Wikileaks, https://perma.cc/CC35-NBCM.

Google Claims Harrassment by Chinese Government, 12 July 2009, Diplomatic cable from the U.S. Embassy in Beijing, No. 09BEIJING1957_a, Wikileaks Public Library of U.S. Diplomacy, Wikileaks, https://perma.cc/XS3P-ZV6H.

Google Update: PRC Role in Attacks and Response Strategy, 26 January 2010, Diplomatic cable from the U.S. Embassy in Beijing, No. 10BEIJING207_a, Wikileaks Public Library of U.S. Diplomacy, Wikileaks, https://perma.cc/L2WS-SAR8.

Russian Bear Hug Squeezes Estonian Economy, 29 May 2007, Diplomatic cable from the U.S. Embassy in Tallinn, No. 07TALLINN347_a, Wikileaks Public Library of U.S. Diplomacy, Wikileaks, https://perma.cc/F383-N7JQ.

Secretary's Internet Freedom Speech: China Reaction, 25 January 2010, Diplomatic cable from the U.S. Embassy in Beijing, No. 10BEIJING183_a, Wikileaks Public Library of U.S. Diplomacy, Wikileaks, https://perma.cc/6VZB-W4DM.

The Sony Archives contain documents and emails stolen from Sony Pictures Entertainment (SPE). According to the U.S. government, the documents were stolen by hackers under the direction of the North Korean government (see case study). SPE is in the business of producing movies and is a U.S. subsidiary of the Japanese corporation Sony. So far, no forgeries were reported in this data set. The emails observed further indicated authenticity, as various copies of emails are concurrently present (multiple recipients). Additionally, the full headers of the emails allow one to verify that they were cryptographically signed by the respective domain owners (DKIM), which further enhances trust into their authenticity.

The following email from the Sony Archives is cited in this book:

> Notice to Sony Pictures Entertainment Inc., 21 November 2014, Email from 'God'sApstls' (dfrank1973.david@gmail.com) to five Sony executives, Email ID 83432, Sony Archive, Wikileaks, https://perma.cc/6YB5-DVMY.

Snowden Archives

In June 2013, Edward Snowden, a contractor for the National Security Agency, leaked a large cache of documents to two journalists (Glenn Greenwald and Laura Poitras). The total number of documents is in dispute. At the upper end, the worst-case analysis by the U.S. government claims that Snowden removed 1.5 million documents sourced from two classified networks, NSANet and JWICS (both cleared at Top Secret/Sensitive Compartmented Information). The documents referred to in this book as sourced from the 'Snowden Archives' are documents that were previously released into the public domain by journalists. Because the documents were released in support of stories written by journalists, they are scattered around the world and hosted online by various news organizations. Sometimes, one organization would release a part of the document, whilst another would release a different part. This makes piecing together the source documents a tedious task that requires much contextual knowledge.

Some online repositories have sprung up to facilitate the task. Three websites are worth mentioning. 'IC off the Record' maintains one of the most complete timelines of the Snowden leaks, as far as can be verified. Two other websites, one operating in support of the leaker (edwardsnowden.com), the other operated by the Canadian Journalists for Free Expression (cjfie.org), host better indexed and searchable versions of Snowden documents.

One problem encountered is that of multiple leakers. There is enough evidence pointing to other leakers having been active since 2013 to shed doubt on the sourcing of a subset of the documents released into the public domain.[4]

I judged the documents used to be authentic. As far as I know, none of the documents in the archives I examined were identified as forgeries. However, to interpret the meaning of the documents, a deep contextual knowledge of the SIGINT organizations producing them is required. This was acquired by reading up on the histories of these organizations, reading and listening to contextualization offered by the officials making public representations (e.g. in congressional hearings), reading oversight reports, speaking to practitioners, and familiarizing myself with the legal frameworks governing the activities.

The following leaked documents are cited in this book:[5]

'Analytic Challenges from Active-Passive Integration', S324, National Security Agency: Der Spiegel, 28 December 2014, https://perma.cc/H7K8-JCUE.

'Bullrun Classification Guide', Government Communications Headquarters: The Guardian, 6September 2013 (Dated: 16 June 2010), https://perma.cc/BK74-QG3Q.

'Bullrun Col—Briefing Sheet', Government Communications Headquarters: Der Spiegel, 28 December 2014, https://perma.cc/DL6X-EDB3.

'Bullrun Presentation', Government Communications Headquarters: Der Spiegel, 28 December 2014, https://perma.cc/2X7W-BDYE.

'BYZANTINE HADES: An Evolution of Collection', NTOC, V225, National Security Agency: Der Spiegel, 17 January 2015 (Dated: June 2010), https://perma.cc/H79D-PMXA.

'Chinese Exfiltrate Sensitive Military Technology', National Security Agency: Der Spiegel, 17 January 2015, https://perma.cc/LW4W-R7ZQ.

'Computer Network Operations—SIGINT Enabling Project', National Security Agency: Pro Publica, 5 September 2013, https://perma.cc/U7EZ-SSFZ.

'CSEC SIGINT Cyber Discovery: Summary of the Current Effort', Cyber-Counterintelligence, Communications Security Establishment Canada: Der Spiegel, 17 January 2015 (Dated: November 2010), https://perma.cc/JQ3V-K4TK.

'Hackers Are Humans Too—Cyber Leads to CI Leads', Communications Security Establishment Canada: The Intercept, 2 August 2017, https://perma.cc/Y6TS-DCG5.

'Iran—Current Topics, Interaction with GCHQ', S2E4, Iran Division Chief, National Security Agency: The Intercept, 10 February 2015 (Dated: 12 April 2013), https://perma.cc/E4XS-X3XR.

'Network Shaping 101', National Security Agency: The Intercept, 28 June 2016, https://perma.cc/PKM5-QWVB.

'PRISM (US-984XN) Expanded Its Impact on NSA's Reporting Mission in FY12 Through Increased Tasking, Collection and Operational Improvements', National Security Agency: Henry Holt and Company, 13 May 2014, https://perma.cc/8QRE-NEZ5:111.

'PRISM/US-984XN Overview or the SIGAD Used Most in NSA Reporting Overview', National Security Agency: Washington Post, 6 June 2013 (Dated: April 2013), http://www.washingtonpost.com/wp-srv/special/politics/prism-collection-documents/.

'SID Today: '4th Party Collection': Taking Advantage of Non-Partner Computer Network Exploitation Activity', National Security Agency: Der Spiegel, 17 January 2015 (Dated: 2008), https://perma.cc/X85G-7NGW.

'SID Today: Digital Network Exploitation (DNE), Digital Network Intelligence (DNI) and Computer Network Exploitation (CNE)', Deputy Director for Data Acquisition, National Security Agency: The Intercept, 10 August 2016 (Dated: 16 July 2003), https://perma.cc/W9K4-ZSHG.

'SIGINT Mission Strategic Plan FY 2008–2013', National Security Agency: New York Times, 2 November 2013 (Dated: 3 October 2007), http://www.nytimes.com/interactive/2013/11/03/world/documents-show-nsa-efforts-to-spy-on-both-enemies-and-allies.html.

'SIGINT Strategy 2012–2016', National Security Agency: New York Times, 23 November 2013 (Dated: 23 February 2012), https://perma.cc/3NEH-SGDH.

'SSO Corporate Portfolio Overview', National Security Agency: New York Times, 15 August 2015 (Dated: 2012), https://perma.cc/WEB2-PZR4.

'Tempora—News', Government Communications Headquarters: Der Spiegel, 18 June 2014 (Dated: May 2012), https://perma.cc/Z6ML-X54V.

'Transgression Overview for Pod58', S31177, National Security Agency: Der Spiegel, 17 January 2015 (Dated: 7 February 2010), https://perma.cc/HMD3-7DTS.

'Turbulence—Apex Active/Passive Exfiltration', S32354, T112, National Security Agency: Der Spiegel, 28 December 2014 (Dated: August 2009), https://perma.cc/DTZ9-DA5X.

'Turbulence—Turmoil VPN Processing', National Security Agency: Der Spiegel, 28 December 2014 (Dated: 27 October 2009), https://perma.cc/5U2N-BJZD.

'Tutelage 411', NTOC, National Security Agency: Der Spiegel, 17 January 2015, https://perma.cc/5NWD-TDVV.

'United States SIGINT System January 2007 Strategic Mission List', National Security Agency: New York Times, 2 November 2013 (Dated: January 2007), http://www.nytimes.com/interactive/2013/11/03/world/documents-show-nsa-efforts-to-spy-on-both-enemies-and-allies.html.

Acknowledgements

This book is the result of many years of research and thinking and many stimulating conversations. Particular thanks go to Lucas Kello, Corneliu Bjola, and Richard Harknett, who encouraged me to transform my research findings into a book.

I have grown as a scholar by engaging with Thomas Biersteker, Aaron Brantly, Dennis Broeders, Ian Brown, Nathan Canestaro, Rodrigo Carvalho, Myriam Dunn Cavelty, Jamie Collier, Sadie Creese, Alex Darer, Ronald J. Deibert, Neil MacFarlane, Oliver Farnan, Miguel Gomez, Emily Goldman, Stephanie Hofmann, Andy Hogan, Dominic Johnson, Rob Johnson, Monica Kaminska, Keith Krause, Alexander Leveringhaus, Ariel E. Levite, Jon Lindsay, Jonathan Lusthaus, Andrew Martin, Lennart Maschmeyer, Tim Maurer, Lilly Pijnenburg Muller, Joseph Nye, George Perkovich, Thomas Rid, Joshua Rovner, David Sanger, James Shires, Max Smeets, Timo Steffens, Katerina Tertychnaya, Claire Vergerio, Greg Walton, Michael Warner, Andreas Wenger, and JD Work. Without you, I would not have written this book.

Countless government officials, analysts, business leaders, policymakers, and members of the intelligence and the wider security community have given me their feedback and assessments of the phenomena I study. I value your input, feedback, and exchange.

Archives and libraries are what makes research possible. Thank you to the supportive library staff at the Bodleian Library, the British Library, the National Archives, and the ETH Library. Thank you to the Earl of Clarendon for the permission to use and quote from the Clarendon Archives. Thank you also to Sadie Creese, whose keen attention to and promotion of my work led to the forwarding of my work to the Lord High Admiral, HRH The Duke of Edinburgh—a special honour for any project involving British naval history.

Thank you to TeleGeography for the permission to use their charts. And thank you to the online communities involved with tracking and tracing new documents.

This research was only possible due to the financial support of the Clarendon Fund, an institution the University of Oxford is rightly proud of. Special thanks also to Pembroke College, whose partnership award enables the Clarendon Fund to support even more students. Thanks also to the Centre for Doctoral Training in Cyber Security and the Department of Politics and International Relations at the University of Oxford for contributing to my research. Lastly, the Center for Security Studies at ETH Zürich provided an optimal environment to write this book.

Thank you to my editors at Oxford University Press for an enriching collaboration throughout the book project.

And finally, thank you to my family, who lovingly supported me throughout this project, and who, show me every day what's important in life.

Zurich, October 2021

Notes

Chapter 1

1. John Scott-Railton, Adam Hulcoop, Bahr Abdul Razzak, Bill Marczak, Siena Anstis, and Ron Deibert, 'Dark Basin: Uncovering a Massive Hack-for-Hire Operation', Citizen Lab, 2020.
2. Joseph S. Nye, Jr., *The Future of Power*, 1st ed. (New York: PublicAffairs, 2011), 151.
3. These and further questions revisit a 'new medievalism' lens raised by Hedley Bull over 40 years ago. See Hedley Bull, *The Anarchical Society: A Study of Order in World Politics* (London: Macmillan, 1977), 254–66. Before him, Arnold Wolfers had alluded to the new medievalism analogy in 1962 but dismissed these 'novel developments, which deserve theoretical as well as practical attention' since the 'traditional problems of intersovereign relations, predominant for the last four centuries, continue to occupy the center of the political stage'. See Arnold Wolfers, *Discord and Collaboration: Essays on International Politics* (Baltimore: Johns Hopkins Press, 1962), 242. The new medievalism frame is part of a larger body of literature questioning the adequacy of state-centric research paradigms in a world that is increasingly populated by influential semi- and non-state actors and where the categories of the public/private are very diverse, with significant security implications. See Julia Costa Lopez, 'Political Authority in International Relations: Revisiting the Medieval Debate', *International Organization* 74, no.2 (2020).
4. Gabriella Coleman, *Hacker, Hoaxer, Whistleblower, Spy: The Many Faces of Anonymous* (London: Verso, 2014); Maura Conway, 'Reality Check: Assessing the (Un)Likelihood of Cyberterrorism', in *Cyberterrorism: Understanding, Assessment, and Response*, ed. Thomas M. Chen, Lee Jarvis, and Stuart MacDonald (New York: Springer, 2014); Nigel Inkster, 'Chinese Intelligence in the Cyber Age', *Survival: Global Politics and Strategy* 55, no. 1 (2013); Gartzke and Lindsay, 'Weaving Tangled Webs: Offense, Defense, and Deception in Cyberspace', *Security Studies* 24, no. 2 (2015); Jon R. Lindsay, 'The Impact of China on Cybersecurity: Fiction and Friction', *International Security* 39, no. 3 (2015); Jon R. Lindsay, Tai Ming Cheung, and Derek S. Reveron, *China and Cybersecurity: Espionage, Strategy, and Politics in the Digital Domain* (New York: Oxford University Press, 2015); Lior Tabansky and Isaac Ben Israel, *Cybersecurity in Israel*, Springer Briefs in Cybersecurity (Cham, Switzerland: Springer, 2015); Ben Buchanan, *The Hacker and the State: Cyber Attacks and the New Normal of Geopolitics* (Cambridge, MA: Harvard University Press, 2020; Richard J. Harknett and Max Smeets, 'Cyber Campaigns and Strategic Outcomes', *Journal of Strategic Studies* (2020); Joshua Rovner, 'Cyber War as an Intelligence Contest', War on the Rocks, 16 September 2019, https://perma.cc/B4HS-4YAF; Robert Chesney, Max Smeets,

Joshua Rovner, Michael Warner, Jon R. Lindsay, Michael P. Fischerkeller, Richard J. Harknett, and Nina Kollars, 'Policy Roundtable: Cyber Conflict as an Intelligence Contest', *Texas National Security Review* (2020); Jon R. Lindsay, 'Cyber Conflict vs. Cyber Command: Hidden Dangers in the American Military Solution to a Large-Scale Intelligence Problem'. *Intelligence and National Security* 36, no. 2 (2020).

5. Proxy relationships can describe some, but not all, of the phenomena evaluated in this book. A limitation of the research on proxy actors is that it often conceptualizes the relationship as one-sided and often assumes a fixed actor identity (e.g. state or non-state). The best treatment of the subject is Tim Maurer, *Cyber Mercenaries: The State, Hackers, and Power* (Cambridge: Cambridge University Press, 2018). See further Jamie Collier, 'Proxy Actors in the Cyber Domain: Implications for State Strategy', *St Antony's International Review* 13, no. 1 (2017); Tim Maurer, '"Proxies" and Cyberspace', *Journal of Conflict and Security Law* 21, no. 3 (2016).

6. For an examination of the domain analogy, see Jordan Branch, 'What's in a Name? Metaphors and Cybersecurity', *International Organization* 75, no.1 (2021).

7. Janice E. Thomson, *Mercenaries, Pirates, and Sovereigns: State-Building and Extraterritorial Violence in Early Modern Europe*, Princeton Studies in International History and Politics (Princeton: Princeton University Press, 1994). Interestingly, while Thomson's narrative highlighted the idiosyncrasies of the process of eradication of private violence, she was unable or unwilling to expand beyond a Weberian notion of the modern state, see Jeremy Larkins, 'Book Review: Janice E. Thomson, *Mercenaries, Pirates, and Sovereigns: State-Building and Extraterritorial Violence in Early Modern Europe*', *Millennium—Journal of International Studies* 24, no. 2 (1995). Thomson's work has been usefully reevaluated in Alejandro Colás and Bryan Mabee, *Mercenaries, Pirates, Bandits and Empires: Private Violence in Historical Context* (London: C Hurst & Co., 2010). On mercantile companies, see in particular Andrew Phillips and J. C. Sharman, *Outsourcing Empire: How Company-States Made the Modern World* (Princeton: Princeton University Press, 2020), building on the insights of Philip J. Stern, *The Company-State: Corporate Sovereignty and the Early Modern Foundation of the British Empire in India* (Oxford: Oxford University Press, 2011).

8. Hendrik Spruyt, *The Sovereign State and Its Competitors: An Analysis of Systems Change*, Princeton Studies in International History and Politics (Princeton: Princeton University Press, 1994).

9. A point aptly made in Anna Leander, 'From Cookbooks to Encyclopaedias in the Making: Methodological Perspectives for Research of Non-State Actors and Processes', in *Researching Non-State Actors in International Security: Theory and Practice*, ed. Andreas Kruck and Andrea Schneiker (Milton Park, Abingdon, Oxon; New York: Routledge, 2017). See further, Michael C. Williams, 'The Public, the Private and the Evolution of Security Studies', *Security Dialogue* 41, no. 6 (2010).

10. Brandon Valeriano and Ryan C. Maness, *Cyber War Versus Cyber Realities: Cyber Conflict in the International System* (New York: Oxford University Press, 2015).

11. See, e.g., Lucas Kello, *The Virtual Weapon and International Order* (New Haven: Yale University Press, 2017).

12. See, e.g., Keith Krause, 'Critical Theory and Security Studies: The Research Programme of "Critical Security Studies"', *Cooperation and Conflict* 33, no. 3 (1998); Keith Krause and Michael C. Williams, *Critical Security Studies: Concepts and Cases* (London: UCL Press, 1997). More recently, a group of scholars has extended the original questioning of theoretical claims to methodological approaches. See Claudia Aradau et al., *Critical Security Methods: New Frameworks for Analysis*, New International Relations (London: Routledge, Taylor & Francis Group, 2015).

13. Simon Dalby, 'Contesting an Essential Concept: Reading the Dilemmas in Contemporary Security Discourse', in *Critical Security Studies: Concepts and Cases*, ed. Keith Krause and Michael C. Williams (London: UCL Press, 1997), 13.

14. Krause, 'Critical Theory and Security Studies'.

15. Further terminological explanations are *cyberattack* is understood as the 'use of code to interfere with the functionality of a computer system for a political or strategic purpose' (Lucas Kello, 'The Meaning of the Cyber Revolution: Perils to Theory and Statecraft', *International Security* 38, no. 2 (2013), 19). Thus, the term cyberattack captures the intentional use of cyberspace to achieve a political or strategic goal by bringing about the effects achieved through cyberspace. This is to be distinguished from *cyber espionage*, which penetrates a computer system for the purpose of exfiltrating data (Kello calls this cyber exploitation, see Kello, 'The Meaning of the Cyber Revolution', 20). Distinguishing the two is important, as cyber espionage, even if done at a large scale, will generally not pass the threshold of an act of war. This is different for cyberattacks. Cyberattacks that 'amplify or are equivalent to major kinetic violence' can be captured by the term *cyberwar* (Nye, 'Nuclear Lessons for Cyber Security?', *Strategic Studies Quarterly* 5, no.4 [2011]). So far, no cyberattack has produced the physical destruction or loss of life so as to be classified by the victim state as an act of war (though one might argue that Stuxnet, a sabotage operation affecting the uranium-enrichment centrifuges in Natanz, could have been classified by the Iranian government as an act of war). To describe these activities below the threshold of war, one could use the umbrella term *cyber conflict*. Cyber conflict, which occurs below the threshold of war, yet outside the normally agreed activities of peaceful conduct, has also been labelled as a state of 'unpeace' (Kello, *The Virtual Weapon and International Order*, 77–78). This book is interested in cyber conflict below the threshold of war, including measures that fall into the state of 'unpeace'.

16. Attribution generally refers to the process of establishing the authorship and responsibility of an action to a particular entity.

17. Nye, *The Future of Power*.

18. Nye, *The Future of Power*, 118.

19. Nye, *The Future of Power*, 122.

20. Note that the category of 'private' actors is, of course, one that changes its meaning across the historical period observed. See, e.g., Patricia Owens, 'Distinctions, Distinctions: "Public" and "Private" Force?', in *Mercenaries, Pirates, Bandits and Empires: Private Violence in Historical Context*, ed. Alejandro Colás and Bryan Mabee (London: C Hurst & Co., 2010).

21. For very short analogical examinations, see Robert Axelrod, 'A Repertory of Cyber Analogies', in *Cyber Analogies*, ed. Emily O. Goldman and John Arquilla (Monterey, CA: Naval Postgraduate School, 2014), 108; Peter W. Singer and Allan Friedman, *Cybersecurity and Cyberwar: What Everyone Needs to Know* (New York: Oxford University Press, 2014), 177–80. Focused on cyberwarfare, see J. Laprise, 'Cyber-Warfare Seen through a Mariner's Spyglass', *Technology and Society Magazine, IEEE* 25, no. 3 (2006). For privateering as a policy option, see Michael Lesk, 'Privateers in Cyberspace: Aargh!', *Security & Privacy, IEEE* 11, no. 3 (2013).

22. Davis B. Bobrow, 'Complex Insecurity: Implications of a Sobering Metaphor: 1996 Presidential Address', *International Studies Quarterly* 40, no. 4 (1996): 436.

23. Betz and Stevens, 'Analogical Reasoning and Cyber Security', *Security Dialogue* 44, no. 2 (April 2013): 147–64, 147; George Perkovich and Ariel Levite, eds., *Understanding Cyberconflict: Fourteen Analogies* (Washington DC: Georgetown University Press, 2017).

24. Noah Shachtman and Peter W. Singer, 'The Wrong War: The Insistence on Applying Cold War Metaphors to Cybersecurity Is Misplaced and Counterproductive', Brookings, 15 August 2011, [Blog], https://perma.cc/SCC5-NW4Y.

25. The three time periods were selected based on the secondary historical literature.

Chapter 2

1. 'Analogy', in *Oxford English Dictionary Online* (Oxford: Oxford University Press, 2017).

2. For a summary and overview of important studies in the field of cognitive psychology, see Dedre Gentner and Linsey A. Smith, 'Analogical Learning and Reasoning', in *The Oxford Handbook of Cognitive Psychology*, ed. Daniel Reisberg (Oxford: Oxford University Press, 2013).

3. George Lakoff and Mark Johnson, *Metaphors We Live By* (Chicago: University of Chicago Press, 1980).

4. Theodore L. Brown, *Making Truth: Metaphor in Science* (Urbana: University of Illinois Press, 2003), 12.

5. Paul A. Chilton, *Security Metaphors: Cold War Discourse from Containment to Common House*, Conflict and Consciousness (New York: Peter Lang, 1996), 409; Richard Little, *The Balance of Power in International Relations: Metaphors, Myths, and Models* (Cambridge: Cambridge University Press, 2007), 35.

6. David Bohm and F. David Peat, *Science, Order and Creativity* (London: Routledge, 1988), 102.

7. Deibert, 'Exorcismus Theoriae: Pragmatism, Metaphors and the Return of the Medieval in IR Theory', *European Journal of International Relations* 3, no. 2 (1997): 170.

8. Roger Tourangeau, 'Metaphor and Cognitive Structure', in *Metaphor: Problems and Perspectives*, ed. David S. Miall (Brighton: Harvester, 1982), 17.

9. Donald A. Schön, 'Generative Metaphor: A Perspective on Problem-Setting in Social Policy', in *Metaphor and Thought*, ed. Andrew Ortony (Cambridge: Cambridge University Press, 1979); Little, *The Balance of Power in International Relations*; Richard H. Brown, 'Social Theory as Metaphor: On the Logic of Discovery for the Sciences of Conduct', *Theory and Society* 3, no. 2 (1976).

10. Michael P. Marks, *The Prison as Metaphor: Re-Imagining International Relations* (Oxford: P. Lang, 2004); Michael P. Marks, *Metaphors in International Relations Theory* (Basingstoke: Palgrave Macmillan, 2011); Little, *The Balance of Power in International Relations*.

11. Martin Hollis and Steve Smith, *Explaining and Understanding International Relations* (Oxford: Clarendon Press, 1990).

12. Marks, *The Prison as Metaphor*, 167.

13. Emphasis in original, Marks, *Metaphors in International Relations Theory*, 195.

14. Closely related, see Deibert's explanation of Richard Rorty's 'therapeutic redescription'. Deibert, 'Exorcismus Theoriae', 180–83.

15. On usefulness as a criterion see also Ulrich Franke and Ralph Weber, 'At the Papini Hotel: On Pragmatism in the Study of International Relations', *European Journal of International Relations* 18, no. 4 (2011).

16. By using this conceptual form of argument, the book engages in 'explaining what'. See Alexander Wendt, 'On Constitution and Causation in International Relations', *Review of International Studies* 24, no. 5 (1998): 110–13; William Dray, '"Explaining What" in History', in *Theories of History*, ed. Patrick L. Gardiner (London: Collier Macmillan, 1959).

17. Deibert, 'Exorcismus Theoriae', 183.

18. Robert W. Cox, 'Social Forces, States and World Orders: Beyond International Relations Theory', *Millennium—Journal of International Studies* 10, no. 2 (1981): 129.

19. This mirrors Patricia Owens observations of how actors are rendered 'public' or 'private'. See Patricia Owens, 'Distinctions, Distinctions: "Public" and "Private" Force?', in *Mercenaries, Pirates, Bandits and Empires: Private Violence in Historical Context*, ed. Alejandro Colás and Bryan Mabee (London: C. Hurst, 2010).

20. Kornprobst, 'Comparing Apples and Oranges?', 33.

21. Kornprobst, 'Comparing Apples and Oranges?', 33–34.

22. Kornprobst, 'Comparing Apples and Oranges?', 34.

23. Kornprobst, 'Comparing Apples and Oranges?', 34.

24. Kornprobst, 'Comparing Apples and Oranges?', 34.

25. Kornprobst, 'Comparing Apples and Oranges?', 34.

26. Halvard Leira, 'Political Change and Historical Analogies', *Global Affairs* 3, no. 1 (2017).

27. David J. Betz and Tim Stevens, 'Analogical Reasoning and Cyber Security', *Security Dialogue* 44, no. 2 (2013); Myriam Dunn Cavelty and Reimer A. Van der Vlugt, 'A Tale of Two Cities: Or How the Wrong Metaphors Lead to Less Security', *Georgetown Journal of International Affairs* 16 (2015); Sean Lawson, 'Putting the "War" in Cyberwar: Metaphor, Analogy, and Cybersecurity Discourse in the United States', *First Monday* 17, no. 7 (July 2012); Helen McLure, 'The Wild, Wild Web: The

Mythic American West and the Electronic Frontier', *Western Historical Quarterly* 31, no. 4 (2000); Constantine J. Petallides, 'Cracking the Digital Vault: A Study of Cyber Espionage', *Inquiries Journal/Student Pulse* 4, no. 4 (2012), https://perma.cc/J6NT-7359.

28. Betz and Stevens, 'Analogical Reasoning and Cyber Security', 157–59.

29. For an examination of the domain analogy, see Jordan Branch, 'What's in a Name? Metaphors and Cybersecurity', *International Organization* 75, no.1 (2021).

30. Whilst the domain qualifies as a commons, security in it, analytically, was not always nor is presently a global public good. See Alex Gould, 'Global Assemblages and Counter-Piracy: Public and Private in Maritime Policing', *Policing and Society* 27, no. 4 (2017).

31. Tim Stevens, *Cyber Security and the Politics of Time* (Cambridge: Cambridge University Press, 2016), 129. Stevens persuasively argues that policymakers are not just ignorant of history (and hence, they do not just need to be taught more history) but that they also use analogies to aid their policymaking and decision-making processes. Stevens's opponents in this argument are Yuen Foong Khong, *Analogies at War: Korea, Munich, Dien Bien Phu, and the Vietnam Decisions of 1965* (Princeton: Princeton University Press, 1992); Richard E. Neustadt and Ernest R. May, *Thinking in Time: The Uses of History for Decision-Makers* (London: Collier Macmillan, 1986).

32. J. Laprise, 'Cyber-Warfare Seen through a Mariner's Spyglass', *Technology and Society Magazine, IEEE* 25, no. 3 (2006): 29.

33. Laprise, 'Cyber-Warfare Seen through a Mariner's Spyglass', 31.

34. Michael Lesk, 'Privateers in Cyberspace: Aargh!', *Security & Privacy, IEEE* 11, no. 3 (2013). For an example of advocating for the private sector in the U.S. to be given letters of marque, analogizing the privateers as a solution to the pirate problem, see Michael Tanji, 'Buccaneer.Com: Infosec Privateering as a Solution to Cyberspace Threats', *Journal of Cyber Conflict Studies* 1, no. 1 (2007).

35. Robert Axelrod, 'A Repertory of Cyber Analogies', in *Cyber Analogies*, ed. Emily O. Goldman and John Arquilla (Monterey, CA: Naval Postgraduate School, 2014), 108; Peter W. Singer and Allan Friedman, *Cybersecurity and Cyberwar: What Everyone Needs to Know* (New York: Oxford University Press, 2014), 177–80.

36. Noah Shachtman and Peter W. Singer, 'The Wrong War: The Insistence on Applying Cold War Metaphors to Cybersecurity Is Misplaced and Counterproductive', Brookings, 15 August 2011, [blog], https://perma.cc/SCC5-NW4Y.

37. A similar time focused on is Matteo G. Martemucci, 'Unpunished Insults—the Looming Cyber Barbary Wars', *Case Western Reserve Journal of International Law* 47, no. 1 Spring (2015).

38. B. Nathaniel Garrett, 'Taming the Wild Wild Web: Twenty-First Century Prize Law and Privateers as a Solution to Combating Cyber-Attacks', *University of Cincinnati Law Review* 81, no. 2 (2013); Paul Rosenzewig, 'International Law and Private Actor Active Cyber Defensive Measures', *Stanford Journal of International Law* 50 (2014); Scott Shackelford and Scott Russell, 'Risky Business: Lessons for Mitigating Cyber Attacks from the International Insurance Law on Piracy', *Minnesota Journal of International Law* 24, no. 1 (2015).

39. See, e.g., Thomas Dullien, 'Piracy, Privateering . . . And the Creation of a New Navy', keynote speech presented at the SOURCE Conference, Dublin, May 2013; Davi Ottenheimer. 'Eventually Navies Take Over', 11 February 2015 [blog], https://perma. cc/VU35-B6ZC; Christopher Ford. 'Here Come the Cyber-Privateers', Science and Technology, 19 July 2010 [blog],https://perma.cc/XE8S-J2TJ.

40. Halvard Leira, 'Political Change and Historical Analogies', *Global Affairs* 3, no. 1 (2017).

41. The following paragraphs on the risks of using the analogy were originally developed for Florian Egloff, 'Cybersecurity and the Age of Privateering', in *Understanding Cyberconflict: Fourteen Analogies*, ed. George Perkovich and Ariel Levite (Washington, DC: Georgetown University Press, 2017).

42. A development various scholars have warned about, see, e.g., Jonathan Zittrain, '"Netwar": The Unwelcome Militarization of the Internet Has Arrived', *Bulletin of the Atomic Scientists* 73, no. 5 (2017); Myriam Dunn Cavelty, 'The Militarisation of Cyber Security as a Source of Global Tension', in *Strategic Trends 2012*, ed. Daniel Möckli (Zürich: Center for Security Studies, ETH Zurich, 2012); Myriam Dunn Cavelty, 'Breaking the Cyber-Security Dilemma: Aligning Security Needs and Removing Vulnerabilities', *Science and Engineering Ethics* 20, no. 3 (2014); Myriam Dunn Cavelty and Florian J. Egloff. 'Hyper-Securitization, Everyday Security Practice and Technification: Cyber-Security Logics in Switzerland'. *Swiss Political Science Review* 27, no. 1 (2021).

43. Ronald J. Deibert, *Reset: Reclaiming the Internet for Civil Society* (Canada: House of Anansi Press, 2020); see also Ronald J. Deibert, 'The Geopolitics of Cyberspace after Snowden', *Current History* 114, no. 768 (2015).

44. Ersel Aydinli, 'Assessing Violent Nonstate Actorness in Global Politics: A Framework for Analysis', *Cambridge Review of International Affairs* 28, no. 3 (2015); Krause and Milliken, 'Introduction: The Challenge of Non-State Armed Groups', *Contemporary Security Policy* 30, no. 2 (2009): 202–20; Mulaj, 'Introduction: Violent Non-State Actors: Exploring Their State Relations, Legitimation, and Operationality', in *Violent Non-State Actors in World Politics*, ed. Kledja Mulaj (New York: Columbia University Press, 2010); Robert Mandel, *Global Security Upheaval: Armed Nonstate Groups Usurping State Stability Functions*, Stanford Security Studies (Stanford: Stanford University Press, 2013).

45. Although there is some debate about the level of violence computer code can incur as well as whether it can be considered a weapon. A good starting point for this debate is found in Thomas Rid, *Cyber War Will Not Take Place* (London: Hurst, 2013). For a perspective of violence in information ethics see Luciano Floridi, *The Ethics of Information* (Oxford: Oxford University Press, 2013). For my view, see Florian J. Egloff and James Shires, 'The Better Angels of Our Digital Nature? Offensive Cyber Capabilities and State Violence', *European Journal of International Security*, forthcoming. doi: 10.1017/eis.2021.20.

46. Aydinli, 'Assessing Violent Nonstate Actorness in Global Politics'.

47. Recent historical research shows that in the 17th and early 18th centuries, the companies could also be classified as non-state actors with respect to their autonomy

from the home government. See, e.g., Philip J. Stern, *The Company-State: Corporate Sovereignty and the Early Modern Foundation of the British Empire in India* (Oxford: Oxford University Press, 2011). This debate will be picked up in Chapter 3.

48. 'Privateer', in *The Oxford Companion to Ships and the Sea*, 2nd edition, ed. I. C. B. Dear and Peter Kemp (Oxford: Oxford University Press, 2006), https://perma.cc/5G2V-P5U2. In maritime history, privateer can also refer to a person who is engaged in privateering.

49. 'Pirate', in *Oxford English Dictionary Online* (Oxford: Oxford University Press, 2017).

50. Kello, 'The Meaning of the Cyber Revolution: Perils to Theory and Statecraft', *International Security* 38, no. 2 (2013): 36–37; idem, *The Virtual Weapon and International Order* (New Haven: Yale University Press, 2017), 12–13.

51. For arguments regarding case selection see the section 'Methodology' in the Introduction. For an extensive discussion of the case selection, see Florian J. Egloff, 'Cybersecurity and Non-State Actors: A Historical Analogy with Mercantile Companies, Privateers, and Pirates', DPhil Thesis, University of Oxford, 2018.

52. Jörg Friedrichs and Friedrich Kratochwil, 'On Acting and Knowing: How Pragmatism Can Advance International Relations Research and Methodology', *International Organization* 63, no. 4 (2009): 718.

53. Here I am using 'Google' as it was used at the time, denoting the entire corporation. The corporation has since restructured into a holding company named Alphabet, only one division of which is now called 'Google'.

54. Costa Lopez, 'Political Authority in International Relations: Revisiting the Medieval Debate', *International Organization* 74, no. 2 (2020).

55. Dunn Cavelty, Myriam, and Florian J. Egloff. 'The Politics of Cybersecurity: Balancing Different Roles of the State', *St Antony's International Review* 15, no. 1 (2019).

Chapter 3

1. This chapter draws on and refines arguments originally introduced in Florian Egloff, 'Cybersecurity and the Age of Privateering', in *Understanding Cyberconflict: Fourteen Analogies*, ed. George Perkovich and Ariel Levite (Washington, DC: Georgetown University Press, 2017).

2. Paul M. Kennedy, *The Rise and Fall of British Naval Mastery* (London: Penguin, 2004).

3. The two realms are settled in the Treaty of Tordesillas (1494) and Treaty of Saragossa (1529). There is some dispute about the exact lines, see Garrett Mattingly, 'No Peace Beyond What Line?', *Transactions of the Royal Historical Society* 13 (1963).

4. Arguing for only a limited *mare clausum* and for a *mare liberum* on the high seas, see original Hugo Grotius and Louis Elzevir, *Mare Liberum Sive De Iure Quod Batavis Competit Ad Indicana Commercia Dissertatio* (Lugduni Batauorvm: Ludovici Elzevirij, 1609). Arguing for a *mare clausum*, but theorized from effective control

of the land, see the original John Selden, *Mare Clausum Seu De Dominio Maris* (London: W. Stanesbeius pro R. Meighen, 1635).

5. 'Narrow Seas', in *The Oxford Companion to Ships and the Sea*, ed. I. C. B. Dear and Peter Kemp (Oxford: Oxford University Press, 2006), https://perma.cc/4XSN-DECB.

6. In February 1603, the government proposed a scheme for the formation of an auxiliary fleet of private ships to protect commerce in the Narrow Seas, tacitly admitting the inability of the Royal Navy to manage this duty, From Kenneth R. Andrews, *Elizabethan Privateering: English Privateering During the Spanish War, 1585–1603* (Cambridge: Cambridge University Press, 1964), 238.

7. David J. Starkey, 'Voluntaries and Sea Robbers: A Review of the Academic Literature on Privateering, Corsairing, Buccaneering and Piracy', *The Mariner's Mirror* 97, no. 1 (2011): 143–46.

8. See e.g. 'Pirates and Markets', in *Bandits at Sea: A Pirates Reader*, ed. C. Richard Pennell (New York: New York University Press, 2001); John L. Anderson, 'Piracy and World History: An Economic Perspective on Maritime Predation', in *Bandits at Sea: A Pirates Reader*, ed. C. Richard Pennell (New York: New York University Press, 2001).

9. Anne Pérotin-Dumon, 'The Pirate and the Emperor: Power and the Law on the Seas, 1450–1850', in *Bandits at Sea: A Pirates Reader*, ed. C. Richard Pennell (New York: New York University Press, 2001), 26.

10. Lauren Benton, 'Toward a New Legal History of Piracy: Maritime Legalities and the Myth of Universal Jurisdiction', *International Journal of Maritime History* 23, no. 1 (2011): 233.

11. Pérotin-Dumon, 'The Pirate and the Emperor', 41.

12. Robert C. Ritchie, *Captain Kidd and the War against the Pirates* (Cambridge, MA: Harvard University Press, 1986), 128. This shift from the primary interest in imperial conquest to the reliance on trade was previously pointed out by Lane's analysis of the shift of profit derived from tribute (i.e. payment in excess of cost of protection) vs. profit derived in the form of protection rents (i.e. cheaper protection for one's own companies than for competitors). See Frederic C. Lane, 'The Economic Meaning of War and Protection', *Journal of Social Philosophy & Jurisprudence* 7, no. 3 (1942). Supportive of the economic driver to the end of piracy, see Alejandro Colás and Bryan Mabee, 'The Flow and Ebb of Private Seaborne Violence in Global Politics', in *Mercenaries, Pirates, Bandits and Empires: Private Violence in Historical Context*, ed. Alejandro Colás and Bryan Mabee (London: C Hurst, 2010). See also Arne Bialuschewski, 'Pirates, Markets and Imperial Authority: Economic Aspects of Maritime Depredations in the Atlantic World, 1716–1726', *Global Crime* 9, nos. 1–2 (2008).

13. Janice E. Thomson, *Mercenaries, Pirates, and Sovereigns: State-Building and Extraterritorial Violence in Early Modern Europe*, Princeton Studies in International History and Politics (Princeton: Princeton University Press, 1994).

14. Mark Shirk, 'How Does Violence Threaten the State? Four Narratives on Piracy', *Terrorism and Political Violence* 29, no. 4 (2017). See also: Mark Shirk, 'Pirates, Anarchists, and Terrorists: Violence and the Boundaries of Sovereign Authority' (PhD Thesis, University of Maryland, 2014).

15. Shirk, 'How Does Violence Threaten the State?', 62.
16. Lauren Benton, *A Search for Sovereignty: Law and Geography in European Empires, 1400–1900* (Cambridge: Cambridge University Press, 2010), 137–48.
17. Benton, *A Search for Sovereignty*, 161.
18. Starkey, 'Voluntaries and Sea Robbers'. 145.
19. B. Richard Burg, *Sodomy and the Pirate Tradition: English Sea Rovers in the Seventeenth Century Caribbean* (New York: New York University Press, 1983); Kenneth J. Kinkor, 'Black Men under the Black Flag', in *Bandits at Sea: A Pirates Reader*, ed. C. Richard Pennell (New York: New York University Press, 2001); C. Richard Pennell, *Bandits at Sea: A Pirates Reader* (New York: New York University Press, 2001); Marcus Rediker, 'Liberty beneath the Jolly Roger: The Lives of Anne Bonny and Mary Read, Pirates', in *Bandits at Sea: A Pirates Reader*, ed. C. Richard Pennell (New York: New York University Press, 2001); Jo Stanley et al., *Bold in Her Breeches: Women Pirates across the Ages* (London: Pandora, 1995).
20. Extensive primary source material is available in commented editions of primary sources, such as Kenneth R. Andrews and Hakluyt Society, *English Privateering Voyages to the West Indies, 1588–1595: Documents Relating to English Voyages to the West Indies from the Defeat of the Armada to the Last Voyage of Sir Francis Drake*, Works Issued by the Hakluyt Society, 2nd Series, No. 111 (Cambridge: Cambridge University Press for Hakluyt Society, 1959).
21. Starkey, 'Voluntaries and Sea Robbers', 130–31.
22. Nicholas A. M. Rodger, *The Safeguard of the Sea: A Naval History of Britain, vol. 1, 660–1649* (London: HarperCollins in association with the National Maritime Museum, 1997), 200; Starkey, 'Voluntaries and Sea Robbers', 130.
23. Primary sources identified from consultations of secondary sources and archival catalogues for the late 17th-century case are Hendrik Carel Vos Leibbrandt, Willem Adriaan van der Stel, and Cape of Good Hope Archives, *Journal, 1699–1732* (Cape Town: Richards, 1896), 228–32; East India Company Original Correspondence, IOR/E/3/52, IOR, British Library. Letter 16 November 1695; Calendar of State Papers Colonial Series America and West Indies, Vere Harmsworth Library. Entries on 28 Nobember 1697 and 1 September 1698; Factory Records Bombay: Copies of Letters Despatched between 21 August 1699 and 30 January 1703, 1699–1703, IOR/G/3/17, IOR, British Library. Letter of 23 July 1700; East India Company Original Correspondence, 1700, IOR/E/3/57, IOR, British Library. Letters of 10 May 1700 and 28 December 1700.

Consulted secondary sources include Peter Earle, *The Pirate Wars* (London: Methuen, 2003), 120–24; John Keay, *The Honourable Company: A History of the East India Company* (London: Harper Collins, 1991), 189; Charles Grey and George Fletcher MacMunn, *Pirates of the Eastern Seas (1618–1723): A Lurid Page of History* (London: Sampson Low, Marston, 1933), 123; Philip J. Stern, *The Company-State: Corporate Sovereignty and the Early Modern Foundation of the British Empire in India* (Oxford: Oxford University Press, 2011).
24. Matthew Norton, 'Classification and Coercion: The Destruction of Piracy in the English Maritime System', *American Journal of Sociology* 119, no. 6 (2014);

Nicholas A. M. Rodger, *The Command of the Ocean: A Naval History of Britain 1649–1815* (New York: W.W. Norton, 2006); Nuala Zahedieh, *The Capital and the Colonies: London and the Atlantic Economy, 1660–1700* (Cambridge: Cambridge University Press, 2010).

25. John B. Hattendorf et al., 'Part IV 1648–1714', in *British Naval Documents, 1204–1960*, ed. John B. Hattendorf, et al. (Aldershot: Scholar Press for the Navy Records Society, 1993), 189–92.

26. Consulted primary sources include the Clarendon Archives and UK National Archives holdings on decision-making at the time. An excellent comprehensive secondary source is Jan Martin Lemnitzer, *Power, Law and the End of Privateering* (Basingstoke: Palgrave Macmillan, 2014).

27. Jan Martin Lemnitzer, *Power, Law and the End of Privateering* (Basingstoke: Palgrave Macmillan, 2014).

28. The second-largest naval power at the time, though considerably weaker than Britain, was France.

29. Kenneth R. Andrews, *Drake's Voyages: A Re-Assessment of Their Place in Elizabethan Maritime Expansion* (London: Weidenfeld & Nicolson, 1967), 117.

30. However, this entailed significant risks. As Paul Kennedy pointed out, the privateers were 'prone to alter carefully formulated plans in favour of rash enterprises and all too easily tempted by the prospect of plunder and glory into forgetting the national strategy'. As an example he points to Sir Francis Drake's attack on the *Rosario*, abandoning the chase of the Armada. Kennedy, *The Rise and Fall of British Naval Mastery*, 38. See also Andrews, *Drake's Voyages*, 130–31.

31. As an example of such a bond see Benjamin Wood for the Challenger, 1959, HCA 25/3, 9, English privateering voyages to the West Indies, 1588–1595: documents relating to English voyages to the West Indies from the defeat of the Armada to the last voyage of Sir Francis Drake, Cambridge University Press for Hakluyt Society, 2nd ser., no. 111, Hakluyt Society.

32. Andrews, *Elizabethan Privateering*, 30.

33. Calendar of State Papers, Domestic Series, of the Reigns of Elizabeth and James I, Addenda, 1580–1625, ed. Mary Anne Everett Green. London: Longman & Co., 1872, State Papers Online, Gale, Cengage Learning, 274.

34. Andrews, *Elizabethan Privateering*, 26–27.

35. Andrews, *Elizabethan Privateering*, 112.

36. Rodger, *The Safeguard of the Sea*, 295.

37. Rodger, *The Safeguard of the Sea*, 343.

38. Andrews, *Drake's Voyages*, 183.

39. Willard Mosher Wallace, *Sir Walter Raleigh* (Princeton: Princeton University Press, 1959); For Ralegh's defence of his actions see Apology in Walter Ralegh, *Miscellaneous Works*, ed. William Oldys and Thomas Birch, 8 vols., vol. 8, *The Works of Sir Walter Ralegh* (Oxford: Oxford University Press, 1829), 479–520.

40. See, e.g., Thomson, *Mercenaries, Pirates, and Sovereigns*.

41. Jan Glete, *Warfare at Sea, 1500–1650: Maritime Conflicts and the Transformation of Europe* (London: Routledge, 2000), 161.

42. Glete, *Warfare at Sea*, 163–64.

43. Matthew S. Anderson, *War and Society in Europe of the Old Regime, 1618–1789* (Stroud: Sutton, 1998), 57; Michael Arthur Lewis, *The History of the British Navy* (Harmondsworth: Penguin Books, 1957), 74–75.

44. Fernand Braudel, *The Mediterranean and the Mediterranean World in the Age of Philip II*, 2 vols. (Berkeley: University of California Press, 1995), 865.

45. On the Barbary corsairs, see Oded Löwenheim, *Predators and Parasites: Persistent Agents of Transnational Harm and Great Power Authority* (Ann Arbor: University of Michigan Press, 2007).

46. Alfred P. Rubin, *The Law of Piracy*, International Law Studies (Newport, RI: Naval War College Press, 1988).

47. Rubin, *The Law of Piracy*, 20.

48. Claire Vergerio, 'Alberico Gentili's De Iure Belli: An Absolutist's Attempt to Reconcile the Jus Gentium and the Reason of State Tradition', *Journal of the History of International Law* 19 (2017): 14.

49. Walter Rech, *Enemies of Mankind: Vattel's Theory of Collective Security*, ed. Martti Koskenniemi, vol. 18, the Erik Castrén Institute Monographs on International Law and Human Rights (Leiden: Martinus Nijhoff, 2013), 53.

50. Rech, *Enemies of Mankind*, 54.

51. Rech, *Enemies of Mankind*, 101.

52. For more on the debate of the status of the United Provinces see C. G. Roelofsen, 'Grotius and the International Politics of the Seventeenth Century', in *Hugo Grotius and International Relations*, ed. Hedley Bull, Benedict Kingsbury, and Adam Roberts (Oxford: Clarendon Press, 1990).

53. Rech, *Enemies of Mankind*, 18, 59.

54. Rech, *Enemies of Mankind*, 56.

55. Rubin, *The Law of Piracy*, 66.

56. Amedeo Policante, *The Pirate Myth: Genealogies of an Imperial Concept*, Glasshouse Book (New York: Routledge, 2015), 138.

57. Rech, *Enemies of Mankind*, 18.

58. *Postliminum* is a Roman law concept referring to the rights to the spoils of war. It is especially important in this context, for whether property can be transferred by the warring party or not (in Roman law, pirates cannot transfer property). Rech, *Enemies of Mankind*, 18.

59. Gijs A. Rommelse, 'An Early Modern Naval Revolution? The Relationship between "Economic Reason of State" and Maritime Warfare', *Journal for Maritime Research* 13, no. 2 (2011): 143.

60. Andrews, *Drake's Voyages*, 185.

61. Andrews, *Drake's Voyages*, 185.

62. Of relevance for the Dutch is the Treaty of Münster in 1648 acknowledging their sovereignty and right to trade in the New World, whereas for the English the Treaties of Madrid (1667, 1670) recognized the English territories. Matthew Norton, 'Culture and Coercion: Piracy and State Power in the Early Modern English Empire', PhD Thesis, Yale University, 2012, 81–82.

63. Norton, 'Culture and Coercion', 83–86.

64. Anderson, *War and Society in Europe of the Old Regime*, 97–98, 147.

65. Kennedy, *The Rise and Fall of British Naval Mastery*, 79.

66. The degree of choice should not be overstated, however, as the French did not have the financial means to invest in a navy comparable with the British. In addition, there was much enthusiasm for privateering. For more details, see Halvard Leira and Benjamin de Carvalho, 'Privateers of the North Sea: At Worlds End—French Privateers in Norwegian Waters', in *Mercenaries, Pirates, Bandits and Empires: Private Violence in Historical Context*, ed. Alejandro Colás and Bryan Mabee (London: C. Hurst, 2010), 60–62.

67. For an account making this argument based on extensive data sources, see Zahedieh, *The Capital and the Colonies*.

68. Stern, *The Company-State*.

69. Stern, *The Company-State*. For an in-depth treatment on how company-states built and interacted with the first international system, see Andrew Phillips and J. C. Sharman, *Outsourcing Empire: How Company-States Made the Modern World* (Princeton: Princeton University Press, 2020); Andrew Phillips and J. C. Sharman, 'Company-States and the Creation of the Global International System', *European Journal of International Relations* 26, no. 4 (2020).

70. An example of the absolutist political vision of the state can be found in Thomas Hobbes's Leviathan.

71. Thomson, *Mercenaries, Pirates, and Sovereigns*, 67. On how 'violence' relates to trade, and how it can be conceived as one of the main exports of the European states, see J. C. Sharman, 'Power and Profit at Sea: The Rise of the West in the Making of the International System', *International Security* 43, no. 4 (2019).

72. Stern, *The Company-State*, 12.

73. Andrew Phillips and Jason C. Sharman, 'Explaining Durable Diversity in International Systems: State, Company, and Empire in the Indian Ocean', *International Studies Quarterly* 59, no. 3 (2015): 444. See further J. C. Sharman, *Empires of the Weak: The Real Story of European Expansion and the Creation of the New World Order* (Princeton: Princeton University Press, 2019).

74. Sharman, 'Power and Profit at Sea'.

75. Phillips and Sharman, 'Explaining Durable Diversity in International Systems', 444.

76. Stern, *The Company-State*, 122.

77. Thomson, *Mercenaries, Pirates, and Sovereigns*, 61–62.

78. Anderson, 'Piracy and World History', 91.

79. Stern, *The Company-State*, 15. Other companies went bankrupt, had their royal charters removed, or merged with other companies.

80. Starkey, 'Voluntaries and Sea Robbers', 140–41; Mark Shirk, '"Bringing the State Back in" to the Empire Turn: Piracy and the Layered Sovereignty of the Eighteenth Century Atlantic', *International Studies Review* 19, no. 2 (2017).

81. Ritchie, *Captain Kidd and the War against the Pirates*, 128. However, the East India Company also applied for privateering licenses, see, e.g., Commission for Taking French Ships, 1694, IOR/H/36, 63–64, Miscellaneous papers, IOR, British Library.

82. *Imperium* is used here in the sense of the early modern period: described as sovereignty by David Armitage, *Foundations of Modern International Thought* (Cambridge: Cambridge University Press, 2012), 124. Keene captures *imperium* (as opposed to *dominium*) as 'rights to ruleship over people', Edward Keene, *International Political Thought: A Historical Introduction* (Cambridge: Polity, 2005), 103.

83. Stern, *The Company-State*, 136.

84. Stern, *The Company-State*, 136.

85. Rodger, *The Command of the Ocean*, 162.

86. Extract of Letters Sent [to] the East India Company from Severall [*sic*] Parts of India, 1697, IOR/H/36, 323–325, Miscellaneous papers, IOR, British Library.

87. Surat to London, 9 September 1696, IOR/E/3/52, 147, East India Company Original Correspondence, IOR, British Library.

88. Ritchie, *Captain Kidd and the War against the Pirates*, 132.

89. Registered Declaration for the Letter of Marque for the Adventure Galley, 11 December 1695, HCA 26/3, 59, HCA, National Archives. See also Bond for the Letter of Marque for the Adventure Galley, 1695, HCA 25/12, Part 2, HCA, National Archives.

90. High Court of Admiralty, *The Arraignment, Tryal, and Condemnation of Captain William Kidd, for Murther and Piracy, Upon Six Several Indictments, at the Admiralty-Sessions, Held by His Majesty's Commission at the Old-Baily, on Thursday the 8th. And Friday the 9th. Of May, 1701* (London: Printed for J. Nutt, 1701).

91. Narrative of the Voyage of Captain William Kidd Commander of the Adventure Galley from London to the East Indies, Received in London 20 September 1699, 7 July 1699, CO 5/860, 200, CO, National Archives.

92. To the Kings Most Excellent Majestie. The Humble Petition of the Governors of the Company of Merchants of London Trading into the East Indies, 1698, IOR/H/36, 420–421, Miscellaneous papers, IOR, British Library.

93. Company Letters from India to London, 1698, IOR/H/36, 385–391, Miscellaneous papers, IOR, British Library.

94. Letter to Mr. Blackburn Secretary of the East Indies Company, 2 August 1698, CO 324/6, 313–314 (old marking: 157–158), CO, National Archives; Proclamation About Pirates in East India, 8 December 1698, PC 2/77, 276–277, PC, National Archives.

95. Vernon to Blackbourn, 21 November 1698, IOR/H/36, 392, Miscellaneous papers, IOR, British Library.

96. The passes were sent from America by his sponsor, Lord Bellomont. See long abstract of items sent in the letter dated 26 July 1699, received in London on 20 September 1699 (158). Among the items are the two 'missing' French passes (159–62), as well as witness statements from various mariners, including a narrative of the voyage by Capt. Kidd himself (199–202). See Lord Bellomont to London, 7 July 1699, *letter and materials re Kidd's activities*, CO 5/860, 158–202, CO, National Archives.

97. High Court of Admiralty, *The Arraignment, Tryal, and Condemnation of Captain William Kidd*.

98. Benton, 'Toward a New Legal History of Piracy', 231.

99. Benton, 'Toward a New Legal History of Piracy', 239.

100. On the expansion of the Royal Navy see the very useful appendices which reflect the build-up of the Royal Navy in the conflict with France during the last two decades of the 17th century. In Rodger, *The Command of the Ocean*.

101. See Stern, *The Company-State*.

102. Benton, 'Toward a New Legal History of Piracy'. 227.

103. To Their Exellencies the Lords Justices of England. The Humble Petition of the Governour & Company of Merchants of London Trading into the East Indies, 16 July 1696, IOR/H/36, 191, Miscellaneous papers, IOR, British Library.

104. Kennedy, *The Rise and Fall of British Naval Mastery*, 164–65, 71; Earle, *The Pirate Wars*.

105. Ritchie, *Captain Kidd and the War against the Pirates*, 146–51.

106. Bryan Mabee, 'Pirates, Privateers and the Political Economy of Private Violence', *Global Change, Peace & Security* 21, no. 2 (2009).

107. Ritchie, *Captain Kidd and the War against the Pirates*, 158.

108. Charles Tilly, 'War Making and State Making as Organized Crime', in *Bringing the State Back In*, ed. Peter B. Evans, Dietrich Rueschemeyer, and Theda Skocpol (Cambridge: Cambridge University Press, 1985); Charles Tilly, *Coercion, Capital, and European States, A.D. 990–1990* (Oxford: Basil Blackwell, 1990).

109. Shirk, ' "Bringing the State Back in" to the Empire Turn'.

110. On the importance of changes in law crystallizing piracy as an object of action see Norton, 'Classification and Coercion'; Norton, 'Culture and Coercion', 148; on the effect this had on colonial autonomy, see Rebecca A. Simon, 'The Problem and Potential of Piracy: Legal Changes and Emerging Ideas of Colonial Autonomy in the Early Modern British Atlantic, 1670–1730', *Journal for Maritime Research* 18, no. 2 (2016).

111. Shirk, ' "Bringing the State Back in' to the Empire Turn', 156.

112. Shirk, 'Pirates, Anarchists, and Terrorists', 133.

113. Quotation was found in Daniel Heller-Roazen, *The Enemy of All: Piracy and the Law of Nations* (New York: Zone, 2009), 117. Original quotation from Christian Wolff, *Jus Gentium Methodo Scientifica Pertractatum*, ed. James Brown Scott, trans. Joseph Horace Drake and Otfried Nippold, vol. 2, Classics of International Law (Oxford: Clarendon Press, 1934), 319. §627.

114. Shirk, 'Pirates, Anarchists, and Terrorists'. 131–32.

115. Earle, *The Pirate Wars*, 205; Shirk, 'Pirates, Anarchists, and Terrorists', 132.

116. Benton, *A Search for Sovereignty*, 152–53.

117. David J. Starkey, E. S. van Eyck van Hesling, and Jaap A. de Moor, *Pirates and Privateers: New Perspectives on the War on Trade in the Eighteenth and Nineteenth Centuries*, Exeter Maritime Studies (Exeter: University of Exeter Press, 1997).

118. Great Britain, *The Statutes Relating to the Admiralty, Navy, Shipping, and Navigation of the United Kingdom from 9 Hen. III to 3 Geo. IV Inclusive: With Notes, Referring in Each Case to the Subsequent Statutes, and to the Decisions in the Courts of Admiralty, Common Law, and Equity, in England, and to the Scotch Law* (London: s.n., 1823), 104–106.

119. Daniel A. Baugh, *The Global Seven Years War, 1754–1763: Britain and France in a Great Power Contest*, Modern Wars in Perspective (Harlow: Longman, 2011).

120. 32 George II, c.25. ('Naval Prize Act' of 1758). For a recent study of privateering in that period, see Thomas M. Truxes, 'The Breakdown of Borders: Commerce Raiding During the Seven Years' War, 1756–1763', in *Commerce Raiding: Historical Case Studies, 1755–2009*, ed. Bruce A. Elleman and Sarah C. M. Paine (Newport, RI: Naval War College Press, 2013).

121. Richard Harding, *Modern Naval History: Debates and Prospects* (London: Bloomsbury, 2016).

122. Nicholas A. M. Rodger, 'Mobilizing Seapower in the Eighteenth Century', in *Essays in Naval History, from Medieval to Modern*, ed. Nicholas A. M. Rodger (Farnham: Ashgate, 2009), 4.

123. Rodger, 'Mobilizing Seapower in the Eighteenth Century'.

124. For more on armed neutrality, see the forum on neutrality, e.g. Silvia Marzagalli and Leos Müller, '"In Apparent Disagreement with All Law of Nations in the World': Negotiating Neutrality for Shipping and Trade During the French Revolutionary and Napoleonic Wars', *International Journal of Maritime History* 28, no. 1 (2016).

125. Thomson, *Mercenaries, Pirates, and Sovereigns*, 26.

126. On the efforts against the Barbary states, see Caitlin M. Gale, 'Barbary's Slow Death: European Attempts to Eradicate North African Piracy in the Early Nineteenth Century', *Journal for Maritime Research* 18, no. 2 (2016).

127. Great Britain, 'British Declaration with Reference to Neutrals and Letters of Marque', in *British Foreign and State Papers*, vol. 46 (London: H. M. S. O.), 36–37.

128. Clarendon to Palmerston, 6 April 1856, draft letter, MSS. Clar. Dep. C. 135, 510–511, Clarendon Papers, Bodleian Library, University of Oxford.

129. Clarendon to Palmerston, 6 April 1856, Clarendon Papers.

130. Lemnitzer, *Power, Law and the End of Privateering*, 39–40.

131. Palmerston to Clarendon, 5 April 1856, letter, MSS. Clar. Dep. C. 49, 241–242, Clarendon Papers, Bodleian Library, University of Oxford.

132. Lemnitzer, *Power, Law and the End of Privateering*, 48–51. See also Clarendon to Palmerston, 6 April 1856, Clarendon Papers.

133. Lemnitzer, *Power, Law and the End of Privateering*, 70.

134. The option of other powers acceding was important to Lord Palmerston. See Palmerston to Clarendon, 12 April 1856, Clarendon Papers.

Chapter 4

1. European Union Agency for Network and Information Security (ENISA), 'CERT Cooperation and Its Further Facilitation by Relevant Stakeholders', Heraklion: ENISA, 2006.

2. Nazli Choucri, Stuart Madnick, and Jeremy Ferwerda, 'Institutions for Cyber Security: International Responses and Global Imperatives', *Information Technology*

for Development 20, no. 2 (2014): 106; on the international governance more broadly, see Joseph S. Nye, Jr., 'The Regime Complex for Managing Global Cyber Activities', in *Paper Series*, Ontario and London: Global Commission on Internet Governance (CIGI) and Chatham House, 2014; Joseph S. Nye, Jr., 'Deterrence and Dissuasion in Cyberspace', *International Security*, 41, no. 3 (2017).

3. William H. Gates, III, 'Trustworthy Computing', email communication to Microsoft staff, Microsoft Company Timeline, 15 January 2002, Microsoft webpage, https://perma.cc/78NQ-EZSM.

4. Myriam Dunn Cavelty, *Cyber-Security and Threat Politics: U.S. Efforts to Secure the Information Age*, CSS Studies in Security and International Relations (London: Routledge, 2008).

5. That year, there were at least two other operations that caused a stir. One was Solar Sunrise, traced back an Israeli hacker and two Californian teenagers. The other was Digital Demon, about which nothing is publicly known to date. Director of Central Intelligence, 'Annual Report for the United States Intelligence Community', Washington DC, 1999.

6. The best source detailing the Moonlight Maze investigation is Thomas Rid, *Rise of the Machines: A Cybernetic History*, 1st ed. (New York: W. W. Norton, 2016). For technical details see Thomas Rid, 'Back to the Future—Moonlight Maze', talk presented at the Security Analyst Summit, Tenerife, Spain, 8 February, 2016.

7. Seymour M. Hersh, 'The Intelligence Gap—How the Digital Age Left Our Spies out in the Cold', *The New Yorker*, 6 December 1999.

8. The programme later transitioned to FISA authority. Best sources are the declassified court documents found at Office of the Director of National Intelligence, 'DNI Announces the Declassification of the Existence of Collection Activities Authorized by President George W. Bush Shortly after the Attacks of September 11, 2001', Office of the Director of National Intelligence, 21 December 2013, https://perma.cc/34E8-AT8B.

9. See 'SID Today: Digital Network Exploitation (DNE), Digital Network Intelligence (DNI) and Computer Network Exploitation (CNE)', Deputy Director for Data Acquisition, National Security Agency, *The Intercept*, 10 August 2016 (dated 16 July 2003), https://perma.cc/W9K4-ZSHG. For a Canadian program, which claims to be an eight-year development effort, see 'CSEC SIGINT Cyber Discovery: Summary of the Current Effort', Cyber-Counterintelligence, Communications Security Establishment Canada, *Der Spiegel*, 17 January 2015 (dated November 2010), https://perma.cc/JQ3V-K4TK.

10. Richard J. Aldrich, *GCHQ: The Uncensored Story of Britain's Most Secret Intelligence Agency* (London: HarperPress, 2011), 488.

11. This tension also existed previously with regard to communications security of telephone calls. For example, NSA's internal history documented the debates on whether to extend encryption to businesses, which the Soviet Union was suspected to be spying on, in the 1970s. See David G. Boak, *A History of U.S. Communications Security*, vol. 2 (Fort George G. Meade, Maryland: National Security Agency, 1981), 27–30. On 'undermining' cryptography, see on Crypto AG, Fiona Endres, and

Nicole Vögele, 'Weltweite Spionage-Operation Mit Schweizer Firma Aufgedeckt.' *SRF*, 11 February 2020, https://perma.cc/44P8-FH8V; Elmar Theveßen, Peter F. Müller, and Ulrich Stoll, '#Cryptoleaks: Wie BND Und CIA Alle Täuschten', *ZDF*, 11 February 2020, https://perma.cc/D9WX-BTJ6; Greg Miller, 'The Intelligence Coup of the Century', *Washington Post*, 11 February 2020, https://perma.cc/6HJJ-YVX6.

12. We know much about the evolution of the U.S. tracking this specific threat actor from the documents leaked in *Der Spiegel* in January 2015. See 'BYZANTINE HADES: An Evolution of Collection', National Threat Operations Center (NTOC), V225, National Security Agency, *Der Spiegel*, 17 January 2015 (dated June 2010), https://perma.cc/H79D-PMXA; 'Chinese Exfiltrate Sensitive Military Technology', National Security Agency, *Der Spiegel*, 17 January 2015, https://perma.cc/LW4W-R7ZQ. See also Gordon Corera, *Intercept: The Secret History of Computers and Spies* (London: Weidenfeld & Nicolson, 2015), 176–201. For a list of publicly reported intrusions attributed to China between 2005 and 2015, see Jon R. Lindsay and Tai Ming Cheung, 'From Exploitation to Innovation: Acquisition, Absorption, and Application', in *China and Cybersecurity: Espionage, Strategy, and Politics in the Digital Domain*, ed. Jon R. Lindsay, Tai Ming Cheung, and Derek S. Reveron (New York: Oxford University Press, 2015), 58–60.

13. BBC, 'MI5 Warns over China Spy Threat', BBC, 2 December 2007, https://perma.cc/2E22-GQVJ.

14. Earlier examples might be the spy plane accident in 2001 (U.S. and China), Turkish vs. Kurdish, Israeli-Palestinian hacking. An excellent source on Estonia is Andreas Schmidt, 'The Estonian Cyberattacks', in *A Fierce Domain: Conflict in Cyberspace 1986–2012*, ed. Jason Healey (Vienna, VA: Cyber Conflict Studies Association, 2013)..

15. Information Warfare Monitor, 'Tracking Ghostnet: Investigating a Cyber Espionage Network', 2009, https://perma.cc/H27G-9RWX. See further Shishir Nagaraja and Ross Anderson, 'The Snooping Dragon: Social-Malware Surveillance of the Tibetan Movement', Technical Report No. 746, Computer Laboratory, Cambridge University, March 2009, https://perma.cc/83Q2-446D.

16. The best account of Stuxnet is Kim Zetter, *Countdown to Zero Day: Stuxnet and the Launch of the World's First Digital Weapon*, 1st ed. (New York: Crown, 2014). For other states, see, e.g., the Dutch involvement in recruiting and making available a human agent, see Kim Zetter, and Huib Modderkolk, 'How a Secret Dutch Mole Aided the U.S.-Israeli Stuxnet Cyberattack on Iran', *Yahoo News*, 2 September 2019, https://perma.cc/DR6J-57A2.

17. See, e.g., Equation Group, APT28, APT29, Turla, Careto, Balibar. A collection of links to industry reports of operations associated with these various threat actors can be found under http://apt.threattracking.com and https://github.com/aptnotes/. On the politics of attribution, see further Florian J. Egloff, 'Public Attribution of Cyber Intrusions', *Journal of Cybersecurity* 6, no.1 (2020); Florian J. Egloff, 'Contested Public Attributions of Cyber Incidents and the Role of Academia', *Contemporary Security Policy* 41, no. 1 (2020).

18. Organisation for Economic Co-operation and Development (OECD), 'Cybersecurity Policy Making at a Turning Point: Analysing a New Generation of National Cybersecurity Strategies for the Internet Economy', Paris, 2012.

19. By Western activities, I do not think they mean 'only' Stuxnet, which happened years earlier. See talking points memo for the director of the NSA and the director of Signals Intelligence: 'Iran—Current Topics, Interaction with GCHQ', S2E4, Iran Division Chief, National Security Agency, *The Intercept*, 10 February 2015 (dated 12 April 2013), https://perma.cc/E4XS-X3XR. The same memo also details that Iran retaliated separately to a wiper attack against its oil infrastructure by launching a wiper attack against Saudi Aramco.

20. United States of America v. Fathi et al., 16-348 (2016).

21. United States of America v. Su Bin, 14-1318M (2014). Criminal Complaint (14-1318M, CDC, 33–34). Importantly, such calculations leave out the analysis, distribution, and management cost of running the espionage campaign. See, e.g., The Grugq, 'Cyber: Ignore the Penetration Testers', 17 September 2016 [blog], https://perma.cc/Q6DS-NNA7.

22. Even private sector assessments are blacked out in official publications. See, e.g., U.S. Congress, House of Representatives, Committee on Oversight and Government Reform, *The OPM Data Breach: How the Government Jeopardized Our National Security for More Than a Generation*, 114th Cong., Washington, DC: Government Printing Office, 2016, https://perma.cc/BZ8T-88Q3. For a detailed case study of the knowledge-making proceses in the case of OPM, see Florian J. Egloff and Myriam Dunn Cavelty, 'Attribution and Knowledge Creation Assemblages in Cybersecurity Politics', *Journal of Cybersecurity* 7, no. 1 (2021), doi: 10.1093/cybsec/tyab002.

23. PWC and BAE Systems, 'Operation Cloud Hopper', April 2017, https://perma.cc/MV3L-FEPW. The origin would later be confirmed in an indictment, see United States of America v. Zhu Hua and Zhang Shilong, 18-891–Indictment (2018).

24. Note I am using the (less-often used) wider 'digital network exploitation' category, as opposed to 'computer network exploitation', as the latter strictly involves active (read surreptitious) endpoint manipulation to facilitate collection (either directly from the endpoint or facilitating midpoint collection). The wider category is important, as the access to information also includes cooperative, non-surreptitious access arrangements.

25. 'Overt' and 'covert' in this usage are terms of art. Overt means the government is the identifiable counterparty; covert means efforts are undertaken to make the access unattributable to the government. Both can be undertaken secretly (out of the public's purview).

26. Some research efforts are trying to externalize security services to the network to reduce the possibility of users inadvertently engaging in 'unsafe' behaviour. See, e.g., D. Montero et al., 'Virtualized Security at the Network Edge: A User-Centric Approach', *IEEE Communications Magazine* 53, no. 4 (2015).

27. Myriam Dunn Cavelty and Florian J. Egloff, 'The Politics of Cybersecurity: Balancing Different Roles of the State', *St Antony's International Review* 15, no. 1 (2019).

Chapter 5

1. Even today, taking over *one* merchant ship is relatively easy (if it is not accompanied by armed guards). However, generating persistent offensive success is made hard by the naval capabilities sent to secure areas of naval predation (e.g. anti-piracy mission in the Gulf of Aden).

2. On the notion of offensive persistence, see also Michael P. Fischerkeller and Richard J. Harknett, 'Deterrence Is Not a Credible Strategy for Cyberspace', *Orbis* 61, no. 3 (2017). On cyber offense-defence balance more generally, see Rebecca Slayton, 'What Is the Cyber Offense-Defense Balance? Conceptions, Causes, and Assessment', *International Security* 41, no. 3 (2017).

3. The problem of attribution will be further discussed in Chapter 6. The three-part split is standard practice. See, e.g., Herbert Lin, 'Attribution of Malicious Cyber Incidents: From Soup to Nuts', *Journal of International Affairs* 70, no. 1 (2016).

4. Note there is a difference between the true false-flag attack, where an attacker tries to deceive a victim into assigning blame to a specific other party, and the use of foreign tactics, techniques, and procedures to muddy attribution, but not directly induce blame on a specific party. On false-flag attacks see Brian Bartholomew and Juan Andrés Guerrero-Saade, 'Wave Your False Flags! Deception Tactics Muddying Attribution in Targeted Attacks' (paper presented at the Virus Bulletin Conference, Denver, CO, 5. October 2016); Christopher Porter, 'Toward Practical Cyber Counter Deception', *Journal of International Affairs* 70, no. 1 (2016). See also Juan Andrés Guerrero-Saade and Costin Raiu, 'Walking in Your Enemy's Shadow: When Fourth-Party Collection Becomes Attribution Hell', paper presented at the Virus Bulletin Conference, Madrid, 4 October 2017; Timo Steffens, *Attribution of Advanced Persistent Threats: How to Identify the Actors Behind Cyber-Espionage* (Berlin: Springer Vieweg, 2020).

5. On attribution see also discussion in Chapter 6. See further my own body of work on the subject: Florian J. Egloff, 'Contested Public Attributions of Cyber Incidents and the Role of Academia', *Contemporary Security Policy* 41, no. 1 (2020); Florian J. Egloff, 'Public Attribution of Cyber Intrusions', *Journal of Cybersecurity* 6, no.1 (2020); Florian J. Egloff and Myriam Dunn Cavelty, 'Attribution and Knowledge Creation Assemblages in Cybersecurity Politics', *Journal of Cybersecurity* 7, no.1 (2021), doi: 10.1093/cybsec/tyab002; Florian J. Egloff and Max Smeets. 'Publicly Attributing Cyber Attacks: A Framework', *Journal of Strategic Studies* (2021), doi: 10.1080/01402390.2021.1895117.

6. Reflecting on the impact of faster knowledge diffusion on cyber capabilities, see Max Smeets, 'A Matter of Time: On the Transitory Nature of Cyberweapons', *Journal of Strategic Studies* 41, nos. 1–2 (2018).

7. United Nations Protocol and Liaison Service, 'The Blue Book—Permanent Missions to the United Nations (St/Pls/Ser.A/306)', March 2021, United Nations.

8. More accurately, it changed very little. The biggest changes are the addition of new canals (e.g. Suez, Panama, Volga-Don, and Kiel canals), which made new shipping lanes possible and decreased the importance of other strategic choke points.

9. They are the dependence of actors on domain, attribution problems, offensive and defensive cost over time, geography, and the mix of public and private capabilities.

10. Mark Shirk, 'How Does Violence Threaten the State? Four Narratives on Piracy', *Terrorism and Political Violence* 29, no. 4 (2017); Mark Shirk, 'Pirates, Anarchists, and Terrorists: Violence and the Boundaries of Sovereign Authority', PhD thesis, University of Maryland, 2014.

11. On this issue more broadly, see, e.g., James A. Lewis, 'Put China's Intellectual Property Theft in a Larger Context', Center for Strategic & International Studies, 15 August 2017, https://perma.cc/M6JV-SJJ7.

12. Such stickiness is often highlighted in the literature on historical institutionalism. See, e.g., Orfeo Fioretos, 'Historical Institutionalism in International Relations', *International Organization* 65, no. 2 (2011).

13. Philip J. Stern, *The Company-State: Corporate Sovereignty and the Early Modern Foundation of the British Empire in India* (Oxford: Oxford University Press, 2011).

14. Alejandro Colás and Bryan Mabee, 'The Flow and Ebb of Private Seaborne Violence in Global Politics', in *Mercenaries, Pirates, Bandits and Empires: Private Violence in Historical Context*, ed. Alejandro Colás and Bryan Mabee (London: C Hurst, 2010), 97.

15. This mirrors the Dutch development. See Jan Glete, *War and the State in Early Modern Europe: Spain, the Dutch Republic and Sweden as Fiscal-Military States, 1500–1660* (London: Routledge, 2002). See also Gijs A. Rommelse, 'An Early Modern Naval Revolution? The Relationship between 'Economic Reason of State' and Maritime Warfare', *Journal for Maritime Research* 13, no. 2 (2011).

16. On the multitude of roles of the state, see Myriam Dunn Cavelty and Florian J. Egloff, 'The Politics of Cybersecurity: Balancing Different Roles of the State', *St Antony's International Review* 15, no. 1 (2019).

Chapter 6

1. There are examples of criminal sites, which exclude content that 'can adversely affect the Russian Federation, the Ukraine, and Belorussia'. Example from Max Goncharov, 'Criminal Hideouts for Lease: Bulletproof Hosting Services', Trend Micro, Cupertino, CA, 2015, 11.

2. Meaning-making is understood as the 'production of facts, images, and spectacles aimed at influencing socio-political uncertainty and conflict generated by crises'. This public function is distinguished from the governmental sense-making processes, which establish what is happening. See Arjen Boin et al., *The Politics of Crisis Management: Public Leadership under Pressure* (Cambridge: Cambridge University Press, 2005), 88. I further developed meaning-making through public attribution in Florian J. Egloff, 'Public Attribution of Cyber Intrusions', *Journal of Cybersecurity* 6 no. 1 (2020).

3. Külliki Korts, 'Inter-Ethnic Attitudes and Contacts between Ethnic Groups in Estonia', *Journal of Baltic Studies* 40 no. 1 (2009).

4. For an Estonian personal account and analysis that highlights the depth of the diverging interpretations, see Enn Soosaar, 'The Bronze Soldier and Its Deportation

to a Military Cemetery', *Diplomaatia* 46 (2007). For a scholarly analysis providing context and depth see Martin Ehala, 'The Bronze Soldier: Identity Threat and Maintenance in Estonia', *Journal of Baltic Studies* 40 no. 1 (2009).

5. Ehala, 'The Bronze Soldier', 142.
6. Eneken Tikk, Kadri Kaska, and Liis Vihul, 'International Cyber Incidents—Legal Considerations', Tallinn, Estonia, 2010. They categorize the attacks into two phases (27–29 April and 30 April—18 May 2007).
7. Andreas Schmidt, 'The Estonian Cyberattacks', in *A Fierce Domain: Conflict in Cyberspace 1986–2012*, ed. Jason Healey (Vienna, VA: Cyber Conflict Studies Association, 2013).
8. Atlantic Council, 'Building a Secure Cyber Future', Atlantic Council, 23 May 2012 [transcript], https://perma.cc/5KMR-G9SF.
9. 'Estonia: Demonstrators Quit Estonian Embassy as Ambassador Returns to Tallinn', 4 May 2007, Diplomatic cable from the U.S. Embassy in Moscow no. 07MOSCOW2065_a, Wikileaks Public Library of U.S. Diplomacy, Wikileaks, https://perma.cc/LHZ5-GCFP. See also Estonian Ministry of Foreign Affairs, 'Estonian Ambassador Is Going on Vacation', Republic of Estonia, 3. May 2007 [Press release], https://perma.cc/95Z7-64WM.
10. International Centre For Defence and Security, 'Russia's Involvement in the Tallinn Disturbances', 11 May 2007 [blog], https://perma.cc/A7DS-QH6A.
11. Estonian Government, 'Possible Misinformation Spreading in Electronic Channels', Republic of Estonia, 28 April 2007 [press release], https://perma.cc/Q9NF-3ER4.
12. Estonian Government, 'Malicious Cyber Attacks against Estonia Come from Abroad', Republic of Estonia, 29 April 2007 [press release], https://perma.cc/787B-ZVBZ.
13. Estonian Government, 'Declaration of the Minister of Foreign Affairs of the Republic of Estonia', Republic of Estonia, 1 May 2007 [press release], https://perma.cc/4C5X-JZJ7.
14. In the discussion of attribution, it is worth noting that the Estonian Foreign Minister highlighted *computers and persons in Russian government agencies*, who—one presumes—were authorized to act in the name of the state, and consequently, the state is responsible for their actions. For an elaboration of political discourse of state action and responsibility, see Sean Fleming, 'Artificial Persons and Attributed Actions: How to Interpret Action-Sentences About States', *European Journal of International Relations* 23 no. 4 (2017).
15. Toomas Hendrik Ilves, 'Statement of the President of the Republic Hendrik Toomas Ilves: We Can Agree Upon a Common Future', Office of the President, 2 May 2007 [transcript], https://perma.cc/SUV5-B7Q5.
16. Estonian President of the Republic, 'US Secretary to the President of Estonia: US Supports Estonia', Republic of Estonia, 3 May 2007 [press release, GoogleTranslate], https://perma.cc/X57G-V2SS.
17. Estonian Ministry of Foreign Affairs, 'Address by Minister of Foreign Affairs of Estonia Urmas Paet', Republic of Estonia, 11 May 2007 [transcript], https://perma.cc/FG3N-S8P5.

18. European Parliament, European Parliament Resolution of 24 May 2007 on Estonia, 2007, http://www.europarl.europa.eu. (P6_TA(2007)0215).

19. Jaak Aaviksoo, 'Cyber Defense—The Unnoticed Third World War', speech presented at the 24th International Workshop of the Series on Global Security, June 2007, Paris.

20. 'Police Conclude Probe into Alleged Riot Ringleaders', *The Baltic Times*, 6 September 2007, https://perma.cc/3SY9-7T3Q.

21. Lucas Kello, *The Virtual Weapon and International Order* (New Haven: Yale University Press, 2017), 185.

22. Alfred P. Rubin, *The Law of Piracy*, International Law Studies (Newport, RI: Naval War College Press, 1988), 20.

23. Rubin, *The Law of Piracy*, 66.

24. Rubin, *The Law of Piracy*, 66.

25. European Union Presidency, 'EU Presidency Statement on the Situation in Front of the Estonian Embassy in Moscow', 2 May 2007 [press release], https://perma.cc/99JQ-XQ2D; North Atlantic Treaty Organization, 'EU Presidency Statement on the Situation in Front of the Estonian Embassy in Moscow', 3 May 2007 [press release], https://perma.cc/99JQ-XQ2D.

26. 'Russian Bear Hug Squeezes Estonian Economy', 29 May 2007, Diplomatic cable from the U.S. Embassy in Tallinn no. 07TALLINN347_a, Wikileaks Public Library of U.S. Diplomacy, Wikileaks, https://perma.cc/F383-N7JQ.

27. 'Estonia's Cyber Attacks: World's First Virtual Attack against Nation State', 4 June 2007, Diplomatic cable from the U.S. Embassy in Tallinn no. 07TALLINN366_a, Wikileaks Public Library of U.S. Diplomacy, Wikileaks, https://perma.cc/CC35-NBCM.

28. 'Estonia's Cyber Attacks: Lessons Learned', 6 June 2007, Diplomatic cable from the U.S. Embassy in Tallinn no. 07TALLINN374_a, Wikileaks Public Library of U.S. Diplomacy, Wikileaks, https://perma.cc/3ABQ-6J7D.

29. Note: official corruption remains a problem in all levels of government in Russia in 2021, see U.S. Department of State, 'International Narcotics Control Strategy Report—Money Laundering and Financial Crimes', Washington, DC, 2021, 159.

30. See Eli Jellenc and Kimberly Zenz, 'Global Threat Research Report: Russia', iDefense, Chantilly, VA, 2007.

31. See authoritative account Brian Krebs, *Spam Nation: The Inside Story of Organized Cybercrime—from Global Epidemic to Your Front Door* (Naperville: Sourcebooks, 2014).

32. See also Jose Nazario, 'Politically Motivated Denial of Service Attacks', in *The Virtual Battlefield: Perspectives on Cyber Warfare*, ed. Christian Czosseck and Kenneth Geers (Amsterdam: IOS Press, 2009).

33. Andrëi Soldatov and Irina Borogan, *The New Nobility: The Restoration of Russia's Security State and the Enduring Legacy of the KGB*, 1st ed. (New York: PublicAffairs, 2010), Chapter 18. Soldatov and Borogan also mention kavkazcenter.com. Interestingly, the Chechen Islamist site stayed in the Russian state's purview. In 2014 APT28, a cyberespionage group associated with the Russian state's interest, used the domain in a spear-phishing campaign, registering their own site on kavkazcentr.info.

See FireEye, 'APT28: A Window into Russia's Cyber Espionage Operations?', Milpitas, CA, 2014. Thanks to Juan Andrés Guerrero-Saade for pointing this out to me.

34. Soldatov and Borogan, *The New Nobility*, Chapter 18.

35. Soldatov and Borogan, *The New Nobility*, Chapter 18.

36. The certificate was awareded for the defacement of the Jewish website www.evrey. com. The text of the certificate includes (as translated by Jellenc and Zenz): 'As Deputy of the State Duma and member of the Security Committee, I want to present you with the thanks and appreciation of the Information department of the NSD 'Slavic Union' for your vigilance and your recent suppression of Russophobe and others on the Internet, Russophobes that fan the flames of inter-religious discord and provide related materials. I hope that from now on your work will not become any less productive or ideologically adjusted', Jellenc and Zenz, 'Global Threat Research Report: Russia', 47.

37. Andreï Soldatov and Irina Borogan, *The Red Web: The Struggle between Russia's Digital Dictators and the New Online Revolutionaries*, 1st ed. (New York: PublicAffairs, 2015), 151.

38. According to Marina Kaljurand, the mutual assistance treaty was invoked by Estonia in June 2007, but no Russian cooperation was forthcoming. Kello, *The Virtual Weapon and International Order*, 185.

39. Federation Council of the Federal Assembly of the Russian Federation, 'Address of the Federation Council of the Federal Assembly of the Russian Federation (No. 15-SF)', 24 January 2007 [press release, GoogleTranslate], https://perma.cc/M46P-DWKM.

40. Russian Public Opinion Research Center (VCIOM), 'Monuments and Burial of Soviet Warriors in Estonia', 12 March 2007 [GoogleTranslate], https://perma.cc/7ZQJ-5VTY. See also Veiko Spolitis, 'Russland Und Die Baltischen Staaten. Denkmalstreit Und Russische Minderheit in Estland', *Russland Analysen* no. 134 (2007).

41. 'Here We Go Again', *The Baltic Times*, 4 April 2007, https://perma.cc/JT4M-LZ9L.

42. Ministry of Foreign Affairs of the Russian Federation, 'Remarks and Replies to Media Questions by Russian Minister of Foreign Affairs Sergey Lavrov at Joint Press Conference with Spanish Minister of Foreign Affairs Miguel Angel Moratinos after Their Talks, Madrid, April 18, 2007', Russian Federation, 19 April 2007 [transcript], https://perma.cc/PWQ5-XA5J.

43. Ministry of Foreign Affairs of the Russian Federation, 'On the Note of the Ministry of Foreign Affairs of Russia to the Foreign Ministry of Estonia', Russian Federation, 23 April 2007 [press release, GoogleTranslate], https://perma.cc/YWE5-KPU2. Russia also raised the objections to the removal of the statue by one of the daughters of the soldiers buried at the grave site.

44. Ministry of Foreign Affairs of the Russian Federation, 'Statement by the Permanent Representative of the Russian Federation, AN Borodavkin, at the Meeting of the OSCE Permanent Council', Russian Federation, 3 May 2007 [transcript, GoogleTranslate], https://perma.cc/2W8A-5WML.

45. 'The Lavrov Letter in Full', 12 May 2007, A lamb with no guiding light [blog], https://perma.cc/2A2T-VX2E. The translation from Finnish, provided by the blogger, can be independently corroborated by concurrent newspaper accounts at the time.

46. President of Russia, 'Speech at the Military Parade Celebrating the 62nd Anniversary of Victory in the Great Patriotic War', Russian Federation, 9 May 2007 [transcript], https://perma.cc/KHE8-TSE8.

47. BBC, 'Estonia Hit by 'Moscow Cyber War', BBC, 17 May 2007, https://perma.cc/ U98H-J4YF; quote from Mark Landler and John Markoff, 'Digital Fears Emerge after Data Siege in Estonia', New York Times, 29 May 2007.

48. Nicole Perlroth, 'Online Security Experts Link More Breaches to Russian Government', New York Times, 29 October 2014; Nargiz Asadova, 'We, the Russian Overseas, Do Not Need Foreigners', 5 March 2009 [blog, GoogleTranslate], https:// perma.cc/ANR2-CHCZ; Andrey Zlobin and Xenia Bolletskaya, 'Electronic Bomb— Who Is Behind the Cyberwar between Russia and Estonia?', Vedomosti, 28 May 2007 [GoogleTranslate], https://perma.cc/9CW6-UZRD.

49. Highlighting the impact of the missing attributive evidence on securitization, see Lene Hansen and Helen Nissenbaum, 'Digital Disaster, Cyber-Security, and the Copenhagen School', International Studies Quarterly no. 53 (2009): 1170.

50. See also Amir Lupovici, 'The "Attribution Problem" and the Social Construction of "Violence": Taking Cyber Deterrence Literature a Step Forward', International Studies Perspectives 17, no. 3 (2016); Hansen and Nissenbaum, 'Digital Disaster, Cyber-Security, and the Copenhagen School'.

51. This section builds on my own work in Egloff, 'Public Attribution of Cyber Intrusions', and Florian J. Egloff, 'Contested Public Attributions of Cyber Incidents and the Role of Academia', Contemporary Security Policy 41, no. 1 (2020).

52. Thomas Rid and Ben Buchanan, 'Attributing Cyber Attacks', Journal of Strategic Studies 38, nos. 1–2 (2015); Clement Guitton, Inside the Enemy's Computer: Identifying Cyber-Attackers (London: Hurst, 2017); Herbert Lin, 'Attribution of Malicious Cyber Incidents: From Soup to Nuts', Journal of International Affairs 70, no. 1 (2016); Ashley Coward and Corneliu Bjola, 'Cyber-Intelligence and Diplomacy: The Secret Link', in Secret Diplomacy: Concepts, Contexts and Cases, ed. Corneliu Bjola and Stuart Murray, Routledge New Diplomacy Studies (Abingdon: Routledge, 2016), 207; Marcus Schulzke, 'The Politics of Attributing Blame for Cyberattacks and the Costs of Uncertainty', Perspectives on Politics 16, no. 4 (2018): 954–68. For literature on how attribution links to deterrence, see Jon R. Lindsay, 'Tipping the Scales: The Attribution Problem and the Feasibility of Deterrence against Cyberattack', Journal of Cybersecurity 1, no. 1 (2015); Sandeep Baliga, Ethan Bueno De Mesquita, and Alexander Wolitzky, 'Deterrence with Imperfect Attribution', American Political Science Review 114, no. 4 (2020).

53. Rid and Buchanan, 'Attributing Cyber Attacks', 7, 32.

54. On misattribution, see also Miguel Alberto Gomez, 'Past behavior and future judgements: seizing and freezing in response to cyber operations', Journal of Cybersecurity 5, no. 1 (2019). Monica Kaminska, 'Restraint under conditions of uncertainty: Why the United States tolerates cyberattacks', Journal of Cybersecurity 7, no. 1 (2021).

55. Guitton, Inside the Enemy's Computer, 82. See also 'Achieving Attribution', PhD Thesis, King's College London, 2014, 98–122.

56. Lin, 'Attribution of Malicious Cyber Incidents'.

57. Steffens, *Auf Der Spur Der Hacker Wie Man Die Täter Hinter Der Computer-Spionage Enttarnt* (Berlin: Springer Vieweg, 2018). See also the updated English version, Timo Steffens, *Attribution of Advanced Persistent Threats: How to Identify the Actors Behind Cyber-Espionage* (Berlin: Springer Vieweg, 2020).

58. See Egloff, 'Public Attribution of Cyber Intrusions, originally introduced in Florian J. 'Cybersecurity and Non-State Actors: A Historical Analogy with Mercantile Companies, Privateers, and Pirates, DPhil Thesis, University of Oxford, 2018. For further elaboration on sense-making see Florian J. Egloff and Myriam Dunn Cavelty, 'Attribution and Knowledge Creation Assemblages in Cybersecurity Politics, *Journal of Cybersecurity* 7, no. 1 (2021), doi: 10.1093/cybsec/tyab002; Egloff, 'Public Attribution of Cyber Intrusions'.

59. See Egloff, 'Public Attribution of Cyber Intrusions'.

60. For further depth on these contestations following public attributions, see Egloff, 'Contested Public Attributions of Cyber Incidents and the Role of Academia'.

61. The full-length theoretical argument for this can be found in Egloff, 'Public Attribution of Cyber Intrusions'.

62. My own view of how to think about public attribution as a means of response, see Florian J. Egloff and Max Smeets, 'Publicly Attributing Cyber Attacks: A Framework, *Journal of Strategic Studies* (2021); see further, Gil Baram and Uri Sommer, 'Covert or Not Covert: National Strategies During Cyber Conflict, paper presented at the 2019 11th International Conference on Cyber Conflict (CyCon), 28–31 May 2019; Kristen E. Eichensehr, 'The Law and Politics of Cyberattack Attribution, *UCLA Law Review* 67 (2020); Andrew J. Grotto, 'Deconstructing Cyber Attribution: A Proposed Framework and Lexicon, *IEEE Security & Privacy* 18, no. 1 (2020); Xander Bouwman, Harm Griffioen, Jelle Egbers, Christian Doerr, Bram Klievink, and Michel van Eeten, 'A Different Cup of TI? The Added Value of Commercial Threat Intelligence, in *Proceedings of the 29th USENIX Security Symposium*, San Diego, CA: USENIX Association, 2020; Sasha Romanosky and Benjamin Boudreaux, 'Private-Sector Attribution of Cyber Incidents: Benefits and Risks to the U.S. Government, *International Journal of Intelligence and CounterIntelligence* 34, no. 3 (2021); Lennart Maschmeyer, Ronald J. Deibert, and Jon R. Lindsay, 'A Tale of Two Cybers—How Threat Reporting by Cybersecurity Firms Systematically Underrepresents Threats to Civil Society, *Journal of Information Technology & Politics* 18, no. 1 (2021); Martha Finnemore and Duncan B. Hollis, 'Beyond Naming and Shaming: Accusations and International Law in Cybersecurity, *European Journal of International Law* (2020).

63. For an analysis focusing only on state responsibility, see Jason Healey, 'The Spectrum of National Responsibility for Cyberattacks, *Brown Journal of World Affairs* 18, no. 1 (2011).

64. Joel Brenner and Jon R. Lindsay, 'Correspondence: Debating the Chinese Cyber Threat, *International Security* 40, no. 1 (2015): 192.

65. Federal Bureau of Investigation, 'Wanted by the FBI: Joshua Samuel Aaron, news release, 2 June 2015, https://perma.cc/AY3N-6UFJ. On the return, see 'American in Russia to Return to Face U.S. Charges in J.P. Morgan Hacking Case, Reuters News, 14 December 2016. https://perma.cc/L2CR-J443.

66. Some even say cyber operations are particularly badly suited for signalling. See, e.g., Ben Buchanan, *The Hacker and the State: Cyber Attacks and the New Normal of Geopolitics* (Cambridge, MA: Harvard University Press, 2020). For my own view, see Florian J. Egloff and Lennart Maschmeyer, 'Shaping Not Signaling: Understanding Cyber Operations as a Means of Espionage, Attack, and Destabilization', *International Studies Review* 23, no. 3 (2021).

67. Andrew Higgins, 'Maybe Private Russian Hackers Meddled in Election, Putin Says', *New York Times*, 1 June 2017. Note, the Mueller investigation and indictments leave little doubt as to the Russian origin of the interference attempts in the 2016 elections. See Robert S. Mueller, III, *Report on the Investigation into Russian Interference in the 2016 Presidential Election*, vol. 1, Washington, DC: US Department of Justice, 2019.

68. The importance and function of such top-level cover in Russian organized crime more generally is well explained in Mark Galeotti, *The Vory: Russia's Super Mafia* (New Haven: Yale University Press, 2018).

69. On Russia's cooperation with organized crime more broadly, see contemporarily Mark Galeotti, 'Crimintern: How the Kremlin Uses Russia's Criminal Networks in Europe', policy brief, European Council on Foreign Relations, London, 2017. For a major work on the Russian mafia covering the turbulent 1990s, see Federico Varese, *The Russian Mafia: Private Protection in a New Market Economy* (Oxford: Oxford University Press, 2001).

70. Misha Glenny, *Darkmarket: Cyberthieves, Cybercops, and You*, 1st U.S. ed. (New York: Alfred A. Knopf, 2011); Krebs, *Spam Nation*; Goncharov, 'Criminal Hideouts for Lease'; idem, 'Russian Underground 2.0', Trend Micro, Cupertino, CA, 2015, 7; Joseph Menn, *Fatal System Error: The Hunt for the New Crime Lords Who Are Bringing Down the Internet* (New York, London: PublicAffairs, 2010); Nikolas K. Gvosdev, 'The Bear Goes Digital: Russia and Its Cyber Capabilities', in *Cyberspace and National Security Threats, Opportunities, and Power in a Virtual World*, ed. Derek S. Reveron (Washington, DC: Georgetown University Press, 2012). On patriotic hackers, see also Soldatov and Borogan, *The New Nobility*, Chapter 18.

71. Sarmistha Acharya, 'Dyre Malware Disrupted after Russian Authorities Raid Moscow Film Company Office', *International Business Times*, 7 February 2016, https://perma. cc/79RP-RKV2; Ruslan Stoyanov, 'The Hunt for Lurk', Kaspersky, 30 August 2016, https://perma.cc/5VFR-RK5L.

72. This case relies heavily on U.S. court documents. As such, it privileges the U.S. governmental discourse over potentially alternative discourses from the individuals involved. Research commitments of symmetry and generosity towards all stakeholders meant that efforts were made to corroborate the accounts through other sources and research alternative narratives by the accused individuals themselves. In the case of Roman Seleznev, there exist court filings on his behalf. In the case of Bogachev and Dokuchaev et al., no evidence documenting their perspective was found. Hence, the analysis presented here is a snapshot of the discourses available at the time of this writing and may be revised upon availability of a future Russian account of the two cases.

73. For a profile of the Seleznev case see Nicole Perlroth, 'Russian Hacker Sentenced to 27 Years in Credit Card Case', *New York Times*, 21 April 2017.

74. United States of America v. Roman V. Seleznev, CR11-0070RAJ —Sentencing Memorandum (Document No. 464), 5-6 (2017). Indeed, diplomatic requests for assistance had failed already in earlier cybercrime cases. For an early case, see, e.g., Kevin Poulsen, *Kingpin: How One Hacker Took over the Billion-Dollar Cybercrime Underground*, 1st ed. (New York: Crown, 2011), 51.

75. Ministry of Foreign Affairs of the Russian Federation, 'Foreign Minister Sergey Lavrov's Interview to Komsomolskaya Pravda Newspaper and Radio, Moscow', Russian Federation, 31 May 2016 [transcript], https://perma.cc/938U-XQTA.

76. Ministry of Foreign Affairs of the Russian Federation, 'Briefing by Foreign Ministry Spokesperson Maria Zakharova, Moscow', Russian Federation, 27 April 2017 [transcript], https://perma.cc/5DWJ-E86Z.

77. United States of America v. Roman V. Seleznev, CR11-0070RAJ—Letter (Document No. 463) (2017).

78. 18 U.S. Code Chapter 209: Extradition. Title 18 Part II.

79. Excellent profiles on the Bogachev case were published by *Wired* and the *New York Times*, see Garret M. Graff and Chad Hagen, 'Inside the Hunt for Russia's Most Notorious Hacker', *Wired*, April 2017; Michael Schwirtz and Joseph Goldstein, 'Russian Espionage Piggybacks on a Cybercriminal's Hacking', *New York Times*, 12 March 2017.

80. Federal Bureau of Investigation, 'Wanted by the FBI: Evgeniy Mikhailovich Bogachev', news release, 10 May 2017, https://perma.cc/66T4-YSH9. For the charges see United States of America v. Evgeniy Bogachev, CR14-00127-AJS— Indictment (Document No. 1) (2014). The one case known to the author, in which a bounty was successful, is the arrest of Sasser Worm author Sven Jaschan. Thanks to Clement Guitton for pointing this out.

81. Michael Sandee, Tillmann Werner, and Elliott Peterson, 'Gameover Zeus— Bad Guys and Backends', paper presented at the Black Hat USA, Las Vegas, 5–6 August 2015.

82. Michael Sandee, 'Gameover Zeus. Backgrounds on the Badguys and the Backends', Delft:Fox-IT, 2015, 2.

83. Sandee, 'Gameover Zeus', 21–23. Note that the coordination between criminals and intelligence agencies is a significant challenge for both parties involved. See for example The Grugq, 'Cyber Operators — Differences Matter', 29 September 2017 [blog], https://perma.cc/JA9R-MAVP. See also The Grugq, 'How Very APT', presentation at the 10th Troopers Conference, Heidelberg, Germany, 23 March, 2017.

84. This is a confirmed assessment. For a contemporary example of two sources confirming this to Meduza, see Daniil Turovsky, 'America's Hunt for Russian Hackers: How FBI Agents Tracked Down Four of the World's Biggest Cyber-Criminals and Brought Them to Trial in the U.S', translated to English by Kevin Rothrock, Meduza, 9 September 2017, https://perma.cc/VNX9-KU4T.

85. In a newspaper article by a cybersecurity reporter with a credible track record, SecureWorks analyst Alex Tilley is quoted assessing Dyre to be 'some or all of the same people including Bogachev', The same article quotes anonymous sources

saying that many Dyre operators were 'released without being charged' and are back in the cybercriminal business. See Thomas Fox-Brewster, 'Behind the Mystery of Russia's "Dyre" Hackers Who Stole Millions from American Business', *Forbes*, 4 May 2017, https://perma.cc/HR3P-344A. If the claims were true, it would further substantiate the depth of the relationship between the state and cybercriminals.

86. United States of America v. Dmitry Dokuchaev et al., CR17-103—Indictment (2017). Note for context: Dokuchaev together with three others, including Kaspersky employee Ruslan Stoyanov, were arrested for high treason in Russia on 4 December 2016. Not many details are known about their cases, though there is some speculation about suspected links to Western intelligence agencies. Hence, though Dokuchaev et al. provides the most detailed substantiation of FSB and cybercriminal cooperation to date, and no reason to question the veracity of the allegations exists, there is a question why the U.S. government chose to reveal that level of detail in February 2017. For background and coverage of their cases, see, e.g., Brian Krebs, 'A Shakeup in Russia's Top Cybercrime Unit', krebsonsecurity.com, 28 January 2017 [blog], https://perma.cc/GX9Z-6VQY; 'Russia Federal Agents Suspected of Treason Reportedly Passed Secrets to the CIA', *Moscow Times*, 31 January 2017; Brian Krebs, 'Four Men Charged with Hacking 500m Yahoo Accounts', krebsonsecurity.com, 15 March 2017 [blog], https://perma.cc/PAK6-UL9Q.

87. U.S. Department of Justice, 'U.S. Charges Russian FSB Officers and Their Criminal Conspirators for Hacking Yahoo and Millions of Email Accounts', U.S. Department of Justice, 15 March 2017, https://perma.cc/688M-8UY2.

88. United States of America v. Dmitry Dokuchaev et al., 10.

89. United States of America v. Dmitry Dokuchaev et al., 1–2.

90. United States of America v. Dmitry Dokuchaev et al., 2.

91. The tactics, techniques, and procedures of Belan's intrusions in 2012–2013 are described in detail in Chris McNab, 'Alexsey's TTPs', Medium, 19 March 2017 [blog], https://perma.cc/3G55-KR9H.

92. United States of America v. Dmitry Dokuchaev et al., 11–13.

93. United States of America v. Dmitry Dokuchaev et al., 14–16.

94. United States of America v. Dmitry Dokuchaev et al., 16.

95. Krebs, 'Four Men Charged with Hacking 500m Yahoo Accounts'.

96. Washington Post Staff, 'Full Testimony of FBI Director James Comey in Front of the Senate Judiciary Committee on FBI Oversight', *Washington Post*, 3 May 2017 [transcript], https://perma.cc/3KDP-6TDK. The head of the UK national crime agency puts it more diplomatically: Having previously referred to the overrepresentation of highly sophisticated cybercriminals in Russia and neighbouring countries, they are often operating in 'jurisdictions with relatively weak cybercrime-fighting capability, or where the mechanisms and/or policies required to facilitate effective bilateral law enforcement action are immature', Jamie Saunders, 'Tackling Cybercrime—The UK Response', *Journal of Cyber Policy* 2, no. 1 (2017): 11.

97. These are questions first raised and discussed by Marcy Wheeler, 'Why Would FSB Officer Dmitry Dokuchaev Use a Yahoo Email Account to Spy for Russia?', emptywheel.net blog, 18 March 2017 [blog], https://perma.cc/5BHD-XTVE.

98. Paul M. Kennedy, *The Rise and Fall of British Naval Mastery* (London: Penguin, 2004), 38.

99. Kennedy, *The Rise and Fall of British Naval Mastery*, 38.

100. First reported in Kogershin Sagieva, 'Arrested in the Case of State Treasury, the Top Manager of Kaspersky Lab Asked the Authorities', TV Rain, 12 April 2017 [GoogleTranslate], https://perma.cc/G8G6-AY78. Partial letters were published in Eva Merkacheva, 'The Internet as a Territory Where One Might Become a Super Villain', Moskovsky Komsomolets, 17 April 2017 [GoogleTranslate], https://perma.cc/V7LS-4J8V. (A professional translation of these excerpts is available in 'Paper Publishes Bits of Arrested Russian Lab Employee Memoir', BBC Monitoring Former Soviet Union, 11 May 2017.)

101. Being in pretrial arrest at the time of making the statements makes Ruslan Stoyanev a source with a peculiar motivation, which, for an outsider, is difficult to assess. Nothing is known as to why Stoyanev decided to give his account to the newspaper and why he was able to do so. Hence, his account, while plausible, on its own is to be assigned low trustworthiness. However, in combination with the rest of the data presented in this book, it confirms the interpretation of state-criminal nexus in the area of cybercrime. For the best analysis of the treason case, see Kimberely Zenz, 'Infighting Among Russian Security Services in the Cyber Sphere', Paper presented at Black Hat USA, Las Vegas, 2019.

102. Andrew E. Kramer, 'How Russia Recruited Elite Hackers for Its Cyberwar', *New York Times*, 29 December 2016; Brian Krebs, 'The Download on the DNC Hack', krebsonsecurity.com, 3 January 2017 [blog], https://perma.cc/S7XF-7ATZ; Daniil Turovsky, 'Russian Cyber Army: How the State Creates Military Detachments of Hackers', Meduza, 7 November 2016 [GoogleTranslate], https://perma.cc/9K4T-PF64.

103. On Dmitry Dokuchaev being a former criminal hacker, see Svetlana Reiter, 'What the Arrest of the Russian Intel Top Cyber-Crime Expert Has to Do with American Elections', The Bell, 8 December 2017, https://perma.cc/8P56-G5FR; Alexander Boreiko and Yulia Belous, 'Face to Face with a Hacker', Vedomosti, 2 November 2004 [GoogleTranslate], https://perma.cc/HTV4-S7G5. On the hacker 'Forb' being the Dmitry Dokuchaev of interest, see Mike and Forb, 'Perl Bruteforce', xakep.ru, 17 January 2002 [GoogleTranslate], https://perma.cc/7NS9-WS8S; Dmitry Dokuchaev (aka Forb), 'Dedicated for the Hacker', xakep.ru, 2006 [GoogleTranslate], https://perma.cc/9MBP-Z994.

104. 'Hackers Are Humans Too—Cyber Leads to CI Leads', Communications Security Establishment Canada, *The Intercept*, 2 August 2017, https://perma.cc/Y6TS-DCG5.

105. For an account detailing the reassertion of the state over organized crime in the late 1990s, see Varese, *The Russian Mafia*. For the broader political context, see Mark Galeotti, 'Moscow's Mercenaries Reveal the Privatisation of Russian Geopolitics', openDemocracy, 29 August 2017, https://perma.cc/PL7R-TY88; Mark Galeotti, 'Stolypin: Russia Has No Grand Plans, but Lots of "Adhocrats"', intellinews, 18 January 2017,https://perma.cc/6VCV-Z47R; Thomas E. Graham, 'The Sources of Russian Conduct', *The National Interest*, 24 August 2016, https://

perma.cc/FZ5C-XC6Y; see also Joss I. Meakins, 'Squabbling Siloviki: Factionalism within Russia's Security Services', *International Journal of Intelligence and CounterIntelligence* 31, no. 2 (2018).

106. The firm is referred to by the cryptonym ENFER and, as can be deduced from the report, does not refer to Kaspersky, see Winnona DeSombre et al., 'Countering Cyber Proliferation: Zeroing in on Access-as-a-Service', Atlantic Council, New York, 2021.

107. See the industry reports on APT28, APT29, Turla, or the Sandworm team (links to the various reports are best found on http://apt.threattracking.com). More generally on Russia's intelligence services, see a contemporary account in Mark Galeotti, 'Putin's Hydra: Inside Russia's Intelligence Services', policy brief, European Council on Foreign Relations, London, 2016. For the long history, one of the best sources is Christopher M. Andrew and Vasili Mitrokhin, *The Sword and the Shield: The Mitrokhin Archive and the Secret History of the KGB*, 1st ed. (New York: Basic Books, 1999).

108. Ben Buchanan, *The Cybersecurity Dilemma: Hacking, Trust and Fear between Nations* (Oxford: Oxford University Press, 2017).

109. Lucas Kello, 'The Security Dilemma of Cyberspace: Ancient Logic, New Problems', Lawfare, 28 August 2017 [blog], https://perma.cc/V2Y4-EMZP.

110. Kello, *The Virtual Weapon and International Order*.

111. Kello, *The Virtual Weapon and International Order*, 176. However, the four degrees of closeness are not further developed. See, e.g., the 2-by-2 matrix on p. 183, which splits the actors into state and private actors, not incorporating the nuance introduced with the four degrees of closeness.

112. Kello, *The Virtual Weapon and International Order*, 183, 230.

113. Specifically, one could say criminologists start with studying crime, whilst this book starts with the political rendering of the activity of hacking, which is sometimes rendered criminal and sometimes not. Different focal points lead to different types of analyses. For an example of a criminologists' work on cybercrime, see Jonathan Lusthaus's excellent work on Eastern European cybercrime that focuses on the sociology and economics of cybercrime but brackets the interrogation of the political constitution of its presence. Jonathan Lusthaus, 'Honour among (Cyber)Thieves?', Extra Legal Governance Institute Working Paper No. 2016-1, https://perma.cc/UF99-2AS8; see further, Jonathan Lusthaus, *Industry of Anonymity: Inside the Business of Cybercrime* (Cambridge, MA: Harvard University Press, 2018).

114. Lauren Benton, 'Legal Spaces of Empire: Piracy and the Origins of Ocean Regionalism', *Comparative Studies in Society and History* 47, no. 4 (2005).

Chapter 7

1. Stine Jacobsen, 'Silicon Valley Giants Outrank Many Nations, Says First "Techplomat"', Reuters News, 19 June 2017. The first (now former) Danish technology ambassador was hired by Microsoft in 2020.

2. Though some senior technology executives voiced their interest in creating their own lawless zones of experimentation. See, e.g., Larry Page's comments regarding regulations: 'we also haven't maybe built mechanisms to allow experimentation. There's many, many exciting and important things you could do that you just can't do 'cause they're illegal or they're not allowed by regulation'. TechHive Staff, 'Hello, Larry! Google's Page on Negativity, Laws, and Competitors', PC World, 15 May 2013 [transcript of keynote address at Google I/O], https://perma.cc/B4LB-HSDH. Another prominent libertarian initiative working towards zones outside the state system is funded by technology billionaire Peter Thiel. See comments on 'Seasteading' in George Packer, 'No Death, No Taxes', The New Yorker, 28 November 2011.

3. Arguing for more research on mercantile companies for a better understanding of the resurgence of private violence today, see Andrew Phillips, 'Company Sovereigns, Private Violence and Colonialism', in Routledge Handbook of Private Security Studies, ed. Rita Abrahamsen and Anna Leander (New York: Routledge, 2016), 46–47. See further J. C. Sharman, Empires of the Weak: The Real Story of European Expansion and the Creation of the New World Order (Princeton: Princeton University Press, 2019); Andrew Phillips and J. C. Sharman, Outsourcing Empire: How Company-States Made the Modern World (Princeton: Princeton University Press, 2020); Andrew Phillips and J. C. Sharman, 'Company-States and the Creation of the Global International System', European Journal of International Relations 26, no. 4 (2020).

4. For an explanation why the statist organized Portuguese Estado da India failed, whilst the Dutch and English East India Companies succeeded, see Andrew Phillips and Jason C. Sharman, 'Explaining Durable Diversity in International Systems: State, Company, and Empire in the Indian Ocean', International Studies Quarterly 59, no. 3 (2015): 440–41.

5. Gordon Corera, Intercept: The Secret History of Computers and Spies (London: Weidenfeld & Nicolson, 2015).

6. Michael Joseph Gross, 'Enter the Cyber-Dragon', Vanity Fair, 1 September 2011.

7. Gross, 'Enter the Cyber-Dragon'.

8. Bryan Krekel, Patton Adams, and George Bakos, 'Occupying the Information High Ground: Chinese Capabilities for Computer Network Operations and Cyber Espionage', West Falls Church, VA, Northrop Grumman, 2012, 98. See also John Markoff, 'Cyberattack on Google Said to Hit Password System', New York Times, 19 April 2010.

9. Gross, 'Enter the Cyber-Dragon'; Markoff, 'Cyberattack on Google Said to Hit Password System'.

10. Bruce Schneier, 'U.S. Enables Chinese Hacking of Google', CNN, 23 January 2010, https://perma.cc/Y2SB-DL4U. Schneier's account is corroborated by further reporting, see Ellen Nakashima, 'Chinese Hackers Who Breached Google Gained Access to Sensitive Data, U.S. Officials Say', Washington Post, 20 June 2013, https://perma.cc/G8UR-5SY2.

11. See, e.g., 'PRISM/US-984XN Overview or the SIGAD Used Most in NSA Reporting Overview', National Security Agency, Washington Post, 6 June 2013

(dated April 2013), http://www.washingtonpost.com/wp-srv/special/politics/prism-collection-documents/.

12. Nakashima, 'Chinese Hackers Who Breached Google Gained Access to Sensitive Data'.

13. ' "What we found was the attackers were actually looking for the accounts that we had lawful wiretap orders on," Aucsmith says. "So if you think about this, this is brilliant counter-intelligence. You have two choices: If you want to find out if your agents, if you will, have been discovered, you can try to break into the FBI to find out that way. Presumably that's difficult. Or you can break into the people that the courts have served paper on and see if you can find it that way. That's essentially what we think they were trolling for, at least in our case" '. Kenneth Corbin, '"Aurora" Cyber Attackers Were Really Running Counter-Intelligence', CIO.com, 22 April 2013, https://perma.cc/LJ8Y-E2GX.

14. Nakashima, 'Chinese Hackers Who Breached Google Gained Access to Sensitive Data'.

15. David E. Sanger and John Markoff, 'After Google's Stand on China, U.S. Treads Lightly', New York Times, 14 January 2010.

16. The exact nature and circumstance of such access also remain shrouded in secrecy. Access could have been gained, e.g., by (a) asking the owner of the system (b) gaining authority to access the system through the government, or (c) accessing the system directly. Shane Harris quotes a former intelligence official saying, 'Google broke into the server' but notes that it's still unclear how the company's investigators 'gained access to the server'. Shane Harris, @War: The Rise of the Military-Internet Complex (Boston: Houghton Mifflin Harcourt, 2014), 172.

17. Eric Schmidt and Jonathan Rosenberg, How Google Works (London: John Murray, 2014), 148.

18. Eric Schmidt and Jared Cohen, The New Digital Age: Reshaping the Future of People, Nations and Business (London: John Murray, 2013), 109.

19. Michael Riley, 'U.S. Agencies Said to Swap Data with Thousands of Firms', Bloomberg, 15 June 2013, https://perma.cc/5NT2-6QQJ.

20. This debate was already spelled out in public when Google entered the Chinese market in 2006. Google, 'Testimony: The Internet in China by Google Inc. (Represented by Eliot Schrage) before the Subcommittee on Asia and the Pacific, and the Subcommittee on Africa, Global Human Rights, and International Operations. Committee on International Relations, United States House of Representatives', Google Inc., 15 February 2006 [transcript], https://perma.cc/B3U9-CUP5.

21. Schmidt and Rosenberg, How Google Works, 144–45.

22. Corera, Intercept, 258. Evidence of censorship is self-reported by Google both publicly on its website and privately to U.S. government officials. Google, 'Google Transparency Report: Known Disruptions of Traffic to Google Products and Services', Google Inc., 2017, https://perma.cc/R9WC-TJZS; 'Google Claims Harrassment by Chinese Government', 12 July 2009, diplomatic cable from the U.S. embassy in Beijing, No. 09BEIJING1957_a, Wikileaks Public Library of U.S. Diplomacy, Wikileaks, https://perma.cc/XS3P-ZV6H.

23. Sergey Brin. 'It Was a Real Step Backward', interview by Philip Bethge. Der Spiegel, 30 March 2010.

24. Schmidt and Rosenberg, *How Google Works*, 144.
25. Schmidt and Rosenberg, *How Google Works*, 146.
26. Schmidt and Rosenberg, *How Google Works*, 148.
27. Schmidt and Rosenberg, *How Google Works*, 149.
28. Google, 'A New Approach to China', Google Inc., 12 January 2010 [blog], https://perma.cc/L9GP-BN5X.
29. See U.S. Congress, U.S.-China Economic and Security Review Commission, Annual Report to Congress, 111th Cong., 1st sess., Washington, DC, U.S. Government Printing Office, 2009, http://www.uscc.gov, 163–65.
30. Google, 'A New Approach to China'; Bryan Krekel, 'Capability of the People's Republic of China to Conduct Cyber Warfare and Computer Network Exploitation', McLean, VA, Northrop Grumman, 2009.
31. Information Warfare Monitor, 'Tracking Ghostnet: Investigating a Cyber Espionage Network', 2009, https://perma.cc/H27G-9RWX; Nart Villeneuve. Malware Explorer [Blog], https://perma.cc/YX34-Q8JA.
32. Google, 'A New Approach to China: An Update', Google Inc., 22 March 2010 [blog], https://perma.cc/R86E-SUJ2.
33. For current DNS-based censorship technology used in China, see Oliver Farnan, Alexander Darer, and Joss Wright, 'Poisoning the Well: Exploring the Great Firewall's Poisoned DNS Responses', In *Proceedings of the 2016 ACM on Workshop on Privacy in the Electronic Society*, Vienna, Austria, ACM, 2016.
34. Harris, *@War*, 173.
35. Hillary Clinton, 'Statement on Google Operations in China', U.S. Department of State, 12 January 2010 [Press release], https://perma.cc/H3FQ-RTMY.
36. See 'Re: 12/21 Revisions to Internet Freedom Speech', email chain documenting the revision history of the internet freedom speech, Doc No. C05763238, U.S. Department of State, FOIA Case No. F-2014-20439, 29 December 2009, https://foia.state.gov/Search/Results.aspx?collection=Clinton_Email. The email references an email from Tomicah S. Tillemann dated 21 December 2009 with the subject line: 'Fw: 12/21 Revisions to Internet Freedom Speech'.
37. See, e.g., U.S. Department of State, 'Daily Press Briefing by the Assistant Secretary Philip J. Crowley', 14 January 2010, https://perma.cc/T265-PGUP.
38. Hillary Clinton, 'Remarks on Internet Freedom', U.S. Department of State, 21 January 2010 [transcript], https://perma.cc/HX6B-ZZY4.
39. Clinton, 'Remarks on Internet Freedom'.
40. Gross, 'Enter the Cyber-Dragon'.
41. To a great extent they still are unclear. See Madeline Carr, 'Public–Private Partnerships in National Cyber-Security Strategies', *International Affairs* 92, no. 1 (2016); Madeline Carr, *US Power and the Internet in International Relations* (Basingstoke: Palgrave Macmillan, 2016), 102–107; Myriam Dunn Cavelty and Florian J. Egloff, 'The Politics of Cybersecurity: Balancing Different Roles of the State', *St Antony's International Review* 15, no. 1 (2019); Florian J. Egloff and Myriam Dunn Cavelty, 'Attribution and Knowledge Creation Assemblages in Cybersecurity Politics', *Journal of Cybersecurity*, 7, no. 1 (2021), doi: 10.1093/cybsec/tyab002.

42. Two accounts report on the existence of such an agreement: Ellen Nakashima, 'Google to Enlist NSA to Help It Ward Off Cyberattacks', *Washington Post*, 4 February 2010, https://perma.cc/VZ4T-2ESS; Siobhan Gorman and Jessica E. Vascellaro, 'Google Working with NSA to Investigate Cyber Attack', *Wall Street Journal*, 4 February 2010, https://perma.cc/TYC9-ES5B.

43. Harris, *@War*, 175–76.

44. Harris, *@War*, 176; The direct quotation is from Nakashima, 'Chinese Hackers Who Breached Google Gained Access to Sensitive Data'.

45. From 10 to ca. 29%, see 'Percentage of Individuals using the Internet between 2000–2016' 'Statistics', ITU, 2017, https://perma.cc/ZKX8-RNQY.

46. Adam Segal, *The Hacked World Order: How Nations Fight, Trade, Maneuver, and Manipulate in the Digital Age* (New York: PublicAffairs, 2016), 29.

47. Segal, *The Hacked World Order*, 29.

48. Jon R. Lindsay, 'The Impact of China on Cybersecurity: Fiction and Friction', *International Security* 39, no. 3 (2015): 15.

49. In Chinese Communist Party terminology, the three evils are terrorism, secessionism, and extremism, and they are currently represented by the five poisons, the Uighur and Tibetan independence movement, the regime critical Falun Gong, the Chinese democracy movement, and the Taiwan independence movement. See Lindsay, 'The Impact of China on Cybersecurity', 38; Bundesministerium des Innern, 'Verfassungsschutzbericht', Berlin, 2016, 271.

50. Ministry of Foreign Affairs of the People's Republic of China, 'Foreign Ministry Spokesperson Jiang Yu's Regular Press Conference on January 14, 2010', People's Republic of China, 15 January 2010 [press release], https://perma.cc/PC2F-YAS8. See also 'China Says Its Web Open, Welcomes Int'l Companies', Xinhua, 14 January 2010, https://perma.cc/HLF4-YE5U. The Chinese embassies around the world, including in the United States, usually reposted the Xinhua articles on their websites.

51. 'Google Claims Harrassment by Chinese Government', 12 July 2009, Wikileaks Public Library of U.S. Diplomacy.

52. Ministry of Foreign Affairs of the People's Republic of China, 'Minister Xie Feng of the Chinese Embassy in the United States Reiterated China's Principled Position in Response to the Recent Announcement by Google on Possible Adjustment of Its Business in China', People's Republic of China, 18 January 2010 [press release], https://perma.cc/773D-GDZF.

53. 'China Says Google Case Should Not Be Linked to Ties with U.S.', Xinhua, 21 January 2010, https://perma.cc/U8WE-VM99.

54. 'Secretary's Internet Freedom Speech: China Reaction', 25 January 2010, diplomatic cable from the U.S. embassy in Beijing, No. 10BEIJING183_a, Wikileaks Public Library of U.S. Diplomacy, Wikileaks, https://perma.cc/6VZB-W4DM.

55. 'China Urges U.S. to Stop Accusations on So-Called Internet Freedom', Xinhua, 22 January 2010, https://perma.cc/U7EX-UTGS.

56. 'China Urges U.S. To Stop Accusations on So-Called Internet Freedom'.

57. 'Commentary: Don't Impose Double Standards on "Internet Freedom"', Xinhua, 24 January 2010, https://perma.cc/8FAJ-XLGA.

58. 'Commentary'.

59. 'Accusation of Chinese Government's Participation in Cyber Attack "Groundless": Ministry', Xinhua, 25 January 2010, https://perma.cc/A4D2-QNTF.

60. 'Google Update: PRC Role in Attacks and Response Strategy', 26. January 2010, dip-lomatic cable from the U.S. Embassy in Beijing, No. 10BEIJING207_a, Wikileaks Public Library of U.S. Diplomacy, Wikileaks, https://perma.cc/L2WS-SAR8.

61. Christopher Helman, 'Microsoft's Ballmer Calls out Google over China Stance', Forbes, 22 January 2010, https://perma.cc/ML39-SBA9.

62. David Morgan, 'Bill Gates Says Internet Needs to Thrive in China', Reuters News, 25. January 2010.

63. Steve Lohr, 'Bill Gates Defends Google, Then Pans It', New York Times, 25 January 2010.

64. Lohr, 'Bill Gates Defends Google, Then Pans It'.

65. Steve Ballmer, 'Microsoft & Internet Freedom', Microsoft on the Issues, 25 April 2010, [blog], https://perma.cc/28CG-L4A6.

66. Bobbie Johnson and Ian Katz, 'Google Co-Founder Sergey Brin Urges US to Act over China Web Censorship', The Guardian, 24 March 2010.

67. Phillips and Sharman, 'Explaining Durable Diversity in International Systems', 444.

68. Phillips and Sharman, 'Explaining Durable Diversity in International Systems', 444.

69. On the history of the large Western technology companies' relations with the Chinese government from a business ethics perspective, see Gary Elijah Dann and Neil Haddow, 'Just Doing Business or Doing Just Business: Google, Microsoft, Yahoo! and the Business of Censoring China's Internet', Journal of Business Ethics 79, no. 3 (2008); Justin Tan and Anna E. Tan, 'Business under Threat, Technology under Attack, Ethics under Fire: The Experience of Google in China', Journal of Business Ethics 110, no. 4 (2012).

70. Internet Society of China, 'Public Pledge of Self-Regulation and Professional Ethics for China Internet Industry', 26 March 2002, https://perma.cc/M95N-HSQG.

71. Florian J. Egloff, 'Public Attribution of Cyber Intrusions', Journal of Cybersecurity 6, no. 1 (2020); see further Florian J. Egloff and Max Smeets, 'Publicly Attributing Cyber Attacks: A Framework', Journal of Strategic Studies (2021), doi: 10.1080/01402390.2021.1895117; Florian J. Egloff and Andreas Wenger, 'Public Attribution of Cyber Incidents', in CSS Analysis ed. Fabien Merz (Zurich: Center for Security Studies, 2019).

72. Gross, 'Enter the Cyber-Dragon'.

73. Google, 'Google Cloud Security and Compliance: Google Has a Strong Security Culture', Google Inc., 2017, https://perma.cc/D2GP-K86Z.

74. Harris, @War, 175–77.

75. The discussion of hacking-back extends and refines arguments originally published in Florian Egloff, 'Cyber Privateering: A Risky Policy Choice for the United States', Lawfare, 17 November 2016 [blog], https://perma.cc/ME95-WAXZ. Plenty of evidence exists as to why a state might adopt offensive measures against attackers, see 'SID Today: "4th Party Collection": Taking Advantage of Non-Partner Computer Network Exploitation Activity', National Security Agency, Der Spiegel, 17 January

2015 (dated 2008), https://perma.cc/X85G-7NGW; 'Tutelage 411', NTOC, National Security Agency, *Der Spiegel*, 17 January 2015, https://perma.cc/5NWD-TDVV; 'Transgression Overview for Pod58', S31177, National Security Agency, *Der Spiegel*, 17 January 2015 (dated 7 February 2010), https://perma.cc/HMD3-7DTS.

76. It captures what Lucas Kello defines as active defensive measures. See Lucas Kello, *The Virtual Weapon and International Order* (New Haven: Yale University Press, 2017), 231–34.

77. One of the most extensive treatments of hacking-back identifies information gathering, which potentially leads to criminal prosecution and the publication of the gathered information to shame other governments as the purpose. Jeremy Rabkin and Ariel Rabkin, 'Hacking Back without Cracking Up', Hoover Institution, Stanford Universtiy, 2016. For the broader debate on authorizing private hack-back, see Kello, *The Virtual Weapon and International Order*, 229–46; Paul Rosenzewig, 'International Law and Private Actor Active Cyber Defensive Measures', *Stanford Journal of International Law* 50 (2014); Paul Rosenzweig, Steven P. Bucci, and David Inserra, 'Next Steps for U.S. Cybersecurity in the Trump Administration: Active Cyber Defense', Heritage Foundation, Washington DC, 2017; Dave Aitel, 'Cyber Deterrence "at Scale"', 10 June 2016 [blog], https://perma.cc/9YEN-P6UC; Dave Aitel, 'How "Active Defense" Would Work', CyberSecPolitics, 1 December 2016, [blog], https://perma.cc/2KLB-P2NK; Center for Cyber & Homeland Security, 'Into the Gray Zone—The Private Sector and Active Defense against Cyber Threats', Washington DC, 2016; Joseph Cox, 'Inside the Shadowy World of Revenge Hackers', Daily Beast, 19 September 2017, https://perma.cc/C9S8-UNUD; Dennis Broeders, 'Private Active Cyber Defense and (International) Cyber Security—Pushing the Line?' *Journal of Cybersecurity* 7, no. 1 (2021).

78. Leslie R. Caldwell, 'Assistant Attorney General Leslie R. Caldwell Delivers Remarks at the Georgetown Cybersecurity Law Institute', Department of Justice, 20 May 2015, https://perma.cc/M2AE-VWYD. For information how the U.S. tries to boost cooperation with industry see Department of Homeland Security, 'Enhanced Cybersecurity Services (ECS)', Department of Homeland Security, 2017, https://perma.cc/DU43-BDLF. For the background history of the precursor to the ECS program see Milton Mueller and Andreas Kuehn, 'Einstein on the Breach: Surveillance Technology, Cybersecurity and Organizational Change', paper presented at the 12th Workshop on the Economics of Information Security (WEIS), Washington DC, 2013.

79. The motivations can be the same as when states engage in hack-back, see Ben Buchanan, *The Cybersecurity Dilemma: Hacking, Trust and Fear between Nations* (Oxford: Oxford University Press, 2017).

80. There is anecdotal evidence of such hacking-back occurring. See, e.g., Cox, 'Inside the Shadowy World of Revenge Hackers'; Craig Timberg, Ellen Nakashima, and Danielle Douglas-Gabriel, 'Cyberattacks Trigger Talk of "Hacking Back"', *Washington Post*, 9 October 2014, https://perma.cc/2H4V-BM2V; Hannah Kuchler, 'Cyber Insecurity: Hacking Back', *Financial Times* (2015), https://perma.cc/U8UM-VLBY; malware.lu and itrust consulting, 'APT1: Technical Backstage—Malware Analysis', malware.lu, 27 March 2013, https://perma.cc/56GS-QTLB. For people

with moderate offensive skills, hack-back of command-and-control servers is some-times a realistic possibility, see Waylon Grange, 'Digital Vengeance: Exploiting the Most Notorious C&C Toolkits', briefing presented at the Black Hat USA, Las Vegas, 27 July, 2017.

81. John Scott-Railton, Adam Hulcoop, Bahr Abdul Razzak, Bill Marczak, Siena Anstis, and Ron Deibert, 'Dark Basin: Uncovering a Massive Hack-for-Hire Operation'. Citizen Lab, 2020.

82. For an excellent book-length elaboration of the analysis of the security dilemma be-tween states see Buchanan, *The Cybersecurity Dilemma*.

83. Palmerston to Clarendon, 5 April 1856, letter, MSS. Clar. Dep. C. 49, 241–242, Clarendon Papers, Bodleian Library, University of Oxford.

84. The introduction to the case overview has previously been published in Florian J. Egloff, 'Contested Public Attributions of Cyber Incidents and the Role of Academia', *Contemporary Security Policy* 41, no. 1 (2020). 'Notice to Sony Pictures Entertainment Inc.', 21 November 2014, email from 'God'sApstls' (dfrank1973. david@gmail.com) to five Sony executives, email ID 83432, Sony Archive, Wikileaks, https://perma.cc/6YB5-DVMY. Note: although no authenticity guar-antee is given, the email originates from the GMT + 0900 time zone.

85. 'Spokesman of Policy Department of NDC Blasts S. Korean Authorities' False Rumor About DPRK', *KCNAWatch*, 7 December 2014.

86. Sean Gallagher, 'Sony Pictures Attackers Demand: "Stop the Terrorist Film!"', *ars technica*, 8 December 2014.

87. David Perera, 'DHS: No Credible Threat to Sony Movie Launch', *Politico*, 16 December 2014; Mark Seal, 'An Exclusive Look at Sony's Hacking Saga', *Vanity Fair*, 28 February 2015. The threat assessment was reiterated on the 24 December 2014, see U.S. Department of Homeland Security and Federal Bureau of Investigation, 'November 2014 Cyber Intrusion on USPER I and Related Threats', *Joint Intelligence Bulletin* (2014), https://perma.cc/X6YN-XY26.

88. White House, 'Press Briefing by the Press Secretary Josh Earnest', 18 December 2014 [press briefing], https://perma.cc/JS4N-JTYL.

89. Federal Bureau of Investigation, 'Update on Sony Investigation', 19 December 2014 [news release], https://perma.cc/Z745-YR3S Later, more details were released, see James B. Comey, 'Adressing the Cyber Security Threat', paper presented at the International Conference on Cyber Security, Fordham University, New York, 7 January 2015.

90. Barack Obama, 'Remarks by the President in Year-End Press Conference', White House, 19 December 2014 [transcript], https://perma.cc/AQ6V-MEXN.

91. Jim Cowie, 'Someone Disconnects North Korea—Who?', Dyn Research, 23 December 2014 [blog], https://perma.cc/SA39-YDJK; Center for Applied Internet Data Analysis, 'View of Internet Outages in North Korea: Visible BGP Prefixes', University of California San Diego, https://perma.cc/K8C7-KCEL.

92. U.S. Department of the Treasury, 'Treasury Imposes Sanctions against the Government of the Democratic People's Republic of Korea', 2 January 2015 [news release], https://perma.cc/C7WV-HREF.

93. Sony Corporation, 'Consolidated Financial Results for the Fiscal Year Ended March 31 2015', 30 April 2015, No. 15-039E, https://perma.cc/SH42-EK4K. The total costs are estimated in Travis Sharp, 'Theorizing Cyber Coercion: The 2014 North Korean Operation against Sony', *Journal of Strategic Studies* 40, no. 7 (2017): 18.

94. United States of America v. Park Jin Hyok, No. MJ18-1479. (2018), U.S. District Court, Central District of California, https://perma.cc/SQA4-DUXR. In 2021, the U.S. issued an indictment extending the original complaint to two other North Korean Citizens, see United States of America v. Jon Chang Hyok et al., No. 2:20-cr-00614-DMG (2020). U.S. District Court, Central District of California, https://perma.cc/Z5WH-K78Z. For a discussion of the public contestation of the attribution in this case, see Egloff, 'Contested Public Attributions'.

95. Penetration of North Korean networks had been a priority of U.S. signals intelligence for a long time (See Appendix B in 'SIGINT Mission Strategic Plan FY 2008–2013', National Security Agency, *New York Times*, 2 November 2013 (dated 3 October 2007), http://www.nytimes.com/interactive/2013/11/03/world/docume nts-show-nsa-efforts-to-spy-on-both-enemies-and-allies.html. See also Enduring Targets—North Korea in 'United States SIGINT System January 2007 Strategic Mission List', National Security Agency, *New York Times*, 2 November 2013 (dated January 2007), http://www.nytimes.com/interactive/2013/11/03/world/docume nts-show-nsa-efforts-to-spy-on-both-enemies-and-allies.html. According to press reports the U.S. had indeed penetrated North Korean networks years earlier. See David E. Sanger and Martin Fackler, 'N.S.A. Breached North Korean Networks before Sony Attack, Officials Say', *New York Times*, 18 January 2015.

96. White House, 'Press Briefing by the Press Secretary Josh Earnest'.

97. U.S. Department of State, 'Daily Press Briefing by the Deputy Spokesperson Marie Harf', 23 December 2014, https://perma.cc/SPX8-L7J4.

98. U.S. Department of State, 'Daily Press Briefing'.

99. Dan Holden, 'North Korea Goes Offline', Arbor Networks, 22 December 2014, https://perma.cc/GK3E-LPNS. John Carlin's book further reinforces the interpreatation that the U.S. government was not behind the DDoS, but watched activists from the sidelines, see John P. Carlin and Garrett M. Graff, *The Dawn of the Code War: America's Battle against Russia, China, and the Rising Global Cyber Threat* (New York: PublicAffairs, 2018), 340.

100. Comey, 'Adressing the Cyber Security Threat'; James Clapper, 'National Intelligence, North Korea, and the National Cyber Discussion', paper presented at the International Conference on Cyber Security, Fordham University, New York, 7 January 2015. Note: just as in the Estonia case, the contention of the public attribution claim is worthy of study. However, it is not the focus of this case study, and hence no further analysis is performed here. For a case analysis see Egloff, 'Contested Public Attributions'.

101. White House, 'Statement by the Press Secretary on the Executive Order Entitled "Imposing Additional Sanctions with Respect to North Korea"', White House, 2 January 2015 [press release], https://perma.cc/ET5V-VGSM.

102. 'U.S. Can Never Justify Screening and Distribution of Reactionary Movie: Policy Department of NDC of DPRK', *KCNA*, 27 December 2014.

103. For reporting on the discussions with the Chinese at the time, see David E. Sanger, Nicole Perlroth, and Eric Schmitt, 'U.S. Asks China to Help Rein in Korean Hackers', *New York Times*, 20 December 2014.

104. Eric Lipton, David E. Sanger, and Scott Shane, 'The Perfect Weapon: How Russian Cyberpower Invaded the U.S.', *New York Times*, 13 December 2016. I highlight this account, as the first reports about this option were published a day before the actual outage took place. The discussions hinged on an American operation necessarily touching on Chinese sovereignty. Additional corroboration is offered by James Clapper in Shaun Waterman, 'Clapper: U.S. Shelved "Hack Backs" Due to Counterattack Fears', CyberScoop, 2 October 2017, https://perma.cc/6JX3-TY4Y.

105. United States of America v. Wang Dong et al., 14–118 (2014).

106. Walter Isaacson, David E. Sanger, and Michael Rogers, 'Beyond the Build: Leveraging the Cyber Mission Force', Aspen Institute, 23 July 2015 [transcript], https://perma.cc/DBV6-EMGT.

107. Isaacson, Sanger, and Rogers, 'Beyond the Build.' Advocating for a digital right to self-defence due to the state not protecting private actors, see Bryan Reinicke, Jeffrey Cummings, and Howard Kleinberg, 'The Right to Digital Self-Defense', *IEEE Security & Privacy* 15, no. 4 (2017).

108. On the administrative changes, see Nicholas A. M. Rodger, *The Command of the Ocean: A Naval History of Britain 1649–1815* (New York: W.W. Norton, 2006), 291–311.

109. On the navies involvement in the counter-piracy operations in the 1820s see Peter Earle, *The Pirate Wars* (London: Methuen, 2003), 183–208.

110. For this point on SPE's response and more broadly on the diverging expectations between the government and the private sector of investment into security, see Carr, *US Power and the Internet in International Relations*, 104.

111. 'Spokesman of Policy Department of NDC Blasts S. Korean Authorities' False Rumor About DPRK', *KCNAWatch*, 7 December 2014.

112. Note: just because the Snowden archives have given us extraordinary access and insight into Five-Eyes SIGINT operations, this does not mean that other states do not engage in the same types of operations.

113. 'Top 100 Digital Companies 2019', *Forbes*, 29 January 2020, https://perma.cc/V76P-D6S3. They used to be the biggest in 2017, Antoine Gara et al., 'The World's Biggest Public Companies', *Forbes*, 24 May 2017, https://perma.cc/NZ4C-Y49H.

114. ITU, 'Statistics'.

115. Facebook, 'Facebook Reports Third Quarter 2019 Results', 30 October 2019, https://perma.cc/GS6C-TKFZ.

116. Ross Miller, 'Gmail Now Has 1 Billion Monthly Active Users', TheVerge, 1 February 2016, https://perma.cc/NBP7-UP9A.

117. Kif Leswing, 'Investors Are Overlooking Apple's Next $50 Billion Business', Business Insider, 4 April 2016, https://perma.cc/3N27-WAQB.

118. Global Bandwith Research Service, 'Executive Summary', TeleGeography, 2016, 1 https://perma.cc/SG9J-FZK6..

119. Global Bandwith Research Service, 'Executive Summary', 1, 4. See also Craig Labovitz et al., 'Internet Inter-Domain Traffic', *SIGCOMM Computer Communication Review* 40, no. 4 (2010).

120. For the 2015 statistic see Global Bandwith Research Service, 'Executive Summary', 4; On new capacity, see Alan Mauldin, 'Shaping the Global Wholesale Bandwidth Market', PriMetrica, 28 July 2017 [blog], https://perma.cc/A7QQ-XBQX.

121. Global Bandwith Research Service, 'Executive Summary', TeleGeography, 2020, https://perma.cc/Y3PV-WEBX.

122. Michael V. Hayden, 'FISA for the 21st Century. Testimony to the United States Judiciary Committee of the US Senate', 26 July 2006 [transcript], https://perma.cc/CTN9-RXRP. Note also the title of Hayden's autobiography reflecting the motivation to use their legal powers to the fullest extent possible Michael V. Hayden, *Playing to the Edge: American Intelligence in the Age of Terror* (New York: Penguin Press, 2016).

123. 'PRISM/US-984XN Overview or the SIGAD Used Most in NSA Reporting Overview'. The date for Yahoo has been established to be demonstrably wrong. Rather than 3/12/08 it should read 5/12/08. Hence, the exactness of the dates, unless corroborated by other sources, should be read with caution; the order can be assumed to be broadly accurate. The existence of collection with these providers can be established with various other sources.

124. 'PRISM/US-984XN Overview or the SIGAD Used Most in NSA Reporting Overview'. The type of information collected is corroborated, among other documents, in the Privacy and Civil Liberties Oversight Board, 'Report on the Surveillance Program Operated Pursuant to Section 702 of the Foreign Intelligence Surveillance Act', 2, July 2014, https://perma.cc/2RZC-RC4F.

125. 'SIGINT Strategy 2012–2016', National Security Agency, *New York Times*, 23 November 2013 (dated 23 February 2012), https://perma.cc/3NEH-SGDH.

126. Google, 'Google Transparency Report: HTTPS Usage', Google Inc., 2021, https://perma.cc/B8ZX-53E8.

127. Jenna McLaughlin, 'Spy Chief Complains That Edward Snowden Sped up Spread of Encryption by 7 Years', *The Intercept*, 25 April 2016.

128. 'PRISM (US-984XN) Expanded Its Impact on NSA's Reporting Mission in FY12 Through Increased Tasking, Collection and Operational Improvements', National Security Agency, Henry Holt and Company, 13 May 2014, 111 https://perma.cc/8QRE-NEZ5. The importance was also highlighted in 'SSO Corporate Portfolio Overview', National Security Agency, *New York Times*, 15 August 2015 (dated 2012), https://perma.cc/WEB2-PZR4.

129. 'United States SIGINT System January 2007 Strategic Mission List'; 'What Is Known About NSA's PRISM Program', Electrospaces, 23 April 2014 [blog], https://perma.cc/2EJD-JATV.

130. 'SIGINT Strategy 2012–2016'.

131. Fiona Endres and Nicole Vögele, 'Weltweite Spionage-Operation Mit Schweizer Firma Aufgedeckt', *SRF*, 11 February 2020, https://perma.cc/44P8-FH8V; Elmar Theveßen, Peter F. Müller, and Ulrich Stoll, '#Cryptoleaks: Wie BND Und CIA Alle Täuschten', *ZDF*, 11 February 2020, https://perma.cc/D9WX-BTJ6; Greg Miller,

'The Intelligence Coup of the Century', *Washington Post*, 11 February 2020, https://perma.cc/6HJJ-YVX6.

132. 'Computer Network Operations—SIGINT Enabling Project', National Security Agency, *Pro Publica*, 5 September 2013, 115 https://perma.cc/U7EZ-SSFZ.

133. 'Computer Network Operations, 115–16.

134. Jeff Larson, Nicole Perlroth, and Scott Shane, 'Revealed: The NSA's Secret Campaign to Crack, Undermine Internet Security', *ProPublica*, 5 September 2013; Nicole Perlroth, Jeff Larson, and Scott Shane, 'N.S.A. Able to Foil Basic Safeguards of Privacy on Web', *New York Times*, 5.September 2013; James Ball, Julian Borger, and Glenn Greenwald, 'Revealed: How US and UK Spy Agencies Defeat Internet Privacy and Security', *The Guardian*, . September 2013. The exact quote is taken from *ProPublica* and *New York Times* articles.

135. I use the term 'backdoor' following other experts, such as Stephen Checkoway and Daniel J. Bernstein, who describe it as a backdoor. Dan Shumow and Niels Ferguson, 'On the Possibility of a Back Door in the NIST SP800-90 Dual EC PRNG', paper presented at the Proc. Crypto, 2007; Stephen Checkoway et al., 'On the Practical Exploitability of Dual EC in TLS Implementations', paper presented at the Proceedings of the 23rd USENIX Conference on Security Symposium, San Diego, CA, 2014.

136. Daniel J. Bernstein, Tanja Lange, and Ruben Niederhagen, 'Dual EC: A Standardized Back Door', in *The New Codebreakers*, ed. Peter Y. A. Ryan, David Naccache, and Jean-Jacques Quisquater (Springer, 2016).

137. Joseph Menn, 'Exclusive: Secret Contract Tied NSA and Security Industry Pioneer', Reuters News, 20 December 2013. See also further reporting in Joseph Menn, 'Exclusive: NSA Infiltrated RSA Security More Deeply Than Thought—Study', Reuters News, 31 March 2014.

138. RSA, 'RSA Response to Media Claims Regarding NSA Relationship', 22 December 2013 [blog], https://perma.cc/LSE5-GY6E.

139. Shumow and Ferguson, 'On the Possibility of a Back Door in the NIST SP800-90 Dual EC PRNG'.

140. For a list of implementations before the Snowden revelations see National Institute of Standards and Technology, 'DRBG Validation List', 1 June 2013, https://perma.cc/3LQP-8YCJ.

141. Stephen Checkoway et al., 'A Systematic Analysis of the Juniper Dual EC Incident', paper presented at the Proceedings of the 2016 ACM SIGSAC Conference on Computer and Communications Security, Vienna, Austria, 2016.

142. Derrick Scholl, 'Important Announcement About ScreenOS', Security Incident Response, 17 December 2015, https://perma.cc/MSC9-APX9. This vulnerability was given the CVE 2015-7756. For the Buchanan claim, see Buchanan, 'The Hacker and the State', 76. Jordan Robertson, 'Juniper Breach Mystery Starts to Clear With New Details on Hackers and U.S. Role', *Bloomberg*, 2. September 2021, https://perma.cc/42L8-BPHB. Someone also added an undocumented administrator password to the ScreenOS source code (CVE 2015-7755). See HD Moore, 'CVE-2015-7755: Juniper ScreenOS Authentication Backdoor', Rapid7Community, 20

December 2015, https://perma.cc/78EE-6TDU. Buchanan dates this to 2014 and at-
tributes it to 'Chinese hackers', see Buchanan, 'The Hacker and the State', 79.

143. James Clapper, Worldwide Threat Assessment of the U.S. Intelligence
Community Hearing at the U.S. Senate Select Committee on Intelligence, 114th
Cong., Washington DC, Government Printing Office, 2016. https://perma.cc/
Y4UR-6TZU.

144. 'SSO Corporate Portfolio Overview', 5. See also Julia Angwin et al., 'AT&T Helped
U.S. Spy on Internet on a Vast Scale', *New York Times*, 15 August 2015.

145. On active passive integration see also 'Analytic Challenges from Active-Passive
Integration', S324, National Security Agency, *Der Spiegel*, 28 December 2014, https://
perma.cc/H7K8-JCUE; 'Network Shaping 101', National Security Agency, *The
Intercept*, 28 June 2016, https://perma.cc/PKM5-QWVB. Specifically with regard to
VPN IKE interception, see 'Turbulence—Apex Active/Passive Exfiltration', S32354,
T112, National Security Agency, *Der Spiegel*, 28 December 2014 (dated August
2009), https://perma.cc/DTZ9-DA5X; 'Turbulence—Turmoil VPN Processing',
National Security Agency, *Der Spiegel*, 28 December 2014 (dated 27. October 2009),
https://perma.cc/5U2N-BJZD.

146. This assessment is based in part on the literature on NSA and supported by the
Snowden archives. Note also that Verizon sold much of its data centre infrastructure,
which is suspected to have a key role in the U.S. government's traffic monitoring and
interception, in 2017. Equinix, 'Equinix Completes Acquisition of 29 Data Centers
from Verizon', 1 May 2017, [news release] https://perma.cc/JY4H-W8VU.

147. Frederik Obermaier et al., 'Der Lohn Der Lauscher', *Süddeutsche Zeitung*, 21
November 2014.

148. On the effects of the divestiture and its impact on NSA, see 'The AT&T Divestiture
& National Security', *Cryptolog* 11, nos. 8–9 (1984). Quotation first found in Corera,
Intercept, 208.

149. For a primary source on Shamrock, see Church Committee's counsel's recollections in L. Britt Snider, 'Recollections from the Church Committee's Investigation
of NSA: Unlucky Shamrock', *Studies in Intelligence* (Winter 1999–2000), https://
perma.cc/8PXD-KXSJ. Best multi-sourced accounts are found in James Bamford,
*Body of Secrets: How America's NSA and Britain's GCHQ Eavesdrop on the
World* (London: Arrow, 2002). A shorter discussion but with an integration
into the modern packet-switched interception, see James Bamford, *The Shadow
Factory: The Ultra-Secret NSA from 9/11 to the Eavesdropping on America*, 1st ed.
(New York: Doubleday, 2009).

150. *Commission on CIA Activities Within the United States, Report on Inquiry into CIA-
Related Electronic Surveillance Activities*, Washington DC, Rockefeller Commission,
1976, 32–36. 32–36, https://perma.cc/A7DM-A99J.

151. Shamrock, see Church Committee's counsel's recollections in Snider, 'Recollections
from the Church Committee's Investigation of NSA.'

152. For AT&T's involvement, see, e.g., Angwin et al., 'AT&T Helped U.S. Spy on Internet
on a Vast Scale'.

153. Bamford, *The Shadow Factory*, 181.On remuneration of telecommunication companies for services provided, in this case GCHQ, see Obermaier et al., 'Der Lohn Der Lauscher'.

154. Corera, *Intercept*, 347.

155. On the late 19th-century British strategic telegraph politics, see Paul M. Kennedy, 'Imperial Cable Communications and Strategy, 1870–1914', *The English Historical Review* 86, no. 341 (1971).

156. Richard J. Aldrich, *GCHQ: The Uncensored Story of Britain's Most Secret Intelligence Agency* (London: HarperPress, 2011), 240. Of course, back then, it would not have been called GCHQ; it first was known as 'Room 40' and then as 'Government Code and Cypher School'.

157. Corera, *Intercept*, 337.

158. Aldrich, *GCHQ*, 543–46. Note especially Aldrich's discussion on the 'Internet Modernisation Programme' and the 'Mastering the Internet' project.

159. Ewen MacAskill et al., 'Mastering the Internet: How GCHQ Set out to Spy on the World Wide Web', *The Guardian*, 21 June 2013 2013, https://perma.cc/P7Q5-ZCR5.

160. 'Tempora—News', Government Communications Headquarters, *Der Spiegel*, 18 June 2014 (dated May 2012), https://perma.cc/Z6ML-X54V.

161. See quote on matching NSA's investment in building capabilities in Malaysia and India in MacAskill et al., 'Mastering the Internet'.

162. 'Bullrun Presentation', Government Communications Headquarters, *Der Spiegel*, 28 December 2014, https://perma.cc/2X7W-BDYE. See further 'Bullrun Col—Briefing Sheet', Government Communications Headquarters, *Der Spiegel*, 28 December 2014, https://perma.cc/DL6X-EDB3.

163. IC stands for Intelligence Community, 'Bullrun Classification Guide', Government Communications Headquarters, *The Guardian*, 6 September 2013 (dated 16 June 2010), https://perma.cc/BK74-QG3Q.

164. Bruce Schneier, *Data and Goliath: The Hidden Battles to Collect Your Data and Control Your World* (New York: W.W. Norton, 2016), 92.

165. To further explore this point in book-length format, see Shawn M. Powers and Michael Jablonski, *The Real Cyber War: The Political Economy of Internet Freedom*, History of Communication (Urbana: University of Illinois Press, 2015).

166. There is some substantiation of the claim of patriotism offered by people involved in the cooperation. See, e.g., statements from the ex-CEO of HP (from 1999–2004) in Michael Isikoff, 'Carly Fiorina Defends Bush-Era Torture and Spying, Calls for More Transparency', Yahoo News, 28 September 2015, https://perma.cc/PW45-5D2U.

167. *In Re Directives to Yahoo! Inc. Pursuant to Section 105B of the Foreign Intelligence Surveillance Act*, 105B(G) 07-01 (2008).

168. *In Re Directives to Yahoo! Inc.*

169. For the same tension in the law enforcement space, see the battle between Microsoft and the U.S. government about U.S. compelled access to data stored in Ireland in United States of America v. Microsoft Corporation, U.S. Supreme Court Docket No. 17-2 (Case Nr. 14-2985).

170. Hannah Kuchler and Max Seddon, 'Apple Removes Apps That Bypass China's Censors', *Financial Times*, 30 July 2017, https://perma.cc/FQ3X-RYEH.

Conclusion

1. As we suggested in Florian J. Egloff and Andreas Wenger, 'Public Attribution of Cyber Incidents', ed. Fabien Merz, Center for Security Studies (CSS), ETH Zurich, 2019 and started to do in Florian J. Egloff, 'Contested Public Attributions of Cyber Incidents and the Role of Academia', *Contemporary Security Policy* 41, no. 1 (2020); Florian J. Egloff, 'Public Attribution of Cyber Intrusions', *Journal of Cybersecurity* 6 (2020); Florian J. Egloff and Max Smeets, 'Publicly Attributing Cyber Attacks: A Framework', *Journal of Strategic Studies* 7, no. 1 (2021), doi: 10.1080/01402390.2021.1895117; Florian J. Egloff and Myriam Dunn Cavelty, 'Attribution and Knowledge Creation Assemblages in Cybersecurity Politics', *Journal of Cybersecurity* (2021), doi: 10.1093/cybsec/tyab002.

2. On implausible deniability, see Rory Cormac and Richard J. Aldrich, 'Grey Is the New Black: Covert Action and Implausible Deniability', *International Affairs* 94, no. 3 (2018). On contestation, see further Egloff, 'Contested Public Attributions of Cyber Incidents and the Role of Academia'; on self-attribution see Michael Poznansky and Evan Perkoski, 'Rethinking Secrecy in Cyberspace: The Politics of Voluntary Attribution', *Journal of Global Security Studies* 3, no. 4 (2018).

3. For a discussion of the norms construction process in cybersecurity, see Toni Erskine and Madeline Carr, 'Beyond "Quasi-Norms": The Challenges and Potential of Engaging with Norms in Cyberspace', in *International Cyber Norms: Legal, Policy and Industry Perspectives*, ed. Anna-Maria Osula and Henry Rõigas (Tallinn: NATO CCD COE, 2016); Martha Finnemore and Duncan B. Hollis, 'Constructing Norms for Global Cybersecurity', *American Journal of International Law* 110, no. 3 (2017).

4. Dennis Broeders. *The Public Core of the Internet: An International Agenda for Internet Governance* (n.p.: Amsterdam University Press, 2016).

5. See, e.g., Microsoft's statement after the WannaCry attacks Brad Smith. 'The Need for Urgent Collective Action to Keep People Safe Online: Lessons from Last Week's Cyberattack', Microsoft On the Issues, 14 May 2017 [blog], https://perma.cc/E5NT-3H6M. For an empirical overview, see also Jacqueline Eggenschwiler 'International Cybersecurity Norm Development: The Roles of States Post-2017', Research in Focus, EU Cyber Direct, 2019; for research on the matter, see Louise Marie Hurel and Luisa Cruz Lobato, 'Unpacking Cyber Norms: Private Companies as Norm Entrepreneurs', *Journal of Cyber Policy* 3, no. 1 (2018).

6. With regard to the mirror-imaging argument, an actor aliased ENFER may be instructive, see Winnona DeSombre et al., 'Countering Cyber Proliferation: Zeroing in on Access-as-a-Service', Atlantic Council, New York, 2021.

7. Examples are Dokuchaev's collaboration with Karim Baratov (Canadian), the UAE recruitment attempt of Simone Margaritelli, or the Saudi Arabian recruitment attempt of Moxie Marlinspike. See Jenna McLaughlin, 'Spies for Hire', *The Intercept*, 24 October 2016; Moxie Marlinspike, 'A Saudi Arabia Telecom's Surveillance Pitch', moxie.org, 13 May 2013 [blog], https://perma.cc/RTP5-XH5A; Simone Margaritelli, 'How the United Arab Emirates Intelligence Tried to Hire Me to Spy on Its People', evilsocket.net, 27 July 2016 [blog], https://perma.cc/MC6S-5ABZ.

8. Joseph Cox, 'Inside the Shadowy World of Revenge Hackers', Daily Beast, 19 September 2017, https://perma.cc/C9S8-UNUD.

9. John Scott-Railton et al., 'Dark Basin: Uncovering a Massive Hack-for-Hire Operation', Citizen Lab, 2020.

10. Lucas Kello, *The Virtual Weapon and International Order* (New Haven: Yale University Press, 2017).

11. Brandon Valeriano and Ryan C. Maness, *Cyber War Versus Cyber Realities: Cyber Conflict in the International System* (New York: Oxford University Press, 2015).

12. As indeed I have started, see Egloff, 'Contested Public Attributions of Cyber Incidents and the Role of Academia'; Egloff, 'Public Attribution of Cyber Intrusions'.

13. For the notion of historical redescription, see Ronald J. Deibert, 'Exorcismus Theoriae: Pragmatism, Metaphors and the Return of the Medieval in IR Theory', *European Journal of International Relations* 3, no. 2 (1997).

14. Indeed there is some indication that this is not the case for physical violence either, see, e.g., the struggle for control by the Mexican drug cartels. Keith Krause, 'From Armed Conflict to Political Violence: Mapping & Explaining Conflict Trends', *Daedalus* 145, no. 4 (2016). Note: there is an active discussion whether some of the harms generated as a result of offensive cyber operations should be classified as violent, see Florian J. Egloff and James Shires, 'The Better Angels of Our Digital Nature? Offensive Cyber Capabilities and State Violence', *European Journal of International Security*, 2021, first view. Doi: 10.1017/eis.2021.20; Florian J. Egloff and James Shires, 'Offensive Cyber Capabilities and State Violence: Three Logics of Integration', *Journal of Global Security Studies*, forthcoming. doi: 10.1093/jogss/ogab028.

15. Joseph S. Nye, Jr., *The Future of Power*, 1st ed. (New York: PublicAffairs, 2011), 118.

16. Kello's framework shares intellectual similarities with that offered by James N. Rosenau, *Turbulence in World Politics: A Theory of Change and Continuity* (London: Harvester Wheatsheaf, 1990).

17. For a narrative treatment of the Citizen Lab's research, see Ronald J. Deibert, *Black Code: Surveillance, Privacy, and the Dark Side of the Internet*, exp. ed. (Toronto: Signal, 2013). See also https://citizenlab.ca/publications/.

18. On cyber privateers, see for example Facebook's litigation, supported by Microsoft and Google, against NSO group.

19. Egloff and Shires, 'The Better Angels of Our Digital Nature?'; Egloff and Shires, 'Offensive Cyber Capabilities and State Violence'.

A Note on Sources

1. Freedom of the Press Foundation, 'United States v. PFC Bradley E. Manning. Vol. 10, Unofficial Draft. Morning Session. Witness Patrick Kennedy', 5 August 2013 [unofficial court transcript], https://perma.cc/5YYA-JN8T.

2. 'United States V. PFC Bradley E. Manning. Vol. 10, Unofficial Draft. Morning Session. Witness Charles Wisecarver', 26 June 2013 [unofficial court transcript], https://perma.cc/46A5-PWTU.

3. Michael Gill and Arthur Spirling, 'Estimating the Severity of the Wikileaks U.S. Diplomatic Cables Disclosure,' *Political Analysis* 23, no. 2 (2015).

4. One of the best overviews of those discussions is given in 'Leaked Documents That Were Not Attributed to Snowden'. Electrospaces, 20 April 2017 [blog], https://perma.cc/M7FR-HYEL.

5. The date indicates the time the document was made publicly available, the original date is provided if available in the document itself. Both the originating source and the publisher are provided.

Bibliography

Archival Sources

The British Library, 96 Euston Road, London

IOR   India Office Records and Private Papers.

The National Archives, Kew, Richmond, Surrey

Calendar of State Papers   Calendar of State Papers, Domestic Series, of the Reigns of Elizabeth and James I, Addenda, 1580–1625, Ed. Mary Anne Everett Green. London: Longman & Co., 1872. Also accessible under State Papers Online, Gale, Cengage Learning.

CO   Records of the Colonial Office, Commonwealth and Foreign and Commonwealth Offices, Empire Marketing Board, and Related Bodies.

HCA   Records of the High Court of Admiralty and Colonial Vice-Admiralty Courts.

PC   Records of the Privy Council and other records collected by the Privy Council Office.

The Special Collections Archives, Bodleian Libraries, University of Oxford, Oxford

Clarendon Papers   Papers of George William Frederick Villiers, 4th Earl of Clarendon, 1820–1870. Also includes correspondence, diaries and papers of Lady Katharine Clarendon, with some correspondence of her husband, George, 4th Earl of Clarendon, and some miscellaneous family papers, 1815–92.

Snowden Archives

Snowden Archives   For the leaked documents, the date indicates the time it was made publicly available. Both the originating source and the publisher are provided. A list of all the cited documents is available in the 'Note on Sources'.

U.S. Court Cases

In Re Directives to Yahoo! Inc. Pursuant to Section 105B of the Foreign Intelligence Surveillance Act, 105B(G) 07-01 (2008).

United States of America v. Dmitry Dokuchaev et al., CR17-103 (2017).

United States of America v. Evgeniy Bogachev, CR14-00127-AJS (2014).

United States of America v. Fathi et al., 16-348 (2016).

United States of America v. Jon Chang Hyok et al., 2:20-cr-00614-DMG (2020).

United States of America v. Microsoft Corporation, U.S. Supreme Court Docket No. 17-2 (Case Nr. 14-2985).

United States of America v. Park Jin Hyok, MJ18-1479—Criminal Complaint (2018).

United States of America v. Roman V. Seleznev, CR11-0070RAJ (2017).

United States of America v. Su Bin, 14-1318M (2014).
United States of America v. Wang Dong et al., 14-118 (2014).
United States of America v. Zhu Hua and Zhang Shilong, 18-891—Indictment (2018).

U.S. Department of State

U.S. Department of State Records of the U.S. Department of State FOIA Case No. F-2014-20439, U.S. State Department.

Wikileaks Archives

WikileaksPublic Library of U.S. Diplomacy. A list of all the cited documents is available in the 'Note on Sources'.
Sony Email Archives. A list of all the cited documents is available in the 'Note on Sources'.

Main Bibliography

Aaviksoo, Jaak. 'Cyber Defense—The Unnoticed Third World War'. Speech presented at the 24th International Workshop of the Series on Global Security, Paris, June 2007.
Abrahamsen, Rita, and Michael C. Williams. 'Securing the City: Private Security Companies and Non-State Authority in Global Governance'. *International Relations* 21, no. 2 (June 2007): 237–53.
Abrahamsen, Rita, and Michael C. Williams. 'Security Beyond the State: Global Security Assemblages in International Politics'. *International Political Sociology* 3, no. 1 (2009): 1–17.
Abrahamsen, Rita, and Michael C. Williams. *Security Beyond the State: Private Security in International Politics*. Cambridge: Cambridge University Press, 2011.
'Accusation of Chinese Government's Participation in Cyber Attack "Groundless": Ministry'. Xinhua, 25 January 2010. https://perma.cc/A4D2-QNTF.
Acharya, Sarmistha. 'Dyre Malware Disrupted after Russian Authorities Raid Moscow Film Company Office'. *International Business Times*, 7 February 2016. https://perma.cc/79RP-RKV2.
Aitel, Dave. 'Cyber Deterrence "at Scale" '. Washington, DC: Lawfare, 10 June 2016 [Blog]. https://perma.cc/9YEN-P6UC.
Aitel, Dave. 'How "Active Defense" Would Work'. CyberSecPolitics, 1 December 2016 [Blog]. https://perma.cc/2KLB-P2NK.
Aldrich, Richard J. *GCHQ: The Uncensored Story of Britain's Most Secret Intelligence Agency*. London: HarperPress, 2011.
'American in Russia to Return to Face U.S. Charges in J.P. Morgan Hacking Case'. Reuters News, 14 December 2016.
Anderson, John L. 'Piracy and World History: An Economic Perspective on Maritime Predation'. In *Bandits at Sea: A Pirates Reader*, edited by C. Richard Pennell, 82–106. New York: New York University Press, 2001.
Anderson, Matthew S. *War and Society in Europe of the Old Regime, 1618–1789*. Stroud: Sutton, 1998.
Anderson, Ross. *Security Engineering: A Guide to Building Dependable Distributed Systems*. 2nd ed. Indianapolis: Wiley, 2008.
Andrew, Christopher M., and Vasili Mitrokhin. *The Sword and the Shield: The Mitrokhin Archive and the Secret History of the KGB*. 1st ed. New York: Basic Books, 1999.

Andrews, Kenneth R. *Drake's Voyages: A Re-Assessment of Their Place in Elizabethan Maritime Expansion*. London: Weidenfeld & Nicolson, 1967.

Andrews, Kenneth R. *Elizabethan Privateering: English Privateering During the Spanish War, 1585–1603*. Cambridge: Cambridge University Press, 1964.

Andrews, Kenneth R., and Hakluyt Society. *English Privateering Voyages to the West Indies, 1588–1595: Documents Relating to English Voyages to the West Indies from the Defeat of the Armada to the Last Voyage of Sir Francis Drake*. Works issued by the Hakluyt Society, 2nd Series, No. 111. Cambridge: Cambridge University Press for Hakluyt Society, 1959.

Angwin, Julia, Charlie Savage, Jeff Larson, Henrik Moltke, Laura Poitras, and James Risen. 'AT&T Helped U.S. Spy on Internet on a Vast Scale'. *New York Times*, 15 August 2015.

Aradau, Claudia, Jef Huysmans, Andrew W. Neal, and Nadine Voelkner. *Critical Security Methods: New Frameworks for Analysis*. The New International Relations. London: Routledge, Taylor & Francis Group, 2015.

Armitage, David. *Foundations of Modern International Thought*. Cambridge: Cambridge University Press, 2012.

Arquilla, John. 'Can Information Warfare Ever Be Just?'. *Ethics and Information Technology* 1, no. 3 (September 1999): 203–12.

Asadova, Nargiz. 'We, the Russian Overseas, Do Not Need Foreigners'. Moscow: Echo of Moscow, 5 March 2009 [Blog, GoogleTranslate]. https://perma.cc/ANR2-CHCZ.

'The AT&T Divestiture & National Security'. *Cryptolog* 11, no. 8-9 (1984): 10–12.

Atlantic Council. 'Building a Secure Cyber Future'. Atlantic Council, 23 May 2012 [Transcript]. https://perma.cc/5KMR-G9SF.

Axelrod, Robert. 'A Repertory of Cyber Analogies'. In *Cyber Analogies*, edited by Emily O. Goldman and John Arquilla, 108–17. Monterey, CA: Naval Postgraduate School, 2014.

Aydinli, Ersel. 'Assessing Violent Nonstate Actorness in Global Politics: A Framework for Analysis'. *Cambridge Review of International Affairs* 28, no. 3 (2015): 424–44.

Baldwin, David A. 'The Concept of Security'. *Review of International Studies* 23, no. 1 (1997): 5–26.

Baldwin, David A. 'Security Studies and the End of the Cold War'. *World Politics* 48, no. 1 (1995): 117–41.

Ball, James, Julian Borger, and Glenn Greenwald. 'Revealed: How US and UK Spy Agencies Defeat Internet Privacy and Security'. *The Guardian*, 6 September 2013.

Ballmer, Steve. 'Microsoft & Internet Freedom'. Microsoft on the Issues, Microsoft Inc., Redmond, WA, 25 April 2010. [Blog]. https://perma.cc/28CG-L4A6.

Baliga, Sandeep, Ethan Bueno De Mesquita, and Alexander Wolitzky. 'Deterrence with Imperfect Attribution'. *American Political Science Review* 114, no. 4 (2020): 1155–78.

Bamford, James. *Body of Secrets: How America's NSA and Britain's GCHQ Eavesdrop on the World*. London: Arrow, 2002.

Bamford, James. *The Shadow Factory: The Ultra-Secret NSA from 9/11 to the Eavesdropping on America*. 1st ed. New York: Doubleday, 2009.

Baram, Gil, and Uri Sommer. 'Covert or Not Covert: National Strategies During Cyber Conflict'. Paper presented at the 11th International Conference on Cyber Conflict (CyCon), 28–31 May 2019.

Barkawi, Tarak. 'Of Camps and Critiques: A Reply to "Security, War, Violence"'. *Millennium—Journal of International Studies* 41, no. 1 (September 2012): 124–30.

Bartholomew, Brian, and Juan Andrés Guerrero-Saade. 'Wave Your False Flags! Deception Tactics Muddying Attribution in Targeted Attacks'. In *Virus Bulletin Conference*, 1–9. Denver, CO: Virus Bulletin, 2016.

Baugh, Daniel A. *The Global Seven Years War, 1754–1763: Britain and France in a Great Power Contest*. Modern Wars in Perspective. Harlow: Longman, 2011.

BBC. 'Estonia Hit by "Moscow Cyber War"'. 17 May 2007. https://perma.cc/U98H-J4YF.

BBC. 'MI5 Warns over China Spy Threat'. 2 December 2007. https://perma.cc/2E22-GQVJ.

BBC. '"One Billion" Affected by Yahoo Hack'. 15 December 2016. https://perma.cc/J566-AJEV.

Benton, Lauren. 'Legal Spaces of Empire: Piracy and the Origins of Ocean Regionalism'. *Comparative Studies in Society and History* 47, no. 04 (2005): 700–24.

Benton, Lauren. *A Search for Sovereignty: Law and Geography in European Empires, 1400–1900*. Cambridge: Cambridge University Press, 2010.

Benton, Lauren. 'Toward a New Legal History of Piracy: Maritime Legalities and the Myth of Universal Jurisdiction'. *International Journal of Maritime History* 23, no. 1 (June 2011): 225–40.

Berdal, Mats. 'The "New Wars" Thesis Revisited'. In *The Changing Character of War*, edited by Hew Strachan and Sibylle Scheipers. Oxford Leverhulme Programme on the Changing Character of War, 109–33. Oxford: Oxford University Press, 2011.

Bernstein, Daniel J., Tanja Lange, and Ruben Niederhagen. 'Dual EC: A Standardized Back Door'. In *The New Codebreakers*, edited by Peter Y. A. Ryan, David Naccache, and Jean-Jacques Quisquater, 256–81. Springer, 2016.

Betz, David J., and Tim Stevens. 'Analogical Reasoning and Cyber Security'. *Security Dialogue* 44, no. 2 (April 2013): 147–64.

Bialuschewski, Arne. 'Pirates, Markets and Imperial Authority: Economic Aspects of Maritime Depredations in the Atlantic World, 1716–1726'. *Global Crime* 9, nos. 1–2 (February 2008): 52–65.

Biersteker, Thomas J., and Cynthia Weber. *State Sovereignty as Social Construct*. Cambridge Studies in International Relations. Cambridge: Cambridge University Press, 1996.

Bigo, Didier. 'The Möbius Ribbon of Security(ies)'. In *Identities, Borders, Orders: Rethinking International Relations Theory*, edited by Mathias Albert, David Jacobson and Yosef Lapid, 91–116. Minneapolis: University of Minnesota Press, 2001.

Bigo, Didier, and Rob B. J. Walker. 'Political Sociology and the Problem of the International'. *Millennium—Journal of International Studies* 35, no. 3 (September 2007): 725–39.

Boak, David G. *A History of U.S. Communications Security*. Vol. 2. Fort George G. Meade, Maryland: National Security Agency, 1981.

Bobrow, Davis B. 'Complex Insecurity: Implications of a Sobering Metaphor: 1996 Presidential Address'. *International Studies Quarterly* 40, no. 4 (1996): 435–50.

Bohm, David, and F. David Peat. *Science, Order and Creativity*. London: Routledge, 1988.

Boin, Arjen, Paul t' Hart, Eric Stern, and Bengt Sundelius. *The Politics of Crisis Management: Public Leadership under Pressure*. Cambridge: Cambridge University Press, 2005.

Booth, Ken. *Theory of World Security*. Cambridge: Cambridge University Press, 2007.

Boreiko, Alexander, and Yulia Belous. 'Face to Face with a Hacker'. Vedomosti, 2 November 2004 [GoogleTranslate]. https://perma.cc/HTV4-S7G5.

Bouwman, Xander, Harm Griffioen, Jelle Egbers, Christian Doerr, Bram Klievink, and Michel van Eeten. 'A Different Cup of TI? The Added Value of Commercial Threat Intelligence'. In *Proceedings of the 29th USENIX Security Symposium*, 433–50. San Diego, CA: USENIX Association, 2020.

Branch, Jordan. 'What's in a Name? Metaphors and Cybersecurity'. *International Organization* 75, no. 1 (2021): 39–70.

Braudel, Fernand. *The Mediterranean and the Mediterranean World in the Age of Philip II.* 2 vols. Berkeley: University of California Press, 1995.

Brenner, Joel, and Jon R. Lindsay. 'Correspondence: Debating the Chinese Cyber Threat'. *International Security* 40, no. 1 (2015): 191–95.

Brin, Sergey. 'It Was a Real Step Backward'. Interview by Philip Bethge. *Der Spiegel*, 30 March 2010.

Broeders, Dennis. *The Public Core of the Internet: An International Agenda for Internet Governance.* Amsterdam: Amsterdam University Press, 2016. doi: 10.26530/oapen_610631.

Broeders, Dennis. 'Private Active Cyber Defense and (International) Cyber Security—Pushing the Line?'. *Journal of Cybersecurity* 7, no. 1 (2021): 1–14.

Brown, Richard H. 'Social Theory as Metaphor: On the Logic of Discovery for the Sciences of Conduct'. *Theory and Society* 3, no. 2 (1976): 169–97.

Brown, Theodore L. *Making Truth: Metaphor in Science.* Urbana: University of Illinois Press, 2003.

Buchanan, Ben. *The Cybersecurity Dilemma: Hacking, Trust and Fear between Nations.* Oxford: Oxford University Press, 2017.

Buchanan, Ben. *The Hacker and the State: Cyber Attacks and the New Normal of Geopolitics.* Cambridge, MA: Harvard University Press, 2020.

Bueger, Christian. 'Doing Europe: Agency and the European Union in the Field of Counter-Piracy Practice'. *European Security* 25, no. 4 (October 2016): 407–22.

Bueger, Christian. 'Learning from Piracy: Future Challenges of Maritime Security Governance'. *Global Affairs* 1, no. 1 (January 2015): 33–42.

Bueger, Christian. 'Making Things Known: Epistemic Practices, the United Nations, and the Translation of Piracy'. *International Political Sociology* 9, no. 1 (2015): 1–18.

Bueger, Christian. 'Piracy Studies: Academic Responses to the Return of an Ancient Menace'. *Cooperation and Conflict* 49, no. 3 (September 2013): 406–16.

Bueger, Christian. 'Practice, Pirates and Coast Guards: The Grand Narrative of Somali Piracy'. *Third World Quarterly* 34, no. 10 (November 2013): 1811–27.

Bueger, Christian, Jan Stockbruegger, and Sascha Werthes. 'Pirates, Fishermen and Peacebuilding: Options for Counter-Piracy Strategy in Somalia'. *Contemporary Security Policy* 32, no. 2 (August 2011): 356–81.

Bull, Hedley. *The Anarchical Society: A Study of Order in World Politics.* London: Macmillan, 1977.

Bundesministerium des Innern. 'Verfassungsschutzbericht'. Berlin, 2016.

Burg, B. Richard *Sodomy and the Pirate Tradition: English Sea Rovers in the Seventeenth Century Caribbean.* New York: New York University Press, 1983.

Buzan, Barry. 'New Patterns of Global Security in the Twenty-First Century'. *International Affairs* 67, no. 3 (1991): 431–51.

Buzan, Barry, Ole Waever, and Jaap De Wilde, eds. *Security: A New Framework for Analysis.* Boulder: Lynne Rienner, 1998.

Caldwell, Leslie R. 'Assistant Attorney General Leslie R. Caldwell Delivers Remarks at the Georgetown Cybersecurity Law Institute'. Department of Justice, 20 May 2015. https://perma.cc/M2AE-VWYD.

Carlin, John P., and Garrett M. Graff. *The Dawn of the Code War: America's Battle against Russia, China, and the Rising Global Cyber Threat.* New York: PublicAffairs, 2018.

Carr, Madeline. 'Public–Private Partnerships in National Cyber-Security Strategies'. *International Affairs* 92, no. 1 (2016): 43–62.

Carr, Madeline. *US Power and the Internet in International Relations*. Basingstoke: Palgrave Macmillan, 2016.

Center for Applied Internet Data Analysis. 'View of Internet Outages in North Korea: Visible BGP Prefixes'. University of California San Diego. https://perma.cc/K8C7-KCEL.

Center for Cyber & Homeland Security, 'Into the Gray Zone—The Private Sector and Active Defense against Cyber Threats'. George Washington University, Washington DC, 2016.

Checkoway, Stephen, Matthew Fredrikson, Ruben Niederhagen, Adam Everspaugh, Matthew Green, Tanja Lange, Thomas Ristenpart, Daniel J. Bernstein, Jake Maskiewicz, and Hovav Shacham. 'On the Practical Exploitability of Dual EC in TLS Implementations'. In *Proceedings of the 23rd USENIX Conference on Security Symposium*, 319–35. San Diego, CA: USENIX Association, 2014.

Checkoway, Stephen, Jacob Maskiewicz, Christina Garman, Joshua Fried, Shaanan Cohney, Matthew Green, Nadia Heninger, Ralf-Philipp Weinmann, Eric Rescorla, Hovav Shacham. 'A Systematic Analysis of the Juniper Dual EC Incident'. In *Proceedings of the 2016 ACM SIGSAC Conference on Computer and Communications Security*, 468–79. Vienna, Austria: ACM, 2016.

Chesney, Robert, Max Smeets, Joshua Rovner, Michael Warner, Jon R. Lindsay, Michael P. Fischerkeller, Richard J. Harknett, and Nina Kollars. 'Policy Roundtable: Cyber Conflict as an Intelligence Contest'. Special issue: Cyber Competition, *Texas National Security Review* (2020).

Chilton, Paul A. *Security Metaphors: Cold War Discourse from Containment to Common House*. Conflict and Consciousness. New York: Peter Lang, 1996.

'China Says Google Case Should Not Be Linked to Ties with U.S.'. Xinhua, 21 January 2010. https://perma.cc/U8WE-VM99.

'China Says Its Web Open, Welcomes Int'l Companies'. Xinhua, 14 January 2010. https://perma.cc/HLF4-YE5U.

'China Urges U.S. To Stop Accusations on So-Called Internet Freedom'. Xinhua, 22 January 2010. https://perma.cc/U7EX-UTGS.

Choucri, Nazli, Stuart Madnick, and Jeremy Ferwerda. 'Institutions for Cyber Security: International Responses and Global Imperatives'. *Information Technology for Development* 20, no. 2 (2014): 96–121.

Clapper, James. 'National Intelligence, North Korea, and the National Cyber Discussion'. Paper presented at the International Conference on Cyber Security, Fordham University, New York, 7 January 2015,

Clapper, James. *Worldwide Threat Assessment of the U.S. Intelligence Community Hearing at the U.S. Senate Select Committee on Intelligence*. 114th Cong., Washington, DC: Government Printing Office, 2016. https://perma.cc/Y4UR-6TZU.

Clarke, Richard A., and Robert K. Knake. *Cyber War: The Next Threat to National Security and What to Do about It*. New York: Ecco, 2010.

Clinton, Hillary. 'Remarks on Internet Freedom'. U.S. Department of State, 21 January 2010 [Transcript]. https://perma.cc/HX6B-ZZY4.

Clinton, Hillary. 'Statement on Google Operations in China'. U.S. Department of State, 12 January 2010 [Press release]. https://perma.cc/H3FQ-RTMY.

Coker, Christopher. 'Outsourcing War'. In *Non-State Actors in World Politics*, edited by Daphne Josselin and William Wallace, 189–202. Basingstoke: Palgrave, 2001.

Colás, Alejandro, and Bryan Mabee. 'The Flow and Ebb of Private Seaborne Violence in Global Politics'. In *Mercenaries, Pirates, Bandits and Empires: Private Violence in Historical Context*, edited by Alejandro Colás and Bryan Mabee, 83–106. London: C Hurst, 2010.

Colás, Alejandro, and Bryan Mabee. *Mercenaries, Pirates, Bandits and Empires: Private Violence in Historical Context*. London: C Hurst, 2010.

Coleman, E. Gabriella. *Hacker, Hoaxer, Whistleblower, Spy: The Many Faces of Anonymous*. London: Verso, 2014.

Collier, Jamie. 'Proxy Actors in the Cyber Domain: Implications for State Strategy'. *St Antony's International Review* 13, no. 1 (May 2017): 25–47.

Comey, James B. 'Addressing the Cyber Security Threat'. Paper presented at the International Conference on Cyber Security, 7 January 2015, Fordham University, New York.

'Commentary: Don't Impose Double Standards on "Internet Freedom"'. Xinhua, 24 January 2010. https://perma.cc/8FAJ-XLGA.

Commission on CIA Activities Within the United States. *Report on Inquiry into CIA-Related Electronic Surveillance Activities*. Rockefeller Commission, Washington, DC, 1976. https://perma.cc/A7DM-A99J.

Conway, Maura. 'Reality Check: Assessing the (Un)Likelihood of Cyberterrorism'. In *Cyberterrorism: Understanding, Assessment, and Response*, edited by Thomas M. Chen, Lee Jarvis and Stuart MacDonald, 103–22. New York: Springer, 2014.

Corbin, Kenneth. '"Aurora" Cyber Attackers Were Really Running Counter-Intelligence'. CIO.com, 22 April 2013. https://perma.cc/LJ8Y-E2GX.

Corera, Gordon. *Intercept: The Secret History of Computers and Spies*. London: Weidenfeld & Nicolson, 2015.

Cormac, Rory, and Richard J. Aldrich. 'Grey Is the New Black: Covert Action and Implausible Deniability'. *International Affairs* 94, no. 3 (2018): 477–94.

Costa Lopez, Julia. 'Political Authority in International Relations: Revisiting the Medieval Debate'. *International Organization* 74, no. 2 (2020): 222–52.

Coward, Ashley, and Corneliu Bjola. 'Cyber-Intelligence and Diplomacy: The Secret Link'. In *Secret Diplomacy: Concepts, Contexts and Cases*, edited by Corneliu Bjola and Stuart Murray. Routledge New Diplomacy Studies, 201–28. Abingdon: Routledge, 2016.

Cowie, Jim. 'Someone Disconnects North Korea—Who?' Dyn Research, 23 December 2014 [Blog]. https://perma.cc/SA39-YDJK.

Cox, Joseph. 'Inside the Shadowy World of Revenge Hackers'. Daily Beast, 19 September 2017. https://perma.cc/C9S8-UNUD.

Cox, Robert W. 'Social Forces, States and World Orders: Beyond International Relations Theory'. *Millennium—Journal of International Studies* 10, no. 2 (1981): 126–55.

Dalby, Simon. 'Contesting an Essential Concept: Reading the Dilemmas in Contemporary Security Discourse'. In *Critical Security Studies: Concepts and Cases*, edited by Keith Krause and Michael C. Williams, 3–32. London: UCL Press, 1997.

Dann, Gary Elijah, and Neil Haddow. 'Just Doing Business or Doing Just Business: Google, Microsoft, Yahoo! And the Business of Censoring China's Internet'. *Journal of Business Ethics* 79, no. 3 (May 2008): 219–34.

Davis, Diane E., and Anthony W. Pereira. *Irregular Armed Forces and Their Role in Politics and State Formation*. Cambridge: Cambridge University Press, 2003.

De Landa, Manuel. *A New Philosophy of Society: Assemblage Theory and Social Complexity.* London: Continuum, 2006.

Dear, I. C. B., and Peter Kemp. *Oxford Companion to Ships and the Sea.* Oxford: Oxford University Press, 2006.

Deibert, Ronald J. 'Black Code: Censorship, Surveillance, and the Militarisation of Cyberspace'. *Millennium—Journal of International Studies* 32, no. 3 (2003): 501–30.

Deibert, Ronald J. *Black Code: Surveillance, Privacy, and the Dark Side of the Internet.* Exp. ed. Toronto: Signal, 2013.

Deibert, Ronald J. 'Circuits of Power: Security in the Internet Environment'. In *Information Technologies and Global Politics: The Changing Scope of Power and Governance*, edited by James N. Rosenau and J. P. Singh. SUNY Series in Global Politics, 115–42. Albany: State University of New York Press, 2002.

Deibert, Ronald J. 'Exorcismus Theoriae: Pragmatism, Metaphors and the Return of the Medieval in IR Theory'. *European Journal of International Relations* 3, no. 2 (1997): 167–92.

Deibert, Ronald J. 'The Geopolitics of Cyberspace after Snowden'. *Current History* 114, no. 768 (January 2015): 9–15.

Deibert, Ronald J. *Reset: Reclaiming the Internet for Civil Society.* Canada: House of Anansi Press, 2020.

Department of Homeland Security. 'Enhanced Cybersecurity Services (ECS)'. Department of Homeland Security, 2017. https://perma.cc/DU43-BDLF.

Der Derian, James. 'The Question of Information Technology in International Relations'. *Millennium—Journal of International Studies* 32, no. 3 (2003): 441–56.

DeSombre, Winnona, James Shires, JD Work, Robert Morgus, Patrick Howell O'Neill, Luca Allodi, and Trey Herr. 'Countering Cyber Proliferation: Zeroing in on Access-as-a-Service'. Atlantic Council, New York, 2021.

Director of Central Intelligence. 'Annual Report for the United States Intelligence Community'. Washington, DC, 1999.

Dokuchaev, Dmitry (aka Forb). 'Dedicated for the Hacker'. xakep.ru 2006 [GoogleTranslate]. https://perma.cc/9MBP-Z994.

Dray, William. '"Explaining What" in History'. In *Theories of History*, edited by Patrick L. Gardiner, 403–8. London: Collier Macmillan, 1959.

Dullien, Thomas. 'Piracy, Privateering . . . And the Creation of a New Navy'. Keynote speech presented at the SOURCE Conference, May 2013, Dublin.

Dunn Cavelty, Myriam. 'Breaking the Cyber-Security Dilemma: Aligning Security Needs and Removing Vulnerabilities'. *Science and Engineering Ethics* 20, no. 3 (September 2014): 701–15.

Dunn Cavelty, Myriam. *Cyber-Security and Threat Politics: U.S. Efforts to Secure the Information Age.* CSS Studies in Security and International Relations. London: Routledge, 2008.

Dunn Cavelty, Myriam. 'From Cyber-Bombs to Political Fallout: Threat Representations with an Impact in the Cyber-Security Discourse'. *International Studies Review* 15, no. 1 (2013): 105–22.

Dunn Cavelty, Myriam. 'The Militarisation of Cyber Security as a Source of Global Tension'. In *Strategic Trends 2012*, edited by Daniel Möckli, 103–24. Zürich: Center for Security Studies, ETH Zurich, 2012.

Dunn Cavelty, Myriam, and Florian J. Egloff. 'Hyper-Securitization, Everyday Security Practice and Technification: Cyber-Security Logics in Switzerland'. *Swiss Political Science Review* 27, no. 1 (2021): 139–49.

Dunn Cavelty, Myriam, and Florian J. Egloff. 'The Politics of Cybersecurity: Balancing Different Roles of the State'. *St Antony's International Review* 15, no. 1 (2019): 37–57.

Dunn Cavelty, Myriam, and Reimer A. Van der Vlugt. 'A Tale of Two Cities: Or How the Wrong Metaphors Lead to Less Security'. *Georgetown Journal of International Affairs* 16 (2015): 21–29.

Dunn, Kevin C. 'Historical Representations'. In *Qualitative Methods in International Relations: A Pluralist Guide*, edited by Audie Klotz and Deepa Prakash. Research Methods Series, 78–92. Basingstoke: Palgrave Macmillan, 2008.

Earle, Peter. *The Pirate Wars*. London: Methuen, 2003.

Ebert, Hannes, and Tim Maurer. 'Cyber Security'. Oxford University Press, 11 January 2017 [Annotated Bibliography]. https://perma.cc/Y74K-WXKH.

Eggenschwiler, Jacqueline. 'International Cybersecurity Norm Development: The Roles of States Post-2017', Research in Focus, EU Cyber Direct, 2019.

Egloff, Florian J. 'Contested Public Attributions of Cyber Incidents and the Role of Academia'. *Contemporary Security Policy* 41, no. 1 (2020): 55–81.

Egloff, Florian J. 'Cyber Privateering: A Risky Policy Choice for the United States'. Lawfare, 17 November 2016 [Blog]. https://perma.cc/ME95-WAXZ.

Egloff, Florian J. 'Cybersecurity and the Age of Privateering'. In *Understanding Cyberconflict: Fourteen Analogies*, edited by George Perkovich and Ariel Levite, 231–47. Washington, DC: Georgetown University Press, 2017.

Egloff, Florian J. 'Cybersecurity and the Age of Privateering: A Historical Analogy'. University of Oxford Cyber Studies Working Papers, no. 1, 2015. Published electronically 4 March 2015. https://perma.cc/XC33-GT7W.

Egloff, Florian J. 'Cybersecurity and Non-State Actors: A Historical Analogy with Mercantile Companies, Privateers, and Pirates'. DPhil Thesis, University of Oxford, 2018.

Egloff, Florian J. 'Intentions and Cyberterrorism'. In *Oxford Handbook of Cyber Security*, edited by Paul Cornish. Oxford: Oxford University Press, 2022.

Egloff, Florian J. 'Public Attribution of Cyber Intrusions'. *Journal of Cybersecurity* 6, no.1 (2020): 1–12.

Egloff, Florian J., and Andreas Wenger. 'Public Attribution of Cyber Incidents'. *CSS Analysis* edited by Fabien Merz: Center for Security Studies (CSS), ETH Zurich, 2019: 1–4.

Egloff, Florian J., and Myriam Dunn Cavelty, 'Attribution and Knowledge Creation Assemblages in Cybersecurity Politics'. *Journal of Cybersecurity* 7, no. 1 (2021): 1–12. doi: 10.1093/cybsec/tyab002.

Egloff, Florian J., and James Shires. 'The Better Angels of Our Digital Nature? Offensive Cyber Capabilities and State Violence', *European Journal of International Security*, first view (2021): 1–20. doi: 10.1017/eis.2021.20.

Egloff, Florian J., and James Shires. 'Offensive Cyber Capabilities and State Violence: Three Logics of Integration', *Journal of Global Security Studies*, forthcoming. doi: 10.1093/jogss/ogab028.

Egloff, Florian J., and Lennart Maschmeyer. 'Shaping Not Signaling: Understanding Cyber Operations as a Means of Espionage, Attack, and Destabilization'. *International Studies Review* 23, no. 3 (2021): 997–98.

Egloff, Florian J., and Max Smeets. 'Publicly Attributing Cyber Attacks: A Framework'. *Journal of Strategic Studies* (2021): 1–32. doi: 10.1080/01402390.2021.1895117.

Egloff, Florian J., and Max Smeets. 'Sandworm: A New Era of Cyberwar and the Hunt for the Kremlin's Most Dangerous Hackers'. *Journal of Cyber Policy* 5, no. 2 (2020): 326–27.

Ehala, Martin. 'The Bronze Soldier: Identity Threat and Maintenance in Estonia'. *Journal of Baltic Studies* 40, no. 1 (2009): 139–58.

Eichensehr, Kristen E. 'The Law and Politics of Cyberattack Attribution'. *UCLA Law Review* 67 (2020): 520–98.

Endres, Fiona, and Nicole Vögele. 'Weltweite Spionage-Operation Mit Schweizer Firma Aufgedeckt'. *SRF*, 11 February 2020, https://perma.cc/44P8-FH8V.

Equinix. 'Equinix Completes Acquisition of 29 Data Centers from Verizon'. news release, 1 May 2017, https://perma.cc/JY4H-W8VU.

Eriksson, Johan, and Giampiero Giacomello. 'The Information Revolution, Security, and International Relations: (IR) Relevant Theory?'. *International Political Science Review / Revue internationale de science politique* 27, no. 3 (2006): 221–44.

Erskine, Toni, and Madeline Carr. 'Beyond "Quasi-Norms": The Challenges and Potential of Engaging with Norms in Cyberspace'. In *International Cyber Norms: Legal, Policy and Industry Perspectives*, edited by Anna-Maria Osula and Henry Rõigas, 87–109. Tallinn: NATO CCD COE, 2016.

Estonian Government. 'Declaration of the Minister of Foreign Affairs of the Republic of Estonia'. Republic of Estonia, 1 May 2007 [Press release]. https://perma.cc/4C5X-JZJ7.

Estonian Government. 'Malicious Cyber Attacks against Estonia Come from Abroad'. Republic of Estonia, 29 April 2007 [Press release]. https://perma.cc/787B-ZVBZ.

Estonian Government. 'Possible Misinformation Spreading in Electronic Channels'. Republic of Estonia, 28 April 2007 [Press release]. https://perma.cc/Q9NF-3ER4.

Estonian Ministry of Foreign Affairs. 'Address by Minister of Foreign Affairs of Estonia Urmas Paet'. Republic of Estonia, 11 May 2007 [Transcript]. https://perma.cc/FG3N-S8P5.

Estonian Ministry of Foreign Affairs. 'Estonian Ambassador Is Going on Vacation'. Republic of Estonia, 3 May 2007 [Press release]. https://perma.cc/95Z7-64WM.

Estonian President of the Republic. 'US Secretary to the President of Estonia: US Supports Estonia'. Republic of Estonia, 3 May 2007 [Press release, GoogleTranslate]. https://perma.cc/X57G-V2SS.

European Parliament. *European Parliament Resolution of 24 May 2007 on Estonia.* Strasbourg, 2007. http://www.europarl.europa.eu/. (P6_TA(2007)0215).

European Union Agency for Network and Information Security (ENISA). 'CERT Cooperation and Its Further Facilitation by Relevant Stakeholders'. ENISA, Heraklion: ENISA, 2006.

European Union Presidency. 'EU Presidency Statement on the Situation in Front of the Estonian Embassy in Moscow'. 2 May 2007 [Press release]. https://perma.cc/99JQ-XQ2D.

Evron, Gadi. 'Battling Botnets and Online Mobs. Estonia's Defence Efforts during the Internet War'. *Georgetown Journal of International Affairs* 9, no. 1 (2008): 121–26.

Facebook, 'Facebook Reports Third Quarter 2019 Results'. 30 October 2019 [Press release]. https://perma.cc/GS6C-TKFZ.

Farnan, Oliver, Alexander Darer, and Joss Wright. 'Poisoning the Well: Exploring the Great Firewall's Poisoned DNS Responses'. In *Proceedings of the 2016 ACM on Workshop on Privacy in the Electronic Society*, 95–98. Vienna, Austria: ACM, 2016.

Federal Bureau of Investigation. 'Update on Sony Investigation'. News release. 19 December 2014. https://perma.cc/Z745-YR3S.

Federal Bureau of Investigation. 'Wanted by the FBI: Evgeniy Mikhailovich Bogachev'. News release. 10 May 2017. https://perma.cc/66T4-YSH9.

Federal Bureau of Investigation. 'Wanted by the FBI: Joshua Samuel Aaron'. News release. 2 June 2015. https://perma.cc/AY3N-6UFJ.

Federation Council of the Federal Assembly of the Russian Federation. 'Address of the Federation Council of the Federal Assembly of the Russian Federation (No. 15-SF)'. 24 January 2007 [Press release, GoogleTranslate]. https://perma.cc/M46P-DWKM.

Finnemore, Martha, and Duncan B. Hollis. 'Beyond Naming and Shaming: Accusations and International Law in Cybersecurity'. *European Journal of International Law* 31, no. 3 (2020): 969–1003.

Finnemore, Martha, and Duncan B. Hollis. 'Constructing Norms for Global Cybersecurity'. *American Journal of International Law* 110, no. 3 (2017): 425–79.

Fioretos, Orfeo. 'Historical Institutionalism in International Relations'. *International Organization* 65, no. 2 (2011): 367–99.

FireEye, 'APT28: A Window into Russia's Cyber Espionage Operations?'. Milpitas, CA, 2014.

Fischerkeller, Michael P., and Richard J. Harknett. 'Deterrence Is Not a Credible Strategy for Cyberspace'. *Orbis* 61, no. 3 (2017): 381–93.

Fleming, Sean. 'Artificial Persons and Attributed Actions: How to Interpret Action-Sentences about States'. *European Journal of International Relations* 23, no. 4 (2017): 930–50.

Floridi, Luciano. *The Ethics of Information*. Oxford: Oxford University Press, 2013.

Ford, Christopher. 'Here Come the Cyber-Privateers'. Science and Technology, Hudson Institute, Washington DC, 19 July 2010 [Blog]. https://perma.cc/XE8S-J2TJ.

Fox-Brewster, Thomas. 'Behind the Mystery of Russia's "Dyre" Hackers Who Stole Millions from American Business'. Forbes, 4 May 2017. https://perma.cc/HR3P-344A.

Franke, Ulrich, and Ralph Weber. 'At the Papini Hotel: On Pragmatism in the Study of International Relations'. *European Journal of International Relations* 18, no. 4 (December 2011): 669–91.

Freedom of the Press Foundation. 'United States v. PFC Bradley E. Manning. Vol. 10, Unofficial Draft. Morning Session. Witness Charles Wisecarver'. 26 June 2013 [Unofficial court transcript]. https://perma.cc/46A5-PWTU.

Freedom of the Press Foundation. 'United States v. PFC Bradley E. Manning. Vol. 10, Unofficial Draft. Morning Session. Witness Patrick Kennedy'. 5 August 2013 [Unofficial court transcript]. https://perma.cc/5YYA-JN8T.

Friedrichs, Jörg, and Friedrich Kratochwil. 'On Acting and Knowing: How Pragmatism Can Advance International Relations Research and Methodology'. *International Organization* 63, no. 4 (2009): 701–31.

Gaddis, John Lewis. 'History, Science, and the Study of International Relations'. In *Explaining International Relations since 1945*, edited by Ngaire Woods, 32–48. Oxford: Oxford University Press, 1996.

Gale, Caitlin M. 'Barbary's Slow Death: European Attempts to Eradicate North African Piracy in the Early Nineteenth Century'. *Journal for Maritime Research* 18, no. 2 (2016): 139–54.

Galeotti, Mark, 'Crimintern: How the Kremlin Uses Russia's Criminal Networks in Europe'. Policy brief, European Council on Foreign Relations, London, 2017.

Galeotti, Mark, 'Moscow's Mercenaries Reveal the Privatisation of Russian Geopolitics'. openDemocracy, 29 August 2017. https://perma.cc/PL7R-TY88.

Galeotti, Mark, 'Putin's Hydra: Inside Russia's Intelligence Services'. Policy brief, European Council on Foreign Relations, London, 2016.

Galeotti, Mark. 'Stolypin: Russia Has No Grand Plans, but Lots of "Adhocrats" '. intellinews, 18 January 2017. https://perma.cc/6VCV-Z47R.

Galeotti, Mark. *The Vory: Russia's Super Mafia*. New Haven: Yale University Press, 2018.

Gallagher, Sean. 'Sony Pictures Attackers Demand: "Stop the Terrorist Film!" '. *ars technica*, 8 December 2014.

Gara, Antoine, Lauren Gensler, Maggie McGrath, Kristin Stoller, Ashlea Ebeling, Grace L. Williams, and Corinne Jurney. 'The World's Biggest Public Companies'. *Forbes*, 24 May 2017. https://perma.cc/NZ4C-Y49H.

Garrett, B. Nathaniel. 'Taming the Wild Wild Web: Twenty-First Century Prize Law and Privateers as a Solution to Combating Cyber-Attacks'. *University of Cincinnati Law Review* 81, no. 2 (2013): 683–707.

Gartzke, Erik. 'The Myth of Cyberwar: Bringing War in Cyberspace Back Down to Earth'. *International Security* 38, no. 2 (2013): 41–73.

Gartzke, Erik, and Jon R. Lindsay. 'Weaving Tangled Webs: Offense, Defense, and Deception in Cyberspace'. *Security Studies* 24, no. 2 (2015): 316–48.

Gates, William H. III. 'Trustworthy Computing'. 15 January 2002, e-mail communication to Microsoft Staff, Microsoft Company Timeline, Microsoft Webpage, https://perma.cc/78NQ-EZSM.

Geertz, Clifford, ed. *The Interpretation of Cultures: Selected Essays*. New York: Basic Books, 1973.

Gentner, Dedre, and Linsey A. Smith. 'Analogical Learning and Reasoning'. In *The Oxford Handbook of Cognitive Psychology*, edited by Daniel Reisberg, 668–81. Oxford: Oxford University Press, 2013.

Gill, Michael, and Arthur Spirling. 'Estimating the Severity of the Wikileaks U.S. Diplomatic Cables Disclosure'. *Political Analysis* 23, no. 2 (2015): 299–305.

Glenny, Misha. *Darkmarket: Cyberthieves, Cybercops, and You*. 1st U.S. ed. New York: Alfred A. Knopf, 2011.

Glete, Jan. *War and the State in Early Modern Europe: Spain, the Dutch Republic and Sweden as Fiscal-Military States, 1500–1660*. London: Routledge, 2002.

Glete, Jan. *Warfare at Sea, 1500–1650: Maritime Conflicts and the Transformation of Europe*. London: Routledge, 2000.

Global Bandwith Research Service. 'Executive Summary'. TeleGeography, 2016. https://perma.cc/SG9J-FZK6.

Global Bandwith Research Service. 'Executive Summary'. TeleGeography, 2020, https://perma.cc/Y3PV-WEBX.

Global Internet Research Service. 'Global Internet Geography Report'. TeleGeography, 2020, www.telegeography.com.

Gomez, Miguel Alberto, 'Past Behavior and Future Judgements: Seizing and Freezing in Response to Cyber Operations'. *Journal of Cybersecurity* 5, no. 1 (2019).

Goncharov, Max. 'Criminal Hideouts for Lease: Bulletproof Hosting Services'. Trend Micro, Cupertino, CA, 2015.

Goncharov, Max, 'Russian Underground 2.0'. Trend Micro, Cupertino, CA, 2015.

Google. 'Google Cloud Security and Compliance: Google Has a Strong Security Culture'. Google Inc. 2017. https://perma.cc/D2GP-K86Z.

Google. 'Google Transparency Report: HTTPS Usage'. Google Inc., 2021, https://perma.cc/B8ZX-53E8.

Google. 'Google Transparency Report: Known Disruptions of Traffic to Google Products and Services'. Google Inc. 2017. https://perma.cc/R9WC-TJZS.

Google. 'A New Approach to China'. Google Inc., 12 January 2010 [Blog]. https://perma. cc/L9GP-BN5X.

Google. 'A New Approach to China: An Update'. Google Inc., 22 March 2010 [Blog]. https://perma.cc/R86E-SUJ2.

Google. 'Testimony: The Internet in China by Google Inc. (Represented by Eliot Schrage) before the Subcommittee on Asia and the Pacific, and the Subcommittee on Africa, Global Human Rights, and International Operations. Committee on International Relations, United States House of Representatives'. Google Inc., 15 February 2006 [Transcript]. https://perma.cc/B3U9-CUP5.

Gorman, Siobhan, and Jessica E. Vascellaro. 'Google Working with NSA to Investigate Cyber Attack'. Wall Street Journal, 4 February 2010. https://perma.cc/TYC9-ES5B.

Gould, Alex. 'Global Assemblages and Counter-Piracy: Public and Private in Maritime Policing'. Policing and Society 27, no. 4 (2017): 408–18.

Graff, Garret M., and Chad Hagen. 'Inside the Hunt for Russia's Most Notorious Hacker'. Wired, April 2017.

Graham, Thomas E. 'The Sources of Russian Conduct'. The National Interest, 24 August 2016. https://perma.cc/FZ5C-XC6Y.

Grange, Waylon. 'Digital Vengeance: Exploiting the Most Notorious C&C Toolkits'. Briefing presented at Black Hat USA, Las Vegas, 27 July 2017.

Great Britain. The Statutes Relating to the Admiralty, Navy, Shipping, and Navigation of the United Kingdom from 9 Hen. III to 3 Geo. IV Inclusive: With Notes, Referring in Each Case to the Subsequent Statutes, and to the Decisions in the Courts of Admiralty, Common Law, and Equity, in England, and to the Scotch Law. London: s.n., 1823.

Grey, Charles, and George Fletcher MacMunn. Pirates of the Eastern Seas (1618–1723): A Lurid Page of History. London: Sampson Low, Marston, 1933.

Gross, Michael Joseph. 'Enter the Cyber-Dragon'. Vanity Fair, 1 September 2011.

Grotius, Hugo, and Louis Elzevir. Mare Liberum Sive De Iure Quod Batavis Competit Ad Indicana Commercia Dissertatio. Lugduni Batauorvm: Ludovici Elzevirij, 1609.

The Grugq. 'Cyber: Ignore the Penetration Testers'. Medium, 17 September 2016 [Blog]. https://perma.cc/Q6DS-NNA7.

The Grugq. 'Cyber Operators—Differences Matter'. Medium, 29 September 2017 [Blog]. https://perma.cc/JA9R-MAVP.

The Grugq. 'How Very APT'. Presentation presented at the 10th Troopers Conference, Heidelberg, Germany, 23 March, 2017.

Grotto, Andrew J. 'Deconstructing Cyber Attribution: A Proposed Framework and Lexicon'. IEEE Security & Privacy 18, no. 1 (2020): 12–20.

Guerrero-Saade, Juan Andrés, and Costin Raiu. 'Walking in Your Enemy's Shadow: When Fourth-Party Collection Becomes Attribution Hell'. In Virus Bulletin Conference, 1–9. Madrid: Virus Bulletin, 2017.

Guitton, Clement. 'Achieving Attribution'. PhD Thesis, King's College London, 2014.

Guitton, Clement. Inside the Enemy's Computer: Identifying Cyber-Attackers. London: Hurst, 2017.

Guitton, Clement, and Elaine Korzak. 'The Sophistication Criterion for Attribution'. The RUSI Journal 158, no. 4 (2013): 62–68.

Gvosdev, Nikolas K. 'The Bear Goes Digital: Russia and Its Cyber Capabilities'. In Cyberspace and National Security Threats, Opportunities, and Power in a Virtual World, edited by Derek S. Reveron, 173–90. Washington, DC: Georgetown University Press, 2012.

Hall, Rodney Bruce, and Thomas J. Biersteker. *The Emergence of Private Authority in Global Governance*. Cambridge: Cambridge University Press, 2002.

Hansen, Lene, and Helen Nissenbaum. 'Digital Disaster, Cyber-Security, and the Copenhagen School'. *International Studies Quarterly*, no. 53 (2009): 1155–75.

Harding, Richard. *Modern Naval History: Debates and Prospects*. London: Bloomsbury, 2016.

Harknett, Richard J., and Max Smeets. 'Cyber Campaigns and Strategic Outcomes'. *Journal of Strategic Studies* (2020): 1–34. doi: 10.1080/01402390.2020.1732354.

Harris, Shane. *@War: The Rise of the Military-Internet Complex*. Boston: Houghton Mifflin Harcourt, 2014.

Hattendorf, John B., David Aldrige, J. D. Davies, Sari Hornstein, Brian Lavery, Peter Le Fevre, A. W. H. Pearsall, and R. V. Saville. 'Part IV 1648–1714'. In *British Naval Documents, 1204–1960*, edited by John B. Hattendorf, R. J. B. Knight, A. W. H. Pearsall, Nicholas A. M. Rodger and Geoffrey Till, 187–311. Aldershot: Scholar Press for the Navy Records Society, 1993.

Hay, Colin. *Why We Hate Politics*. Cambridge: Polity, 2007.

Hayden, Michael V. 'FISA for the 21st Century. Testimony to the United States Judiciary Committee of the US Senate'. 26 July 2006 [Transcript]. https://perma.cc/CTN9-RXRP.

Hayden, Michael V. *Playing to the Edge: American Intelligence in the Age of Terror*. New York: Penguin Press, 2016.

Healey, Jason. *Beyond Attribution: Seeking National Responsibility for Cyber Attacks*. Washington DC: Atlantic Council, 2011.

Healey, Jason. 'The Spectrum of National Responsibility for Cyberattacks'. *Brown Journal of World Affairs* 18, no. 1 (2011): 57–69.

Heller-Roazen, Daniel. *The Enemy of All: Piracy and the Law of Nations*. New York: Zone, 2009.

Helman, Christopher. 'Microsoft's Ballmer Calls out Google over China Stance'. *Forbes*, 22 January 2010. https://perma.cc/ML39-SBA9.

Henderson, Scott J. *The Dark Visitor: Inside the World of Chinese Hackers*. 2007.

'Here We Go Again'. *The Baltic Times*, 2007. Published electronically 4 April 2007. https://perma.cc/JT4M-LZ9L.

Hersh, Seymour M. 'The Intelligence Gap—How the Digital Age Left Our Spies out in the Cold'. *The New Yorker*, 6 December 1999, 58–76.

Herzog, Stephan. 'Revisiting the Estonian Cyber Attacks: Digital Threats and Multinational Responses'. *Journal of Strategic Security* 4, no. 2 (2011): 49–60.

Higgins, Andrew. 'Maybe Private Russian Hackers Meddled in Election, Putin Says'. *New York Times*, 1 June 2017.

High Court of Admiralty. *The Arraignment, Tryal, and Condemnation of Captain William Kidd, for Murther and Piracy, Upon Six Several Indictments, at the Admiralty-Sessions, Held by His Majesty's Commission at the Old-Baily, on Thursday the 8th. And Friday the 9th of May, 1701*. London: Printed for J. Nutt, 1701.

Holden, Dan. 'North Korea Goes Offline'. Arbor Networks, 22 December 2014. https://perma.cc/GK3E-LPNS.

Holmwood, John. 'The Challenge of Global Social Inquiry'. *Sociological Research Online* 14, no. 4 (2009): 13.

Hurel, Louise Marie, and Luisa Cruz Lobato. 'Unpacking Cyber Norms: Private Companies as Norm Entrepreneurs'. *Journal of Cyber Policy* 3, no. 1 (2018): 61–76.

Idler, Annette Iris, and James J. F. Forest. 'Behavioral Patterns among (Violent) Non-State Actors: A Study of Complementary Governance'. *Stability: International Journal of Security and Development* 4, no. 1 (2015): 1–19.

Ilves, Toomas Hendrik. 'Statement of the President of the Republic Hendrik Toomas Ilves: We Can Agree Upon a Common Future'. Office of the President, 2 May 2007 [Transcript]. https://perma.cc/SUV5-B7Q5.

Information Warfare Monitor. 'Tracking Ghostnet: Investigating a Cyber Espionage Network'. 2009. https://perma.cc/H27G-9RWX.

Inkster, Nigel. 'Chinese Intelligence in the Cyber Age'. *Survival: Global Politics and Strategy* 55, no. 1 (2013): 45–66.

International Centre for Defence and Security. 'Russia's Involvement in the Tallinn Disturbances'. Tallinn, 11 May 2007 [Blog]. https://perma.cc/A7DS-QH6A.

Internet Society of China. 'Public Pledge of Self-Regulation and Professional Ethics for China Internet Industry'. 26 March 2002. https://perma.cc/M95N-HSQG.

Isaacson, Walter, David E. Sanger, and Michael Rogers. 'Beyond the Build: Leveraging the Cyber Mission Force'. Aspen Institute, 23 July 2015 [Transcript]. https://perma.cc/DBV6-EMGT.

Isikoff, Michael. 'Carly Fiorina Defends Bush-Era Torture and Spying, Calls for More Transparency'. Yahoo News, 28 September 2015. https://perma.cc/PW45-5D2U.

ISO/IEC. 'ISO 27001: Information Technology—Security Techniques—Information Security Management Systems—Requirements'. 2013, ISO, Geneva.

ITU. 'Statistics'. ITU 2021. https://perma.cc/KX4W-36T4.

Jackson, Patrick Thaddeus. 'Thinking Interpretively: Philosophical Presuppositions and the Human Sciences'. In *Interpretation and Method: Empirical Research Methods and the Interpretive Turn*, edited by Dvora Yanow and Peregrine Schwartz-Shea, 267–83. Armonk, NY: M.E. Sharp, 2014.

Jackson, Patrick Thaddeus, and Daniel H. Nexon. 'International Theory in a Post-Paradigmatic Era: From Substantive Wagers to Scientific Ontologies'. *European Journal of International Relations* 19, no. 3 (2013): 543–65.

Jacobsen, Stine. 'Silicon Valley Giants Outrank Many Nations, Says First "Techplomat"'. Reuters News, 19 June 2017.

Jellenc, Eli, and Kimberly Zenz, 'Global Threat Research Report: Russia'. iDefense, Chantilly, VA, 2007.

Johnson, Bobbie, and Ian Katz. 'Google Co-Founder Sergey Brin Urges US to Act over China Web Censorship'. *The Guardian*, 24 March 2010.

Kaldor, Mary. *New and Old Wars: Organized Violence in a Global Era*. Cambridge: Polity Press, 1999.

Kalyvas, Stathis N. *The Logic of Violence in Civil War*. Cambridge: Cambridge University Press, 2006.

Kalyvas, Stathis N. '"New" and "Old" Civil Wars: A Valid Distinction?'. *World Politics* 54, no. 1 (2001): 99–118.

Kaminska, Monica. 'Restraint under Conditions of Uncertainty: Why the United States Tolerates Cyberattacks'. *Journal of Cybersecurity* 7, no. 1 (2021): 1–15.

Keay, John. *The Honourable Company: A History of the East India Company*. London: Harper Collins, 1991.

Keck, Margaret E., and Kathryn Sikkink. *Activists Beyond Borders: Advocacy Networks in International Politics*. Ithaca, NY: Cornell University Press, 1998.

Keene, Edward. *International Political Thought: A Historical Introduction.* Cambridge: Polity, 2005.

Kello, Lucas. 'The Meaning of the Cyber Revolution: Perils to Theory and Statecraft'. *International Security* 38, no. 2 (2013): 7–40.

Kello, Lucas. 'The Security Dilemma of Cyberspace: Ancient Logic, New Problems'. Lawfare, 28 August 2017 [Blog]. https://perma.cc/V2Y4-EMZP.

Kello, Lucas. 'The Virtual Weapon: Dilemmas and Future Scenarios'. *Politique étrangère* 79, no. 4 (2014–2015): 1–12.

Kello, Lucas. *The Virtual Weapon and International Order.* New Haven: Yale University Press, 2017.

Kennedy, Paul M. 'Imperial Cable Communications and Strategy, 1870–1914'. *The English Historical Review* 86, no. 341 (1971): 728–52.

Kennedy, Paul M. *The Rise and Fall of British Naval Mastery.* London: Penguin, 2004.

Khong, Yuen Foong. *Analogies at War: Korea, Munich, Dien Bien Phu, and the Vietnam Decisions of 1965.* Princeton: Princeton University Press, 1992.

Kinkor, Kenneth J. 'Black Men under the Black Flag'. In *Bandits at Sea: A Pirates Reader,* edited by C. Richard Pennell, 195–210. New York: New York University Press, 2001.

Kornprobst, Markus. 'Comparing Apples and Oranges? Leading and Misleading Uses of Historical Analogies'. *Millennium* 36, no. 1 (2007): 29–49.

Korts, Külliki. 'Inter-Ethnic Attitudes and Contacts between Ethnic Groups in Estonia'. *Journal of Baltic Studies* 40, no. 1 (2009): 121–37.

Kramer, Andrew E. 'How Russia Recruited Elite Hackers for Its Cyberwar'. *New York Times,* 29 December 2016.

Krause, Keith. 'Critical Theory and Security Studies: The Research Programme of "Critical Security Studies"'. *Cooperation and Conflict* 33, no. 3 (1998): 298–333.

Krause, Keith. 'From Armed Conflict to Political Violence: Mapping & Explaining Conflict Trends'. *Daedalus* 145, no. 4 (2016): 113–26.

Krause, Keith, and Jennifer Milliken. 'Introduction: The Challenge of Non-State Armed Groups'. *Contemporary Security Policy* 30, no. 2 (2009): 202–20.

Krause, Keith, and Michael C. Williams. 'Broadening the Agenda of Security Studies: Politics and Methods'. *Mershon International Studies Review* 40, no. 2 (1996): 229–54.

Krause, Keith, and Michael C. Williams. *Critical Security Studies: Concepts and Cases.* London: UCL Press, 1997.

Krebs, Brian. 'The Download on the DNC Hack'. krebsonsecurity.com, 3 January 2017 [Blog]. https://perma.cc/S7XF-7ATZ.

Krebs, Brian. 'Four Men Charged with Hacking 500m Yahoo Accounts'. krebsonsecurity.com, 15 March 2017 [Blog]. https://perma.cc/PAK6-UL9Q.

Krebs, Brian. 'A Shakeup in Russia's Top Cybercrime Unit'. krebsonsecurity.com, 28 January 2017 [Blog]. https://perma.cc/GX9Z-6VQY.

Krebs, Brian. *Spam Nation: The Inside Story of Organized Cybercrime—From Global Epidemic to Your Front Door.* Naperville: Sourcebooks, 2014.

Krebs, Ronald R. 'Tell Me a Story: FDR, Narrative, and the Making of the Second World War'. *Security Studies* 24, no. 1 (2015): 131–70.

Krekel, Bryan. 'Capability of the People's Republic of China to Conduct Cyber Warfare and Computer Network Exploitation'. Report prepared for the U.S.-China Economic and Security Review Commission. McLean, VA: Northrop Grumman, 2009.

Krekel, Bryan, Patton Adams, and George Bakos. 'Occupying the Information High Ground: Chinese Capabilities for Computer Network Operations and Cyber Espionage'.

Report prepared for the U.S.-China Economic and Security Review Commission. West Falls Church, VA: Northrop Grumman, 2012.

Kuchler, Hannah. 'Cyber Insecurity: Hacking Back'. *Financial Times*, 27 July 2015. https://perma.cc/U8UM-VLBY.

Kuchler, Hannah, and Max Seddon. 'Apple Removes Apps That Bypass China's Censors'. *Financial Times*, 30 July 2017. https://perma.cc/FQ3X-RYEH.

Labovitz, Craig, Scott Iekel-Johnson, Danny McPherson, Jon Oberheide, and Farnam Jahanian. 'Internet Inter-Domain Traffic'. *SIGCOMM Computer Communication Review* 40, no. 4 (2010): 75–86.

Lakoff, George, and Mark Johnson. *Metaphors We Live By*. Chicago: University of Chicago Press, 1980.

Landler, Mark, and John Markoff. 'Digital Fears Emerge after Data Siege in Estonia'. *New York Times*, 29 May 2007.

Lane, Frederic C. 'The Economic Meaning of War and Protection'. *Journal of Social Philosophy & Jurisprudence* 7, no. 3 (1942): 254–70.

Laprise, J. 'Cyber-Warfare Seen through a Mariner's Spyglass'. *Technology and Society Magazine, IEEE* 25, no. 3 (2006): 26–33.

Larkins, Jeremy. 'Book Review: Janice E. Thomson, Mercenaries, Pirates, and Sovereigns: State-Building and Extraterritorial Violence in Early Modern Europe'. *Millennium—Journal of International Studies* 24, no. 2 (1995): 358–60.

Larson, Jeff, Nicole Perlroth, and Scott Shane. 'Revealed: The NSA's Secret Campaign to Crack, Undermine Internet Security'. *ProPublica*, 5 September 2013.

'The Lavrov Letter in Full'. A lamb with no guiding light, 12 May 2007 [Blog]. https://perma.cc/2A2T-VX2E.

Lawson, Sean. 'Putting the "War" in Cyberwar: Metaphor, Analogy, and Cybersecurity Discourse in the United States'. *First Monday* 17, no. 7 (July 2012).

'Leaked Documents That Were Not Attributed to Snowden'. Electrospaces, 20 April 2017 [Blog]. https://perma.cc/M7FR-HYEL.

Leander, Anna. 'From Cookbooks to Encyclopaedias in the Making: Methodological Perspectives for Research of Non-State Actors and Processes'. In *Researching Non-State Actors in International Security: Theory and Practice*, edited by Andreas Kruck and Andrea Schneiker, Milton Park, 233–44. Abingdon, Oxon; New York: Routledge, 2017.

Lee, Robert M., and Thomas Rid. 'OMG Cyber!'. *The RUSI Journal* 159, no. 5 (September 2014): 4–12.

Leibbrandt, Hendrik Carel Vos, Willem Adriaan van der Stel, and Cape of Good Hope Archives. *Journal, 1699–1732*. Cape Town: Richards, 1896.

Leira, Halvard. 'Political Change and Historical Analogies'. *Global Affairs* 3, no. 1 (2017): 81–88.

Leira, Halvard, and Benjamin de Carvalho. 'Privateers of the North Sea: At Worlds End—French Privateers in Norwegian Waters'. In *Mercenaries, Pirates, Bandits and Empires: Private Violence in Historical Context*, edited by Alejandro Colás and Bryan Mabee, 55–82. London: C. Hurst, 2010.

Lemnitzer, Jan Martin. *Power, Law and the End of Privateering*. Basingstoke: Palgrave Macmillan, 2014.

Lesk, Michael. 'Privateers in Cyberspace: Aargh!' *Security & Privacy, IEEE* 11, no. 3 (2013): 81–84.

Leswing, Kif. 'Investors Are Overlooking Apple's Next $50 Billion Business'. *Business Insider*, 4 April 2016. https://perma.cc/3N27-WAQB.

Lewis, James A. 'Put China's Intellectual Property Theft in a Larger Context'. Center for Strategic & International Studies, 15 August 2017. https://perma.cc/M6JV-SJJ7.

Lewis, Michael Arthur. *The History of the British Navy*. Harmondsworth: Penguin Books, 1957.

Lin, Herbert. 'Attribution of Malicious Cyber Incidents: From Soup to Nuts'. *Journal of International Affairs* 70, no. 1 (Winter 2016): 75–137.

Lindsay, Jon R. 'Cyber Conflict vs. Cyber Command: Hidden Dangers in the American Military Solution to a Large-Scale Intelligence Problem'. *Intelligence and National Security* 36, no. 2 (2021): 260–78.

Lindsay, Jon R. 'The Impact of China on Cybersecurity: Fiction and Friction'. *International Security* 39, no. 3 (2015): 7–47.

Lindsay, Jon R. 'Stuxnet and the Limits of Cyber Warfare'. *Security Studies* 22, no. 3 (2013): 365–404.

Lindsay, Jon R. 'Tipping the Scales: The Attribution Problem and the Feasibility of Deterrence against Cyberattack'. *Journal of Cybersecurity* 1, no. 1 (2015): 53–67.

Lindsay, Jon R., and Tai Ming Cheung. 'From Exploitation to Innovation: Acquisition, Absorption, and Application'. In *China and Cybersecurity: Espionage, Strategy, and Politics in the Digital Domain*, edited by Jon R. Lindsay, Tai Ming Cheung, and Derek S. Reveron, 51–86. New York: Oxford University Press, 2015.

Lindsay, Jon R., Tai Ming Cheung, and Derek S. Reveron. *China and Cybersecurity: Espionage, Strategy, and Politics in the Digital Domain*. New York: Oxford University Press, 2015.

Lipton, Eric, David E. Sanger, and Scott Shane. 'The Perfect Weapon: How Russian Cyberpower Invaded the U.S.'. *New York Times*, 13 December 2016.

Little, Richard. *The Balance of Power in International Relations: Metaphors, Myths, and Models*. Cambridge: Cambridge University Press, 2007.

Lobo-Guerrero, Luis. 'Archives'. In *Research Methods in Critical Security Studies: An Introduction*, edited by Mark B. Salter and Can E. Mutlu, 121–24. New York: Routledge, 2012.

Lobo-Guerrero, Luis. *Insuring War: Sovereignty, Security and Risk*. Interventions. Abingdon: Routledge, 2012.

Lohr, Steve. 'Bill Gates Defends Google, Then Pans It'. *New York Times*, 25 January 2010.

Löwenheim, Oded. *Predators and Parasites: Persistent Agents of Transnational Harm and Great Power Authority*. Ann Arbor: University of Michigan Press, 2007.

Lupovici, Amir. 'The "Attribution Problem" and the Social Construction of "Violence": Taking Cyber Deterrence Literature a Step Forward'. *International Studies Perspectives* 17, no. 3 (2016): 322–42.

Lusthaus, Jonathan. 'Honour among (Cyber)Thieves?' Extra Legal Governance Institute Working Paper No. 2016-1. https://perma.cc/UF99-2AS8.

Lusthaus, Jonathan. *Industry of Anonymity: Inside the Business of Cybercrime*. Cambridge, MA: Harvard University Press, 2018.

Mabee, Bryan. 'Pirates, Privateers and the Political Economy of Private Violence'. *Global Change, Peace & Security* 21, no. 2 (2009): 139–52.

MacAskill, Ewen, Julian Borger, Nick Hopkins, Nick Davies, and James Ball. 'Mastering the Internet: How GCHQ Set out to Spy on the World Wide Web'. *The Guardian*, 21 June 2013. https://perma.cc/P7Q5-ZCR5.

Mallard, Gregoire. 'From Europe's Past to the Middle East's Future: The Constitutive Purpose of Forward Analogies'. Paper presented at the American Sociological Association Annual Meeting, New York, August 2013.

malware.lu, and itrust consulting. 'APT1: Technical Backstage - Malware Analysis'. malware.lu, 27 March 2013. https://perma.cc/56GS-QTLB.

Mandel, Robert. *Global Security Upheaval: Armed Nonstate Groups Usurping State Stability Functions.* Stanford Security Studies. Stanford: Stanford University Press, 2013.

Margaritelli, Simone. 'How the United Arab Emirates Intelligence Tried to Hire Me to Spy on Its People'. evilsocket.net, 27 July 2016 [Blog]. https://perma.cc/MC6S-5ABZ.

Markoff, John. 'Cyberattack on Google Said to Hit Password System'. *New York Times*, 19 April 2010.

Marks, Michael P. *Metaphors in International Relations Theory.* Basingstoke: Palgrave Macmillan, 2011.

Marks, Michael P. *The Prison as Metaphor: Re-Imagining International Relations.* Oxford: P. Lang, 2004.

Marlinspike, Moxie. 'A Saudi Arabia Telecom's Surveillance Pitch'. moxie.org, 13 May 2013 [Blog]. https://perma.cc/RTP5-XH5A.

Martemucci, Matteo G., Col. 'Unpunished Insults -- the Looming Cyber Barbary Wars'. *Case Western Reserve Journal of International Law* 47, no. 1 Spring (2015): 53–62.

Marzagalli, Silvia, and Leos Müller. '"In Apparent Disagreement with All Law of Nations in the World": Negotiating Neutrality for Shipping and Trade During the French Revolutionary and Napoleonic Wars'. *International Journal of Maritime History* 28, no. 1 (2016): 108–17.

Maschmeyer, Lennart, Ronald J. Deibert, and Jon R. Lindsay. 'A Tale of Two Cybers - How Threat Reporting by Cybersecurity Firms Systematically Underrepresents Threats to Civil Society'. *Journal of Information Technology & Politics* 18, no. 1 (2021): 1–20.

Mattingly, Garrett. 'No Peace Beyond What Line?'. *Transactions of the Royal Historical Society* 13 (December 1963): 145–62.

Mauldin, Alan. 'Shaping the Global Wholesale Bandwidth Market'. PriMetrica, 28 July 2017 [Blog]. https://perma.cc/A7QQ-XBQX.

Maurer, Tim. *Cyber Mercenaries: The State, Hackers, and Power.* Cambridge: Cambridge University Press, 2018.

Maurer, Tim. '"Proxies" and Cyberspace'. *Journal of Conflict and Security Law* 21, no. 3 (2016): 383–403.

McLaughlin, Jenna. 'Spies for Hire'. *The Intercept*, 24 October 2016.

McLaughlin, Jenna. 'Spy Chief Complains That Edward Snowden Sped up Spread of Encryption by 7 Years'. *The Intercept*, 25 April 2016.

McLure, Helen. 'The Wild, Wild Web: The Mythic American West and the Electronic Frontier'. *Western Historical Quarterly* 31, no. 4 (2000): 457–76.

McNab, Chris. 'Alexsey's TTPs'. Medium, 19 March 2017 [Blog]. https://perma.cc/3G55-KR9H.

Meakins, Joss I. 'Squabbling Siloviki: Factionalism within Russia's Security Services'. *International Journal of Intelligence and CounterIntelligence* 31, no. 2 (2018: 235–70).

Menn, Joseph. 'Exclusive: NSA Infiltrated RSA Security More Deeply Than Thought - Study'. *Reuters News*, 31 March 2014.

Menn, Joseph. 'Exclusive: Secret Contract Tied NSA and Security Industry Pioneer'. *Reuters News*, 20 December 2013.

Menn, Joseph. *Fatal System Error: The Hunt for the New Crime Lords Who Are Bringing Down the Internet.* New York, London: PublicAffairs, 2010.

Merkacheva, Eva. 'The Internet as a Territory Where One Might Become a Super Villain'. Moskovsky Komsomolets, 17 April 2017 [GoogleTranslate]. https://perma.cc/V7LS-4J8V.

Microsoft. 'Microsoft by the Numbers'. 2016. https://perma.cc/R5X5-CH2S.

Mike, and Forb. 'Perl Bruteforce'. xakep.ru, 17 January 2002 [GoogleTranslate]. https://perma.cc/7NS9-WS8S.

Miller, Greg. 'The Intelligence Coup of the Century'. *Washington Post*, 11 February 2020, https://perma.cc/6HJJ-YVX6.

Miller, Ross. 'Gmail Now Has 1 Billion Monthly Active Users'. TheVerge, 1 February 2016. https://perma.cc/NBP7-UP9A.

Ministry of Foreign Affairs of the People's Republic of China. 'Foreign Ministry Spokesperson Jiang Yu's Regular Press Conference on January 14, 2010'. People's Republic of China, 15 January 2010 [Press release]. https://perma.cc/PC2F-YAS8.

Ministry of Foreign Affairs of the People's Republic of China. 'Minister Xie Feng of the Chinese Embassy in the United States Reiterated China's Principled Position in Response to the Recent Announcement by Google on Possible Adjustment of Its Business in China'. People's Republic of China, 18 January 2010 [Press release]. https://perma.cc/773D-GDZF.

Ministry of Foreign Affairs of the Russian Federation. 'Briefing by Foreign Ministry Spokesperson Maria Zakharova, Moscow'. Russian Federation, 27 April 2017 [Transcript]. https://perma.cc/5DWJ-E86Z.

Ministry of Foreign Affairs of the Russian Federation. 'Foreign Minister Sergey Lavrov's Interview to Komsomolskaya Pravda Newspaper and Radio, Moscow'. Russian Federation, 31 May 2016 [Transcript]. https://perma.cc/938U-XQTA.

Ministry of Foreign Affairs of the Russian Federation. 'On the Note of the Ministry of Foreign Affairs of Russia to the Foreign Ministry of Estonia'. Russian Federation, 23 April 2007 [Press release, GoogleTranslate]. https://perma.cc/YWE5-KPU2.

Ministry of Foreign Affairs of the Russian Federation. 'Remarks and Replies to Media Questions by Russian Minister of Foreign Affairs Sergey Lavrov at Joint Press Conference with Spanish Minister of Foreign Affairs Miguel Angel Moratinos after Their Talks, Madrid, April 18, 2007'. Russian Federation, 19 April 2007 [Transcript]. https://perma.cc/PWQ5-XA5J.

Ministry of Foreign Affairs of the Russian Federation. 'Statement by the Permanent Representative of the Russian Federation, AN Borodavkin, at the Meeting of the OSCE Permanent Council'. Russian Federation, 3 May 2007 [Transcript, GoogleTranslate]. https://perma.cc/2W8A-5WML.

Montero, Diego, Marcelo Yannuzzi, Adrian Shaw, Ludovic Jacquin, Antonio Pastor, Rene Serral-Gracia, Antonio Lioy, Fulvio Risso, Cataldo Basile, Roberto Sassu, et al. 'Virtualized Security at the Network Edge: A User-Centric Approach'. *IEEE Communications Magazine* 53, no. 4 (2015): 176–86.

Moore, Daniel, and Thomas Rid. 'Cryptopolitik and the Darknet'. *Survival* 58, no. 1 (2016): 7–38.

Moore, HD. 'CVE-2015-7755: Juniper ScreenOS Authentication Backdoor'. Rapid7Community, Juniper, 20 December 2015. https://perma.cc/78EE-6TDU.

Morgan, David. 'Bill Gates Says Internet Needs to Thrive in China'. *Reuters News*, 25 January 2010.

Mueller, Milton. *Networks and States: The Global Politics of Internet Governance.* Information Revolution and Global Politics. Cambridge, Mass.: MIT Press, 2010.

Mueller, Milton. *Ruling the Root: Internet Governance and the Taming of Cyberspace.* Cambridge, Mass.: MIT Press, 2002.

Mueller, Milton, and Andreas Kuehn. 'Einstein on the Breach: Surveillance Technology, Cybersecurity and Organizational Change'. Paper presented at the 12th Workshop on the Economics of Information Security (WEIS 2013), Washington DC, 2013.

Mueller, Robert S., III. *Report on the Investigation into Russian Interference in the 2016 Presidential Election*. Vol. 1. Washington, DC: US Department of Justice, 2019.

Mulaj, Kledja. 'Introduction: Violent Non-State Actors: Exploring Their State Relations, Legitimation, and Operationality'. In *Violent Non-State Actors in World Politics*, edited by Kledja Mulaj, 1–26. New York: Columbia University Press, 2010.

Münkler, Herfried, and Patrick Camiller. *The New Wars*. Cambridge: Polity, 2005.

Nagaraja, Shishir, and Ross Anderson. 'The Snooping Dragon: Social-Malware Surveillance of the Tibetan Movement'. Technical Report No. 746, Computer Laboratory, University of Cambridge, March 2009. https://perma.cc/83Q2-446D.

Nakashima, Ellen. 'Chinese Hackers Who Breached Google Gained Access to Sensitive Data, U.S. Officials Say'. *Washington Post*, 20 June 2013. https://perma.cc/G8UR-5SY2.

Nakashima, Ellen. 'Google to Enlist NSA to Help It Ward Off Cyberattacks'. *Washington Post*, 4 February 2010. https://perma.cc/VZ4T-2ESS.

Nazario, Jose. 'Politically Motivated Denial of Service Attacks'. In *The Virtual Battlefield: Perspectives on Cyber Warfare*, edited by Christian Czosseck and Kenneth Geers, 163–81. Amsterdam: IOS Press, 2009.

Neustadt, Richard E., and Ernest R. May. *Thinking in Time: The Uses of History for Decision-Makers*. London: Collier Macmillan, 1986.

National Institute of Standards and Technology. 'DRBG Validation List'. 1 June 2013. https://perma.cc/3LQP-8YCJ.

North Atlantic Treaty Organization. 'EU Presidency Statement on the Situation in Front of the Estonian Embassy in Moscow'. 3 May 2007 [Press release]. https://perma.cc/99JQ-XQ2D.

Norton, Matthew. 'Classification and Coercion: The Destruction of Piracy in the English Maritime System'. *American Journal of Sociology* 119, no. 6 (2014): 1537–75.

Norton, Matthew. 'Culture and Coercion: Piracy and State Power in the Early Modern English Empire'. PhD Thesis, Yale University, 2012.

Nye, Joseph S., Jr. 'Deterrence and Dissuasion in Cyberspace'. *International Security* 41, no. 3 (2017): 44–71.

Nye, Joseph S., Jr. *The Future of Power*. 1st ed. New York: PublicAffairs, 2011.

Nye, Joseph S., Jr. 'Nuclear Lessons for Cyber Security?'. *Strategic Studies Quarterly* 5, no. 4 (2011): 18–38.

Nye, Joseph S., Jr. 'The Regime Complex for Managing Global Cyber Activities'. Global Commission on Internet Governance (CIGI) and Chatham House, Ontario and London, 2014.

Nyman, Jonna. 'What Is the Value of Security? Contextualising the Negative/Positive Debate'. *Review of International Studies* 42, no. 5 (2016): 821–39.

Obama, Barack. 'Remarks by the President in Year-End Press Conference'. White House, 19 December 2014 [Transcript]. https://perma.cc/AQ6V-MEXN.

Obermaier, Frederik, Henrik Moltke, Laura Poitras, and Jan Strozyk. 'Der Lohn Der Lauscher'. *Süddeutsche Zeitung*, 21 November 2014.

Office of the Director of National Intelligence. 'DNI Announces the Declassification of the Existence of Collection Activities Authorized by President George W. Bush Shortly after the Attacks of September 11, 2001'. 21 December 2013. https://perma.cc/34E8-AT8B.

Organisation for Economic Co-operation and Development (OECD). 'Cybersecurity Policy Making at a Turning Point: Analysing a New Generation of National Cybersecurity Strategies for the Internet Economy'. Paris, 2012.

Ottenheimer, Davi. 'Eventually Navies Take Over'. flyingpenguin, 11 February 2015 [Blog]. https://perma.cc/VU35-B6ZC.

Owens, Patricia. 'Distinctions, Distinctions: "Public" and "Private" Force?'. In *Mercenaries, Pirates, Bandits and Empires: Private Violence in Historical Context*, edited by Alejandro Colás and Bryan Mabee, 15–32. London: C Hurst, 2010.

Packer, George. 'No Death, No Taxes'. *The New Yorker*, 28 November 2011.

'Paper Publishes Bits of Arrested Russian Lab Employee Memoir'. BBC Monitoring Former Soviet Union, 11 May 2017.

Pennell, C. Richard. *Bandits at Sea: A Pirates Reader*. New York: New York University Press, 2001.

Percy, Sarah V. *Mercenaries: The History of a Norm in International Relations*. Oxford: Oxford University Press, 2007.

Perera, David. 'DHS: No Credible Threat to Sony Movie Launch'. *Politico*, 16 December 2014.

Perlroth, Nicole. 'Online Security Experts Link More Breaches to Russian Government'. *New York Times*, 29 October 2014.

Perlroth, Nicole. 'Russian Hacker Sentenced to 27 Years in Credit Card Case'. *New York Times*, 21 April 2017.

Perlroth, Nicole, Jeff Larson, and Scott Shane. 'N.S.A. Able to Foil Basic Safeguards of Privacy on Web'. *New York Times*, 5 September 2013.

Pérotin-Dumon, Anne. 'The Pirate and the Emperor: Power and the Law on the Seas, 1450–1850'. In *Bandits at Sea: A Pirates Reader*, edited by C. Richard Pennell, 25–54. New York: New York University Press, 2001.

Petallides, Constantine J. 'Cracking the Digital Vault: A Study of Cyber Espionage'. *Inquiries Journal/Student Pulse* 4, no. 4 (2012). https://perma.cc/J6NT-7359.

Phillips, Andrew. 'Company Sovereigns, Private Violence and Colonialism'. In *Routledge Handbook of Private Security Studies*, edited by Rita Abrahamsen and Anna Leander, 39–48. New York: Routledge, 2016.

Phillips, Andrew, and Jason C. Sharman. 'Explaining Durable Diversity in International Systems: State, Company, and Empire in the Indian Ocean'. *International Studies Quarterly* 59, no. 3 (2015): 436–48.

Phillips, Andrew, and Jason C. Sharman. 'Company-States and the Creation of the Global International System'. *European Journal of International Relations* 26, no. 4 (2020): 1249–72.

Phillips, Andrew, and Jason C. Sharman. *Outsourcing Empire: How Company-States Made the Modern World*. Princeton: Princeton University Press, 2020.

Policante, Amedeo. *The Pirate Myth: Genealogies of an Imperial Concept*. Glasshouse Book. New York: Routledge, 2015.

'Police Conclude Probe into Alleged Riot Ringleaders'. *The Baltic Times*, 6 September 2007. https://perma.cc/3SY9-7T3Q.

Porter, Christopher. 'Toward Practical Cyber Counter Deception'. *Journal of International Affairs* 70, no. 1 (Winter 2016): 161–74.

Poulsen, Kevin. *Kingpin: How One Hacker Took over the Billion-Dollar Cybercrime Underground*. 1st ed. New York: Crown, 2011.

Powers, Shawn M., and Michael Jablonski. *The Real Cyber War: The Political Economy of Internet Freedom*. History of Communication. Urbana: University of Illinois Press, 2015.

Poznansky, Michael, and Evan Perkoski. 'Rethinking Secrecy in Cyberspace: The Politics of Voluntary Attribution'. *Journal of Global Security Studies* 3, no. 4 (2018): 402–16.

President of Russia. 'Speech at the Military Parade Celebrating the 62nd Anniversary of Victory in the Great Patriotic War'. Russian Federation, 9 May 2007 [Transcript]. https://perma.cc/KHE8-TSE8.

Privacy and Civil Liberties Oversight Board. 'Report on the Surveillance Program Operated Pursuant to Section 702 of the Foreign Intelligence Surveillance Act'. 2 July 2014. https://perma.cc/2RZC-RC4F.

PWC and BAE Systems, 'Operation Cloud Hopper'. April 2017. https://perma.cc/MV3L-FEPW.

Rabkin, Jeremy, and Ariel Rabkin, 'Hacking Back without Cracking Up'. Hoover Institution, Stanford University, 2016.

Ralegh, Walter. *Miscellaneous Works*. The Works of Sir Walter Ralegh, edited by William Oldys and Thomas Birch. Vol. 8. Oxford: Oxford University Press, 1829.

Rech, Walter. *Enemies of Mankind: Vattel's Theory of Collective Security*. The Erik Castrén Institute Monographs on International Law and Human Rights, edited by Martti Koskenniemi Vol. 18. Leiden: Martinus Nijhoff Publishers, 2013.

Rediker, Marcus. 'Liberty beneath the Jolly Roger: The Lives of Anne Bonny and Mary Read, Pirates'. In *Bandits at Sea: A Pirates Reader*, edited by C. Richard Pennell, 299–320. New York: New York University Press, 2001.

Reinicke, Bryan, Jeffrey Cummings, and Howard Kleinberg. 'The Right to Digital Self-Defense'. *IEEE Security & Privacy* 15, no. 4 (2017): 68–71.

Reiter, Svetlana. 'What the Arrest of the Russian Intel Top Cyber-Crime Expert Has to Do with American Elections'. The Bell, 8 December 2017. https://perma.cc/8P56-G5FR.

Reno, William. 'Crime Versus War'. In *The Changing Character of War*, edited by Hew Strachan and Sibylle Scheipers. Oxford Leverhulme Programme on the Changing Character of War, 220–37. Oxford: Oxford University Press, 2011.

Rid, Thomas. 'Back to the Future—Moonlight Maze'. Talk presented at the Security Analyst Summit, Tenerife, Spain, 8 February 2016.

Rid, Thomas. *Cyber War Will Not Take Place*. London: Hurst, 2013.

Rid, Thomas. *Rise of the Machines: A Cybernetic History*. 1st ed. New York: W. W. Norton, 2016.

Rid, Thomas. *Active Measures: The Secret History of Disinformation and Political Warfare*. New York: Farrar, Straus and Giroux, 2020.

Rid, Thomas, and Ben Buchanan. 'Attributing Cyber Attacks'. *Journal of Strategic Studies* 38, nos. 1–2 (2015): 4–37.

Riley, Michael. 'U.S. Agencies Said to Swap Data with Thousands of Firms'. Bloomberg, 15 June 2013. https://perma.cc/5NT2-6QQJ.

Risen, James, and Eric Lichtblau. 'Bush Lets U.S. Spy on Callers without Courts'. *New York Times*, 16 December 2005.

Ritchie, Robert C. *Captain Kidd and the War against the Pirates*. Cambridge, MA: Harvard University Press, 1986.

Robertson, Jordan. 'Juniper Breach Mystery Starts to Clear With New Details on Hackers and U.S. Role', *Bloomberg*, 2 September 2021, https://perma.cc/42L8-BPHB.

Rodger, Nicholas A. M. *The Command of the Ocean: A Naval History of Britain 1649–1815*. New York: W.W. Norton, 2006.

Rodger, Nicholas A. M. 'Mobilizing Seapower in the Eighteenth Century'. In *Essays in Naval History, from Medieval to Modern*, edited by Nicholas A. M. Rodger, 1–9. Farnham: Ashgate, 2009.

Rodger, Nicholas A. M. *The Safeguard of the Sea: A Naval History of Britain*. Vol. 1: *660–1649*. London: HarperCollins Publishers in association with the National Maritime Museum, 1997.

Roelofsen, C. G. 'Grotius and the International Politics of the Seventeenth Century'. In *Hugo Grotius and International Relations*, edited by Hedley Bull, Benedict Kingsbury, and Adam Roberts, 95–131. Oxford: Clarendon Press, 1990.

Romanosky, Sasha, and Benjamin Boudreaux. 'Private-Sector Attribution of Cyber Incidents: Benefits and Risks to the U.S. Government'. *International Journal of Intelligence and Counterintelligence* 34, no. 3 (2021): 463–93.

Rommelse, Gijs A. 'An Early Modern Naval Revolution? The Relationship between "Economic Reason of State" and Maritime Warfare'. *Journal for Maritime Research* 13, no. 2 (2011): 138–50.

Rosenau, James N. *Turbulence in World Politics: A Theory of Change and Continuity*. London: Harvester Wheatsheaf, 1990.

Rosenzewig, Paul. 'International Law and Private Actor Active Cyber Defensive Measures'. *Stanford Journal of International Law* 50 (2014): 103.

Rosenzweig, Paul, Steven P. Bucci, and David Inserra, 'Next Steps for U.S. Cybersecurity in the Trump Administration: Active Cyber Defense'. The Heritage Foundation, Washington, DC, 2017.

Rovner, Joshua. 'Cyber War as an Intelligence Contest'. War on the Rocks, 16 September 2019., https://perma.cc/B4HS-4YAF.

RSA. 'RSA Response to Media Claims Regarding NSA Relationship'. Bedford, MA, 22 December 2013 [Blog]. https://perma.cc/LSE5-GY6E.

Rubin, Alfred P. *The Law of Piracy*. International Law Studies. Newport, RI: Naval War College Press, 1988.

'Russia Federal Agents Suspected of Treason Reportedly Passed Secrets to the CIA'. *Moscow Times*, 31 January 2017.

Russian Public Opinion Research Center (VCIOM). 'Monuments and Burial of Soviet Warriors in Estonia'. 12 March 2007 [GoogleTranslate]. https://perma.cc/7ZQJ-5VTY.

Sagieva, Kogershin. 'Arrested in the Case of State Treasury, the Top Manager of Kaspersky Lab Asked the Authorities'. TV Rain, 12 April 2017 [GoogleTranslate]. https://perma.cc/G8G6-AY78.

Sandee, Michael, 'Gameover Zeus. Backgrounds on the Badguys and the Backends'. InTELL, Delft, Fox-IT, 2015.

Sandee, Michael, Tillmann Werner, and Elliott Peterson. 'Gameover Zeus—Bad Guys and Backends'. Paper presented at Black Hat USA, Las Vegas, 2015.

Sanger, David E., and Martin Fackler. 'N.S.A. Breached North Korean Networks before Sony Attack, Officials Say'. *New York Times*, 18 January 2015.

Sanger, David E., and John Markoff. 'After Google's Stand on China, U.S. Treads Lightly'. *New York Times*, 14 January 2010.

Sanger, David E., Nicole Perlroth, and Eric Schmitt. 'U.S. Asks China to Help Rein in Korean Hackers'. *New York Times*, 20 December 2014.

Saunders, Jamie. 'Tackling Cybercrime—The UK Response'. *Journal of Cyber Policy* 2, no. 1 (2017): 4–15.

Schmidt, Andreas. 'The Estonian Cyberattacks'. In *A Fierce Domain: Conflict in Cyberspace 1986–2012*, edited by Jason Healey, 174–93. Vienna, VA: Cyber Conflict Studies Association, 2013.

Schmidt, Eric, and Jared Cohen. *The New Digital Age: Reshaping the Future of People, Nations and Business*. London: John Murray, 2013.

Schmidt, Eric, and Jonathan Rosenberg. *How Google Works*. London: John Murray, 2014.

Schmitt, Michael N. *Tallinn Manual on the International Law Applicable to Cyber Warfare: Prepared by the International Group of Experts at the Invitation of the NATO Cooperative Cyber Defence Centre of Excellence*. Cambridge: Cambridge University Press, 2013.

Schmitt, Michael N., and Liis Vihul. 'Proxy Wars in Cyberspace: The Evolving International Law of Attribution'. *Fletcher Security Review* 1, no. 2 (2014): 54–73.

Schneier, Bruce. *Data and Goliath: The Hidden Battles to Collect Your Data and Control Your World*. New York: W.W. Norton, 2016.

Schneier, Bruce. 'U.S. Enables Chinese Hacking of Google'. CNN, 23 January 2010. https://perma.cc/Y2SB-DL4U.

Scholl, Derrick. 'Important Announcement About ScreenOS'. Security Incident Response, Juniper, 17 December 2015. https://perma.cc/MSC9-APX9.

Schön, Donald A. 'Generative Metaphor: A Perspective on Problem-Setting in Social Policy'. In *Metaphor and Thought*, edited by Andrew Ortony, 254–83. Cambridge: Cambridge University Press, 1979.

Schulzke, Marcus. 'The Politics of Attributing Blame for Cyberattacks and the Costs of Uncertainty'. *Perspectives on Politics* 16, no. 4 (2018): 954–68.

Schwirtz, Michael, and Joseph Goldstein. 'Russian Espionage Piggybacks on a Cybercriminal's Hacking'. *New York Times*, 12 March 2017.

Scott-Railton, John, Adam Hulcoop, Bahr Abdul Razzak, Bill Marczak, Siena Anstis, and Ron Deibert. 'Dark Basin: Uncovering a Massive Hack-for-Hire Operation'. Citizen Lab, 2020, https://web.archive.org/web/20210119103230/https://citizenlab.ca/2020/06/dark-basin-uncovering-a-massive-hack-for-hire-operation/.

Seal, Mark. 'An Exclusive Look at Sony's Hacking Saga'. *Vanity Fair*, 28 February 2015.

Segal, Adam. *The Hacked World Order: How Nations Fight, Trade, Maneuver, and Manipulate in the Digital Age*. New York: PublicAffairs, 2016.

Segal, Adam. 'When China's White-Hat Hackers Go Patriotic'. Net Politics. Council on Foreign Relations, New York:, 13 March 2017 [Blog]. https://perma.cc/6TT6-E39F.

Selden, John. *Mare Clausum Seu De Dominio Maris*. London: W. Stanesbeius pro R. Meighen, 1635.

Shachtman, Noah, and Peter W. Singer. 'The Wrong War: The Insistence on Applying Cold War Metaphors to Cybersecurity Is Misplaced and Counterproductive'. Brookings, 15 August 2011 [Blog]. https://perma.cc/SCC5-NW4Y.

Shackelford, Scott, and Scott Russell. 'Risky Business: Lessons for Mitigating Cyber Attacks from the International Insurance Law on Piracy'. *Minnesota Journal of International Law* 24, no. 1 (2015): 1–15.

Sharman, Jason C. *Empires of the Weak: The Real Story of European Expansion and the Creation of the New World Order*. Princeton: Princeton University Press, 2019.

Sharman, Jason C. 'Power and Profit at Sea: The Rise of the West in the Making of the International System'. *International Security* 43, no. 4 (2019): 163–96.

Sharp, Travis. 'Theorizing Cyber Coercion: The 2014 North Korean Operation against Sony'. *Journal of Strategic Studies* 70, no. 7 (2017): 898–926.

Shirk, Mark. '"Bringing the State Back in" to the Empire Turn: Piracy and the Layered Sovereignty of the Eighteenth Century Atlantic'. *International Studies Review* 19, no. 2 (2017): 143–65.

Shirk, Mark. 'How Does Violence Threaten the State? Four Narratives on Piracy'. *Terrorism and Political Violence* 29, no. 4 (2017): 656–73.

Shirk, Mark. 'Pirates, Anarchists, and Terrorists: Violence and the Boundaries of Sovereign Authority'. PhD Thesis, University of Maryland, 2014.

Shumow, Dan, and Niels Ferguson. 'On the Possibility of a Back Door in the NIST SP800-90 Dual EC PRNG'. Paper presented at the Crypto Rump Session, Santa Barbara CA, 2007.

Simon, Rebecca A. 'The Problem and Potential of Piracy: Legal Changes and Emerging Ideas of Colonial Autonomy in the Early Modern British Atlantic, 1670–1730'. *Journal for Maritime Research* 18, no. 2 (2016): 123–37.

Singer, Peter W. 'Private Military Firms: The Profit Side of VNSAs'. In *Violent Non-State Actors in World Politics*, edited by Kledja Mulaj, 413–40. New York: Columbia University Press, 2010.

Singer, Peter W., and Allan Friedman. *Cybersecurity and Cyberwar: What Everyone Needs to Know*. New York: Oxford University Press, 2014.

Slayton, Rebecca. 'What Is the Cyber Offense-Defense Balance? Conceptions, Causes, and Assessment'. *International Security* 41, no. 3 (2017): 72–109.

Smeets, Max. 'A Matter of Time: On the Transitory Nature of Cyberweapons'. *Journal of Strategic Studies* 41, nos. 1–2 (2018): 6–32.

Smith, Brad. 'The Need for Urgent Collective Action to Keep People Safe Online: Lessons from Last Week's Cyberattack'. Microsoft on the Issues, Redmond, WA, Microsoft Inc., 14 May 2017 [Blog]. https://perma.cc/E5NT-3H6M.

Snider, L. Britt. 'Recollections from the Church Committee's Investigation of NSA: Unlucky Shamrock'. *Studies in Intelligence* (Winter 1999–2000): 43–51. https://perma.cc/8PXD-KXSJ.

Soldatov, Andreï, and Irina Borogan. *The Red Web: The Struggle between Russia's Digital Dictators and the New Online Revolutionaries*. 1st ed. New York: PublicAffairs, 2015.

Soldatov, Andreï, and Irina Borogan. *The New Nobility: The Restoration of Russia's Security State and the Enduring Legacy of the KGB*. 1st ed. New York: PublicAffairs, 2010.

Sony Corporation. 'Consolidated Financial Results for the Fiscal Year Ended 31 March 2015'. 30 April 2015 [No. 15-039E]. https://perma.cc/SH42-EK4K.

Soosaar, Enn. 'The Bronze Soldier and Its Deportation to a Military Cemetery'. *Diplomaatia*, 46 (2007).

'Spokesman of Policy Department of NDC Blasts S. Korean Authorities' False Rumor About DPRK'. *KCNAWatch*, 7 December 2014.

Spolitis, Veiko. 'Russland Und Die Baltischen Staaten. Denkmalstreit Und Russische Minderheit in Estland'. *Russland Analysen*, 134 (2007): 1–16.

Spruyt, Hendrik. *The Sovereign State and Its Competitors: An Analysis of Systems Change*. Princeton Studies in International History and Politics. Princeton: Princeton University Press, 1994.

Stanley, Jo, Anne Chambers, Dian H. Murray, and Julie Wheelwright. *Bold in Her Breeches: Women Pirates across the Ages*. London: Pandora, 1995.

Starkey, David J. 'Pirates and Markets'. In *Bandits at Sea: A Pirates Reader*, edited by C. Richard Pennell, 107–24. New York: New York University Press, 2001.

Starkey, David J. 'Voluntaries and Sea Robbers: A Review of the Academic Literature on Privateering, Corsairing, Buccaneering and Piracy'. *The Mariner's Mirror* 97, no. 1 (2011): 127–47.

Starkey, David J., E. S. van Eyck van Hesling, and Jaap A. de Moor. *Pirates and Privateers: New Perspectives on the War on Trade in the Eighteenth and Nineteenth Centuries*. Exeter Maritime Studies. Exeter: University of Exeter Press, 1997.

Steffens, Timo. *Attribution of Advanced Persistent Threats: How to Identify the Actors Behind Cyber-Espionage*. Berlin: Springer Vieweg, 2020.

Steffens, Timo. *Auf Der Spur Der Hacker Wie Man Die Täter Hinter Der Computer-Spionage Enttarnt*. Berlin: Springer Vieweg, 2018.

Stern, Philip J. *The Company-State: Corporate Sovereignty and the Early Modern Foundation of the British Empire in India*. Oxford: Oxford University Press, 2011.

Stevens, Tim. *Cyber Security and the Politics of Time*. Cambridge: Cambridge University Press, 2016.

Stevens, Tim. 'A Cyberwar of Ideas? Deterrence and Norms in Cyberspace'. *Contemporary Security Policy* 33, no. 1 (2012): 148–70.

Stoyanov, Ruslan. 'The Hunt for Lurk'. Kaspersky, 30 August 2016. https://perma.cc/5VFR-RK5L.

Suter, Manuel. 'The Governance of Cybersecurity. An Analysis of Public-Private Partnerships in a New Field of Security Policy'. PhD Thesis, Eidgenössische Technische Hochschule, Zürich, 2012.

Tabansky, Lior, and Isaac Ben Israel. *Cybersecurity in Israel*. Springer Briefs in Cybersecurity. Cham, Switzerland: Springer, 2015.

Tan, Justin, and Anna E. Tan. 'Business under Threat, Technology under Attack, Ethics under Fire: The Experience of Google in China'. *Journal of Business Ethics* 110, no. 4 (2012): 469–79.

Tanji, Michael. 'Buccaneer.Com: Infosec Privateering as a Solution to Cyberspace Threats'. *Journal of Cyber Conflict Studies* 1, no. 1 (2007): 1–5.

TechHive Staff. 'Hello, Larry! Google's Page on Negativity, Laws, and Competitors'. PC World, 15 May 2013 [Transcript of keynote address at Google I/O]. https://perma.cc/B4LB-HSDH.

Theveßen, Elmar, Peter F. Müller, and Ulrich Stoll. '#Cryptoleaks: Wie BND Und CIA Alle Täuschten'. *ZDF*, 11 February 2020, https://perma.cc/D9WX-BTJ6.

Thomas, Gary. 'A Typology for the Case Study in Social Science Following a Review of Definition, Discourse, and Structure'. *Qualitative Inquiry* 17, no. 6 (2011): 511–21.

Thompson, Peter G. *Armed Groups: The 21st Century Threat*. Lanham: Rowman & Littlefield, 2014.

Thomson, Janice E. *Mercenaries, Pirates, and Sovereigns: State-Building and Extraterritorial Violence in Early Modern Europe*. Princeton Studies in International History and Politics. Princeton: Princeton University Press, 1994.

Tikk, Eneken, and Kadri Kaska. 'Legal Cooperation to Investigate Cyber Incidents: Estonian Case Study and Lessons'. Paper presented at 9th European Conference on Information Warfare and Security, Thessaloniki, 2010.

Tikk, Eneken, Kadri Kaska, and Liis Vihul. 'International Cyber Incidents—Legal Considerations'. Cooperative Cyber Defence Centre of Excellence, Tallinn, Estonia, 2010.

Tilly, Charles. *Coercion, Capital, and European States, A.D. 990–1990.* Oxford: Basil Blackwell, 1990.

Tilly, Charles. 'War Making and State Making as Organized Crime'. In *Bringing the State Back In*, edited by Peter B. Evans, Dietrich Rueschemeyer and Theda Skocpol, 169–91. Cambridge: Cambridge University Press, 1985.

Timberg, Craig, Ellen Nakashima, and Danielle Douglas-Gabriel. 'Cyberattacks Trigger Talk of "Hacking Back"'. *Washington Post*, 9 October 2014. https://perma.cc/2H4V-BM2V.

'Top 100 Digital Companies 2019'. *Forbes*, 29 January 2020, https://perma.cc/V76P-D6S3.

Tourangeau, Roger. 'Metaphor and Cognitive Structure'. In *Metaphor: Problems and Perspectives*, edited by David S. Miall, 14–35. Brighton: Harvester, 1982.

Trachtenberg, Marc. *The Craft of International History: A Guide to Method.* Princeton: Princeton University Press, 2006.

Truxes, Thomas M. 'The Breakdown of Borders: Commerce Raiding During the Seven Years' War, 1756–1763'. In *Commerce Raiding: Historical Case Studies, 1755–2009*, edited by Bruce A. Elleman and Sarah C. M. Paine, 9–26. Newport, RI: Naval War College Press, 2013.

Turovsky, Daniil. 'America's Hunt for Russian Hackers: How FBI Agents Tracked Down Four of the World's Biggest Cyber-Criminals and Brought Them to Trial in the U.S'. Translated to English by Kevin Rothrock, Meduza, 2017. https://perma.cc/VNX9-KU4T.

Turovsky, Daniil. 'Russian Cyber Army: How the State Creates Military Detachments of Hackers'. Meduza, 7 November 2016 [GoogleTranslate]. https://perma.cc/9K4T-PF64.

Twyman-Ghoshal, Anamika A. 'Contemporary Piracy Research in Criminology: A Review Essay with Directions for Future Research'. *International Journal of Comparative and Applied Criminal Justice* 38, no. 3 (2014): 281–303.

'U.S. Can Never Justify Screening and Distribution of Reactionary Movie: Policy Department of NDC of DPRK'. *KCNA*, 27 December 2014.

U.S. Congress, House of Representatives, Committee on Oversight and Government Reform. *The OPM Data Breach: How the Government Jeopardized Our National Security for More Than a Generation.* 114th Cong., 2nd session, Washington, DC: Government Printing Office, 2016. https://perma.cc/BZ8T-88Q3.

U.S. Congress, Senate, Committee on Homeland Security and Governmental Affairs. *Cyber Security: Developing a National Strategy.* 111th Cong., 1st sess. Washington, DC: U.S. Government Printing Office, 2009. (S. Hrg. 111-724).

U.S. Congress, U.S.-China Economic and Security Review Commission. *Annual Report to Congress.* 111th Cong., 1st sess. Washington, DC: U.S. Government Printing Office, 2009. http://www.uscc.gov/.

U.S. Department of Homeland Security and Federal Bureau of Investigation. 'November 2014 Cyber Intrusion on USPER I and Related Threats'. *Joint Intelligence Bulletin* (2014). https://perma.cc/X6YN-XY26.

U.S. Department of Justice. 'U.S. Charges Russian FSB Officers and Their Criminal Conspirators for Hacking Yahoo and Millions of Email Accounts'. 15 March 2017. https://perma.cc/688M-8UY2.

U.S. Department of State. 'Daily Press Briefing by the Assistant Secretary Philip J. Crowley'. 14 January 2010. https://perma.cc/T265-PGUP.

U.S. Department of State. 'Daily Press Briefing by the Deputy Spokesperson Marie Harf'. 22 December 2014. https://perma.cc/H5DK-XG33.

U.S. Department of State. 'International Narcotics Control Strategy Report—Money Laundering and Financial Crimes'. 2019.

U.S. Department of the Treasury. 'Treasury Imposes Sanctions against the Government of the Democratic People's Republic of Korea'. News release, 2 January 2015, https://perma.cc/C7WV-HREF.

United Nations Protocol and Liaison Service. 'The Blue Book—Permanent Missions to the United Nations (St/Pls/Ser.A/306)'. March 2021.

Valeriano, Brandon, and Ryan C. Maness. *Cyber War Versus Cyber Realities: Cyber Conflict in the International System*. New York: Oxford University Press, 2015.

Van Creveld, Martin. *The Rise and Decline of the State*. Cambridge: Cambridge University Press, 1999.

Van Creveld, Martin. *The Transformation of War*. New York: Free Press, 1991.

Varese, Federico. *The Russian Mafia: Private Protection in a New Market Economy*. Oxford: Oxford University Press, 2001.

Vergerio, Claire. 'Alberico Gentili's De Iure Belli: An Absolutist's Attempt to Reconcile the Jus Gentium and the Reason of State Tradition'. *Journal of the History of International Law* 19 (2017): 1–38.

Villeneuve, Nart. Malware Explorer [Blog], 2010. https://perma.cc/YX34-Q8JA.

Vinci, Anthony. *Armed Groups and the Balance of Power: The International Relations of Terrorists, Warlords and Insurgents*. LSE International Studies. London: Routledge, 2009.

Walker, Rob B. J. *Inside/Outside: International Relations as Political Theory*. Cambridge: Cambridge University Press, 1993.

Wallace, Willard Mosher. *Sir Walter Raleigh*. Princeton: Princeton University Press, 1959.

Washington Post Staff. 'Full Testimony of FBI Director James Comey in Front of the Senate Judiciary Committee on FBI Oversight'. *Washington Post*, 3 May 2017 [Transcript]. https://perma.cc/3KDP-6TDK.

Waterman, Shaun. 'Clapper: U.S. Shelved "Hack Backs" Due to Counterattack Fears'. CyberScoop, 2 October 2017. https://perma.cc/6JX3-TY4Y.

Weinstein, Jeremy M. *Inside Rebellion: The Politics of Insurgent Violence*. Cambridge: Cambridge University Press, 2007.

Wendt, Alexander. 'On Constitution and Causation in International Relations'. *Review of International Studies* 24, no. 5 (1998): 101–17.

'What Is Known About NSA's PRISM Program'. Electrospaces, 23 April 2014 [Blog]. https://perma.cc/2EJD-JATV.

Wheeler, Marcy. 'Why Would FSB Officer Dmitry Dokuchaev Use a Yahoo Email Account to Spy for Russia?' emptywheel.net blog, 18 March 2017 [Blog]. https://perma.cc/5BHD-XTVE.

White House. 'Press Briefing by the Press Secretary Josh Earnest'. 18 December 2014 [Press briefing]. https://perma.cc/JS4N-JTYL.

White House. 'Statement by the Press Secretary on the Executive Order Entitled "Imposing Additional Sanctions with Respect to North Korea"'. White House, 2 January 2015 [Press release]. https://perma.cc/ET5V-VGSM.

Williams, Michael C. 'The Public, the Private and the Evolution of Security Studies'. *Security Dialogue* 41, no. 6 (2010): 623–30.

Wolfers, Arnold. *Discord and Collaboration: Essays on International Politics.* Baltimore: Johns Hopkins Press, 1962.

Wolff, Christian. *Jus Gentium Methodo Scientifica Pertractatum.* Translated by Joseph Horace Drake and Otfried Nippold. Classics of International Law, edited by James Brown Scott. Vol. 2. Oxford: Clarendon Press, 1934.

Yanow, Dvora. 'Dear Author, Dear Reader: The Third Hermeneutic in Writing and Reviewing Ethnography'. In *Political Ethnography: What Immersion Contributes to the Study of Power*, edited by Edward Schatz, 275–302. Chicago: University of Chicago Press, 2009.

Yanow, Dvora. 'Thinking Interpretively: Philosophical Presuppositions and the Human Sciences'. In *Interpretation and Method: Empirical Research Methods and the Interpretive Turn*, edited by Dvora Yanow and Peregrine Schwartz-Shea, 5–26. Armonk, New York: M.E. Sharp, 2014.

Yin, Robert K. *Case Study Research: Design and Methods.* 5th ed. Los Angeles: SAGE, 2013.

Zahedieh, Nuala. *The Capital and the Colonies: London and the Atlantic Economy, 1660–1700.* Cambridge: Cambridge University Press, 2010.

Zenz, Kimberley. 'Infighting among Russian Security Services in the Cyber Sphere'. Paper presented at Black Hat USA, Las Vegas, 2019.

Zetter, Kim. *Countdown to Zero Day: Stuxnet and the Launch of the World's First Digital Weapon.* 1st ed. New York: Crown, 2014.

Zetter, Kim, and Huib Modderkolk. 'How a Secret Dutch Mole Aided the U.S.-Israeli Stuxnet Cyberattack on Iran'. Yahoo News, 2 September 2019, https://perma.cc/DR6J-57A2.

Zittrain, Jonathan. '"Netwar": The Unwelcome Militarization of the Internet Has Arrived'. *Bulletin of the Atomic Scientists* 73, no. 5 (September 2017): 300–4.

Zlobin, Andrey, and Xenia Bolletskaya. 'Electronic Bomb—Who Is Behind the Cyberwar between Russia and Estonia?' Vedomosti, 28 May 2007 [GoogleTranslate]. https://perma.cc/9CW6-UZRD.

Zürn, Michael. 'Politisierung Als Konzept Der Internationalen Beziehungen'. In *Die Politisierung Der Weltpolitik—Umkämpfte Internationale Institutionen*, edited by Michael Zürn and Matthias Ecker-Ehrhart, 7–35. Berlin: Suhrkamp, 2013.

Index